COUNTRY LIVING
MAGAZINE

Guide to Rural England

EAST ANGLIA

Norfolk, Suffolk, Essex and Cambridgeshire

By Peter Long

© Travel Publishing Ltd

Published by:

Travel Publishing Ltd

10 Thornbury Road

Cover, Plymouth PL6

Country Living is a registered trademark of The National
Magazine Company Limited.

First Published: 2001
Second Edition: 2004
Third Edition: 2006
Fourth Edition: 2008

COUNTRY LIVING GUIDES:

East Anglia	Scotland
Heart of England	The South of England
Ireland	The South East of England
The North East of England	The West Country
The North West of England	Wales

PLEASE NOTE:

All advertisements in this publication have been accepted in good faith by Travel Publishing and they have not necessarily been endorsed by *Country Living* Magazine.

All information is included by the publishers in good faith and is believed to be correct at the time of going to press. No responsibility can be accepted for errors.

Editor:	Peter Long
Printing by:	Latimer Trend, Plymouth
Location Maps:	© Maps in Minutes ™ (2008) © Collins Bartholomews 2008 All rights reserved.
Walks:	Walks have been reproduced with kind permission of the internet walking site: www.walkingworld.com
Walk Maps:	Reproduced from Ordnance Survey mapping on behalf of the Controller of Her Majesty's Stationery Office, © Crown Copyright. Licence Number MC 100035812
Cover Design:	Lines & Words, Aldermaston
Cover Photo:	Herringfleet Windpump, Somerleyton, Suffolk © Alamy Images
Text Photos:	Text photos have been kindly supplied by the Pictures of Britain photo library © www.picturesofbritain.co.uk and © Bob Brooks, Weston-super-Mare

Foreword

From a bracing walk across the hills and tarns of The Lake District to a relaxing weekend spent discovering the unspoilt hamlets of East Anglia, nothing quite matches getting off the beaten track and exploring Britain's areas of outstanding beauty.

Each month, *Country Living Magazine* celebrates the richness and diversity of our countryside with features on rural Britain and the traditions that have their roots there. So it is with great pleasure that I introduce you to the *Country Living Magazine Guide to Rural England* series. Packed with information about unusual and unique aspects of our countryside, the guides will point both fair-weather and intrepid travellers in the right direction.

Each chapter provides a fascinating tour of the East Anglia area, with insights into local heritage and history and easy-to-read facts on a wealth of places to visit, stay, eat, drink and shop.

I hope that this guide will help make your visit a rewarding and stimulating experience and that you will return inspired, refreshed and ready to head off on your next countryside adventure.

Susy Smith

Susy Smith
Editor, Country Living magazine

PS To subscribe to *Country Living Magazine* each month, call 01858 438844

Introduction

This is the fourth edition of *The Country Living Guide to Rural England – East Anglia* and we are sure that it will be as popular as its predecessors. The guide provides readers with interesting and useful information on places, people and activities in a part of England which definitely offers the visitor some wonderful country landscapes. In the introduction to each village or town we have also summarized and categorized the main attractions to be found there, which makes it easy for readers to plan their visit. Peter Long, the editor, is an experienced travel writer who spent many years as an inspector and writer with Egon Ronay's Hotels & Restaurants Guides before joining the Travel Publishing editorial team. Peter has, of course, completely updated the contents of the guide and ensured that it is packed with vivid descriptions, historical stories, amusing anecdotes and interesting facts on hundreds of places in Norfolk, Suffolk, Cambridgeshire and Essex.

Norfolk is famous for the Norfolk Broads but has a rich and interesting past, gentle hills as well as expansive horizons, delightful pastoral scenes, a beautiful coastline rich in wildlife and many interesting hidden places to visit. Suffolk was made famous by the brush of John Constable and is blessed with incomparable rural beauty which encompasses wide open spaces broken by gentle hills and tidal rivers meandering from a coastline teeming with birdlife. Cambridgeshire is famous for its ancient university and being the birthplace of Oliver Cromwell and Samuel Pepys but offers a wealth of peaceful and attractive countryside with many towns and villages steeped in history. Essex, containing England's oldest recorded town (Colchester), has a strong maritime tradition, pretty villages, a coastline with attractive estuaries and a rich history going back to Roman times.

The advertising panels within each chapter provide further information on places to see, stay, eat, drink and shop. We have also selected a number of walks from walkingworld.com (full details of this website may be found to the rear of the guide) which we highly recommend if you wish to appreciate fully the beauty and charm of the varied rural landscapes and coastlines of East Anglia.

The guide however is not simply an 'armchair tour'. Its prime aim is to encourage the reader to visit the places described and discover much more about the wonderful towns, villages and countryside of East Anglia in person. In this respect we would like to thank all the Tourist Information Centres who helped us to provide you with up-to-date information. Whether you decide to explore this region by wheeled transport or on foot we are sure you will find it a very uplifting experience!

We are always interested in receiving comments on places covered (or not covered) in our guides so please do not hesitate to use the reader reaction forms provided at the rear of this guide to give us your considered comments. This will help us refine and improve the content of the next edition. We also welcome any general comments which will help improve the overall presentation of the guides themselves.

For more information on the full range of travel guides published by Travel Publishing please refer to the order form at the rear of this guide or log on to our website (see below).

Travel Publishing

Did you know that you can also search our website for details of thousands of places to see, stay, eat or drink throughout Britain and Ireland? Our site has become increasingly popular and now receives monthly over 160,000 visits. Try it!

website: www.travelpublishing.co.uk

Contents

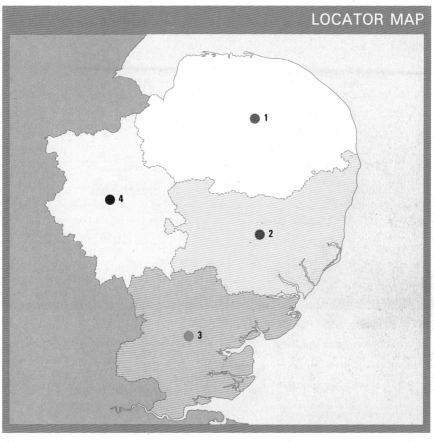

LOCATOR MAP

LOCATOR MAP

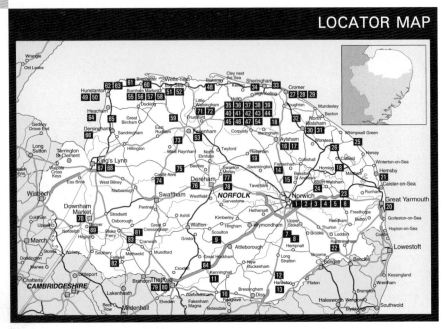

ADVERTISERS AND PLACES OF INTEREST

🏛 historic building   🏚 museum and heritage   🏛 historic site   🗺 scenic attraction   🌿 flora and fauna

1| Norfolk

With two sides bordered by the sea and a third by the Fens, Norfolk has a wealth of attractions for the visitor: miles of sandy beaches, great walking and boating, nature reserves, wonderful villages of thatch and flint, great houses, Norman castles and over 600 medieval churches.

The area that lies between the county capital of Norwich and the border with Suffolk is effectively a plateau, where the

major centres of population include Diss, an old market town with a mix of Tudor, Georgian and Victorian houses, and Wymondham, with its timber-framed houses, picturesque market place and an abbey church that stands up well to comparison even with the majestic Norwich Cathedral. Norwich, once an important centre of the worsted trade, retains many medieval buildings, a number of which now serve as museums

📖 stories and anecdotes 🐾 famous people 🎨 art and craft 🎭 entertainment and sport 🚶 walks

relating the fascinating history of the region.

The area to the east of this fine city contains the unique Norfolk Broads, beautiful stretches of shallow water that form Britain's finest wetland area. On the coast due east of Norwich is the old port and modern holiday resort of Great Yarmouth, where the visitor will find miles of sandy beaches, a breezy promenade, two grand old traditional piers and all the fun of the fair, as well as a rich maritime heritage that lives on to this day.

Upton Dyke in Winter

Miles of sandy beaches, spectacular sea views and fresh sea air are the rewards awaiting visitors to the Norfolk coast, which stretches from Great Yarmouth in the east up to Cromer on the edge of the county, and west to Sheringham, Hunstanton and beyond.

Substantial stretches of the coast are in the care of the National Trust, including the highest point in the county at West Runton, and the North Norfolk coast is renowned for its birdlife. Felbrigg Hall is a superb 17th-century house with Grand Tour paintings and marvellous grounds. The house is near Cromer, a charming resort with a 100-year-old pier and a proud fishing tradition: Cromer crabs are known far and wide for their flavour and succulence.

The northwest coast is an exhilarating coast, with huge skies, ozone-tangy breezes sweeping in from the North Sea, and an abundance of wildlife. An admirable way to experience the area to the full is to walk all or part of the Coastal Footpath which follows the coastline for some 36 miles from Cromer in the east to Holme-next-the-Sea, for most of its route well away from any roads.

King's Lynn, on the Great Ouse three miles inland from The Wash, was one of England's most important ports in medieval times, sitting at the southern end of an underwater maze of sandbanks. To the northeast of King's Lynn is the prosperous market town of Fakenham, around which lie a remarkable variety of places of interest – religious, industrial and scenic. Breckland, which extends for more than 360 square miles in southwest Norfolk and northwest Suffolk, is underlain by chalk with only a light covering of soil. This quiet corner of the county is bounded by the rivers Little Ouse and Waveney, which separate Norfolk from Suffolk.

Norwich

- 🏰 Norwich Castle 🏰 Norwich Cathedral
- 🏛 Bridewell Museum 🏛 Venta Icenorum
- 🏛 City of Norwich Aviation Museum
- 🏛 Castle Museum & Art Gallery ⚒ The Forum
- 🏛 Royal Norfolk Regimental Museum
- 🏛 John Jarrold Printing Museum
- 🏪 The Mustard Shop ⚒ Sainsbury Centre
- 🚶 Whitlingham Country Park

'Norwich has the most Dickensian atmosphere of any city I know,' declared J B Priestley in his *English Journey* of 1933. "What a grand, higgledy-piggledy, sensible old place Norwich is!" More than half a century later, in a European Commission study of 'most habitable' cities, Norwich topped the list of British contenders, well ahead of more favoured candidates such as Bath and York. The political, social and cultural capital of Norfolk, Norwich has an individual charm that is difficult to define, a beguiling atmosphere created in part by its prodigal wealth of sublime buildings, and partly by its intriguing dual personality as both an old-fashioned cathedral town and a vibrant, modern city. Back in prehistoric times, there were several settlements around the confluence of the Rivers Wensum and Yare. By the late 4th century, one of them was important enough to have its own mint. This was Northwic. By the time of the Domesday Book 700 years later, Northwic/Norwich, had become the third-most populous city in England, only outnumbered by London and York. To the Norman conquerors, such a major centre of population (about 5,500 residents) needed a **Castle** to ensure that its

PAINT A PLATE

2 Farmers Avenue, Norwich, Norfolk NR1 3JX
Tel: 01603 616535
e-mil: kat@paintaplate.co.uk
website: www.paintaplate.co.uk

Paint a plate is a contemporary paint your own ceramic studio providing the chance for people of all ages to express their creativity in friendly relaxed surroundings. This creative and stimulating activity is simple, relaxing and fun for adults and kids. You don't have to be an artist to craft a masterpiece!

Customers select from a wide variety of practical or fun, plain ceramic items like plates, cups, money boxes, ornamental animals, fairies or many many more. For a small set fee, customers have the use of brushes, stencils, vibrant paints and the assistance of experienced, qualified staff. Paint a plate will glaze the painted pieces and customers can collect their unique creation three days later or have it posted home. It's a fun, relaxed way to produce a piece to treasure or to give as a present tailor made to suit any occasion.

Throughout school holidays they offer kids workshops and painting activities, please ring or check the website for times and more details. Paint A Plate is located just outside level 4 of the castle mall in Norwich's city centre.

Saxon inhabitants could be kept in order.

The first castle structure, in wood, was replaced in the late 1100s by a mighty fortress in stone which, unlike most blank-walled castles of the period, is decorated with a rich façade of blind arcades and ornamental pilasters. This great fort never saw any military action, and as early as the 13th century was being used as the county gaol, a role it continued to fill until 1889. From its walls, in December 1549, the leader of the rebellion against land enclosures, Robert Kett, was hung in chains and left to starve to death.

The Castle is now home to the **Castle Museum and Art Gallery**, home to some of the most outstanding regional collections of fine art, archaeological exhibits and natural history displays. The former dungeons contain a forbidding display of instruments of torture,

along with the death masks of some of the prisoners who were executed here. Among the countless other fascinating exhibits are those devoted to Queen Boudicca, which features the life of the Iceni tribe with an interactive chariot ride, the Egyptian gallery with its mummy Ankh Hor, and new and interactive displays in the Castle keep and keep basement, recently made accessible to the public, as well as a collection of ceramic teapots.

The Art Gallery has an incomparable collection of paintings by the celebrated Norwich artist, John Sell Cotman (1782-1842), and others in the group known as the Norwich School. Two new decorative arts galleries opened in 2008, tracing 600 years of style and design, from medieval carvings to psychedelic 1960s dresses. Next door to the Castle Museum is the **Royal Norfolk**

ALL'S FAIR

8 St. Gregory's Alley, Norwich, Norfolk NR2 1ER
Tel: 01603 626632
e-mail: inbox@alls-fair.co.uk   website: www.alls-fair.co.uk

All's Fair is a classy little gem of a shop tucked away in the picturesque Norwich Lanes that is perfect for the conscientious shopper looking for fairly traded but lovely goodies and gifts. Remember, when you buy with a conscience, everybody's happy! Think about it. The worker gets a fair deal... happy person no. 1! You get a choice of marvellous products from all over the world... another happy person. And the planet feels healthier too... millions of happy people!

All's Fair strives to bring you the most beautiful, high quality gifts, groceries and home ware products crafted in a variety of materials, including leather, felt, wood, soapstone, silver, glass, ceramics and cotton from all around the World. Carefully selected and displayed beautifully over two floors, it is easy to notice something new to tempt you each time you visit, be it handbags or jewellery, mirrors and lamps, or something from their range of fair trade foodstuffs. Among other items, All's Fair is a stockist for Nkuku - stylish, hand-made journals, photo albums and frames that are both fair trade and eco-friendly. New for 2008, All's Fair now stocks a selection of fantastic fair trade wooden toys. Fun, natural, safe and ethically produced, these are brand new in the UK and bound to go down well with any toddlers you know.

So go forth and shop with a smile on your face, because all the products here are fair trade and eco-friendly. Open Mon-Sat 9am-5.30pm.

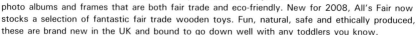

🏛 historic building   🏛 museum and heritage   🏛 historic site   🌄 scenic attraction   🌱 flora and fauna

Regimental Museum on Market Avenue, relating the story of the regiment from its founding in 1685. Exhibits include an extensive collection of medals and other memorabilia and an important photographic collection. The great open space of the Market Square, where every weekday a colourful jumble of traders' stalls can be found, offers just about every conceivable item for sale. Dominating the western side of the Market Square is City Hall, modelled on Stockholm City Hall and opened by King George VI in 1938. Opinions differ about its architectural merits, but there are no such doubts about the nearby Guildhall, a fine example of 15th-century flintwork that now houses a tea room.

Around the corner from London Street, in Bridewell Alley, is the **Bridewell Museum**, a late 14th-century merchant's house now dedicated to Norfolk's crafts and industries. Another museum/shop, this one located in the Royal Arcade, a tiled riot of Art Nouveau fantasy, celebrates the county's great contribution to world cuisine - mustard. Back in the early 1800s, Jeremiah Colman perfected his blend of mustard flours and spice to produce a condiment that was smooth in texture and tart in flavour. Together with his nephew James he founded J & J Colman in 1823; 150 years later **The Mustard Shop** was established to commemorate the company's history. The shop has an appropriately late-Victorian atmosphere and a fascinating display of vintage containers and advertisements,

Norwich Cathedral

12 The Close, Norwich, Norfolk NR1 4DH
Tel: 01603 218300
*The splendour and tranquillity of **Norwich Cathedral** have attracted visitors and pilgrims for over 900 years.*

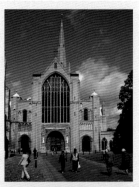

The building remains a place of quiet reflection and prayer as well as for participation in daily worship or the rich pageantry of the Church's festivals. For those with an interest in architecture, **Norwich Cathedral** boasts several superlatives. It is one of the finest complete Romanesque buildings in Europe. It has the second highest spire and largest monastic cloister in England.

The achievements of people, who have prayed, worked and even fought for their beliefs within its walls, live on. Bishop Herbert de Losinga, who began building the Cathedral in 1096, Sir Thomas Erpingham, whose archers secured victory for HenryV at the Battle of Agincourt, and more recently Nurse Edith Cavell, who was executed during WWI for helping prisoners of war to escape, are all buried here. They contribute their part to the living history of Norwich Cathedral.

The Cathedral Close is the largest in England (44 acres). This oasis of tranquillity nestles as a village in the heart of the city. Here can be found a rich mix of domestic buildings ranging from Norman to Dutch gables, flinted frame cottages and Georgian terracing. The Close is often used as a location for period drama.

DRAGON HALL

115-123 King Street, Norwich, Norfolk NR1 1QE
Tel: 01603 663922
e-mail: info@dragonhall.org   website: www.dragonhall.org

The City of Norwich is renowned for its wealth of historic buildings – from the Norman Castle and Cathedral to the Victorian railway station and Shire Hall to name but a few.

Home to almost 1,000 years of history is Dragon Hall, a magnificent medieval trading hall in the heart of Norwich. Dating from c1430 Dragon Hall was the showroom and warehouse of Robert Toppes, a wealthy merchant and mayor of the city.

The secret of Dragon Hall was only discovered in the 1970's when an investigation revealed that above the attics of a row of terraced houses was a stunning timber crown-post roof with an intricately carved and painted dragon. An extensive programme of restoration and development has transformed the site into one of the city's most important heritage attractions. The Great Hall is one of the most spectacular in the UK, the undercroft and cellars reveal earlier layers of the buildings history and the ground floor rooms are as they were in the 19th and 20th centuries.

This famous hall has caught the attention of author Bill Bryson, who said, "It is a joy to see...such a fantastic building, so sensitively restored and made available for public enjoyment."

Visitors of all ages can enjoy a journey through time as they explore this unique legacy of medieval life. Displays, interactive exhibits and a free audio tour tell the story of this intriguing building. Free family packs provide additional activities to engage younger members of the family who will also enjoy hunting out the dragons around the building and dressing up in colourful medieval costumes.

Dragon Hall is also available for hire: hosting weddings, celebrations, meetings and conferences as well as performances and exhibitions. If you want to find out more about what is happening at Dragon Hall you can visit their highly informative website and plan your first visit.

Opening hours: Monday - Friday, 10am-5pm

Sunday and Bank Holiday Mondays 11am - 4pm

some of them from 'Mustard Club' featuring such characters as Lord Bacon of Cookham and Miss Di Gester, created by no less distinguished a writer than Dorothy L Sayers. All in all, a most piquant exhibition.

Millennium Plain, just off Theatre Street, is where visitors will find **The Forum**, an architecturally stunning modern building designed by Sir Michael Hopkins. Combining a unique horseshoe shape with an all-glass façade, this spectacular structure has, at its heart, the Atrium and Bridge, meeting places where you can enjoy a meal or drink anytime through to midnight, seven days a week. At the Origins Visitor Centre, an attractive multi-media display on three floors, affords the opportunity to experience the life and times of Norwich and the wider Norfolk region during the past 2,000 years. Here can also be found the Tourist Information Centre. The Norfolk & Norwich Millennium Library houses 120,000 books and offers the best in information and communication technology.

Also on the site is the Second Air Division Memorial Library, a memorial to the Americans based in East Anglia during the Second World War. The Assembly House in Theatre Street is one of the city's finest historical houses and a leading venue for the arts. With two concert halls, three galleries featuring changing exhibitions, and a restaurant and tea rooms, this magnificent Georgian home must be included in any visit to the city. John Jarrold was a pioneering figure in British printing, and the **John Jarrold Printing Museum** charts the history of the printing industry over the past 160 years.

While the Castle has been used for many purposes over the years, the **Cathedral** (see panel on page 7) remains what it has always been: the focus of ecclesiastical life in the county. It's even older than the castle, its service of consecration taking place over 900 years ago, in 1101. This peerless building, its flint walls clad in creamy-white stone from Caen is, after Durham, the most completely Norman cathedral in England, its appeal enhanced by later Gothic features such as the flying buttresses. The Norman cloisters are the largest in the country and notable for the 400 coloured and gilded bosses depicting scenes from medieval life. Another 1,200 of these wondrous carvings decorate the glorious vaulted roof of the nave.

It's impossible to list all the Cathedral's treasures here, but do seek out the Saxon Bishop's Throne in the Presbytery, the lovely 14th-century altar painting in St Luke's Chapel, and the richly carved canopies in the Choir.

Outside, beneath the slender 315-foot spire soaring heavenwards, the **Cathedral Close** is timeless in its sense of peace. There are some 80 houses inside the Close, some medieval, many Georgian, their residents enjoying an idyllic refuge free from cars. At peace here lie the remains of Nurse Edith Cavell. A daughter of the rector of Swardeston, a few miles south of Norwich, Nurse Cavell worked at a Red Cross hospital in occupied Brussels during the First World War. She helped some 200 Allied soldiers to escape to neutral Holland before being detected and court-martialled by the Germans. As she faced execution by firing squad on 12 October 1915, she spoke her own resonant epitaph: 'Standing as I do, in the view of God and eternity, I realise that patriotism is not enough. I must have no hatred or bitterness towards anyone.'

A stroll around the Close will take you to **Pull's Ferry** with its picturesque flint gateway

COUNTRY & EASTERN

The Old Skating Rink Gallery, 34-36 Bethel Street, Norwich, Norfolk NR2 1NR
Tel: 01603 663890
website: www.countryandeastern.co.uk

Country & Eastern's Gallery is housed in a fine Old Victorian skating rink right in the centre of Norwich together with its own private car park. No need to travel to India or further to feel the lure of the East. Eastern influence is everywhere from huge doors, columns and balconies, to an immense "Yarli" (a mythical beast used in religious processions) and a fierce ceremonial Lion. There is a private collection of everyday South and South East Asian arts and crafts together with pictures and prints dating from the late 18th century. There is also a digital catalogue of over 2000 objects and pictures not yet on display. The owners are direct importers and their policy is to offer interesting and unusual furnishings at fair and affordable prices. They have worked with most of their suppliers and craftspeople for many years and have developed a strong bond of understanding and friendship with them. They offer their customers...

- Indian and Chinese Furniture – Traditional and Antique
- Decorative objects
- Oriental Rugs, Kelims and Textiles
- Handprinted & Handloomed Cotton Table & Bed Linen
- Crewel Curtains & Cushion Covers
- Table Lamps and Ceramics
- Clothes, Shawls and Accessories
- Jewellery
- Indian minature paintings

Pull's Ferry, Norwich

on King Street leads to the only medieval merchants' trading halls known to survive in Western Europe. **Dragon Hall** (see panel on page 8) was built for the merchant Robert Toppes in the mid 15th century.

Norwich is home to some 32 medieval churches in all, every one of them worth attention, although many are now used for purposes other than worship. Outstanding among them are St Peter Mancroft, a masterpiece of Gothic architecture built between 1430 and 1455 (and the largest church in Norwich), and St Peter Hungate, a handsome 15th-century church standing at the top of Elm Hill, a narrow, unbelievably picturesque lane where in medieval times the city's wool merchants built their homes, close to their warehouses beside the River Wensum.

St Gregory's Church in Pottergate is another Norwich church to have been deconsecrated, and its fate might well have been a sad one. Happily, it is now home to an arts centre where local artists, actors, musicians, dancers and other arts groups stage a variety of performances and exhibitions throughout the year.

When the basic structure of the present St Gregory's was built in the late 14th century, the general rule seems to have been that any parish of around 1,000 people would have its own place of worship. St Gregory's was founded on the site of a Saxon church in 1210 and rebuilt in its present form in 1394. The church takes it name from Gregory the Great, the 6th-century Pope best-known for his campaign to convert the heathen Anglo-Saxons of 'Angle-land' to Christianity, despatching a party of 40 monks to Angle-land in AD596, led by Augustine, whom the Pope consecrated as the first Archbishop of Canterbury. St Julian's Church is adjoined by a

fronting the River Wensum. In medieval times a canal ran inland from here so that provisions, goods and, in the earliest days, building materials, could be moved direct to the Cathedral. A short stroll along the riverside walk will bring you to Cow Tower, built around 1378 and the most massive of the old city towers.

At the western end of the Cathedral Close is the magnificent Erpingham Gate, presented to the city in 1420 by a hero of the Battle of Agincourt, Sir Thomas Erpingham. Beyond this gate, in Tombland (originally Toom or wasteland), is Samson and Hercules House, its entrance flanked by two 1674 carvings of these giants. Diagonally opposite stands the 15th-century Maid's Head Hotel. A 14th-century door within a 15th-century opening

rebuilt cell that is the shrine to Mother Julian, whose 14th-century *Revelations of Love Divine* is thought to be the first English book written by a woman.

The Inspire Discovery Centre, housed in the medieval Church of St Michael in Coslany Street, just across the Wensum northeast of the city centre, is full of exciting hands-on displays and activities that make scientific enquiry come to life.

There are also a large number of beautiful and well-maintained parks in the city, some of which offer chess, lawn tennis and hard tennis courts, bowls, pitch and putt, rowing and more, together with a programme of entertainments ranging from theatre to concerts. One worth particular mention is **The Plantation Garden** (see panel below) in Earlham Road, three acres of Victorian plantings restored after having fallen into disrepair, and thought to be the only one in the nation with a Grade II listing.

On the western edge of the city stands the University of East Anglia. It's well worth making your way here to visit the **Sainsbury**

Centre for Visual Arts. Housed in a huge hall of aluminium and glass designed by Norman Foster, the Centre contains the eclectic collection of a 'passionate acquirer' of art, Sir Robert Sainsbury. For more than 50 years, Sir Robert purchased whatever works of art took his fancy, ignoring fashionable trends. Thus the visitor finds sculptures and pictures by Henry Moore, Bacon and Giacometti, along with African and pre-Columbian artefacts, Egyptian, Etruscan and Roman bronzes, works by Native Americans and the Inuit, and sculptures from the Cyclades, the South Seas, the Orient and medieval Europe. This extraordinary collection was donated to the University by Sir Robert and Lady Lisa Sainsbury in 1973; their son David complemented his parents' generosity by paying for the building in which it is housed.

To the south of Norwich in the village of Caistor St Edmund are the remains of **Venta Icenorum**, the Roman town established here after Boudicca's rebellion in AD61. Unusually, this extensive site has not been

The Plantation Garden

Earlham Road, Norwich, Norfolk NR4 7TQ
Tel: 01603621868
e-mail chair@plantationgarden.co.uk
website: www.plantationgarden.co.uk

The Plantation Garden is a hidden treasure of Norwich, a green oasis just a few minutes walk from the city centre. It was created in the 19th century by Henry Trevor, a Norwich business man, who transformed an old chalk quarry into a most unusual and delightful garden. Within its 3 acres can be found a 'Gothic' fountain, Italinate terraces, 'medieval' terrace walls, woodland walkways and a rustic bridge as well as mature trees, flower beds and lawns. This Grade II English Heritage registered garden is open all year round. The entry fee of £2.00 should be placed in the honesty box if the garden is unattended. Teas are served on the lawn on Sundays during the summer.

disturbed by later developments, so archaeologists have been able to identify the full scale of the original settlement. Sadly very little remains above ground, although in dry summers the grid pattern of the streets show up as brown lines in the grass. Most of the finds discovered during excavations in the 1920s and 1930s are now in Norwich Castle Museum, but the riverside site still merits a visit.

Just to the north of the city, on the Cromer road, lies the **City of Norwich Aviation Museum**. A massive Vulcan bomber dominates the collection, which also includes a variety of aircraft both military and civil and displays showing the development of aviation in Norfolk. On the southern outskirts, **Whitlingham Country Park** is a great place for walking, cycling and boating, with woodland, meadows, trails and two broads.

Around Norwich

PORINGLAND
6 miles SE of Norwich on the B1332

The name of this sizable village will be familiar to those who love the paintings of the Norwich artist John Crome (1794-1842), whose Arcadian painting of The Poringland Oak hangs in the Norwich Castle Art Gallery.

To the southwest of Poringland is The Playbarn, an indoor and outdoor adventure centre specially designed for the under-sevens. All the play equipment is based on a farmyard theme, with a miniature farm, bouncy tractors, soft-play sheep pens, and donkey rides among the attractions. Refreshments and light lunches are available, or you can bring along your own picnic.

THE MILL INN

Ipswich Rd, Saxlingham Thorpe, Norwich NR15 1UB
Tel: 01508 470005

The village of Saxlingham Thorpe is situated approximately 7 miles south of Norwich on the main A140 Norwich to Ipswich trunk road. **The Mill Inn** is situated just outside the village centre and a good car park entices the passing motorist to sample the delights of this well located business. The property has undergone significant upgrading to offer a good local drinking house as well as a popular destination food outlet.

There are two main bar areas, one of which is used for bar trade during the week and food trade at the weekend. In addition, there is a delightful brick, timber and glazed conservatory restaurant overlooking the garden with approximately 30 covers and the whole trading area has the capacity to seat 80 plus diners.

GREEN FARM HOLIDAY COTTAGES

Saxlingham Green, Norwich, Norfolk, NR15 1TG
Tel: 01508 499393 e-mail: pennywhyte@hotmail.com
website: www.saxlinghamholidaycottages.co.uk

Nestled in the heart of an old apple orchard in the outstanding conservation area of Saxlingham Green, sit two detached traditional beamed cottages. Just seven miles south of the historic city of Norwich and adjacent to the peaceful village of Saxlingham Nethergate, **Stable Cottage** and **Orchard Cottage** are ideally placed for exploring Norfolk and Suffolk and the beautiful heritage coastline.

Norwich is renowned for its magnificent castle, 11th century cathedral, museums, stylish restaurants, theatres, innovative architecture and superb shopping. The Norfolk Broads are close by providing sailing, boat hire and river trips. Fishing is very popular and golfers have excellent courses locally. The wonderful walks through coastal and country villages, past windmills and lighthouses, beckon bird-watchers, artists, photographers and naturalists alike. Why not bring your bicycles and discover the myriad of wildlife as you venture along tiny peaceful lanes returning to take tea in the summerhouse.

Both cottages have two bedrooms, sleeping three. They are fully self-contained, on one level with minimum low steps, very comfortably furnished with electric central heating, TV, cooker, refrigerator and microwave. They each have their own private, south-facing patios and delightful gardens with BBQ facilities. No smokers or pets.

WYMONDHAM

9 miles SW of Norwich off the A11

🏛 Becket's Chapel 🏛 Railway Station

🏛 Wymondham Heritage Museum 🏛 The Bridewell

The exterior of **Wymondham Abbey** presents one of the oddest ecclesiastical buildings in the county; the interior reveals one of the most glorious. The original building on the site was a Saxon church, replaced when William d'Albini, Chief Butler to Henry I, built a priory for the Benedictine monastery of St Albans. The Benedictines - or Black Monks, as they were known because of the colour of their habits – were the richest and most aristocratic of the monastic orders, who apparently experienced some difficulty in respecting their solemn vows of poverty and humility; especially the latter. Constantly in dispute with the people of Wymondham, the

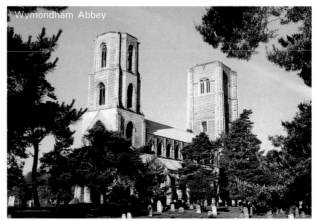
Wymondham Abbey

🏛 historic building 🏛 museum and heritage 🏛 historic site 🔷 scenic attraction 🌿 flora and fauna

dissension between them grew so bitter that in 1249 Pope Innocent IV himself attempted to reconcile their differences. When his efforts failed, a wall was built across the interior of the building, dividing it into an area for the monks and another for the parishioners. Even this drastic measure failed to bring peace, however. Both parties wanted to ring their own bells, so each built a tower. The villagers erected a stately rectangular tower at the west end; the monks an octagonal one over the crossing, thus creating the curious exterior appearance.

Step inside and you find a magnificent Norman nave, 112 feet long. (It was originally twice as long, but the eastern end, along with most of what had become the Abbey buildings, was demolished after the Dissolution of the Monasteries.) The superb hammerbeam roof is supported by 76 beautifully carved angels. There's also an interesting 16th-century tomb, of the last Abbot, in delicate terracotta work, and a striking modern memorial: a gilded and coloured reredos and tester commemorating the local men who lost their lives in the First World War.

The rectangular western tower of the Abbey was the setting for one of the last acts in the ill-fated Kett's Rebellion of 1549. From its walls, William Kett was hung in chains and left to die: his brother Robert, the leading figure in the uprising, suffered the same fate at Norwich Castle.

Although many of Wymondham's oldest houses were lost in the fire of 1615, when some 300 dwellings were destroyed, there are still some attractive Elizabethan buildings in

MANOR FARM BED AND BREAKFAST

Hingham Road, Gt Ellingham, Attleborough, Norfolk, NR17 1JE
Tel: 01953 453388
e-mail: e.rivett@manorfarmnorfolk.co.uk
website: www.manorfarmnorfolk.co.uk

Manor Farm offers spacious comfortable accommodation and hosts Tony and Liz provide a warm welcome ensuring all guests' needs are catered for. The house dates back to the 1640's and has a wealth of exposed beams and an inglenook fireplace in the dining room. All rooms are centrally heated and have views over the garden and fields beyond. Each room is provided with colour TV, hairdryer, radio alarm and tea/coffee making facilities. The conservatory overlooks the garden and there is ample parking for cars, and dry cover for cycles.

Also available is Manor Farm Cottage available through English Country Cottages (www.english-country-cottages.co.uk ref: CXB). With 12 acres of shared woodland to enjoy, this beautiful barn conversion is a delight for lovers of the countryside. Although close to the owners home, **Manor Farm Cottage** stands on its own and is an excellent holiday base for visiting the many attractions of Norfolk and Suffolk.

A pottery can be found in the village itself, whilst Banham Zoo, Bressingham Gardens and the Steam Museum, and Thetford Forest are all within an easy drive. The famous Norfolk Broads and Norwich (with its cathedral, castle, museums, and excellent shops, bars and restaurants) can be reached within an hour. The nearest pub is only 1 mile.

the heart of the town. The Market Place (Friday is market day, and on the first Friday of every month there's an antiques and collectors' fair held in Central Hall) is given dignity by the picturesque octagonal Market Cross, rebuilt two years after the fire. Crowned by a pyramid roof, this appealing timber-framed building is open on all sides on the ground floor, and its upper floor is reached by an outside stairway. Also of interest is **Becket's Chapel**, founded in 1174 and restored in 1559. In its long history it has served as a pilgrim's chapel, grammar school, and coal store. Currently, it houses the town library. The **Bridewell**, or House of Correction, in Bridewell Street, was built as a model prison in 1785 along lines recommended by the prison reformer, John Howard, who had condemned the earlier gaol on the site as 'one of the vilest in the country'. Wymondham's Bridewell is said to have served as a model for the penitentiaries established in the United States. Now owned by the town's Heritage Society, Bridewell is home to several community projects, including the **Wymondham Heritage Museum**. Displays include brushmaking and Kett's rebellion and there are new exhibitions each year (tel: 01953 600205).

Railway buffs will also want to visit the historic **Railway Station**, built in 1845 on the Great Eastern's Norwich-Ely line. At its peak, the station and its section employed over 100 people. Still providing a rail link to Norwich, Cambridge, London and the Midlands, the station has been restored, and its buildings house a railway museum, restaurant and tea room, and a piano showroom. The Mid-Norfolk Railway runs heritage diesels from Wymondham to Dereham (see under Dereham page 97).

DISS
20 miles S of Norwich on the A1066

🏛 St Mary's Church

The much-loved Poet Laureate John Betjeman declared Diss his favourite Norfolk town, and it's easy to understand his enthusiasm. The River Waveney running alongside forms the boundary between Norfolk and Suffolk, but this attractive old market town – winner of Best Kept Market Town in Norfolk, whose town centre is now a designated conservation area – keeps itself firmly on the northern bank of the river. The town is a pleasing mixture of Tudor, Georgian and Victorian houses grouped around The Mere, which gives the town its name, derived from the Anglo-Saxon word for standing water.

The old town grew up on the hill above the Mere, perhaps because, as an 18th-century resident observed, 'all the filth of the town centring in the Mere, beside the many conveniences that are placed over it, make the water very bad and altogether useless ... it stinks exceedingly, and sometimes the fish rise in great numbers, so thick that they are easily taken; they are chiefly roach and eels.' A proper sewerage system was finally installed in 1851 at this six-acre lake, which is said to be the second deepest in the country, counting the depth of water and mud.

There's a public park beside The Mere, and from it a narrow street leads to the small Market Place. This former poultry market is dominated by **St Mary's Church**. The oldest parts date back some 700 years, and the St Nicholas Chapel is particularly appealing with its wonderful corbels, angels in the roof, and gargoyles. In the early 1500s, the Rector here was John Skelton, court poet and tutor to Prince Henry, later Henry VIII. A bitter, quarrelsome man, Skelton was appointed Poet Laureate through the patronage of Cardinal Wolsey, despite the fact that most of Skelton's output has been described as 'breathless doggerel'. Appointed Rector of Diss in 1502, he appears to have been suspended nine years later for having a concubine. Not far from his church is the delightful Victorian Shambles with a cast-iron veranda and a small museum inside.

Bressingham Gardens

BRESSINGHAM
5 miles W of Diss off the A1066

🏛 Bressingham Gardens & Steam Museum

🏛 Fire Museum

Bressingham Gardens and Steam Museum boasts one of the world's finest collections of British and Continental locomotives. All are housed under cover in the museum's extensive

locomotive sheds, which also contain many steam-driven industrial engines, traction engines, a Victorian steam roundabout and The Fire Museum, whose collection of fire engines and fire-fighting equipment could form a complete museum in its own right. Visitors can view the interior of the Royal Coach and ride along five miles of track through the woods and gardens. Three narrow-gauge railways run

OXFOOTSTONE GRANARY

Low Common, South Lopham, Diss, Norfolk IP22 2JS
Tel: 01379 687490
e-mail: mail@oxfoot.co.uk website: www.oxfoot.co.uk

Escape for a weekend, or longer, to South Lopham on the Norfolk-Suffolk border. Let the stress of everyday life evaporate into Norfolk's wide skies. Take time out to recharge your batteries at Oxfootstone Granary situated in quiet open countryside just off the A1066 5 miles from the lovely little market town of Diss and just two miles from the internationally famous gardens of Alan and Adrian Bloom at Bressingham.

We can offer two options: Our comfortable B&B with its two en suite guest rooms situated in a single storey wing in former cart sheds grouped around a central courtyard garden. The rooms, one twin and one double, directly overlook a large pond with waterfowl. Or alternatively, you might prefer to be completely self contained in Piglet Barn, our newly converted building with underfloor heating, wood burner, 2 double bedrooms, fully fitted kitchen and bathroom. Best of all are the long views, the sunsets are just glorious.

Everyone is welcome at Oxfootstone, even your pet. Most of us hate the idea of leaving pets behind or at the kennels, but here you won't have to and there are lots of "walkies".

SUFFOLK POTTERIES

Lopham Road, Kenninghall, Norfolk NR16 2DT
Tel/Fax: 01379 687424
e-mail: suffolkpots@btinternet.com
website: www.suffolkpotteries.co.uk

Suffolk Potteries traditional and contemporary designs combine with the finest materials to produce superb quality handthrown English terracotta pottery for the home and garden.

The simple and traditional kitchenware is equally at home in a modern or country farmhouse kitchen. The attractive and practical pottery is dishwasher safe and can be used in the microwave.

Pots and planters help to add colour and liven up the smallest garden or patio. Suffolk potteries have a wide range of stock and the ability to produce many other designs to order. Safe to leave outside in all but the harshest winters, the range also includes a variety of small bird feeders ideal for winter feeding.

So whether you are looking for a high quality range of kitchenware for your own home, that perfect pot for the garden, or are planning to buy a present (corporate gifts and commemorative items are a speciality!), Suffolk Potteries have the product for you.

PHOENIX GLASSWORKS

3 Gables Yard, The Green, Diss, Norfolk IP21 4SY
Tel: 01379 676 066
e-mail: info@phoenixglassworks.co.uk
website: www.phoenixglassworks.co.uk

Phoenix Glassworks – *Giving Flight to Creativity*

Established just two years ago **Phoenix Glassworks** is a small company with a big presence in decorative glass. Specialists in stained Glass panels and leaded lights, they create stunning hand-crafted stained glass panels or carry out repairs to damaged panels and windows, using traditional and contemporary techniques. Working with warmed glass and fused glass, Phoenix Glassworks produce a colourful range of studio glass ideal as gifts. They are happy to produce Stained Glass commissions working closely with clients. Stained glass can be used to enhance your environment, bringing intense colour and light to your living or work space. It can also be used to disguise an ugly view or to provide privacy whilst allowing light to enter your room. A variety of courses and personal tuition are also available – Please contact for details.

Gables Yard is situated, in the picturesque village of Pulham Market, which is 2 miles east of the A140 between Diss and Norwich. The village amenities include a friendly village store, two public houses, an excellent B&B and two public car parks. For those interested in stained glass a visit to the village Church is a must. Gables Yard has four other studios all with working artists producing unique work. Viewing by appointment

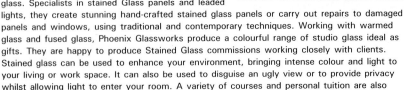

🏛 historic building 🏦 museum and heritage 🏛 historic site 🔱 scenic attraction 🌿 flora and fauna

through the gardens, woods, meadows and lakes. The world-famous six-acre Dell Garden has 47 island beds of perennials, and Foggy Bottom is a seasonal combination of trees, conifers, shrubs, perennials and ornamental grasses. A two-acre plant centre adjoins the gardens and here there are thousands of plant specimens, many of them rare, available for purchase. Another major attraction here is the national *Dads Army* collection – a tribute to TV's Captain Mainwaring and his men at Walmington-on-Sea.

HARLESTON
7 miles NE of Diss off the A143

This pretty market town with some notable half-timbered and Georgian houses, and a splendid 12th-century coaching inn, was a favourite of the renowned architectural authority, Nikolaus Pevsner, who particularly admired the early Georgian Candlers House at the northern end of the town. Another writer has described the area around the marketplace as 'the finest street scene in East Anglia'. The town lies in the heart of the Waveney Valley, a lovely area that inspired many paintings by the locally-born artist, Sir Alfred Munnings.

SCOLE
2 miles E of Diss on the A140

Scole's history goes back to Roman times, since it grew up alongside the Imperial highway from Ipswich to Norwich at the point where it bridged the River Waveney. Traffic on this road (the A140) became unbearable in the 1980s, but a bypass has now mercifully restored some peace to the village. There are two hostelries of note: The Scole Inn, a

---

RUSHALL DOLLS HOUSE

Half Moon Farm, The Street, Rushall, Diss, Norfolk IP21 4QD
Tel: 01379 742557
e-mail: info@rushall-dollshouse-miniatures.co.uk
website: www.rushall-dollshouse-miniatures.co.uk

RUSHALL DOLLS HOUSE is a specialist shop in the world of dolls houses, miniatures and associated accessories in 1:12 and 1:24 scale. The owner, Annette, has stocked her shop from floor to ceiling with an impressive variety of dolls house essentials, from the exclusive, bespoke, one of a kind to the economy range. In fact almost anything you can buy for a real house (including the house itself!) you can buy in miniature for dolls houses, shops and other tiny buildings.

A variety of dolls houses are available from leading brands including Barbara's Mouldings, Sid Cooke, Dolls House Emporium, Streets Ahead to individually made houses, all in a wide range of styles and periods. The furniture and accessories include a selection from Bespaq, Glenowen, McQueenies, SWP, Et Cetera, Mouse House, Sussex Crafts, Phoenix and many carefully selected hand crafted items from expert miniaturists.

The accessories range from DIY to flooring, lighting, fabrics, flowers, food, dolls, pets, musical instruments, seasonal items and all the little bits that make a house a home. Rushall Dolls House also sells signed original paintings, local crafts, handmade greetings cards, Jellycats, Japanese collector's items and selected home ware and gifts.

Annette and her team are warm, welcoming and knowledgeable, adding to the pleasure of a visit to this lovely place, which lies on a farm at Rushall, northeast of Diss and a short drive from the A140 or A143. Opening hours are 10 to 4 Wednesday to Saturday, or by appointment.

---

coaching inn of 1655, built in an extravagant style of Dutch gables, giant pilasters and towering chimney stacks; and the Crossways Inn, which must have a good claim to being the prettiest pub in the county.

THORPE ABBOTS
6 miles E of Diss on a minor road off the A143 or A140 at Dickleburgh bypass

100th Bomb Group Memorial Museum

Veterans of the Second World War and their families and friends will be interested in the **100th Bomb Group Memorial Museum**, a small museum at Common Road on the edge of Dickleburgh Airfield (now disused). The Museum is the Bloody Hundredths tribute to the US 8th Air Force, which was stationed here during the war, and includes displays of USAAF decorations and uniforms, equipment, combat records, wartime photographs and other memorabilia. Facilities include refreshments, a museum shop, visitor centre and a picnic area. The Museum is open Saturdays, Sundays and Bank Holidays, and on Wednesdays from May to September. Closed November, December and January (tel: 01379 740708).

COLTISHALL
8 miles N of Norwich on the B1150/B1354

Ancient Lime Kiln

This charming village beside the River Bure captivates visitors with its riverside setting, leafy lanes, elegant Dutch-gabled houses, village green and thatched church. Coltishall has a good claim to its title of Gateway to Broadland, since for most cruisers this is the beginning of the navigable portion of the Bure. Anyone interested in Norfolk's industrial heritage will want to seek out the

---

LA MAISON WORKSHOP
Unit 3&4 The Paddocks, Frettenham, Horstead, Norwich NR12 7LB Tel: 01603 736184/07930 420967

LA MAISON
5 Bull Street, Holt, Norfolk NR25 6HP Tel: 01263 713418

Nestling in a street in Holt is La Maison, a delightful cottage now turned into a shop with several rooms over two floors supplying restored antique pine furniture to a variety of discerning clientele. La Maison can now be considered as one of the best sources of quality pine furniture around. Also available are many interesting accessories and the shop extends to a delightful garden complete with statues and in the summer months, tables and chairs. Owner David Northcutt has always had an interest in antique furniture and has now been restoring pine for over 10 years. The majority of the pieces are sourced in Holland and France.

In January 2008, the existing workshop had to be replaced with much larger premises to accommodate the growing business and customers are encouraged to visit the new workshop where they can see work in progress and hand pick pieces before restoration. The Showroom adjoining the workshop is stocked with finished pine and accessories for customers to view. Furniture available includes breakdown wardrobes, tables and chairs, chest of drawers, bookcases, bedside cabinets, sideboards and much more.

In addition to the antique pine furniture La Maison also caters for customers who want handmade reclaimed pine i.e. tables, beds and even complete kitchens. All the pieces are done to a high standard in a waxed finish or can be painted or distressed in a colour of your choice. Whatever your needs you will be welcome at **La Maison** and **La Maison Workshop and Showroom** where David or the staff will be happy to discuss your requirements.

---

historic building   museum and heritage   historic site   scenic attraction   flora and fauna

SPIXWORTH HALL COTTAGES

1996

*Grange Farm, Buxton Road,
Spixworth, Norwich NR10 3PR
Tel: 01603 898190*

e-mail: hallcottages@btinternet.com
website: www.hallcottages.co.uk

Spixworth Hall Cottages are a delightful group of cottages and award winning conversions full of character and an ideal base for exploring Norwich, the Norfolk Broads and the marvellous beaches at the coast. The cottages are situated in sheltered seclusion, surrounded by farmland, grazing meadows, ponds and woods. Here you have space to relax and unwind, 500 metres from the nearest road but only 15 minutes from the city centre, with good access to local attractions, historic buildings, gardens, market towns and churches. For those wishing 'to get away from it all', there is plenty to do on site with country walks through bluebell and snowdrop woods, fishing on the lake, tennis, swimming in the summer and cosy log fires in winter, plus an unobtrusive outdoor play area and well stocked games barn that's sure to provide hours of fun for children of all ages. There are a range of 2 and 3 bedroom cottages and a 5 bedroom cottage which sleep from 3 to 12 people.

The Lodge Cottage was the Gatehouse to the hall and is set on its own in a beautiful woodland garden.

Waterside and Granary cottages, *top picture* were originally part of the Spixworth Hall Stables and retain many features including a stable division and some pamment and brick floors. They have lovely views over the farm and parkland and extra seating areas on the landings can be used to relax or as play areas.

The Hayloft, *interior picture*, is a stunning conversion of the old granary with oak flooring in the spacious, light open plan living/dining/kitchen area.

Swallows and Pond Cottages can be let as individual cottages with three and two bedrooms or can be linked together to create an exceptional quality property with five bedrooms and five bathrooms. A far cry from when estate workers had a tin bath in the kitchen of Pond cottage but the cottage still has a cosy intimate feel.

The owners are committed to welcoming all people including the disabled. One of Gaffer's cottages five bedrooms is on the ground floor bedroom and the Lodge is a single storey cottage.

Stables Cottage has level access throughout including into a delightful enclosed courtyard garden. Doors wide enough for cart horses open into generous rooms in which furniture can be repositioned to suit any special needs. Visitors return time and time again to this property.

The thoughtful and sympathetic restoration of the cottages has created quality holiday homes with much style and character but with the luxury of fittings and equipment of the 21st century. These delightful cottages are available throughout the year and offer much to see and do. There is a warm welcome here throughout the year to anyone who loves heritage and the English countryside.

THE OLD PUMP HOUSE
Luxury Bed and Breakfast
Holman Road, Aylsham,
Norfolk NR11 6BY

Tel: *01263 733789*
Fax: *01263 734513*
e-mail:*theoldpumphouse@btconnect.com*
website: *www.theoldpumphouse.com*

A warm, welcoming Georgian House that
is full of character, **The Old Pump House**
is ideally situated close to Norwich, the
Norfolk Broads, the coast, nature reserves
and stately homes (just one mile from
Blickling Hall which is famed for its long
gallery, fine tapestries, paintings and rare
books). Built around 1750, the house has
had a rich and interesting past due to its
history as a farm, boarding school and
rectory. These days it is run by Marc
James, an antiques dealer and Charles
Kirkman, an ex banker, who make for
perfect hosts and your stay an extremely
enjoyable one.

There are five twin or doubles all en-
suite including one four-poster room and
two family rooms. All rooms have wireless
Internet connection, central heating, LCD,
TVs, radio alarm clocks and hairdryers.
The rooms were totally refurbished in
2007 by the owners who have only
recently taken over the establishment and
this could now be straight out of a House
& Gardens magazine. Each room is
themed and tastefully decorated, such as
the 'Oak Room', which as its name
suggests is furnished predominately in
oak. Hospitality trays with teas, coffee,
hot chocolate, biscuits and even a bottle
of water are provided.

Delicious English breakfasts (with local
bacon, sausages and free range eggs) are
freshly cooked to order and served in the
elegant, pine shuttered Georgian Room
where you can watch the birds feeding by the pond in the pretty, tranquil garden. Vegetarian and
Continental breakfasts are served on request. Pre booked evening meals are available outside high
season, and freshly prepared sandwiches and picnic lunches are always available to order.

The unspoilt surrounding countryside with its wealth of attractive villages and historic town
is perfect for walking, bird watching and cycling (local bicycle hire is available) and there are
several steam railways within easy reach.

🏛 historic building 🏛 museum and heritage 🏛 historic site 🏔 scenic attraction 🌿 flora and fauna

Ancient Lime Kiln, next door to the Railway Tavern in Station Road. Lime, formerly an important part of Norfolk's rural economy, is obtained by heating chalk to a very high temperature in a kiln. Most of the county sits on a bed of chalk, but in the area around Coltishall and Horstead it is of a particularly high quality. The kiln at Coltishall, one of the few surviving in the country, is a listed building of finely finished brickwork, built in a style unique to Norfolk.

Blickling Hall, Aylsham

The top of the tapered kiln pot is level with the ground, and down below, a vaulted walkway allowed access to the grills through which the lime was raked out. This was uncomfortable and even dangerous work since fresh lime, when it comes into contact with a moist surface, such as a human body, becomes burning hot. The lime had to be slaked with water before it could be used as a fertiliser, for mortar, or as whitewash. Access to the kiln is by way of the Railway Tavern, but during the months October to March, you may find that the building has been taken over by a colony of hibernating bats which, by law, may not be disturbed.

AYLSHAM
10 miles N of Norwich on the A140

- Blickling Hall
- Mannington
- Bure Valley Railway
- Wolterton Park
- Little Barningham

The attractive market town of Aylsham is set beside the River Bure, the northern terminus of the **Bure Valley Railway**. It has an unspoilt Market Place, surrounded by late 17th- and early 18th-century houses, reflecting the prosperity the town enjoyed in those years

from the cloth trade, and a 14th/15th century church, St Michael's, said to have been built by John O'Gaunt. In the churchyard is the tomb of one of the greatest of the 18th-century landscape gardeners, Humphrey Repton, the creator of some 200 parks and gardens around the country.

One of Repton's many commissions was to landscape the grounds of **Blickling Hall**, a 'dream of architectural beauty', which stands a mile or so outside Aylsham. Many visitors have marvelled at their first sight of the great Hall built for Sir Henry Hobart in the 1620s. 'No-one is prepared on coming downhill past the church into the village, to find the main front of this finest of Jacobean mansions, actually looking upon the road, unobstructedly, from behind its velvet lawns,' enthused Charles Harper in 1904. 'No theatrical manager cunning in all the artful accessories of the stage could devise anything more dramatic.'

Inside, the most dramatic feature is the Long Gallery, which extends for 135 feet and originally provided space for indoor exercise in bad weather. Its glory is the plaster ceiling, an intricately patterned expanse of heraldic panels bearing the Hobart arms, along with others displaying bizarre and inscrutable emblems, such as a naked lady riding a two-legged dragon.

Other treasures at Blickling include a dramatic double-flight carved oak staircase, the Chinese Bedroom lined with 18th-century hand-painted wallpaper, and the dazzling Peter the Great Room. A descendant of Sir Henry Hobart, the 2nd Earl of Buckinghamshire, was appointed Ambassador to Russia in 1746, and he returned from that posting with a magnificent tapestry, the gift of Empress Catherine the Great. This room was redesigned so as to display the Earl's sumptuous souvenir to its full effect, and portraits of himself and his Countess by Gainsborough were added later.

The Earl was a martyr to gout, and his death in 1793 at the age of 50 occurred when, finding the pain unbearable, he thrust his bloated foot into a bucket of icy water, and suffered a heart attack. He was buried beneath the idiosyncratic Egyptian Pyramid in the grounds, a 45-foot structure designed by Ignatius Bonomi that combines Egyptian and classical elements to create a mausoleum which, if nothing else, is certainly distinctive.

Within a few miles of Blickling Hall are two other stately homes, both the properties of Lord and Lady Walpole. **Mannington Gardens and Countryside** are set around a medieval moated manor house and feature a wide variety of plants, trees and shrubs, including thousands of roses, particularly classic varieties. The Heritage Rose Garden and Twentieth-Century Rose Garden are set in small gardens reflecting their period of origin.

BLACK SHEEP

9 Penfold Street, Aylsham, Norfolk NR11 6ET
Tel: 01263 732006 Fax: 01263 735074
e-mail: email@blacksheep.ltd.uk
webiste: www.blacksheep.ltd.uk

Baa baa black sheep, have you any wool? Yes sir...**Black Sheep Ltd** situated in the heart of Aylsham are famous for producing the finest quality knitwear from the best of British wool. Each garment is warm, stylish and above all exclusively designed and produced in England and exported all over the World.

Are 'ewe' looking for something different? Alongside their exclusive knitwear there is a varied range of products. Amongst the ranges in stock are 'Keen' shoes, which have to be worn to be believed! Black Sheep also offer a wide variety of summer and winter ranges for women and men. Mat de Misaine is a classic women's range from France - perfect for summer. Weird Fish offers casual cotton tops for men and women. Chatham, Sebago, Gurteen are other brands that offer a casual look not found on the high street.

Stand out from the flock this year, with Black Sheep jerseys and accessories you always get something truly individual.

Mannington Hall, Aylsham

England's first Prime Minister, stands in grounds landscaped by Humphry Repton. Here can be found walks and trails, orienteering, an adventure playground and various special events, which are held throughout the year. The Hall is open for tours every Friday from April to the end of October.

Over 20 miles of waymarked public footpaths and permissive paths run around Mannington and Wolterton linking into the Weavers Way long-distance footpath and Holt circular walk.

Just north of Mannington Hall stands the village of **Little Barningham**, where St Mary's Church is a magnet for collectors of ecclesiastical curiosities. Inside, perched on the corner of an ancient box pew, stands a

There are also Garden Shops, with plants, souvenirs and crafts, and tea rooms. The Hall itself is open by appointment, while the walks are open every day.

Two miles from Mannington, **Wolterton Park**, the stately 18th-century Hall built for Horatio Walpole, brother of Sir Robert,

---

THE PINK HOUSE

Wickmere, Norfolk NR11 7AL   Tel: 01263 577678
e-mail: info@pinkhousebb.co.uk   website: www.pinkhousebb.co.uk

WILLOW FEN

Ludham Bridge, Norfolk, NR29 5NX   Tel: 01263 577678
e-mail: info@willowfen.co.uk   website: www.willowfen.co.uk

Two contrasting properties; **The Pink House** is a traditional nineteenth century cottage in peaceful countryside which offers comfortable bed and breakfast; **Willow Fen** is a modern dwelling recently completely re-furbished in contemporary style and offers superior self catering accommodation for up to six persons.

Both benefit from their owners attention to detail. Dee and Robert ensure a warm and friendly welcome at The Pink House Bed and Breakfast, with home made cakes, choice of delicious breakfasts (including a daily special), fresh flowers in all the rooms and turn down service with chocolates on the pillow. The Pink House has three double rooms, all of which are comfortably furnished with en suite bathrooms. It has a large conservatory and extensive gardens which guests are welcome to enjoy. Willow Fen has four bedrooms which can be arranged as doubles, twin or single and bathrooms which feature twin basins and power showers. It has a large garden with patio area, barbecue and chiminea.

The Pink House is just five miles from Aylsham in the quiet hamlet of Wickmere, an ideal location for accessing the North Norfolk Coast, local market towns and is very close to Felbrigg Hall and Blickling Hall, two National Trust properties well worth a visit. . Willow Fen Holiday Accommodation is in the heart of the Broads Conservation area and boasts uninterrupted views of marshland overlooking the River Ant. Both properties are wonderful bases for walkers, bird watchers, cyclists and artists. At Willow Fen, Robert can arrange a boat for your entire stay or by the day.

---

stories and anecdotes 🐦 famous people 🌣 art and craft 🖉 entertainment and sport 🕺 walks

Alderford Common

Distance: *3.1 miles (4.8 kilometres)*
Typical time: *90 mins*
Height gain: *20 metres*
Map: *Explorer 238*
Walk: *www.walkingworld.com ID:1504*
Contributor: *Joy & Charles Boldero*

There is no bus route to the car parking area, however there is a bus route to Swannington and the walk could be started at Point 7. The car park is on Alderford Common, which is situated on the Reepham to Hellesdon road three miles southeast of Reepham.

DESCRIPTION:

This is a nice easy short rural walk not far from Norwich. The route is through woodland, along tracks, across meadows and through the rural village of Swannington.

ADDITIONAL INFORMATION:

Alderford Common is a haven for wildlife. Parts of it have been listed as a Site of Special Scientific Interest since 1957. On the south side there is an overgrown Bronze Age barrow. In 1988, the National Nightingale survey stated that this area had more pairs of nightingales than any other in east Norfolk.

Swannington Hall was probably built in the late 1500s for a family named, Richers. Some years ago it became a popular 'pub' but now it is once again a private house; part of the old moat can still be seen. St Margaret's Church has stood here since the 13th century and inside the font is of that age, too.

FEATURES:

Church, Stately Home, Wildlife, Birds, Flowers, Great Views, Butterflies.

WALK DIRECTIONS:

1 | From the car park turn right along the road.

2 | Turn left at the fingerpost sign into a woodland path. It goes through the bracken then across open spaces, at the second of which the path keeps to the top of the bank. The path then goes up and down finally going up steps.

3 | Turn left at the road, then after about 10 paces turn right at the fingerpost along the track.

4 | Turn right along a country lane. Opposite the footpath in Upgate turn left across grass to a yellow marker in the far hedgeline. Go over a plank bridge, up the bank and continue along the field edge.

5 | Turn right at the yellow marker signs, over a bridge and through a gate. Turn left along a meadow, go through a gate and diagonally right under wires to the next gate. Cross the next meadow to a gate ahead.

6 | Turn left along a tarmac lane.

7 | Turn left along a country lane, by a church walking through Swannington. Keep along The Street, then bear right along Broad Lane (near here is the bus stop).

8 | At the bend turn right at the fingerpost along a track.

9 | At a footpath marker on the ground turn left through a hedge gap. Take the path southwestwards across the two fields. Cross the road to the car park.

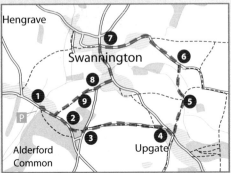

historic building · museum and heritage · historic site · scenic attraction · flora and fauna

remarkable wood-carved skeletal figure of the Grim Reaper. Its fleshless skull stares hollow-eyed at visitors with a defiant, mirthless grin: a scythe gripped in one clutch of bones, and an hour-glass in the other, symbolise the inescapable fate that awaits us all. This gruesomely powerful memento mori was donated to the church in 1640 by one Stephen Crosbie who, for good measure, added the inscription: 'As you are now, even so was I, Remember death for ye must dye.' Those words were a conventional enough adjuration at that time, but what is one supposed to make of Stephen's postscript inscribed on the back of the pew: 'For couples joined in wedlock this seat I did intend'?

GREAT WITCHINGHAM
11 miles NW of Norwich off the A1067

🐾 The Animal Ark and Country Park

🐿 Weston Longville

Set in 25 acres of parkland, the **Animal Ark and Country Centre** is home to an interesting collection of rare and ancient breeds of farm livestock, such as white-faced woodland and Shetland sheep, pygmy goats and Exmoor ponies. The Centre also has tiny deer, Highland cattle, wallabies, llamas, parakeets, pheasants and songbirds. Children can go wild on the Adventure Play, and talks by keepers on the wonders of nature are held twice a day during weekends and school holidays. Open Easter to end October (tel: 01603 872274).

A little further southeast, the Dinosaur Adventure Park near Lenwade doesn't have any living creatures, but as you wander through the woods here you will come across some startlingly convincing life-size models of dinosaurs. One of them, the Climb-a-Saurus, is a children's activity centre. A woodland maze, picnic area with gas-fired barbecues, a play area for toddlers, a restaurant and a Dinostore offering a wide variety of dinosaur models, books and gifts are among the park's other attractions.

Anyone who has ever read Parson Woodforde's enchanting *Diary of a Country Parson* will want to make a short diversion to the tiny village of **Weston Longville**, a mile or so south of the Dinosaur Park. The Rev James Woodforde was vicar of this remote parish from 1774 until his death in 1803, and throughout that time he conscientiously maintained a daily diary detailing a wonderful mixture of the momentous and the trivial. 'Very great Rebellion in France' he notes when, 10 days after the Fall of the Bastille, the dramatic news eventually arrived at Weston Longville. More often he records his copious meals ('We had for dinner a Calf's head, boiled Fowl and Tongue, a saddle of Mutton roasted on the side table, and a fine Swan roasted with Currant Jelly Sauce for the first Course. The Second Course a couple of Wild Fowl, Larks, Blamange, Tarts etc. etc.'), the weather (during the winter of 1785, for example, the frost was so severe that it froze the chamberpots under the beds), and his frequent dealings with the smuggler Andrews, who kept the good parson well-supplied with contraband tea, gin and cognac.

Inside the simple village church there's a portrait of Parson Woodforde, painted by his nephew, and across the road the inn has been named after this beguiling character.

SWANNINGTON
11 miles NW of Norwich off the A1067/B1149

🏛 Swannington Manor

The gardens of **Swannington Manor** are famous for the 300-year-old yew and box topiary hedge. Other features of this small town are the 13th-century St Margaret's church, Swannington Hall – where can be seen the remains of the former moat – and the charming thatched village water pump.

Swannington's Ketts Lane was named after Robert Kett, leader of the peasants' revolt, who reputedly was captured in a barn nearby.

REEPHAM
12 miles NW of Norwich on the B1145

🏃 Marriott's Way

Reepham is an attractive town set in the rich countryside between the Wensum and Bure Valleys. Lovely 18th-century houses border the Market Place, and there is delightful walking along the **Marriott's Way** cycle path. Market day is Wednesdays, and regular antiques fairs are held at the Old Reepham Brewery.

SALLE
13 miles NW of Norwich off the B1145

🏛 Church of St Peter and St Paul

In the village of Salle stands one of Norfolk's finest churches. Norfolk's 'rural cathedral', the Barnack-stone **Church of St Peter and St Paul**, stands in splendid isolation in the Norfolk countryside. Among its many treasures are the seven-sacrament font, the chancel roof with its 160 angels, the carved bosses and a three-decker pulpit.

CAWSTON
12 miles NW of Norwich on the B1145

🏛 St Agnes' Church

'Lovers of the Norfolk churches can never agree which is the best,' wrote Sir John Betjeman. 'I have heard it said that you are

---

VERY NICE THINGS

Market Place, Reepham, nr Norwich,
Norfolk NR10 4JJ
Tel: 01603 873390

Reepham is an attractive village set in rich countryside between the Wensum and Bure Valleys 12 miles northwest of Norwich on the B1145. Handsome 18th century houses border the Market Place, and one of the most prominent properties, standing by the parish church, is home to **Very Nice Things**. Originally a private residence, it offers a relaxed, inviting ambience for browsing among a bright, colourful and uncluttered display space filled with beautiful and interesting homeware and gifts, many of them locally produced.

Owner Sue Cutting personally chooses the constantly changing stock, which includes decorative hand–painted pottery, kitchenware, tea pots, silver jewellery, handbags, silk scarves, candles, soaps, a big selection of cards....and lots more. Browsers are always welcome and every visit will reveal new delights and something special to suit every pocket and every occasion.

Opening hours are 10 to 5 Monday and Tuesday, 10 to 1 and 2 to 5 Wednesday, 10 to 1 Thursday, 10 to 5 Friday and 10 to 4 Saturday; closed Sunday.

🏛 historic building   🏛 museum and heritage   🏛 historic site   🔱 scenic attraction   🌱 flora and fauna

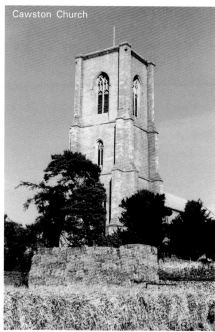

Cawston Church

B1145, stands a huge stone known as the Duelling Stone. It marks the occasion of a duel that took place in 1698 between two local dignitaries, Sir Henry Hobart (see under Aylsham page 21) and Oliver Le Neve.

Great Yarmouth

🏛 Norfolk Nelson Museum 🏛 The Tolhouse

🏛 Elizabethan House Museum 🏛 Yesterday's World

🏛 Time and Tide Museum 🕯 Nelson's Monument

🏛 The Quay 🏛 The Rows 🐚 Sealife centre

The topography of Great Yarmouth is rather curious. Back in Saxon times, it was actually an island, a large sandbank dotted with fishermen's cottages. Later, the narrow estuary of the River Bure at the northern end was blocked off, causing it to flow down the western side of the town. It runs parallel to the sea for two miles before joining the larger River Yare, and then their united waters curve around the southern edge of the town for another three miles before finally entering the sea.

either a Salle man or a Cawston man.' In this county so rich in exceptionally beautiful churches, Salle and Cawston are indeed in a class of their own. **St Agnes' Church** in Cawston, among many other treasures, boasts a magnificent double hammerbeam roof, where angels with protective wings eight feet across float serenely from the roof, and a gorgeous 15th-century rood screen embellished with lovely painted panels of saints and Fathers of the Church. The two churches are just a couple of miles apart, so you can easily decide for yourself whether you are 'a Salle man or a Cawston man'. Surprisingly for such a genial character, Sir John seems to have overlooked the possibility that other visitors to these two remarkable churches might define themselves as either 'a Salle woman or a Cawston woman'.

By the B1149 close to its junction with the

So Yarmouth is now a promontory, its eastern and western sides displaying markedly different characters. The seaward side is a five-mile stretch of sandy beaches, tourist attractions and countless amusements, with a breezy promenade from which one can watch the constant traffic of ships in Yarmouth Roads. There are two fine old traditional piers, the Britannia (810 feet long) and the Wellington (600 feet long), as well as the Jetty, first built in the 16th century for landing goods and passengers. A host of activities are on offer for families: the **Sealife Centre** with many kinds of marine life including octopus and seahorses, and an underwater viewing channel passing through shark-infested

🎞 stories and anecdotes 🕯 famous people 🎨 art and craft ✏ entertainment and sport 🏃 walks

Great Yarmouth Tolhouse

'oceans'; Amazonia, an indoor tropical paradise featuring the largest collection of reptiles in Britain; Merrivale Model Village, which offers an acre of attractive landscaped gardens with over 200 realistic models of town and country in miniature, which are illuminated at dusk; and the Pleasure Beach, featuring over 70 rides and attractions combining all the thrills of modern high-tech amusement park rides with the fun of traditional fairground attractions.

For heritage enthusiasts, Great Yarmouth has a rich and proud maritime history. The **Norfolk Nelson Museum** on South Quay features displays, paintings and contemporary memorabilia relating to the life and times of Horatio Lord Nelson. Also on South Quay is the **Elizabethan House Museum**, built by a wealthy merchant and now a museum of domestic life, with 16th-century panelled rooms and a Victorian kitchen. In Row 117, South Quay, the Old Merchant's House is an excellent example of a 17th-century dwelling and a showplace for local wood and metalwork. Nearby is **The Tolhouse**, originally built in 1262 as a gaol and later used as a courthouse. It is now a museum with original dungeons.

At South Denes, the 144-foot **Nelson's Monument** crowned by a statue, not of

Norfolk's most famous son, but of Britannia.

Most of Yarmouth's older buildings are concentrated in the western, or riverside, part of the town. Here you will find **The Quay**, which moved Daniel Defoe, in 1724, to describe it as 'the finest quay in England, if not Europe'. It is more than a mile long and in places 150 yards wide. The Town Hall is well known for its grand staircase, Court Room and Assembly Room; the building itself is in use by the Local Authority. **The Rows** (see panel opposite), a medieval network of tiny courtyards and narrow alleys, are a mere two feet wide in places. Badly damaged during a bombing raid in 1942, enough remains to show their unique character. There were originally 145 of these rows, about seven miles in total, all of them built at right angles to the sea and therefore freely ventilated by onshore breezes, which, given the urban sanitary conditions of those times, must have been extremely welcome.

The bombing raid of 1942 also completely destroyed the interior of St Nicholas' Church, but left its walls standing. Between 1957 and 1960 this huge building - the largest parish church in England - was completely restored and furnished in traditional style, largely by using pieces garnered from redundant churches and other sources. The partly Norman font, for example, came from Highway church in Wiltshire, the organ from St Mary-the-Boltons in Kensington.

The famous author, Charles Dickens, stayed at the Royal Hotel on Marine Parade in 1847-48 while writing *David Copperfield*. Dickens had visited the town as a child and had actually seen an upturned boat on the beach being used as a dwelling, complete with a chimney emerging from its keel. In his novel, this becomes Peggotty's house to which young

Great Yarmouth Row Houses

Great Yarmouth, Norfolk NR30 2RQ
Tel: 01493 857900
www.english-heritage.org.uk

Experience the sights and sounds of yesterday's Great
Yarmouth. Visit these unique and vividly-presented houses,
one set in c.1870 and the other in 1942, just before
incendiary bombing. Find out how Yarmouth's 'Herring Girls'
lived, hear an original BBC wartime broadcast and 'Mr Rope's
sea shanties'. See the amazing collection of artefacts
rescued from Row houses after World War II bombing, and contrast tenement conditions
with 'respectable' merchant's interiors. Open daily April to September.

Copperfield is brought following the death of his mother. 'One thing I particularly noticed in this delightful house,' he writes, 'was the smell of fish; which was so searching, that when I took out my pocket-handkerchief to wipe my nose, I found it smelt exactly as if it had wrapped up a lobster.'

In fact, the whole town at that time was pervaded with the aroma of smoked herring, the silvery fish that were the basis of Yarmouth's prosperity. Around the time of Dickens' stay here, the author of the town's directory tried to pre-empt any discouraging effect this might have on visitors by claiming that 'The wholesome exhalations arising from the fish during the operation of curing are said to have a tendency to dissipate contagious disorders, and to be generally beneficial to the human constitution which is here sometimes preserved to extreme longevity.'

Then the town would have had some 60 curing houses busy gutting, salting and spicing herrings to produce Yarmouth's great contribution to the English breakfast, the kipper. The process had been invented by a Yarmouth man, John Woodger: a rival of his, a Mr Bishop, developed a different method, which left the fish wonderfully moist and flavoursome, and so created the famous Yarmouth bloater.

For centuries, incredible quantities of herring were landed, nearly a billion in 1913 alone. In earlier years, the trade had involved so many fishermen that there were more boats (1,123) registered at Yarmouth than at London. But the scale of the over-fishing produced the inevitable result: within the space of two decades Yarmouth's herring industry foundered, and by the late 1960s found itself dead in the water. Luckily, the end of that historic trade coincided with the beginning of North Sea oil and gas exploitation, a business that has kept the town in reasonably good economic health up to the present day. The **Time and Tide Museum of Great Yarmouth Life** explains the town's fishing and maritime heritage. Here, too, is the Great Yarmouth Potteries & Herring Smokehouse Museum. Great Yarmouth's newest attraction, opened in 2007 on Marine Parade, is **Yesterday's World**, a spectacular time-travel adventure covering over 100 years of social history and popular culture. Visitors can enjoy stunning sound and light shows and an interactive audience with Queen Victoria, ride on carousels and buy a treat in the traditional English sweet shop and nostalgic gift shop. Described by *Antiques Roadshow's* Eric Knowles as 'a glorious emporium of the past', Yesterday's World is open throughout the year (tel: 01493 331148).

Caister Castle

On the southern outskirts of Great Yarmouth, **Gorleston** boasts a lovely new beachside bandstand, opened in May 2008 after 12 years of hard work and fundraising by the local rotary club. The previous bandstand on the site, built in 1896, was demolished in the 1930s.

Around Great Yarmouth

CAISTER-ON-SEA
3 miles N of Great Yarmouth off the A149

🏛 Caister Castle ❧ Thrigby Hall

In Boudicca's time, this modern holiday resort with its stretch of fine sands was an important fishing port for her people, the Iceni. After the Romans had vanquished her tribe, they settled here sometime in the 2nd century and built a castra, or castle, or Caister, of which only a few foundations and remains have yet been found. **Caister Castle**, which stands in a picturesque setting about a mile to the west of the town, is a much later construction, built in 1432-5 by the legendary Sir John Fastolf with his spoils from the French wars in which he had served, very profitably, as Governor of Normandy and also distinguished himself leading the English bowmen at the Battle of

---

SHEREE'S BOUTIQUE

The Street, Hemsby, nr Great Yarmouth, Norfolk NR29 4EU
Tel: 01493 732903

Sheree Manning took over the premises where her uncle was based, running Joe's Gift Shop for 40 years. The shop, in a village off the A149 north of Great Yarmouth, is now **Sheree's Boutique**, selling a selection of ladies' clothes (sizes 8 to 20), from smart casual and day wear to cruise and holiday wear and clothes for evenings and special occasions. The bright, colourful boutique also stocks a range of bags, hats, jewellery and other accessories, and Uncle Joe's side of the business lives on in an old-world gift section that sells a wide variety of gifts, souvenirs and cards for all occasions. Sheree's Boutique stands next to the parish church a short walk from the beach.

🏛 historic building   🏛 museum and heritage   🏚 historic site   ♧ scenic attraction   ❧ flora and fauna

Agincourt. Academics have enjoyed themselves for centuries disputing whether this Sir John was the model for Shakespeare's immortal rogue, Falstaff. Certainly the real Sir John was a larger-than-life character, but there's no evidence that he shared Falstaff's other characteristics of cowardliness, boastfulness or general over-indulgence.

Caister Castle was the first in England to be built of brick, and is in fact one of the earliest brick buildings in the county. The 90-foot tower remains, together with much of the moated wall and gatehouse, now lapped by still waters and with ivy relentlessly encroaching. The castle is open daily from May to September and, as an additional attraction, there is a Car Collection in the grounds, which features an impressive collection of cars from an 1893 Panhard et Levassor, to Edwardian and vintage cars, an antique fire engine, the original car used in the film of Ian Fleming's *Chitty*

Chitty Bang Bang, Jim Clark's Lotus and the very first Ford Fiesta.

About three miles west of Caister Castle, the pleasantly landscaped grounds surrounding an 1876 Victorian mansion have been transformed into the **Thrigby Hall Wildlife Gardens**, home for a renowned collection of Asian mammals, birds and reptiles. There are snow leopards and rare tigers; gibbons and crocodiles; deer and otters. Other attractions include a tropical house, aviaries, waterfowl lake, willow pattern garden, gift shop and café. The Gardens are open every day, all year round.

FRITTON
6 miles SW of Great Yarmouth off the A143

Fritton Lake Redwings Horse Sanctuary

At **Fritton Lake Countryworld**, visitors will find a large undercover falconry centre with birds-of-prey flying displays twice daily. There

are also heavy horse stables and a children's farm, a nine-hole pitch and putt course, lakeside gardens, boating and a large adventure playground. Open end-March to end-September every day, and weekends and half-term in October. Opposite Countryworld is the Caldecott Visitor Centre of the **Redwings Horse Sanctuary**, where 70 acres of paddocks are home to some very special rescued horses, ponies, donkeys and mules, some of which are available for adoption.

The Broads

The Broads area covers more than 33 square kilometres that include 200 kilometres of waterways. The broads themselves are shallow lakes formed in medieval times when peat was dug out to provide fuel, and over the years the diggings became flooded as the water level rose. These waterways have always been important transport routes, and each village had its own staithe, or quay, many of which are still in use.

The traditional Broads boat, originally used for commercial purposes, was the wherry, a large, single-sail vessel of shallow draught that plied the broads with cargoes of corn, coal and reed. As rail and road transport gradually took over and the holiday trade began to boom, the wherry's original role was lost and many were converted for leisure use or purpose-built for that purpose, with all mod cons. A few - perhaps no more than half a dozen - still survive, available for regular tours or for private charter, and there really is no finer way to savour the delights of the Broads

than from the deck of a wherry.

The Broads, with their wonderful mixture of open water, woodland, fen and marsh, have virtually the status of a National Park; they are protected by the Broads Authority, which is responsible for conservation, recreation and navigation in this unique part of the world. Besides providing peaceful waterborne holidays, the area offers great opportunities for walking and cycling, and there are many points from which fishing is permitted. Some of the individual broads are nature reserves, and the waterways are home to an amazing variety of bird, fish and plant life.

REEDHAM
8 miles SW of Great Yarmouth off the B1140

Here in Reedham is the single remaining car and passenger ferry in the Broads. There's also an interesting craft showroom at the Old Brewery, and a great pub in The Reedham Ferry Inn.

Norfolk Broads

BURGH CASTLE

4 miles W of Great Yarmouth off the A12

When the Romans established their fortress of Garionnonum, now known as Burgh Castle, the surrounding marshes were still under water. The fort then stood on one bank of a vast estuary, commanding a strategic position at the head of an important waterway running into the heart of East Anglia. The ruins are impressive, with walls of alternating flint and brick layers rising 15 feet high in places, and spreading more than 11 feet wide at their base. The Romans abandoned Garionnonum around AD408 and some two centuries later the Irish missionary St Fursey (or Fursa) founded a monastery within its walls. Later generations cannibalised both his building, and much of the crumbling Roman castle, as materials for their own churches and houses.

ACLE

10 miles W of Great Yarmouth off the A47

🏛 Church of St Edmund

A thousand years ago, this small market town, now 10 miles inland, was a small fishing port on the coast. Gradually, land has been reclaimed from the estuaries of the Rivers Bure, Waveney and Yare, so that today large expanses of flat land stretch away from Acle towards the sea. The town's importance as a boating centre began in the 19th century with boat-building yards springing up beside the bridge. When Acle's first Regatta was held in 1890, some 150 yachts took part. The town became known as the Gateway to the Broads and also as the gateway to Windmill Land, a picturesque stretch of the River Bure dotted with windmills. The medieval bridge that formerly crossed the Bure at Acle has less

INSPIRATIONS COUNTRY AND EQUESTRIAN STORE

Norwich Road, Acle, Norwich, Norfolk NR13 3BY
Tel: 01493 754029

At **Inspirations Country and Equestrian Store** you will find everything for horse and rider and country living items all under one roof. This unique store formed by people with a passion for Horses and Country Life with the aim of providing customers with a focal point for availability of products associated with enjoying leisure time in the countryside.

Inspirations stocks a wide range of equestrian products at affordable prices and offer a level of service that is second to none. From jodhpurs and jackets to boots and hats there is a great range of clothing, footwear and accessories available for both children and adults. If you have trouble choosing what's right for you, the knowledgeable staff are always on hand to offer friendly advice.

Inpsirations believes in supporting local crafts people and this is displayed instore where the work of local artists is on sale. The store also stocks many other items to accompany country living such as; traditional foods including jams, marmalades and chutneys, things for the home including Norfolk China and Vanilla Candles, and a wide range of clothing, jewellery and fashion accessories such as handbags, shoes and scarves. Whether you are looking for something for your hobby or something for your home, Inspirations is sure to have it.

agreeable associations, since it was used for numerous executions with the unfortunate victims left to dangle over the river.

Acle was granted permission for a market in 1272, and it's still held every Thursday, attracting visitors from miles around. Others come to see the unusual **Church of St Edmund** with its Saxon round tower, built some time around AD900, crowned with a 15th-century belfry from which eight carved figures look down on the beautifully thatched roof of the nave. The treasures inside include a superbly carved font, six feet high, and inscribed with the date 1410, and a fine 15th-century screen.

WROXHAM
8 miles NE of Norwich on the A1151

Stracey Arms Windmill, Acle

🜋 Wroxham Broad 🜋 Bure Valley Railway

🌱 Hoveton Hall Gardens ⚲ Wroxham Barns

This riverside village, linked to its twin, Hoveton, by a hump-backed bridge over the River Bure, is the self-styled 'capital' of the Norfolk Broads, and as such gets extremely busy during the season. The banks of the river are chock-a-block with boatyards full of cruisers of all shapes and sizes, there's a constant traffic of boats making their way to the open spaces of **Wroxham Broad**, and in July the scene becomes even more hectic when the annual Regatta is under way.

Wroxham is also the southern terminus of the **Bure Valley Railway**, a nine-mile long, narrow-gauge (15-inch) steam train service that closely follows the course of the River Bure through lovely countryside to the market town of Aylsham. It runs along the trackbed of the old East Norfolk Railway, has two half-scale locomotives, and specially constructed passenger coaches with large windows to provide the best possible views.

A couple of miles north of Wroxham is **Wroxham Barns**, a delightful collection of beautifully restored 18th-century barns set in 10 acres of countryside, and housing a community of craftspeople. There are numerous workshops, producing between them a wide range of crafts, from stained glass to woodturning, stitchcraft to handmade children's clothes, pottery to floral artistry, and much more. The complex also includes a cider-pressing centre, a junior farm with lots of hands-on activities, a traditional Family Fair (with individually priced rides), a gift and craft shop, and a tearoom.

A mile or so east of Wroxham Barns, **Hoveton Hall Gardens** offer visitors a splendid combination of plants, shrubs and trees, with rare rhododendrons, azaleas, water plants and dazzling herbaceous borders within a walled garden. There are woodland and lakeside walks, plant sales, gardening books and a tearoom.

Anyone interested in dried flower

🏨 historic building 🏛 museum and heritage 🏚 historic site 🜋 scenic attraction 🌱 flora and fauna

arrangements should make their way to the tiny hamlet of Cangate, another couple of miles to the east, where Willow Farm Flowers provides an opportunity of seeing the whole process, from the flowers in the field to the final colourful displays. The farm shop has an abundance of dried, silk, parchment and wooden flowers, beautifully arranged, and more than 50 varieties of dried flowers are available in bunches or made into arrangements of all shapes and sizes, or to special order. Willow Farm also has a picnic and play area, a guided farm walk, lays on flower arranging demonstrations and also runs one day classes for those interested in learning more about mastering this delicate-fingered skill.

SOUTH WALSHAM
9 miles E of Norwich on the B1140

🏛 St Benet's Abbey   🦆 Fairhaven

🦆 South Walsham Inner Broad

This small village is notable for having two parish churches built within yards of each other. Just to the north of the village is the **Fairhaven Woodland and Water Garden** (see panel below), an expanse of delightful water gardens lying beside the private **South Walsham Inner Broad**. Its centrepiece is the 900-year-old King Oak, lording it over the surrounding displays of rare shrubs and plants, native wild flowers, rhododendrons and giant lilies. There are tree-lined walks, a

Fairhaven Woodland and Water Garden

South Walsham, Norwich,
Norfolk NR13 6HY
Tel: 01603 270449
e-mail: fairhavengarden@btconnect.co.uk
website: www.fairhavengarden.co.uk

Set in the heart of the Norfolk Broads, Fairhaven Woodland and Water Garden is one of the county's best kept secrets. Boasting the UK's finest naturalised collection of Candelabra primulas, a 950 year old Oak Tree (home to a family of ducks), and 130 acres of natural Woodland and Water Garden.

The Garden was developed by the late 2nd Lord Fairhaven Major Henry Broughton, who bought South Walsham Estate in 1946. The Estate had been used as a convalescence home for Officers during the Second World War, and so the Garden had become a jungle. The site was gradually cleared by hand and took 15 years to complete. Lord Fairhaven then set about planting the Garden with shade and water loving plants including Camellias and Rhododendrons specially imported from the Himalayas.

Whether you choose to visit in the height of Summer, or in the depths of Winter there is always something to see.

🎭 stories and anecdotes   🐿 famous people   🎨 art and craft   🎭 entertainment and sport   🚶 walks

Ludham Marshes

Distance: *3.5 miles (5.5 kilometres)*
Typical time: *90 mins*
Height gain: *0 metres*
Map: *Outdoor Leisure 40 The Broads*
Walk: *www.walkingworld.com ID:800*
Contributor: *Stephanie Kedik*

ACCESS INFORMATION:

Ludham can be reached by car from Norwich (A1151/A1062) or by bus (tel: Norfolk Bus Information, 0845 300 6116).

DESCRIPTION:

Ludham is a beautiful, peaceful village at the heart of the Norfolk Broads. A teashop, small restaurant and pub provide a choice of refreshments. The pub with beer garden and children's outside play area, caters for families with young children. The walk takes you from the village centre, down a lane and past a small marina where day boats can be hired. Further down you enter Ludham Marshes Nature Reserve on the edge of the River Thurne. In the summer months the air is buzzing with insects and butterflies, and many varieties of birds are to be seen all year round. Deer can also sometimes be spotted in the nearby wood, while on the river, you will see sailing craft and water birds. The undergrowth can get quite high

along the riverbank in the summer, so leg covering is recommended. Short enough for a gentle afternoon stroll, this walk offers something for everyone.

FEATURES:

River, Pub, Toilets, Play Area, Church, Wildlife, Birds, Flowers, Butterflies, Gift Shop Food Shop, Good for Kids, Nature Trail, Tea Shop.

WALK DIRECTIONS:

1 | After arriving in the centre of Ludham, take the Yarmouth Road, past the Ludham village sign at Bakers Arms Green. Further down, on your right is a little path leading off and alongside the road. Follow this until you get to a right turn where Horse Fen Road meets the main Yarmouth Road.

2 | Turn right, into Horse Fen Road. Continue along the lane, past Womack Staithe boat hire and camping site.

3 | Follow the public bridleway down onto Ludham Marshes National Nature Reserve. As you take the path round the corner and into the reserve, first a garden and then a wood will be on your left beyond the drainage ditch. Deer can sometimes be seen in these woods. On your right, the marshes stretch out across to the River Thurne.

4 | Follow the footpath through the reserve. Where you meet the gravel track, take a turn to the right through the gate (that says, 'Danger unstable road!'). Continue along this track and through another gate. At Horse Fen pumping station, turn right to follow the green footpath sign.

5 | Across the bridge, follow the footpath along the river, keeping the river on your left. This stretch can be a bit overgrown in summer, although it is compensated for by the views of the river. This footpath will take you back from the river, up the creek and out of the reserve at the side of Hunters Yard.

6 | Walk back up Horse Fen Road, past Womack Staithe and the boatyard.

7 | At the top of Horse Fen Road, turn left and onto the road leading back into Ludham.

🏠 historic building   🏛 museum and heritage   🏛 historic site   🏞 scenic attraction   🌿 flora and fauna

bird sanctuary, plants for sale, and a restaurant. A vintage-style riverboat runs trips every half-hour around the Broad.

The best way to see the remains of **St Benet's Abbey** is from a boat along the River Bure (indeed, it's quite difficult to reach it any other way). Rebuilt in 1020 by King Canute, after the Vikings had destroyed an earlier Saxon building, St Benet's became one of the richest abbeys in East Anglia. When Henry VIII closed it down in 1536 he made an unusual deal with its last Abbot. In return for creating the Abbot Bishop of Norwich, the Cathedral estates were to be handed over to the King, but St Benet's properties could remain in the Abbot/Bishop's possession. Even today, the Bishop of Norwich retains the additional title of Abbot of St Benet's, and on the first Sunday in August each year travels the last part of the journey by boat to hold an open-air service near the stately ruins of the Abbey gatehouse.

RANWORTH
9 miles E of Norwich off the B1140

🏛 St Helen's Church

🌿 Broadland Conservation Centre

This beautiful Broadland village is famous for its church and its position on Ranworth Broad. From the tower of **St Helen's Church** it is possible to see five Norfolk Broads, Horsey Mill, the sea at Great Yarmouth and, on a clear day, the spire of Norwich Cathedral. Inside, the church houses one of Norfolk's greatest ecclesiastical treasures, a breathtaking early 15th century Gothic choir screen, the most beautiful and the best preserved in the county. In glowing reds, greens and golds, gifted medieval artists painted a gallery of more than 30 saints and martyrs, inserting tiny cameos of such everyday scenes as falcons seizing hares, dogs chasing ducks and, oddly for Norfolk, lions. Cromwell's

men, offended by such idolatrous images, smothered them with brown paint - an ideal preservative for these wonderful paintings, as became apparent when they were once again revealed during the course of a 19th century restoration of the church.

Just to the north of the village is the **Broadland Conservation Centre** (Norfolk Naturalists Trust), a thatched building floating on pontoons at the edge of Ranworth Broad. It houses an informative exhibition on the history of the Broads, and there's also an interesting Nature Trail which shows how these wetlands gradually developed over the centuries.

HORNING
12 miles NE of Norwich off the A1062

🏛 RAF Air Defence Radar Museum

The travel writer Arthur Mee described Horning as "Venice in Broadland", where "waterways wandering from the river into the gardens are crossed by tiny bridges." With its pretty reed-thatched cottages lining the bank of the River Bure and its position in the heart of the Broads, there are few more attractive places from which to explore this magical area.

At RAF Neatishead, near Horning, the **Air Defence Radar Museum** tells the story of radar and air defence from 1935 to the present day. It is housed in the original 1942 Radar Operations building.

POTTER HEIGHAM
14 miles NE of Norwich off the A149

🏛 Horsey Windpump

Modern Potter Heigham has sprung up around the medieval bridge over the River Thurne, a low-arched structure with a clearance of only seven feet at its highest, a notorious test for novice sailors. The Thurne is a major artery through the Broads, linking them in a continuous waterway from Horsey Mere in the

Horsey Windpump, nr Potter Heigham

east to Wroxham Broad in the west. A pleasant excursion from Potter Heigham is a visit to Horsey Mere, about six miles to the east, and **Horsey Windpump** (both National Trust). From this early 20th-century drainage mill, now restored and fully working, there are lovely views across the Mere. A circular walk follows the north side of Horsey Mere, passes another windmill, and returns through the village. There's a small shop at the Windpump, and light refreshments are available.

WORSTEAD
12 miles NE of Norwich off the A149/B1150

🏛 Norfolk's Golden Fleece Heritage Museum

Hard to imagine now, but Worstead was a busy little industrial centre in the Middle Ages. The village lent its name to the hardwearing cloth produced in the region, and many of the original weavers' cottages can still be seen in the narrow side-streets. Worsted cloth, woven from tightly-twisted yarn, was introduced by Flemish immigrants and became popular throughout England from the 13th century onwards. The Flemish weavers settled happily into the East Anglian way of life and seem to have influenced its

OLD HALL INN
The Coast Road, Sea Palling, Norfolk NR12 0TZ
Tel: 01692 598323

The **Old Hall Inn** run by Barbara Simmons is a substantial building just minutes from the shore in Sea Palling. Dating back to the middle of the 17th century and formerly a farmhouse, the Inn is traditional both from the outside and within.

There are two bars, one adjoining the A la Carte restaurant whilst the second bar has a lounge area & family dining area where children's meals can be served.

The á la carte menu which is available in both dining areas includes a selection of starters. Fish (including lobster & crab when available) steaks and traditional home cooked meals such as steak & ale pie and liver & bacon.

There is some outside seating at the front while at the back of the pub is a delightful beer garden. There is also a car park at the back of the Inn with ample parking space. With six bright, comfortable guest bedrooms, four of them with en-suite facilities, the Inn is a good base for exploring the many attractions that North Norfolk has to offer. Not to mention Sea Palling's stunning beach, this wonderful blue flag, sandy beach is a great place for a walk and a number of reefs have calmed the waves making Sea Palling an ideal place to swim or for children to play.

architecture almost as strongly as its weaving industry.

The lovely 14th-century church of St Mary provides ample evidence of Worstead's former prosperity. Its many treasures include a fine hammerbeam roof, a chancel screen with a remarkable painted dado, and a magnificent traceried font complete with cover. The village stages an annual weekend of events in July to raise money for the restoration of the church.

Norfolk's Golden Fleece Heritage Museum has a collection relating to the place of the Chapel in local life and a collection reflecting the importance of spinning, weaving and dyeing in Norfolk. In the 'Weaver's loft' members of the Worstead Guild of Weavers, Spinners and Dyers can be seen at work.

SUTTON
15 miles NE of Norwich off the A149

🏛 Sutton Windmill and Broads Museum

Sutton Windmill, the tallest in Britain and a famous Norfolk landmark, was built in 1789 and was in commercial use until 1940. On the same site, **The Broads Museum** has numerous displays, including woodworking, the leather trade, razors and shaving, coopers', tinsmiths' and blacksmiths' tools, plumbing, animal traps, taxidermy, medical, veterinary, banknotes and the story of tobacco.

STALHAM
15 miles NE of Norwich off the A149

🏛 Museum of the Broads

🏛 Stalham Fire House Museum

In a range of traditional buildings long

THE STAITHE RESTAURANT

The Staithe, Stalham, Norfolk NR12 9BY
Tel: 01692 580808
website: www.staitherestaurant.co.uk

The Staithe Restaurant offers a unique dining experience in a riverside setting a few steps from the Broads museum. A barn dating from 1837 has been lovingly converted into a beautiful restaurant bursting with character, with lots of honey-coloured reclaimed timber and one wall created from an old flint kiln.

Young, talented head chef Martin Matthews, whose CV includes a spell at the Michelin-starred Morston Hall, has quickly gained a loyal following for producing excellent food served in relaxing surroundings. Classy yet unpretentious, his menus make superb use of prime produce, local as far as possible, putting a contemporary edge on classic dishes using traditional skills and values. Typical dishes on his ever-changing menus might include seared scallops with chilli jam and crème fraîche; chicken liver parfait with pickled courgettes; carpaccio of beef with a truffle dressing; superb pork and pork sausages from Causeway Farm at nearby Ingham; red Thai curry; and, to finish, Eton Mess and pressed chocolate cake.

With its friendly, informal bar area, delightful dining room and riverside terrace, The Staithe is perfect for a variety of occasions: drinks with friends, business lunches, traditional Sunday roasts, snacks and wines on the patio, birthday celebrations, romantic dinner for two, a treat for boaters on the Broads, cruise and dine evenings, and Martin's regular cooking demonstrations. The Staithe is open Tuesday to Sunday from 10.30 to 5 (food served 11.30 to 3) and 6.15 to last orders at 9. Closed on Tuesday out of season.

LITTLE GEMS ROCK SHOP

2a Mount Street, Cromer, Norfolk NR27 9DB
Tel: 01263 519519
e-mail: sales@littlegemrockshop.co.uk
website: www.littlegems.info

The only rock that most seaside resorts can offer is the long, pink, sticky sort. But in Cromer there are rocks of an altogether different kind. **Little Gems Rock Shop** is an Aladdin's Cave filled with thousands of rocks, stones, crystals, fossils, semi-precious stones and gemstone jewellery. The shop is owned and run by Gail Hickling, who established it in 2000 from an idea generated by collecting fossils and stones as a child.

Behind the pink-washed, bow-windowed frontage the shop is light, bright and full of colour, with easy browsing among the items on show, most of which can be handled. These include, in addition to the rocks and crystals and fossils, both familiar and unusual, a 'baby dinosaur' skeleton, dinosaur teeth, prehistoric bones and flies in amber. Visitors to Little gems can be certain of finding something unique, either for a personal collection or for a special gift. Set back from the road, with parking nearby, this super little place is open from 10 to 5 Monday to Saturday, also on Sunday (11 to 4 in winter, 12 to 5 in summer).

SILVER & SALTS

25 Garden Street, Cromer, Norfolk NR27 9HN
Tel: 07920 728482
e-mail: silverandsalts@btconnect.com
website: www.silverandsalts.co.uk

As well as one of Norfolk's most attractive seaside resorts, Cromer is not only famous for its succulent Cromer crabs and its fine seafood restaurants but also for its shopping. Mandi Teagle is the proud owner of **Silver & Salts**.

Established three years ago, this Norfolk gem offers customers a kaleidoscope of items. Whether you are looking for that perfect find for your home, yourself or as a gift, Silver & Salts will have it. Amongst the exclusive treasures are gorgeous locally made jewellery, the legendary seating comfort of Lloyd Loom, hand-made soaps and candles and fairtrade handbags. Worthy of special mention are the extremely handy magnetic notice boards.

A visit to Cromer is not complete without a visit to Silver & Salts.

associated with the wherry trade, **The Museum of the Broads** tells the story of the history, culture and environment of the Broads. Displays include the old racing yacht *Maria* and the steam launch *Falcon*. **The Fire House Museum** relates the history of the Stalham fire service in an 1830s building that housed the town's first fire engine.

Cromer

🏛 Cromer Pier 🕊 Henry Blogg Museum

🎨 Cromer Museum

As you enter a seaside town, what more reassuring sight could there be than to see the pier still standing? **Cromer Pier** is the genuine article, a haven of Edwardian delight, complete with Lifeboat Station and the Pavilion Theatre, which still stages traditional end-of-the-pier shows. The Pier's survival is all the more impressive since it was badly damaged in 1953 and 1989, and in 1993 sliced in two by a drilling rig, which had broken adrift in a storm.

Cromer has been a significant resort since the late 1700s and in its early days even received an unsolicited testimonial from Jane Austen. In her novel *Emma* (1816), a character declares that 'Perry was a week at Cromer once, and he holds it to be the best of all the sea-bathing places.' A succession of celebrities, ranging from Lord Tennyson and Oscar Wilde, to Winston Churchill and the German Kaiser, all came to see for themselves.

The inviting sandy beach remains much as they saw it (horse-drawn bathing machines aside), as does the Church of St Peter & St Paul, which boasts the tallest tower in

---

EDEN

10 High Street, Cromer, Norfolk NR27 9HG
Tel: 01263 515581
e-mail: janet-eden@btconnect.com

With its pier and its two museums, wide-open beaches, spectacular cliffs, there is a lot to enjoy in Cromer. Not to mention the town's Folk Festival and famous Carnival.

Established 2 years ago, **Eden** an exciting new age gift shop where you will find a beautiful range of inspiring products, crystals, relaxation CD's, spiritual books, incense, jewellery and ethically sourced clothing.

Janet Denning, the owner, has extensive knowledge in the healing profession and offers Crystal Healing in the relaxed and tranquil therapy room above the shop. Other therapies presently on offer include, Reiki, Reflexology, Hypno Counselling, Bowen Technique, Indian Head Massage, Palm Reading and private Tarot and Medium sittings.

Holistic workshops are available throughout the year and Janet runs a meditation group during the week.

Eden is a shop that packs plenty of mystical punch and a visit mustn't be missed.

🎬 stories and anecdotes 🕊 famous people 🎨 art and craft 🖋 entertainment and sport 🥾 walks

Norfolk, 160 feet high. And then as now, Cromer crabs were reckoned to be the most succulent in England. During the season, between April and September, crab-boats are launched from the shore (there's no harbour here), sail out to the crab banks about three miles offshore, and there the two-man teams on each boat deal with some 200 pots.

Next to the old boathouse is the **RNLI Henry Blogg Museum**. It tells the dramatic story of the courageous men who manned the town's rescue service. Pre-eminent among them was Henry (Harry) Blogg, who was coxswain of the lifeboat for 37 years, from 1910 to 1947. During those years his boat, the *H F Bailey*, was called out 128 times and saved 518 lives. The most decorated lifeboatman, he won three Gold and four Silver RNLI Gallantry medals, the George Cross and the British Empire Medal. The *H F Bailey* is displayed alongside lifeboat models, historic photographs, paintings and other memorabilia.

Also well worth visiting is the **Cromer Museum**, housed in a row of restored fishermen's cottages near the church, where you can follow the story of Cromer from the days of the dinosaurs, some of whose bones were found nearby, up to the present, and access the computer for thousands of pictures and facts about this attractive town.

Around Cromer

HAPPISBURGH
14 miles SE of Cromer on the B1159

[f] St Mary's Church

The coastal waters off Happisburgh (or Hazeborough, to give the village its correct pronunciation), have seen many a shipwreck over the centuries, and the victims lie buried in the graveyard of **St Mary's Church**. The large grassy mound on the north side of the church contains the bodies of the ill-fated crew of HMS *Invincible*, wrecked on the treacherous sandbanks here in 1801. The ship was on its way to join up with Nelson's fleet at Copenhagen when the tragedy occurred, resulting in the deaths of 119 sailors.

Happisburgh's distinctive lighthouse, built in 1791 and striped like a barber's pole, certainly proved ineffectual on that occasion; as did the soaring 110-foot tower of the church itself, which could normally be relied on as a back-up warning to mariners.

Inside the Church is a splendid 15th-century octagonal font carved

Cromer Pier

with the figures of lions, satyrs and 'wild men'; embedded in the pillars along the aisle are the marks left by shrapnel from German bombs dropped on the village in 1940.

LESSINGHAM
14 miles SE of Cromer off the B1159

From this small village, a lane winds down through spectacular dunes to the sands at Eccles Beach and, a little further north, to Cart Gap with its gently sloping beach and colourful lines of beach huts.

NORTH WALSHAM
9 miles SE of Cromer on the A149

🐿 Paston School 🎨 Alby Crafts

This busy country town with its attractive Market Cross of 1600 has some interesting historical associations. Back in 1381, despite its remoteness from London, North Walsham became the focus of an uprising in support of Wat Tyler's Peasants' Revolt. These North Norfolk rebels were led by John Litester, a local dyer, and their object was the abolition of serfdom. Their actions were mainly symbolic: invading manor houses, monasteries and town halls, and burning the documents that recorded their subservient status. In a mass demonstration they gathered on Mousehold Heath outside Norwich, presented a petition to the King, and then retreated to North Walsham to await his answer. It came in the form of the sanguinary Bishop of Norwich, Henry Despenser, who, as his admiring biographer recorded, led an assault on the rebels, 'grinding his teeth like a wild boar, and sparing neither himself nor his enemies ... stabbing some, unhorsing others, hacking and hewing'. John

WINSTANLEY CAT POTTERY

1 Grammar School Road, North Walsham, Norfolk NR28 9JH
Tel: 01692 402962
e-mail: nickallen07@btinetnet.com
website: www.winstanleycats.uk.com

It's an age-old problem. There's someone special that you want to buy a gift for, for their birthday, an anniversary, for Christmas, or maybe just to show how much you value them.

But what can you get them? Haven't they got just about everything? Okay, so they don't have an Aston Martin, but your finances will not stretch quite that far this year!

But wait...Is your friend a cat lover? Are they owned by a cat? Problem solved!

Jenny Winstanley's workshop in North Walsham is filled with beautiful things. It's a treasure trove of art, and what is quite astonishing is that, Jenny has made everything herself.

Winstanley Cat Pottery is the brainchild of Jenny Winstanley and she has been creating ceramic cats for over 40 years! After firing, each cat is individually hand-painted to ensure that no two are identical. Their unique cathedral glass "follow you" eyes are fitted to finish off these highly desirable collectors pieces, that are also listed in the "Millers Guide" to antiques. They are so lifelike; you can almost hear them purr!

If you would like to learn more about the pottery and handmade production of these animals, or purchase one or two, then log on to the website, every piece created at the pottery bears the Winstanley signature, and size number underwritten on the base.

Bacton Woods

Distance: *3.1 miles (4.8 kilometres)*

Typical time: *90 mins*

Height gain: *20 metres*

Map: *Explorer 25*

Walk: *www.walkingworld.com ID:1208*

Contributor: *Joy & Charles Boldero*

Free car parking at the woodland car/picnic site. Go along the B1150 east from North Walsham and then follow the signs, Bacton Wood and Picnic Centre to the car park.

There has been a woodland here since Saxon times. It is thought that because the soil is so poor, the area was not converted to agriculture. The Forestry Commission bought the wood in the 1950s. In the larch woodlands, goldcrests and warblers can be spotted. There are two sessile oaks standing, they have been there for over 200 years. The sessile and the English oak are true native species. The sessile oak was planted as a crop in centuries past because the wood is so good for making charcoal. Oak bark of course was used for the tanning of leather before manmade chemicals were used. Mountain cycling is permitted, also horse riding by permit.

There is a permanent orienteering course, maps for this and permits are obtained from the Countryside Project Officer at North Norfolk District council (tel: 01263 513811).

This walk is mostly around the ancient Bacton woodland, although the route has a short section along a country lane.

Wildlife, Birds, Flowers, Great Views, Butterflies, Woodland.

1 | Go to the notice board. Turn left along the path with a red and yellow band on a small post.

2 | At the left hand bend, turn right through two small posts and along a narrow path. Turn left along a wider path ignoring all paths off it.

3 | At the T-junction turn right along a track.

4 | At a country lane turn left.

5 | At Wood Mill Farm track, turn left along the bridleway. This leads into the wood. Ignore all the paths off it. Keep along it until you reach the road, then the path curves left still in woodland beside the road.

6 | Turn left, the path takes you back into the wood again.

7 | Take the right fork.

8 | At the T-junction turn left, following red marker posts. Turn right. Turn left downhill. Cross the track and go up the bank opposite and back to the car park.

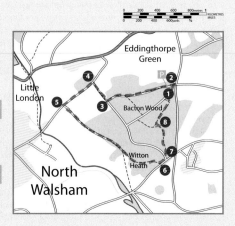

NORFOLK MOTORCYCLE MUSEUM

Rail Yard, North Walsham, Norfolk, NR28 0DS
Tel: 01692 406266
e-mail: info@mc-museum.freeserve.co.uk
website: www.mc-museum.freeserve.co.uk

The goal of the **Norfolk Motorcycle Museum** is to celebrate and preserve the rich tradition of motorcycling in Great Britain. The museum is a shed full of motorbikes - over one hundred of them dating from the 1920s-60s when British motorcycles 'ruled the world' - plus plenty of pushbikes hanging from the rafters. This is a very varied collection, with lots of small machines. It is a place where nostalgia can run riot for the older generations whilst the displays can capture the imagination of younger visitors. There are certainly a lot of different makes of machines here, including some that you my have forgotten about. There is much to be learned and much to see so spend your time marvelling at the wonders of technology and transport in just one place!

The Norfolk Motorcycle Museum has an ongoing policy of restoration and repair, and an ever-watchful eye for interesting new additions to the collection. If you are in the area this museum is well worth a visit.

Open 7 days a week from 10:00 to 16:30.
(Closed Sundays October to Easter)
Admission: Adults £3.00, Senior Citizens £2.50, Children £1.50

Litester was captured, summarily executed and, on the orders of the Bishop, 'divided into four parts, and sent throughout the country to Norwich, Yarmouth, Lynn and to the site of his own house'.

A more glorious fate awaited the town's most famous resident, Horatio Nelson, who came to The Paston School here in 1768 as a boy of 10. Horatio was already dreaming of a naval career and, three years later when he read in the county newspaper that his Uncle Maurice had been appointed commander of a warship, he prevailed on his father to let him join the *Raisonnable*.

The Paston School had been founded in 1606 by Sir William Paston. His ancestors were the writers of the extraordinary collection of more than 1,000 letters, written between 1422 and 1509, which present an astonishingly vivid picture of East Anglian life at the end of the turbulent Middle Ages. Sir William himself is buried in the parish church where he personally supervised (and paid for) the construction of the impressive marble and alabaster monument he desired to be erected in his memory.

About four miles east of North Walsham, near the village of **Erpingham** on the A140, **Alby Crafts & Gardens** has a Crafts Gallery promoting the excellence of mainly East Anglian and British craftsmanship - lacework, woodturning, jewellery, canework and much more. The Plantsman's Garden displays a fine collection of unusual shrubs, plants and bulbs in a four-acre site; there are also workshops where you can watch craftsmen at work, a Bottle Museum and a tearoom.

WILDS COTTAGE B&B

Cromer Road, Antingham, North Walsham,
Norfolk NR28 0NJ
Tel: 01692 500321
e-mail: info@wildscottage.co.uk
website: www.wildscottage.co.uk

Looking for Holiday or Business accommodation in North Norfolk, Look no further! We offer B&B that's special!

Your hosts, Glenda and Mike Toll, provide a warm welcome to their countrysideretreat. The venue is a 18th century farmhouse **Wilds Cottage**, set in 1.5 acres of well established gardens, close to the beautiful Norfolk coastline, only a mile from North Walsham and six miles from Cromer.

We offer a variety of accommodation in our very relaxing B&B or Holiday Cottage Annex. Delicious home cooking makes for a very pleasant break. You can take afternoon tea in the lovely courtyard area and enjoy the lovely garden.

We can suggest ideas for holiday activities why not visit our website www.wildscottage.co.uk/attractions.html which offers a variety of options.

Want to indulge your artistic side, where art and comfort combine perfectly? We can offer a wide range arts and crafts courses call for further details. Please note we are a non smoking establishment.Smoking is allowed in the grounds. Sorry no pets.

We look forward to meeting you.

PASTON

9 miles SE of Cromer on the B1159

It was in this small village that the Paston family entered historical record. The vivid collection of letters they wrote to each other during the years that England was being wracked by the Wars of the Roses has already been mentioned (see page 47), and the village boasts another magnificent legacy from this remarkable family. In 1581, Sir William Paston built a cavernous tithe barn here with flint walls and a thatched roof. It still stands, its roof still thatched: 160 feet long, almost 60 feet high - the longest, most imposing barn in Norfolk. In the nearby church, the most striking of the family memorials is the one dedicated to Katherine Paston. Sculpted in alabaster by Nicholas Stone in 1628, Katherine lies dressed to kill in her Jacobean finery of starched ruff, embroidered bodice, puffed sleeves and pearl necklaces. The monument cost £340, a staggering sum of money at that time. In the nearby village of Bacton are the remains of Bromholm Priory, founded in the 12th century and once one of the grandest and most famous of European ecclesiastical buildings.

MUNDESLEY

7 miles SE of Cromer on the B1159

 Maritime Museum

'The finest air in the kingdom has been wasted for centuries,' said a speaker celebrating the arrival of the railway at Mundesley in 1898, 'because nobody had the courage to bring the people to the district.' The railway has been and gone, but the fresh breezes off the North Sea remain as invigorating as ever.

The Norfolk Shire Horse Centre

West Runton, Cromer, Norfolk NR27 9QH
Tel: 01263 837339 Fax: 01263 837132
e-mail: bakewell@norfolkshirehorse.fsnet.co.uk
website: www.norfolk-shirehorse-centre.co.uk

Shires, Suffolk Punches and Clydesdales are among the stars of the show at the **Norfolk Shire Horse Centre**, and visitors can meet these wonderful, gentle giants at close quarters in the front yard stables. Two large museum sheds contain a video room and an indoor demonstration area, and also on show are carts, coaches, gypsy caravans and farm machinery of yesteryear. Next to the museum is a children's play area.

A short walk through a meadow brings visitors to the area where the small animals are kept in their sheds and pens and aviaries. This really is a paradise for animal lovers: native pony mares with their foals, donkeys, Dexter cows, pigs, goats, lambs, guinea pigs, rabbits, chipmunks, chinchillas, cage birds. The ducks and geese have a great time in their own little pond. Twice a day the centre's proprietor, David Blakewell, accompanies demonstrations with a friendly, informative talk about the heavy horses; themes include harnessing and working the horses with the old machinery. Children can have a ride in a cart and join in the feeding of small animals. Numerous specials events are held throughout the summer, including foal days, blacksmiths days, sheepdog days, plough days and harvesting with the heavy horses. Dogs are welcome on leads; the site has a two-acre car park, a café and a gift shop.

After the hazards of the coastline, immediately to the north where cliffs, fields and houses have all been eroded by the relentless sea, it's a pleasure to arrive at this unassuming holiday resort with its superb sandy beach, considered by many the very best in Norfolk. Mundesley village is quite small (appropriately, its **Maritime Museum**, housed in a former coastguard lookout, is believed to be the smallest museum in the country), but it provides all the facilities conducive to a relaxing family holiday. Best of all, there is safe swimming in the sea, and when the tide is out, children can spend many a happy hour exploring the many 'lowes', or shallow lagoons, left behind.

WEST RUNTON
3 miles W of Cromer on the A149

♋ Beacon Hill ♞ Norfolk Shire Horse Centre

The parish of West Runton can boast that within its boundaries lies the highest point in Norfolk - **Beacon Hill**. This eminence is all of 330 feet high, so you won't be needing any oxygen equipment to reach the summit, but there are some excellent views. Nearby is the Roman Camp (National Trust), a misleading name since there's no evidence that the Romans ever occupied these 70 acres of heathland. Excavations have shown, however, that in Saxon and medieval times this was an iron-working settlement.

West Runton's major tourist attraction is

undoubtedly the **Norfolk Shire Horse Centre** (see panel on page 49), where twice a day, during the season, these wonderful, gentle giants are harnessed and give a half-hour demonstration of the important role they played in agricultural life right up until the 1930s. They are the largest (19 hands/6 feet 4 inches high) and heaviest horses in the world, weighing more than a ton, and for generations were highly valued both as war-horses and draught animals. Several other heavy breeds, such as the Suffolk Punch, Clydesdale and Percheron, also have their home here, along with no fewer than nine different breeds of pony. The Centre also has a video room showing a 30-minute film, a small animals' enclosure and an adventure playground for children, a cafe and gift shop. A horse-drawn cart will transport you around the village and at the West Runton Riding School (on site) you can hire riding horses by the hour or obtain instruction in riding.

AYLMERTON

3 miles W of Cromer on minor road off the A148

🏛 Felbrigg Hall

Aylmerton is home to one of Norfolk's grandest houses, **Felbrigg Hall**. Thomas Windham began rebuilding the old manor house at Felbrigg in the 1620s, erecting in its place a grand Jacobean mansion with huge mullioned windows, pillared porch, and at roof-level a dedication in openwork stone: Gloria Deo in Excelsis, - Glory to God in the Highest. Later that century, Thomas' grandson William Windham I married a wealthy heiress and added the beautifully proportioned Carolean West Wing, where visitors can see portraits of the happily married couple painted by Sir Peter Lely. Their son, William

Windham II, returning from his four-year-long Grand Tour, filled the house with treasures he had collected - so many of them that he had to extend the Hall yet again.

The Windham family's ownership of Felbrigg Hall came to a tragi-comic end in the 1860s when William Frederick Windham inherited the estate. William was one of the great English eccentrics. He loved uniforms. Clad in the Felbrigg blue and red livery, he would insist on serving at table; in guard's uniform he caused chaos on the local railway with his arbitrary whistle-blasts; dressed as a policeman, he sternly rounded up the ladies of easy virtue patrolling London's Haymarket. Inevitably, 'Mad' Windham fell prey to a pretty fortune-hunter and Felbrigg was only saved from complete bankruptcy by his death at the age of 26.

The Hall was acquired by the National Trust in 1969, complete with its 18th-century furnishings, collection of paintings by artists such as Kneller and van der Velde, and a wonderful Gothic library. There are extensive grounds, which include a Walled Garden containing an elegant octagonal dove-house, an Orangery, built in 1707, sheltering an outstanding collection of camellias, as well as many woodland and lakeside walks, and a restaurant, tea room and shop.

SHERINGHAM

5 miles W of Cromer on the A149

🌿 The Poppy Line (North Norfolk Railway)

🌿 Pretty Corner   🌿 Sheringham Park

Sheringham has made the transition from fishing village to popular seaside resort with grace and style. There are plenty of activities on offer, yet Sheringham has managed to avoid the brasher excesses of many English seaside towns. The beach here is among the

MISS MADELEINE'S GIFTWARE EMPORIUM AT THE SEWING ROOM OF SHERINGHAM

3 & 4 The Courtyard, Sheringham, Norfolk NR26 8RF
Tel: 01263 821990 Fax: 01263 823021
e-mail: sewing-room@hotmail.com
website: www.sewing-room.net

Miss Madeleine's Giftware Emporium and **The Sewing Room** are located in adjacent premises in a glass-covered arcade in a little courtyard, close to the centre of Sheringham yet away from the bustle of the high street. What began as a small dressmaking and gift shop has become the perfect place for making any occasion extra special. These occasions can be anything from weddings and anniversaries to birthdays, New Baby, Christmas and New Home.

Mary Kirby started in a small way sewing and dressmaking, and with growing demand and leftover materials she expanded and began to specialise in wedding dresses. She opened The Sewing Room in 1994 when her dressmaking room at home overspilled. Initially she offered just a dressmaking and alteration service, but soon realised the potential for expansion. She took that chance when the shop next door came up for sale, creating two bright, beautiful shops under one roof, with ground-floor sales areas and an upstairs work room. Over the years she has carefully sourced more products, assisted by input and reactions from customers and from her family – husband Robert, daughters Sacha and Nina and granddaughter Madeleine.

Madeleine, who arrived just after Mary took the shop next door, was the inspiration for the name of the Giftware Emporium and for its best-known product. Madeleine's fairies and pixies, each one unique in design and handmade using vintage materials and jewellery, make the perfect gift for a special person to treasure. They can also be co-ordinated with a bridesmaid's dress or a favourite colour scheme. Among other gifts and homeware in the Emporium are bed and table linen, French silk flowers, Beatrix Potter clocks, magnets and bookends, organic baby wear, gifts from Nature's Purest and wonderful Christmas decorations, including their own range of one-offs created using vintage fabrics.

Wedding services include bespoke dressmaking and alterations for the bride and bridesmaids, tiaras, function room design, setting up marquees, table settings and decorations, favours, keepsakes, hand-crafted stationery unique to the occasion and card and paper materials from Artoz of Switzerland for making your own invitations. Christening gowns are another speciality.

The Sewing Room and Miss Madeleine's Giftware attracts a constant stream of visitors, many of whom return time and again to browse, to buy or to commission a handmade gift. Opening times are 9.30 to 5 Monday to Saturday, 11 to 4 Sunday.

cleanest in England, and markedly different from the shingle beaches elsewhere on this part of the coast. Consisting mainly of gently sloping sand, it is excellent for bathing and the team of lifeguards makes it ideal for families with children. Rainfall at Sheringham is one of the lowest in the county, and the bracing air has also recommended the town to sufferers from rheumatism and respiratory problems.

A small fleet of fishing boats still operates from here, mostly concentrating on crabs and lobsters, but also bringing in catches of cod, skate, plaice, mackerel and herring. Several original fishermen's cottages remain, some with lofts where the nets were mended. Sheringham has never had a harbour, so boats are launched from the shore where stacks of creels stand as they have for generations. A golden lobster in the town's coat of arms celebrates this traditional industry.

Like so many other former fishing villages in England, Sheringham owes its transformation into a resort to the arrival of the railway. During the Edwardian peak years of rail travel, some 64 trains a day steamed into the station, but the line became yet another victim of the Beeching closures of the 1960s. Devotees of steam trains joined together and, by dint of great effort and enthusiasm, managed to re-open the line in 1975 as the North Norfolk Railway, better known as **The Poppy Line**.

The name refers to 'Poppyland', a term given to the area by the Victorian journalist Clement Scott, who visited in pre-herbicide days when the summer fields were ablaze with poppies. In 1883, Scott travelled to Cromer on the newly-opened Great Eastern Railway's extension from Norwich. Walking out of the town, he was entranced by the tranquillity of the countryside. In his dispatch to *The Daily Telegraph* he wrote: 'It is difficult to convey an idea of the silence of the fields through which I passed, or the beauty of the prospect that surrounded me - a blue sky without a cloud across it, a sea sparkling under a haze of heat, wild flowers in profusion around me, poppies predominating everywhere ...' Spurred by Scott's enthusiasm, a succession of notable Victorians made their way here - painters, writers, actors, even a youthful Winston Churchill. Later, during the Second World War, Churchill returned to the area, staying at Pear Tree Cottage in Mundesley.

Although greatly diminished in number, plenty of brilliant poppies can still be seen when travelling the scenic five-mile journey from Sheringham to Holt. The railway operates up to eight trains daily in each direction during the season, March to October, and there are special Saturday evening and Sunday lunchtime services when you can dine in style in one of the Pullman coaches from the old Brighton Belle. On West Slipway, the Henry Ramey Upcher Lifeboat Museum houses this private lifeboat built in 1894 and in service until 1935. It is housed in its original boatshed.

Just to the west of the town, at Upper Sheringham, footpaths lead to the lovely grounds of **Sheringham Park** (National Trust). The Park was landscaped by Humphry Repton, who declared it to be his 'favourite and darling child in Norfolk'. There are grand views along the coast, dense growths of oak, beech and fir trees and banks of rhododendrons, which are at their most dazzling in late May and June.

There's yet more grand scenery at the aptly-named **Pretty Corner**, just to the east of the A1082 at its junction with the A148. This is a particularly beautiful area of woodland and also offers superb views over the surrounding countryside.

WEYBOURNE
9 miles W of Cromer on the A149

🏛 The Muckleburgh Collection

Here, the shingle beach known as Weybourne Hope (or Hoop) slopes so steeply that an invading fleet could bring its ships right up to the shore. Which is exactly what the Danes did many times during the 9th and 10th centuries. A local adage states that 'He who would Old England win, Must at Weybourne Hoop begin,' and over the centuries care has been taken to protect this stretch of the coast. A map dated 1st May 1588 clearly shows 'Waborne Fort', and Holt's Parish Register for that year of the Armada notes that 'in this yeare was the town of Waborne fortified with a continuall garrison of men bothe of horse and foote with sconces (earthworks)

Muckleburgh Collection, Weybourne

ordinaunce and all manner of appoyntment to defend the Spannyards landing theare'.

As it turned out, the 'Spannyards' never got close, but during both World Wars the same concern was shown for defending this vulnerable beach. The garrison then became the Anti-Aircraft Permanent Range and Radar Training Wing, providing instruction for National Servicemen until the camp finally closed in 1959. It was reckoned that by then some 1,500,000 shells had been fired out to sea. The site has since been returned to agricultural use, but the original NAAFI building remains and now houses **The Muckleburgh Collection**, a fascinating museum of military vehicles, weapons and equipment, most of which have seen action in battlefields all over the world. All of the tanks, armoured cars and amphibious vehicles on display can be inspected at close quarters, and there are regular tank demonstrations and rides on various vehicles. Meals and snacks are available, served in a NAAFI-style canteen. Incidentally, despite its exposed position, Weybourne has in fact only been attacked once, by the Luftwaffe on 11th July 1940. A stick of bombs landed in the main street and badly damaged two cottages.

HOLT
10 miles W of Cromer on the A148

🏛 Gresham's School

A perennial finalist in the Anglia in Bloom competition, Holt's town centre always looks a picture, with hanging baskets and flowers everywhere. Back in 1892, a guide-book to the county described Holt as 'A clean and very prettily situated market town, being planted in a well undulating and very woody neighbourhood'. More than a century later, one can't quarrel with that characterisation.

CHAPEL YARD HOLT
Albert St, Holt, Norfolk NR25 6HG

In the Historic market town of Holt just off the main street there is a courtyard full of colour and variety, products old and new, offering something for everyone. Artwork, woodwork, antiques, furniture, clothing and jewellery sourced from all over the world. Take your time to see everything that is on offer, ask for advice on wildlife gardening and why not treat yourself to a manicure. With ample parking next to the courtyard take a relaxing browse around these shops where personal service is given with a smile and nothing is too much trouble.

BIRD VENTURES
Tel: 01263 710203
website: www.birdventures.co.uk

The premier shop for Wild Bird Care Products, Insect Habitats and Nature Study Equipment. Helping wildlife is the ethos of Bird Ventures and we not only provide hundreds of wildlife products but also offer expert advice on all aspects of wildlife gardening.

SILK CONNECTIONS
Tel: 01263 711444
website: silkconnections@hotmail.co.uk

Finest quality handpainted silk scarves, authentic Chinese Ming style furniture. Soft furnishings, jewellery, boxes, porcelain and ceramic artworks plus many more original gift ideas from China. Mention this advert and receive a 10% discount.

PAST CARING
Tel: 01263 713771

Good selection of ORIGINAL vintage clothing - 1800's - 1950's always available. Also period handbags, hats, shoes, gloves and jewellery. Plus Fine ANTIQUE linen and christening gowns. Items wanted for purchase. Established 1988.

REFLEX HAIR STUDIO
Tel: 01263 710202

Reflex Hair Studio and Fuchsia Beauty Salon is a friendly and buzzing salon where you can come to relax. Offering a range of different treatments from cut to colours and facials to manicures.

🏚 historic building 🏛 museum and heritage 🏛 historic site 🌄 scenic attraction 🐾 flora and fauna

PACHAMAMA

Tel: 01263 713080
website: www.itchycoopark.biz

We stock indoor and outdoor clothing from Weirdfish, Deal cottons and Pachamama handknits. The latest designs and colours are stocked and a vast choice is available. See you there!

LIBRA SILVER JEWELLERY

Tel: 01263 712920

A little shop with a big heart; a mix of delicious amber, silver, semi-previous stones and crystal jewellery along with pure cotton night dresses. Mention this advert and receive 10% discount. cottage.collectables@virgin.net

WOOD N THINGS

Tel: 01263 713720
e-mail: hyattbruin@aol.com
website: www.wood-n-things.co.uk

Antiques, affordable furniture and collectables. Bespoke furniture made to order. Royal Doulton "Norfolk"; largest stock in Eastern Countries.

CASA ANDALUS

Tel: 01263 712889
e-mail: info@casaandalus.co.uk
website: www.casaandalus.co.uk

The shop to visit for exclusive Spanish lighting, Moroccan and Turkish lanterns, colourful pottery and cushions. Also photographic prints of north Norfolk, framed or on canvas.

GREAT TO BE GREEN

Tel: 01263 711733
e-mail: clare@greattobegreen.co.uk
website: www.greattobegreen.co.uk

To prove ethical can also be chic; we provide a wide range of British made and Fair Trade products for the home and garden including soft furnishings and vintage collectables.

MORSTON TOWN & COUNTRY SPORTS – CLOTHES FOR LIFE

9 Shirehall Plain, Holt, Norfolk NR25 6HT
Tel: 01263 713545
e-mail: nikola@morstontowncountrysports.co.uk

'Country Clothing with City Style' is the motto of **Morston Town & Country Sports**, a bright, beautiful retail shop in rural North Norfolk. Behind the double frontage of the late-Victorian building, the oak-floored display space is stocked with an impressive variety of sporting, outdoor and country clothes and accessories that are stylish, practical and durable, and definitely smart enough to turn heads in town. The stock, which changes constantly, includes all the best-known brands in country clothing and accessories.

- REALLY WILD Berkshire-based company making a wide range of coats, jumpers, shirts, waistcoats, leisure & sporting footwear and the famous Lindsey caps in corduroy or tweed

- BERETTA American manufacturer of hunting, shooting, outdoor and leisure clothes, from shorts and T-shirts to jackets, breeks, caps and gloves

- DUBARRY Based in Ireland, Dubarry produces a range of top-quality clothes (superb tweeds), bags and sporting footwear

- HUNTER A British firm known throughout the world for its rubber wellington boots, available in several colours as well as the classic green

- BELSTAFF Italian-designed high-tech leather jackets (some with canvas and wax elements) guaranteed to turn heads on or off a Harley-Davidson

- FARLOWS Country clothing and shooting wear, including cord trousers, Tattershall shirts, V-neck sweaters and moleskin waistcoats

- SASTA A Finnish firm making high-quality clothes and accessories for hunting, country and outdoor life

- STETSON German-based company famous for its hats in felt, straw, wool and beaver fur

- BARONS Swedish maker of bags. The Country Collection includes travel, duffel, shoulder, game, cartridge and wash bags and backpacks

People come from many miles around to spend time in the pretty market town of Holt, and for those looking for the latest in top-quality country wear Morston Town & Country Sports is definitely the place to head for. Owner Nikola Taylor and her team are always on hand with help and advice at this outstanding shop, which is open from 10 to 5 Monday to Saturday.

The worst day in the town's history was May 1st 1708, when a raging fire consumed most of the town's ancient houses. The consequent rebuilding in the 1770s replaced them with some elegant Georgian houses - gracious buildings that played a large part in earning the town its designation as a Conservation Area.

The town's most famous building, **Gresham's School**, somehow escaped the disastrous conflagration of 1708. Founded in 1555 by Sir John Gresham, the school began

---

THE PIED PIPER SHOP

8 Station Road, Holt, Norfolk NR25 6BS
Tel: 01263 711124
e-mail: ppshop@btopenworld.com
website: www.justjellycat.co.uk

The **Pied Piper Shop** has been a fixture in Holt for more than 25 years, and the owners have established a fine reputation for quality and friendly, efficient service. The shop is a browser's delight, with a wide variety of gifts to suit all pockets, toys, dolls, games, books, watches, clocks, metal magnets, drawer knobs, light pulls and other useful things for the house. It also holds a selection of cotton fabrics and quilt-making supplies and is a major stockist of the Jelly Cat range. See the website for a comprehensive selection of goods stocked by and available on line from this lovely little shop.

BIRCHAM GALLERY

14 Market Place, Holt, Norfolk NR25 6BW
Tel: 01263 713312
e-mail: birchamgal@aol.com
website: www.birchamgallery.co.uk

Bircham Gallery is located in the Market Place of the Georgian town of Holt. It was established in 1988 by Christopher and Deborah Harrison, and has since built up an enviable reputation locally and nationally for the quality of its artists and exhibitions. Managed by Gail Richardson, the Gallery stocks the works of upwards over 200 artists and craftspeople – a wide range of beautiful modern and contemporary art, from paintings, prints and photographs to ceramics, glass, jewellery, paper craft and wood.

An innovative exhibition programme includes the work of established artists, acclaimed modern masters and emerging new talent, with the artists chosen for the quality or their work and imagination. The aim is to make viewing and collecting original art an enjoyable and rewarding experience.

The Gallery is a founder member (2004) of the Own Art scheme offering interest-free loans to make it easy for everyone to buy high-quality art. The Gallery also sells art books and magazines, cards, gifts and gift vouchers. Opening times are 9 to 5 Monday to Saturday, 10 to 4 Bank Holidays; closed Sundays. Customers who cannot get to the gallery can visit the comprehensive website and order online.

HEATHFIELD ANTIQUES

Candlestick Lane, Thornage Road, Holt, Norfolk NR25 6SU
Tel/Fax: 01263 711609
e-mail: sarahheathfield@onetel.com
website: www.antique-pine.net

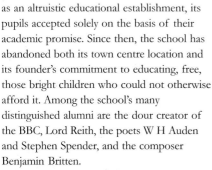

Established in 1988, **Heathfield Antiques** is a family-run business located on the B1110 Holt to Guist road. In the showroom is a large collection of pine furniture – original antiques, reproduction, restored, reclaimed or painted – and pieces in oak, ash, elm, beech and leather. Restoration, repair and replacement work, carried out on site, uses authentic materials whenever possible, and other services include French polishing, bespoke paint finishes and commercial work, and commissions are accepted for made-to-order pieces of furniture. Heathfield Antiques is open from 8.30 to 5 Monday to Saturday.

as an altruistic educational establishment, its pupils accepted solely on the basis of their academic promise. Since then, the school has abandoned both its town centre location and its founder's commitment to educating, free, those bright children who could not otherwise afford it. Among the school's many distinguished alumni are the dour creator of the BBC, Lord Reith, the poets W H Auden and Stephen Spender, and the composer Benjamin Britten.

Look out for one of Holt's most unusual buildings, Home Place. Designed and built between 1903 and 1905 by E S Prior, an architect and follower of the Arts and Crafts movement, the exterior of the house is completely covered with an ingeniously contrived cladding of local pebbles. The parish Church of St Andrew, virtually destroyed by the 1708 fire, was rebuilt in 1720 and fully restored in 1863 by the great church architect William

Butterfield. Chapel Yard is a pretty area of small shops that includes a row of 16th-century cottages.

CLEY-NEXT-THE-SEA
12 miles W of Cromer on the A149

🏠 St Mary's Church 🌿 Blakeney Point

Cley's full name is no longer appropriate. Cley-a-mile-away-from-the-Sea would be more truthful. But in early medieval times, Cley (pronounced Cly, and meaning clay) was a more important port than King's Lynn, with a busy trade exporting wool to the Netherlands. In return, Cley imported a

Cley-next-the-Sea Windmill

predilection for houses with curved gables, Flemish bricks and pantiles. The windmill overlooking the harbour adds to the sense that a little piece of Holland has strayed across the North Sea. This is the famous Cley Mill, the subject of thousands of paintings. Built in 1713 and in use until 1921, the Mill is open to visitors during the season (afternoons only), and also offers bed and breakfast.

The village's prosperity in the past is reflected in the enormous scale of its 14th/15th-century parish church, **St Mary's**, whose south porch is particularly notable for its fine stonework and 16 armorial crests. The gorgeous fan-vaulted roof is decorated with bosses carved with angels, flowers, and a lively scene of an old woman throwing her distaff at a fox running away with her chickens.

From Cley it's possible to walk along the shoreline to **Blakeney Point**, the most northerly extremity of East Anglia. This spit of land that stretches three miles out into the sea is a birdwatcher's paradise. Some 256 species of birds have been spotted here, and the variety of flora is scarcely less impressive: almost 200 flowering species have been recorded.

BLAKENEY
14 miles W of Cromer on the A149

One of the most enchanting of the North Norfolk coastal villages, Blakeney was a commercial port until the beginning of the 20th century, when silting up of the estuary prevented all but pleasure craft from gaining access. The silting has left a fascinating landscape of serpentine creeks and channels twisting their way through mud banks and sand hills. In a side street off the quay is the 14th-century Guildhall (English Heritage), which was probably a private house and contains an interesting undercroft, or cellar,

ANCHOR SHOP

35 High Street, Blakeney, Norfolk NR25 7NA
Tel: 01263 741555
e-mail: info@theanchorshop.co.uk
website: www.theanchorshop.co.uk

The Anchor Shop is a charming gift shop within a Grade II listed building in the heart of Blakeney a minute or two from the quayside. This is a family run business that was established by Alec and Gill Mellor after they found retirement left them with little to do and so when the lease of 35, High Street, Blakeney, became available in 2005, they took it up. For many years it had been know as the Anchor Shop, the name of the public house it had previously been, but had been trading under a name of less resonance. So they reverted to the earlier name and opened as the Anchor Shop.

Alec and Gill offer an eclectic mix of all things traditional - gifts, greetings, home, garden, toys for kids, babies, children & all with a shabby chic vintage English country living feel.

* Greeting cards * jewellery * handmade decorative items * nautical novelties, commemorative cushions * plus much more!

Blakeney

Distance: *3.1 miles (4.8 kilometres)*
Typical time: *90 mins*
Height gain: *15 metres*
Map: *Explorer 24*
Walk: *www.walkingworld.com ID:2103*
Contributor: *Joy & Charles Boldero*

ACCESS INFORMATION:

Norfolk Bus routes: Freecall 0500 626116, 9am to 5pm, Monday to Friday. Parking in National Trust car park by the quay.

DESCRIPTION:

This is a very pleasurable walk with good paths and no stiles. There are fine views of the coastline. Blakeney is a very popular and pretty village on the North Norfolk coast. The River Glaven is tidal and fills the quayside channel at high tide. It is a place for sailing, safe for small children to bathe and fish, and where the boats wait to take passengers out to Blakeney Point to see the seals. The outer route is along field edges and returns along the Norfolk Coastal Path, which runs beside the marshes.

FEATURES:

River, Pub, Toilets, Church, National Trust/ NTS, Wildlife, Birds, Flowers, Great Views, Butterflies, Food Shop.

WALK DIRECTIONS:

1 | Turn left up the narrow street with its attractive flinted cottages. Just past the Methodist Church and opposite Coronation Cottage turn right along Little Lane. At the T-junction, turn left along New Road, then right along a residential road.

2 | Turn right at a fingerpost sign along a gravel track with pretty flinted cottages. It then becomes a rough path alongside a field.

3 | Turn left along the road and very soon turn right at a fingerpost sign along a driveway. There are fine views here of the marshes. As the driveway goes right keep ahead to a house, and then go left at a yellow marker sign beside the field edge with a hedge on the right. The path winds and the hedge is then on the left with a thatched house on the hill ahead. Just before the gate the path goes left.

4 | Turn right along the road, then left at a fingerpost sign ahead along a grass path leading downhill.

5 | At a T-junction of paths turn right along the Norfolk Coastal Path, which takes you into Blakeney. This path goes beside the marshes where sea lavender and wading birds can be seen.

6 | Turn left along the pavement and walk along beside the Quay.

7 | Turn right up the narrow street with the White House Hotel ahead and back to the car park.

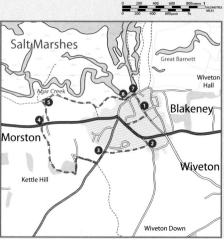

Blakeney Harbour

herb gardens, nurseries, a nature trail alongside the unspoilt River Glaven, and the Centre also organises a wide range of events with a conservation theme. A short walk down the valley from the Centre is the **Glandford Shell Museum**, a lovely Dutch-style building, which houses the private collection of Sir Alfred Jodrell, a unique accumulation of sea shells gathered from beaches all around the world, together with a fascinating variety of artefacts, fossils, scraps of ingeniously carved scrimshaw, tiny figures made out of shells and 19th century cameo brooches.

which is notable as an early example of a brick-built vaulted ceiling.

The beautifully restored Church of St Nicholas, set on a hill overlooking village and marshland, offers the visitor a lovely Early English chancel, built in 1220, and the magnificent west tower, 100 feet high, a landmark for miles around. In a small turret on the northeast corner of the chancel, a light would once burn as a beacon to guide ships safely into Blakeney Harbour.

GLANDFORD
12 miles W of Cromer off the B1156

🏠 Glandford Shell Museum

🌱 Natural Surroundings Wild Flower Centre

Near this delightful village, the **Natural Surroundings Wild Flower Centre** is dedicated to gardening with a strong ecological emphasis. There are wild flower meadows and gardens, organic vegetable and

A couple of miles south of Glandford you'll find a building, dated 1802, which, year after year, has been awarded the title of 'op Tourist Attraction in North Norfolk. **Letheringsett Watermill** stands on the site of an earlier mill recorded in the Domesday Book, and was rescued from near-dereliction in the 1980s. This fully functional, water-powered mill produces 100% wholewheat flour from locally grown wheat; there are regular demonstrations of the milling process, with a running commentary from the miller; and the end product can be purchased in the gift shop.

LANGHAM
14 miles W of Cromer off the A149/A148

🔮 Langham Glass

The minor road south from Morston leads to **Langham Glass**, where, in a wonderful

🎬 stories and anecdotes 🦅 famous people 🔮 art and craft 🖋 entertainment and sport 🚶 walks

collection of restored 18th-century barn workshops, visitors can watch a variety of craftspeople exercising their traditional skills. In addition to the now famous Langham Glass works where a master glass-maker will give a running commentary, there's a pyrographer, wood-turner, stained glass maker, and glass engraver. The Factory Gift Shop is well stocked with their creations, the Antiques & Collectables Shop offers a wide variety of items from Victorian china to Lalique, and there's also a rose and clematis walled garden, a seven-acre maize maze with three miles of walkways through corn maize interspersed with sunflowers, an adventure playground, tea rooms and café.

MORSTON

13 miles W of Cromer on the A149

Great stretches of salt marshes and mud flats lie between this pleasant village and the sea, which is reached by way of a tidal creek that almost disappears at low tide. Morston is a particularly pleasing village with quiet lanes and clusters of cottages built from local flint cobbles. If the church tower looks rather patched-up, that's because it was struck by lightning in 1743. It's said that local people took this as a sign that the Second Coming of Christ was imminent, and that repairing their church was therefore pointless. It was many years before restoration work was finally undertaken, by which time the fabric of the tower had deteriorated even further.

STIFFKEY

16 miles W of Cromer on the A149

🏛 Binham Priory 🌿 Stiffkey Salt Marshes

Regarded as one of the prettiest villages in the county, Stiffkey lies beside the little river of the same name. Pronounced Stewkey, the

name means Island of Tree Stumps and is most likely derived from the marshy river valley of reed beds and fallen trees, which indeed gives the village the appearance of an island. At the east end of the village is the Church of St John the Baptist; from the churchyard there are fine views of the river and of **Stiffkey Hall** to the south. All that now remains of this once-impressive building, built by the Bacon family in 1578, are the towers, one wing of the house, and the 17th-century gatehouse. The stately ruins of the great hall have been transformed into a rose terrace and sunken garden and are open to the public.

The former Rectory is a grand Georgian building, famous as the residence of the Rev Harold Davidson, Rector of Stiffkey during the 1920s and 1930s. Rather like the central

Stiffkey Hall

character in Michael Palin's film *The Missionary*, Harold launched a personal crusade to save the fallen women of London, and caused much gossip and scandal by doing so. Despite the fact that his notoriety regularly filled the church to capacity, he constantly fell foul of the ecclesiastical authorities and eventually lost his living. There is a rather bizarre ending to his story. After handing over the keys of Stiffkey Rectory, Harold joined a travelling show and was later killed by a lion whose cage he was sharing.

To the north of the village are the **Stiffkey Salt Marshes**, a National Trust nature reserve, which turn a delicate shade of purple in July when the sea lavender is in bloom. Here on the sandflats can be found the famous Stewkey blues - cockles that are highly regarded as a delicacy by connoisseurs of succulent bivalve molluscs.

A couple of miles south of Stiffkey stand the picturesque ruins of **Binham Priory** (English Heritage), its magnificent nave still serving as the parish church. This represents only about one-sixth of the original Priory, founded in 1091 by a nephew of William the Conqueror. The church is well worth a visit to see its unusually lofty interior with a Monk's Walk at roof level, its Seven Sacraments font, and noble west front.

Stiffkey Salt Marshes

Hunstanton

🌿 Sea Life Sanctuary

The busy seaside resort of Hunstanton can boast two unique features: one, it has the only cliffs in England made up of colourful levels of red, white and brown strata, and two, it is the only east coast resort that faces west, looking across The Wash to the Lincolnshire coast and the unmistakable tower of the 272-foot Boston Stump (more properly described as the Church of St Botolph).

Hunstanton town is a comparative newcomer, developed in the 1860s by Mr Hamon L'Estrange of nearby Hunstanton Hall to take advantage of the arrival of the railway here, and to exploit the natural appeal of its broad, sandy beaches. The centre is well planned, with mock-Tudor houses grouped around a green that falls away to the shore.

Hunstanton's social standing was assured after the Prince of Wales, later Edward VII, came here to recover from typhoid fever. He stayed at the Sandringham Hotel which, sadly, has since been demolished, along with the grand Victorian pier and the railway. But Hunston, as locals call the town, still has a distinct 19th-century charm about it and plenty to entertain visitors.

The huge stretches of sandy beach, framed

Hunstanton Sea Life Sanctuary

Southern Promenade, Hunstanton,
Norfolk PE36 5BH
Tel: 01485 533576
website: www.sealsanctuary.co.uk

Every year, many sick and abandoned seals are rescued and brought to the **Hunstanton Sea Life Sanctuary** to be nursed back to health. As well as seals, over 30 fascinating marine displays provide a haven for many other fascinating creatures, including otters, seahorses, penguins and sharks. There's fun for all the family with a full programme including talks, feeding displays and demonstrations.

The seals brought to the sanctuary are mostly young pups, ill or orphaned, and their plight is usually reported by concerned members of the public. Their rehabilitation begins in the Seal Hospital as soon as they arrive. In the capable hands of the animal care team, the pups gradually recover, and when they are able to feed, they are transferred to the convalescence pool. Here they build up their strength before returning to the wild. At the Seal Hospital you can learn how they care for a seal pup from rescue through to release.

by those multi-coloured cliffs, are just heaven for children who will also be fascinated by the **Sea Life Sanctuary** (see panel above), on Southern Promenade, where an underwater glass tunnel provides a wonderful opportunity to watch the varied and often weird forms of marine life that inhabit Britain's waters.

A popular excursion from Hunstanton is the boat trip to Seal Island, a sandbank in The Wash where seals can indeed often be seen sunbathing at low tide.

Around Hunstanton

WELLS-NEXT-THE-SEA
17 miles E of Hunstanton on the A149

There's no doubt about the appeal of Wells' picturesque quayside, narrow streets and ancient houses. Wells has been a working port since at least the 13th century, but over the years the town's full name of Wells-next-the-Sea has become increasingly inapt - its harbour now stands more than a mile from the sea. In 1859, to prevent the harbour silting up altogether, Lord Leicester of Holkham Hall built an Embankment cutting off some 600 acres of marshland. This now provides a pleasant walk down to the sea.

The Embankment gave no protection, however, against the great floods of 1953 and 1978. On the 11th January 1978, the sea rose 16 feet 1 inch above high tide, a few inches less than the 16 feet 10 inches recorded on the 31st January 1953, when the flood waters lifted a ship on to the quay. A silo on the harbour is marked with these abnormal levels.

Running alongside the Embankment is the Harbour Railway, which trundles from the quay to the lifeboat station by the beach. The Wells-Walsingham Light Railway carries passengers on a particularly lovely ride along

FISHERS OF HUNSTANTON

2-4 Greengate, Hunstanton, Norfolk, PE36 6BJ
Tel: 01485 532487

This traditional Fish and Chip Shop and Restaurant was established in 1998 and since then has grown to be very popular. Ten welcoming friendly staff keep **Fishers of Hunstanton** running smoothly, and food is cooked in a traditional way. It is also a licensed bar, with a large selection of bottled beers (including Carling, Budweiser, Corona and Magners Cider), red wines and white wines.

There are children's play tables and books to keep them entertained while you finish your meal, and there is also some quality vegetarian options on the menu. Their take-away menu is of a high standard.

The good-looking roof garden (ten tables) has a magnificent view of the sea, especially when the sun is setting. The potatoes used to make their delicious chips are locally sourced, and the salads are locally produced too. They are an eco-friendly restaurant with hardly any wastage as everything is recycled.

The extensive menu includes a Kids Menu (with scampi, chicken nuggets, fishcake and more), Main Courses (massive range from pies to fried chicken, chicken burgers, pastys, savaloy, jacket potatoes, and fishcakes), and most importantly the Fish Menu (cod, haddock, plaice, scampi, eel, lobster tails and a magnificent seafood platter). The Fishers Challenge involves eating a whole giant prime cod with all the extras (including a drink), and those who complete the challenge receive a free dessert of their choice! There is also an impressive Side Orders section and of course Desserts.

Disabled access, child-friendly and ample parking. 100 yards from the lovely Princess Theatre with shows on all year round, and only one minute walk from the sea.

BEACHCOMBER

55 Staithe Street, Wells-Next-The-Sea,
Norfolk NR23 1AN
Tel: 01328 710496

If you find yourself on the coast, in need of a
jacket or fleece due to a sudden breeze or your
walking boots give up the ghost, Beachcomber
is the place to visit!

Set in the charming coastal town of Wells
Next The Sea, town and country enthusiasts
come to this fascinating store on Staithe Street
to purchase a wide selection of gentleman's,
ladies and children's all weather clothing and superb leather
accessories. Stockists include J. Barbour and Sons whose jackets
and knitwear have evolved from clothing rooted in the British
countryside to encompass a unique style that blends fashion with
functionality. Musto is also a big attraction, with its snappy design
and performance materials, ideally suited to life beyond the city.

It is this commitment to quality and durability that makes these
names synonymous with the best of country living.

So pay a visit to this store where not only quality products but a
warm smile and good service awaits you.

ART - NEXT - THE - SEA

26 Staithe Street, Wells-Next-The-Sea, Norfolk NR23 1AF
Tel: 01328 710722 e-mail: info@artnextthesea.co.uk
website: www.artnextthesea.co.uk

This modern gallery features the work of local and national artists,
photographers, potters and crafts people. The gallery combines
this display with antique furniture, sculpture and bronzes.

FAKENHAM ANTIQUES CENTRE

The Old Church, 14 Norwich Road, Fakenham, Norfolk, NR21 8AZ
Tel: 01328 862941 e-mail: info@fakenhamantiques.co.uk
website: www.fakenhamantiques.co.uk

The centre has been run by Julie Hunt and Mandy Allen since
February 1999. The centre now houses over 30 dealers offering
a wide selection of antiques, curious and collectables.

SHIREHALL PLAIN ANTIQUES CENTRE HOLT

2 Shirehall Plain, Holt, Norfolk NR25 6HT
Tel: 01263 711991 e-mail: info@shirehallplainantiques.co.uk
website: shirehallplainantiques.co.uk

This centre in Holt has eight large showrooms, housing over 20
antiques dealers. It specialises in fine period furniture, but also
houses a number of well stocked cabinets offering a wide range
of good quality antiques, collectables and memorabilia.

🏛 historic building 🏚 museum and heritage 🏛 historic site ♨ scenic attraction 🌱 flora and fauna

the route of the former Great Eastern Railway to Little Walsingham. The four-mile journey takes about 30 minutes with stops at Warham St Mary and Wighton. Both the WWR and the Harbour Railway services are seasonal. In a curious change of function, the former GER station at Wells is now home to the Old Station Pottery & Bookshop, the former signal box is now the station, while the old station at Walsingham is now a church!

In addition to being the largest of North Norfolk's ports, Wells is also a popular resort, with one of the best beaches in England, bordered by the curiously named Holkham Meals, a plantation of pines established here in the 1860s to stabilise the dunes.

HOLKHAM
16 miles E of Hunstanton on the A149

🏠 Holkham Hall

If the concept of the Grand Tour ever needed any justification, **Holkham Hall** amply provides it. For six years, from 1712 to 1718, young Thomas Coke (pronounced Cook) travelled extensively in Italy, France and Germany, studying and absorbing at first hand the glories of European civilisation. And,

Holkham Hall

wherever possible, buying them. When he returned to England, Coke realised that his family's modest Elizabethan manor could not possibly house the collection of treasures he had amassed. The manor would have to be demolished and a more worthy building erected in its place.

During his travels in Italy, Coke had been deeply impressed by the cool, classical lines favoured by the Renaissance architect Andrea Palladio. Working with his friend Lord Burlington - another fervent admirer of Palladio - and the architect William Kent, Coke's monumental project slowly took shape. Building began in 1734 but was not completed until 1762, three years after Coke's death.

The completed building, its classical balance and restraint emphasised by the pale honey local brick used throughout, has been described as 'the ultimate achievement of the English Palladian movement'. As you step into the stunning entrance hall, the tone is set for the rest of the house. Modelled on a Roman Temple of Justice, the lofty coved ceiling is supported by 18 huge fluted columns of pink Derbyshire alabaster, transported to nearby Wells by river and sea.

Historically, the most important room at Holkham is the Statue Gallery, which contains one of the finest collections of classical sculpture still in private ownership. In this sparsely furnished room there is nothing to distract one's attention from the sublime statuary that has survived for millennia, among it a bust of Thucydides (one of the earliest portrayals of man) and a statue of Diana, both of which have been dated to 4BC.

Each room reveals new treasures: Rubens and Van Dyck in the Saloon, the Landscape Room with its incomparable collection of paintings by Lorrain, Poussin and other masters, the Brussels tapestries in the State Sitting Room and, on a more domestic note, the vast, high-ceilinged kitchen, which remained in use until 1939 and still displays the original pots and pans.

Astonishingly, the interior of the house remains almost exactly as Thomas Coke planned it, his descendants having respected the integrity of his vision. They concentrated their reforming zeal on improving the enormous estate. It was Coke's great-nephew, Thomas William Coke (1754-1842), who was mainly responsible for the elegant layout of the 3,000-acre park visitors see today. Universally known as Coke of Norfolk, Thomas was a pioneer of the Agricultural Revolution, best known for introducing the idea of a four-crop rotation. He was also a generous patron of agricultural innovations, and the Sheep Shearings he inaugurated - gatherings to which several hundred people came to exchange ideas on all aspects of agriculture - were the direct forerunners of the modern agricultural show.

The Thomas Coke who had built the house had been created Earl of Leicester in 1744, but as his only son died before him, the title lapsed. However, when his grand-nephew, Coke of Norfolk was elevated to the peerage by Queen Victoria in 1837, he adopted the same title.

BURNHAM THORPE
11 miles E of Hunstanton off the B1355

🏛 Creake Abbey

From the tower of All Saints' Church, the White Ensign flaps in the breeze; the only pub in the village is The Lord Nelson. No prizes for deducing that Burnham Thorpe was the birthplace of Horatio Nelson. His father, the Rev Edmund Nelson, was the Rector here for 46 years; Horatio was the sixth of his 11 children.

Parsonage House, where Horatio was born seven weeks' premature in 1758, was demolished during his lifetime, but the pub (one of more than 200 hostelries across the country bearing the hero's name) has become a kind of shrine to Nelson's memory, its walls covered with portraits, battle scenes and other marine paintings.

There's more Nelson memorabilia in the church, among it a crucifix and lectern made with wood from HMS *Victory*, a great chest from the pulpit used by the Rev Nelson, and two flags from HMS *Nelson*. Every year on Trafalgar Day, 21st October, members of the Nelson Society gather at this riverside church for a service in commemoration of the man who had specified in his will that he wanted to be buried in its country graveyard 'unless the King decrees otherwise'. George III did indeed decree otherwise, and the great hero was interred in St Paul's Cathedral.

A little over a mile to the south of Burnham Thorpe stand the picturesque ruins of **Creake Abbey** (English Heritage), an Augustinian monastery founded in 1206. The Abbey's working life came to an abrupt end in 1504 when, within a single week, every one of the monks died of the plague.

BURNHAM MARKET
9 miles E of Hunstanton on the B1155

There are seven Burnhams in all, strung along the valley of the little River Burn. A stone's throw from the glorious North Norfolk coastline, Burnham Market is the largest of them, its past importance reflected in the wealth of Georgian buildings surrounding the green and the two churches

BURNHAM MARKET

Situated a stone's throw away from the glorious North Norfolk coastline with its many stunning beaches, wide open spaces, some of the best coastal walks, renouned restaurants and hotel, it is the perfect place to shop, dine, or simply stay a while and revel in being part of the traditional village atmosphere.

So many towns in Britiain today are dominated by multiples, with one high street looking very much like another. Here in Burnham Market there is a traditional post office, butcher, baker, hardware shop, fish shop and chemist for all the daily necessities, plus over 30 highly original independant and specialist shops, selling a wide range of exciting deli products, vibrant and stylish accessories for home and garden, trendy clothes shops for all the family, and books old and new. There is an exciting array of eateries serving everything from snacks to full meals.

SOWERBYS HOLIDAY COTTAGES

Market Place, Burnham Market, Norfolk PE31 8HD
Tel: 01328 730880
e-mail: info@sowerbysholidaycottages.co.uk
website: www.sowerbysholidaycottages.co.uk

To enjoy all that Burnham Market and the surrounding area has to offer throughout the year, why not stay in one of the delightful holiday cottages available from Sowerbys Holiday Cottages. Sowerbys is a local agency which specialises in letting much-loved second homes sleeping 2 to 16 and available for flexible short breaks in the winter or full weeks during the summer. The properties are all furnished and equipped to an extremely high standard, to give a real "home from home" experience, and range from cosy beamed cottages to spacious contemporary barn conversions .

TILLY'S CAFÉ

Market Place, Burnham Market, Norfolk PE31 8HF
Tel: 01328 730300

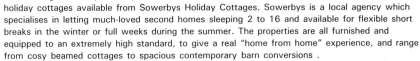

Set in the loveliest village in Norfolk, Tilly's Cafe in Burnham Market offers visitors the very best in hospitality, food and drink. The cafe is well placed for visitors to this area of outstanding beauty to call in and revel in being part of the traditional village atmosphere while enjoying an excellent cup of tea or specialist blended coffee and deliciously prepared light lunch. All through the day Tilly's serve home made cakes, scones and biscuits making the cafe an ideal place to head to for that special afternoon tea. Open 10 am - 4.30 p.m. Monday - Saturday

THE RINGSTEAD GALLERY

Market Place, Burnham Market, Norfolk PE31 8HD
Tel: 01328 738458   e-mail: ringsteadgallery@btconnect.com
website: www.ringsteadgallery.com

Established in Ringstead in 1974, **The Ringstead Gallery** moved to Burnham Market in August 2007. The Gallery's location in the bustling village is perfect for showcasing the talents of local, national and international artists. As well as constantly changing exhibitions from traditional to the more modern paintings, bronzes and fine turned wood, the gallery aims to seek out and showcase new and up-and-coming artists. Fresh 'discoveries' can often be found in the mixed exhibitions, making The Ringstead Gallery an essential destination to discover new and exciting pieces of art by emerging talent. Open Mon-Sat 10am-5pm. Entry to the gallery is free.

GRAPEVINE CONTEMPORARY ARTS

Overy Road, Burnham Market,
Norfolk PE31 8HH
Tel: 01328 730125
website: www.grapevinegallery.co.uk

Grapevine Contemporary Arts in Burnham Market is owned and directed by Alison and Peter Low - both well known in architectural circles - and is sister gallery to Grapevine in Norwich, the city's principal contemporary art gallery.

The work shown at Burnham Market perpetuates the ethos of the Norwich gallery with an eclectic mix of contemporary paintings and ceramics. From the outset our aim has been to make the gallery welcoming and interesting, with a very distinct character. Whilst we show the best of the region's artists and potters, a considerable part of the gallery's portfolio is work by artists from all over the country, frequently including work more usually found in London galleries. The main website www.grapevinegallery.co.uk provides an overview of the artists we represent and is regularly updated. Featured exhibitions are held every 6 to 7 weeks throughout the year; at other times you may expect to see work by a small selection of our many artists with further work available to view on request.

The gallery is to be found in an ancient and very beautiful building, St Andrew's Cottage on Overy Road, close to the well-known Saltwater Gallery. It is open throughout the year, summer opening being Monday to Saturday - and most Sundays - from 10 to 5.30. From November to Easter, openings vary, typically Thursday - Saturday 11am to 5pm with additional openings during holiday periods and by chance.

CRANMER COUNTRY COTTAGES

Home Farm, Cranmer, Fakenham, Norfolk NR21 9HY
Telephone: 01328 823135 Fax: 01328 823136
e-mail: bookings@homefarmcranmer.co.uk
website: www.homefarmcranmer.co.uk

North Norfolk is one of England's coastal treasures and the UK's premier bird watching destination. This part of Norfolk offers a wealth of individuality under its famous big skies and it is all within easy reach of Cranmer. Award winning Cranmer Country Cottages is a small complex of converted Victorian barns at home Farm; set in a gorgeous rural setting close to the sandy beaches and pine woods of Holkham and Wells and the fashionable village of Burnham Market. The sensitively restored barns are all on one level, spacious and well equipped making self catering a pleasure.

The magnificent threshing barn has been converted into a sparkling indoor heated swimming pool providing a year round attraction. There are also 2 all- weather tennis courts, games room, and a large enclosed play area making Home Farm an ideal base for the whole family.

These stylish cottages with their original beamed ceilings are ideal for every occasion. The cottages' living areas boast magnificent views over the open countryside. The whole complex has a relaxed feel and everything is taken care of – from barbecues, cycle hire and free WIFI internet access to baby sitting and bespoke catering. There is easy access to walks, cycling and bird watching. Pensthorpe Nature Reserve, host of BBC's spring watch is within 6 miles. Slightly further a field are the National Trust properties at Blickling, Felbrigg, Brancaster and the Royal retreat at Sandringham. Not least the internationally renowned bird reserves at Titchwell Cley and RSPB Snettisham.

that lie at each end of its broad main street, just 600 yards apart. In the opinion of many, Burnham Market has the best collection of small Georgian houses in Norfolk, and it's a delight to wander through the yards and alleys that link the town's three east-west streets.

BRANCASTER STAITHE
9 miles NE of Hunstanton on the A149

In Roman times a castle was built near Brancaster to try and control the Iceni, Boudicca's turbulent tribe. Nothing of it remains, although a Romano-British cemetery was discovered nearby in 1960. In the 18th century, this delightful village was a port of some standing, hence the Staithe, or quay, in its name. The waterborne traffic in the harbour is now almost exclusively pleasure craft, although whelks are still dredged from the sea bed, 15 miles out, and mussels are farmed in the harbour itself.

From the harbour ,a short boat trip will take you to Scolt Head Island (National Trust), a three-and-a-half mile sand and shingle bar separated from the mainland by a narrow tidal creek. It was originally much smaller, but over the centuries deposits of silt and sand have steadily increased its size, and continue to do so. Scolt Head is home to England's largest colony of Sandwich terns, which flock here to breed during May, June and July. A Nature Trail leads past the ternery (closed during the breeding season) and on to a fascinating area where a rich variety of plantlife and wildlife abounds. During the summer, the sea asters, sea lavender and sea pinks put on a colourful display, attracting many different types of moths and butterflies.

SUSSEX FARM HOLIDAY

Head Office, The Hall, Brancaster,
Kings Lynn, Norfolk PE31 8AF
Tel: 01485 210000
e-mail: info@tbfholidayhomes.co.uk
website: www.tbfholidayhomes.co.uk

Welcome to **Sussex Farm Holiday Cottages** – relax, unwind and treat yourself to a holiday in one of the five beautifully restored, traditional flint farm cottages which are set in a stunning location in unspoilt farmland. Locally there are woodlands, long sandy beaches, marshes and sand dunes, miles of country walks, famous nature reserves, big-wide skies and above all, a real feeling of space and freedom.

Yet the charming country town of Burnham Market is on the doorstep and throughout the countryside you will find cosy pubs, antique shops, local markets and of course Sandringham House, Holkham and Houghton Halls and the King's Lynn Festival during the summer, and so much more.

The cottages are very well equipped, each has splendid views, log fires, barbecues, beautiful gardens with patios, a shared tennis court, high chairs, cots, staffgates, wooden playhouse, beds made up ready for your arrival, laundry, microwaves, television, videos, radios, irons and dishwashers.

Sussex Farm Holiday Cottages are the ideal base from which to explore all that North West Norfolk has to offer. Alternatively you can just wind down on the beach or by the barbecue in summer or relax by the fireside in your cottage in the winter.

⚏ stories and anecdotes ⚑ famous people ♟ art and craft ✍ entertainment and sport ⚐ walks

TITCHWELL

7 miles E of Hunstanton on the A149

🌾 Titchwell Marsh

Perhaps in keeping with the village's name, the Church of St Mary at Titchwell is quite tiny - and very pretty indeed. Its circular, probably Norman, tower is topped by a little 'whisker' of a spire, and inside is some fine late 19th century glass.

Just to the west of the village is a path leading to **Titchwell Marsh** (see panel below), a nationally important RSPB reserve comprising some 420 acres of shingle beach, reed beds, freshwater and salt marsh. These different habitats encourage a wide variety of birds to visit the area throughout the year, and many of them breed on or around the reserve. Brent geese, ringed plovers, marsh harriers, terns, waders and shore larks may all be seen, and two of the three hides available are accessible to wheelchairs.

DOCKING

9 miles SE of Hunstanton on the B1454/B1153

One of the larger inland villages, Docking was at one time called Dry Docking because,

perched on a hilltop 300 feet above sea level, it had no water supply of its own. The nearest permanent stream was at Fring, almost three miles away, so in 1760 the villagers began boring for a well. They had to dig some 230 feet down before they finally struck water, which was then sold at a farthing (0.1p) per bucket. A pump was installed in 1928, but a mains supply didn't reach Docking until the 1930s.

HOLME-NEXT-THE-SEA

3 miles NE of Hunstanton off the A149

🚶 Peddar's Way and Norfolk Coastal Footpath

This village is notable chiefly as the northern end of the **Peddar's Way**, the 50-mile pedestrian trail that starts close to the Suffolk border at Knettisham Heath near Thetford and, almost arrow-straight for much of its length, slices across northwest Norfolk to Holme, with only an occasional deviation to negotiate a necessary ford or bridge. This determinedly straight route was already long-trodden for centuries before the Romans arrived, but they incorporated long stretches of it into their own network of roads. It was from the Latin word

Titchwell Marsh RSPB Reserve

Main Road, Titchwell, King's Lynn, Norfolk PE31 8BB
Tel: 01485 210432
e-mail: titchwell@rspb.org.uk website: www.rspb.org.uk

On the stunning north Norfolk coast, Titchwell Marsh is one of the RSPB's most visited reserves. It has something for everyone, from beginners to seasoned birdwatchers on the lookout for a rarity. Hundreds of thousands of migrating birds pass through in spring and autumn, and many spend winter here, giving you an unrivalled opportunity to see many species of ducks, waders, seabirds and geese. In spring and summer, Titchwell is home to the RSPB's emblem bird, the avocet; this rare wader has nested on the lagoons since 1984. There are RSPB staff and volunteers at the information desk to help you and binoculars can be hired at the visitor centre. The reserve is open all year. Entry to the reserve and the three birdwatching hides is free.

pedester that the route takes its name. With few gradients of any consequence to negotiate, the Peddar's Way is ideal for the casual walker. At Holme, the Peddar's Way meets with the **Norfolk Coastal Footpath**, a much more recent creation. Starting at Hunstanton, it closely follows the coastline all the way to Cromer. Numerous sections of the Peddars Way are open to cyclists, and a special route is available for horse riders. Several lengths of both routes are accessible to wheelchair users.

Holme-next-the-Sea is famous in part as the site of Sea Henge, a 4,500-year-old Bronze Age tree circle discovered on Holme Beach.

RINGSTEAD
3 miles E of Hunstanton off the A149

🏞 Ringstead Downs

Another appealing village, with pink and white-washed cottages built in wonderfully decorative Norfolk carrstone. A rare Norman round tower, all that survives of St Peter's Church, stands in the grounds of the former Rectory and adds to the visual charm.

In a region well-provided with excellent nature reserves, the one on **Ringstead Downs** is particularly attractive, and popular with picnickers. The chalky soil of the valley provides a perfect habitat for the plants that thrive here and for the exquisitely marked butterflies they attract.

OLD HUNSTANTON
1 mile N of Hunstanton off the A149

With its mellow old houses and narrow winding lanes, Old Hunstanton is utterly charming. The sand dunes and creeks provide a perfect habitat for interesting varieties of

---

VIVIEN YOUNG FINE ART
The Old School, Old Hunstanton
Road, Old Hunstanton,
Norfolk PE36 6HZ
Tel: 01485 534828
e-mail: viv@vivienyoungfineart.co.uk
website: www.vivienyoungfineart.co.uk

Located in the lovely village of Old Hunstanton, minutes from the sea, this one-room 1860s school is now a welcoming gallery space for contemporary fine art and ceramics. Owner Vivien Young established her gallery in 2003 and holds regular solo and mixed exhibitions of works by artists from throughout East Anglia and the UK.

The gallery is particularly honoured to represent James Dunbar, a truly outstanding painter, who lives and works in North West Norfolk. His amazing series of "treescapes" and architectural paintings were shown to great success in 2007 and his next major show "Inscape" will be held in Spring 2009.

From October 2008 Vivien will be curating additional regular exhibitions in Sedgeford Hall, a delightful Queen Anne house located on a large country estate in nearby Sedgeford. This lovely venue will also have a permanent but changing collection of paintings, sculpture and ceramics.

To find out more about opening times, information about special exhibitions in both venues and to see a selection of images by the gallery's artists please visit the website or email or telephone Vivien Young who will be delighted to help you.

🏛 stories and anecdotes 👛 famous people 🎨 art and craft 🐾 entertainment and sport 🏃 walks

DRIFTWOOD DELI & POST OFFICE

38 Old Hunstanton Road, Old Hunstanton, Norfolk PE36 6HS
Telephone: 01485 533197

Open 7days week 7.30am – 5.30pm Half day Thursday.

This former coaching inn has recently been given a new lease of life. Pauline Farncombe took over the shop 3years ago and the village store now tastefully combines East Anglias finest foods, the aromas of coffee and baking bread, with friendly old fashioned service. There are samples of cheeses, local and international, olives and homemade cakes to taste and buy. Much of the fruit and veg is sourced from the allotments in the village with a selection of the exotic for variety. Pauline adopted a policy of no plastic bags when she first took over and has encouraged the shoppers to bring their own shopping bags, recycle their egg boxes and refill olive oil bottles. It has taken a while but everyone has caught on now!

The coaching inn was called the Lifeboat and as the village has an active Lifeboat station a small RNLI shop is part of the building allowing goods to be sold through the shop, without relying on hard pressed volunteers to man it. The shop remains the centre of the village and it is said that if you want to know anything or source anything ask in the village shop, if they don't know the answer they will know someone who will.

colourful flora - sea poppies, samphire, marram and sea lavender and more. The glorious sands continue here, and the Norfolk Coastal Footpath leads eastwards all the way to Cromer, some 36 miles distant.

GREAT BIRCHAM
7 miles SE of Hunstanton off the B1153

A couple of miles south of Docking stands the five-storey Great Bircham Windmill, one of the few in Norfolk to have found a hill to perch on, and it's still working. If you arrive on a day when there's a stiff breeze blowing, the windmill's great arms will be groaning around; on calm days, content yourself with tea and home-made cakes in the tearoom,

and take home some bread baked at the Mill's own bakery.

HEACHAM
3 miles S of Hunstanton off the A149

🌱 Norfolk Lavender

Heacham Park Fishery on Pocahontas Lake is set within the original boundary of Heacham Hall. This three-and-a-half acre freshwater lake was re-established in 1996. Spring 1997 saw the introduction to the lake of specimen carp, to be followed in 1998 by rudd, bream, perch and roach. The lake takes its name from the renowned Native American princess, who married into the Rolfe family, owners of Heacham Hall, and lived here in the 1600s.

Norfolk Lavender Field

built of local carrstone in the 19th century that was originally a water mill. On entering the site, visitors instinctively breathe in, savouring the unmistakable aroma that fills the air. Guided tours of the grounds run throughout the day from the Spring Bank Holiday until the end of September, and during the lavender harvest, visitors can tour the distillery and see how the wonderful fragrance is made.

Just outside this charming village is the famous **Norfolk Lavender**, the largest lavender-growing and distilling operation in the country. Established in 1932, it is also the oldest. The information point at the western entrance is sited in an attractive listed building

As well as being a working farm, this is also the home of the National Collection of Lavenders, a living botanical dictionary that displays the many different colours, sizes and smells of this lovely plant. Among other attractions at Norfolk Lavender are a Fragrant Meadow Garden, a Fragrant Plant Centre in the conservatory, a Herb Garden with 55 individual beds of herbs, a gift shop selling a wide variety of products, and a tearoom

FRAN'S PANTRY FAYRE

28 High St, Heacham, King's Lynn, Norfolk PE31 7EP
Tel: 01485 572220

After a good morning's antiques hunting head over to **Fran's Pantry Fayre** for a spot of refreshment. The café is serious about local sourcing and showcases much of the best products currently being produced in the county.

So, if you're looking to relive the taste of your dear granny's lovely homemade cakes and puds then you'll like it at Fran's. It's very traditional in every way, but the big draw is the fact that all of the cakes and meals are homemade including cheesecake, carrot cake and crumbles as well as savoury stuff such as Shepherd's pie and lasagne.

The hardest bit is making up your mind what to order - after all it's greedy to order two puddings...isn't it?

serving cream teas and even lavender-and-lemon scones! Tel: 01485 570384 for details.

SNETTISHAM
5 miles S of Hunstanton off the A149

🐾 RSPB Bird Sanctuary

Snettisham is best known nowadays for its spacious, sandy beaches and the **RSPB Bird Sanctuary**, both about two miles west of the village itself. But for centuries, Snettisham was much more famous as a prime quarry for carrstone, an attractive soft-red building-block that provided the 'light relief' for the walls of thousands of Georgian houses around the country, and for nearby Sandringham House. The carrstone quarry is still working, its product now destined mainly for goldfish ponds and the entrance-banks of the more pretentious type of bungalow. Unfortunately, one has to go to the British Museum in London to see Snettisham's greatest gift to the national heritage: an opulent collection of gold and silver ornaments from the 1st century AD, the largest hoard of treasure trove ever found in Britain, discovered here in 1991. At Snettisham Park, the attractions include a renowned red deer herd, a discovery trail, horse and pony rides, friendly farm animals, a huge adventure playground, a leather workshop, gift and farm shop, visitor centre and tea room.

DERSINGHAM
7 miles S of Hunstanton off the A149

This large village just north of Sandringham was actually the source of the latter's name: in the Domesday Book, the manor was inscribed as 'Sant-Dersingham'. Norfolk tongues found 'Sandringham' much easier to get around. Dersingham village has expanded greatly in

---

QUEEN VICTORIA

19 Lynn Road, Snettisham, King's Lynn, Norfolk, PE31 7LW
Tel: 01485 541344
e-mail: info@queenvictoriasnettisham.co.uk
website: www.queenvictoriasnettisham.co.uk

Set in picturesque village of Snettisham the **Queen Victoria** is "the perfect place to drink, dine and sleep". This distinctive and much loved pub extends a warm welcome to locals and visitors alike.

Guests can choose from the varied and creative menu that offers a blend of the best of World cuisine alongside traditional 'old school' pub favourites. Using the finest local ingredients whenever possible. In better weather guests can take advantage of a large beer garden or move indoors to gather round a cosy fire when the chill sets in.

A stone's throw from the coast, the Queen Victoria is well placed for exploring the many sights and attractions of this beautiful part of Norfolk which is noted for its beaches and nature reserves as well as an abundance of historic sites, castles and activity centres.

A recently converted barn now provides five guest bedrooms. Each of the wonderfully comfortable rooms boasts en-suite facilities, Free-Sat TV, tea and coffee making facilities. Direct access from the car park means that guests can rise at dawn to take in the air without fear of disturbing or being disturbed by others, and by arrangement you can bring along your faithful dog too! In addition to these rooms the Queen Victoria boast an award winning caravan club certified location. The pitches offering all the facilities you could possibly need during your stay here.

🏛 historic building 🏛 museum and heritage 🏛 historic site ♧ scenic attraction 🐾 flora and fauna

THE FEATHERS HOTEL

Manor Road, Dersingham, King's Lynn, Norfolk PE31 6LN
Tel: 01485 540207

On approach to Dersingham by-passing lovely lavender fields, visitors could easily imagine they were driving through the abundant lavender lands of southern France, but this is not so for Dersingham is a typical Norfolk village with a very English heather covered landscape of heathland.

Included in the amenities of the village is the historic church of St.Nicholas and in contrast to this is the almost equally historic **Feathers Hotel**, a former coaching inn originally serving the Norwich to York route. The inn can justifiably claim Royal connections; it was part of the Sandringham House Estate purchased in 1882 as a home for Albert Edward, the then Prince of Wales. At the time it was known as The Lamb, but the name was changed to the "Feathers" in honour of the Prince. Edward VII is known to have brought his mistress Lillie Langtree to the inn, as well as many of his other friends and associates.

Today the Feather Hotel is a family run hotel where the facilities include 2 Bars, a Restaurant, a private function room, en-suite accommodation and two large gardens with play area and seating, one garden is private with a pond that is perfect for outside functions. The Hotel and Gardens also provide the perfect setting for Wedding Receptions or private functions.

The region is idyllic for its wonderful beaches, bird watching and cycling. Attractions include a tour of Sandringham House, its gardens, museum, country park and visitor centre. Hunstanton, just a short drive away offers sandy beaches backed by multi-coloured cliffs, a funfair, amusements and lovely gardens. King's Lynn lies to the south of Dersingham, this is full of medieval charm and a wealth of fine old buildings.

For keen birdwatchers there is the RSPB reserve at Snettisham, this has several hides overlooking the watching areas. The Norfolk Coast Path, Nar Valley Way and Peter Scott Path offer wonderful opportunities for solitude and the enjoyment of nature at her very best. Or just relax on the Hotel terrace to watch the sunset, a treat not to be missed!

recent years and modern housing has claimed much of Dersingham Common, although there are still many pleasant walks here through Dersingham Wood and the adjoining Sandringham Country Park.

SANDRINGHAM
8 miles S of Hunstanton off the A149/B1140

🏠 Sandringham House

🌳 Sandringham Country Park

A couple of miles north of Castle Rising is the entrance to **Sandringham Country Park** and **Sandringham House**, the Royal Family's country retreat. Unlike the State Rooms at Windsor Castle and Buckingham Palace, where visitors marvel at the awesome trappings of majesty, at Sandringham they can savour the atmosphere of a family home. The rooms the visitor sees here are those used by the Royal Family when in residence, complete with family portraits and photographs, and comfy armchairs. Successive royal owners have furnished the house with an intriguing medley of the grand, the domestic and the unusual. Entering the principal reception room, The Saloon, for example, you pass a weighing-machine with a leather-covered seat, apparently a common amenity in great houses of the 19th century. In the same room, with its attractively carved Minstrels' Gallery, hangs a fine family portrait by one of Queen Victoria's favourite artists, Heinrich von Angeli. It shows the Prince of Wales (later Edward VII), his wife Alexandra and two of their children, with

Sandringham in the background. The numerous porcelain, jade and crystal oriental figures were collected by Queen Alexandra and Queen Mary, and the collection of oriental arms and armour was brought back from the Far East by the Prince in 1876.

The Prince first saw Sandringham on 4th February 1862. At Victoria's instigation, the 20-year-old heir to the throne had been searching for some time for a country property, a refuge of the kind his parents already enjoyed at Balmoral and Osborne. A courtier accompanying the Prince reported back that although the outside of the house was ugly, it was pleasant and convenient within, and set in 'pretty grounds'. The surrounding countryside was plain, he went on, but the property was in excellent order and the opportunity of securing it should not be missed. Within days, the purchase was completed.

Most of the 'ugly' house disappeared a few years later when the Prince and Princess rebuilt

Sandringham House

the main residence in 1870; the 'pretty grounds' have matured into one of the most beautiful landscaped areas in the country. And the 'plain' countryside around - open heath and grassland overrun by rabbits - has been transformed into a wooded country park, part of the coastal Area of Outstanding Natural Beauty.

One of the additions the Prince made to the house in 1883 was a Ballroom, much to the relief of Princess Alexandra. 'It is beautiful I think & a great success.' she wrote, '& avoids pulling the hall to pieces each time there is a ball or anything.' This attractive room is now used for cinema shows and the estate workers' Christmas party. Displayed on the walls is a remarkable collection of Indian weapons, presented to the Prince during his state visit in 1875-6; hidden away in a recess are the two flags planted at the South Pole by the Shackleton expedition.

Just across from the house, the old coach-houses and stables have been converted into a fascinating museum. There are some truly splendid royal vehicles here, including the first car bought by a member of the royal family - a 1900 Daimler Phaeton. There's also a splendid 1939 Merryweather fire engine used by the Estate's own fire brigade, several childen's cars and the old estate game cart. There are Arts and Crafts ceramic tiles and plaques, commemorative china, an exhibition of the Sandringham Company of the 5th Norfolk Regiment and an evocative series of old photographs depicting the life of the royal family at Sandringham from 1862 until Christmas 1951. Other attractions at Sandringham include a visitor centre,

adventure playground, nature walks, souvenir shop, restaurant and tearoom. The beautiful medieval church where the Royal Family worships is open during the visitor season.

King's Lynn

🏛 Custom House 🏛 Guildhall of the Holy Trinity
🏛 St George's Guildhall 🏛 The Old Gaol House
🎨 Caithness Crystal 🏛 Hanseatic Warehouse
🏛 Town House Museum of Lynn Life
🎭 Church of St Margaret 🎨 King's Lynn Arts Centre
🏛 South Gate 🏛 Greenland Fishery Building

In the opinion of James Lee-Milne, the National Trust's architectural authority, 'The finest old streets anywhere in England' are to be found at King's Lynn. Tudor, Jacobean and Flemish houses mingle harmoniously with grand medieval churches and stately civic buildings. It's not surprising that the BBC chose the town to represent early 19th-century London in their production of *Martin Chuzzlewit*. It seems, though, that word of this ancient sea port's many treasures has not yet been widely broadcast, so most visitors to the area tend to stay on the King's Lynn bypass

King's Lynn Tudor Guildhall

while making their way to the better-known attractions of the north Norfolk coast. They are missing a lot.

The best place to start an exploration of the town is at the beautiful **Church of St Margaret**, founded in 1101 and with a remarkable leaning arch of that original building still intact. The architecture is impressive, but the church is especially famous for its two outstanding 14th-century brasses, generally reckoned to be the two largest and most monumental in the kingdom. Richly engraved, one shows workers in a vineyard, the other, commemorating Robert Braunche, represents the great feast that Robert hosted at King's Lynn for Edward III in 1364.

Marks on the tower doorway indicate the church's, and the town's, vulnerability to the waters of the Wash and the River Great Ouse. They show the high-water levels reached during the great floods of 11th March 1883 (the lowest), 31st January 1953, and 11th January 1978.

The organist at St Margaret's in the mid 18th century was the celebrated writer on music, Dr Charles Burney, but his daughter Fanny was perhaps even more interesting. She wrote a best-selling novel, *Evelina*, at the age of 25, became a leading light of London society, a close friend of Dr Johnson and Sir Joshua Reynolds and, at the age of 59, underwent an operation for breast cancer without anaesthetic. She only fainted once during the 20-minute operation, and went on to continue her active social life until her death at the ripe old age of 87.

Alongside the north wall of St Margaret's is the Saturday Market Place, one of the town's two market places, where visitors can explore the **Old Gaol House** (see panel opposite), an

---

BRADLEY'S WINE BAR & RESTAURANT

Bradleys
WINE BAR & RESTAURANT

*10 South Quay, King's Lynn,
Norfolk PE30 5DT
Tel: 01553 819888
e-mail: relax@bradleysbytheriver.co.uk
website: www.bradleysbytheriver.co.uk*

Fine cuisine matched with correctly served wines in an elegant but relaxed atmosphere is the best way to describe **Bradley's Wine Bar and Restaurant** on King's Lynn's historic waterfront.

The ground floor is given over to a relaxed wine bar and lounge where customers are invited to enjoy a light meal or a quiet drink while they watch the sunset over the river. The stylish restaurant is on the first floor with views of the river and is served by a customer lift. At the rear of the premises there is an enclosed courtyard for warm summer evenings.

The building itself has a colourful history. It was originally a Georgian Merchant's house, hence the Belvedere on the top floor. The first floor restaurant has the elegance of a Georgian dining room. Fine furnishings, crystal chandeliers, quality cutlery and beautiful drapes that frame views across the river, combine to make this a very special venue for that intimate dinner, business lunch or family celebration.

Open: Monday - Friday 12 noon - 2:30pm and 5:30pm - 11pm; Saturday 12 noon - 11pm; Sunday 12 noon - 4pm. Free parking on the quayside.

🏛 historic building 🏛 museum and heritage 🏛 historic site ⚘ scenic attraction 🌱 flora and fauna

Tales of the Old Gaol House

Market Place, King's Lynn, Norfolk PE30 5DQ
Tel: 01553 774297
e-mail: gaolhouse@west-norfolk.gov.uk
website: www.west-norfolk.gov.uk

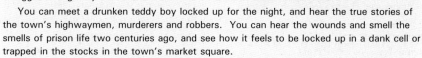

Let your imagination run riot as your personal stereo guide takes you through King's Lynn's 1930s police station and into the old cells beyond, where smugglers caught by the revenue men of the Custom House would be thrown.

You can meet a drunken teddy boy locked up for the night, and hear the true stories of the town's highwaymen, murderers and robbers. You can hear the wounds and smell the smells of prison life two centuries ago, and see how it feels to be locked up in a dank cell or trapped in the stocks in the town's market square.

Your guide describes how 'witches' were identified and punished, and you can hear the crowds shout as one poor woman is captured to be taken to her fate! Enjoy an atmospheric visit with the sounds and smells of prison life two centuries ago at the Old Gaol House.

experience complete with the sights and sounds of the ancient cells, and tales of local witches, murderers and highwaymen. Also here are the borough archives and the Regalia Rooms, where the civic treasures include the King John Cup. This dazzling piece of medieval workmanship is adorned with coloured enamel scenes set in gold. The Cup was said to be part of King John's treasure, which had been lost in 1215 when his overburdened baggage train was crossing the Nene Estuary and sank into the treacherous quicksands. This venerable legend is sadly undermined by the fact that the Cup was not made until 1340, more than a century after John's death.

A few steps further on is one of the most striking sights in the town, the **Guildhall of the Holy Trinity** with its distinctive chequerboard design of black flint and white stone. The Guildhall was built in 1421 and extended in 1624, and its Great Hall is still used today for wedding ceremonies and various civic events.

Next door to the Guildhall is the Town Hall of 1895, which in a good-neighbourly way is constructed in the same flint-and-stone pattern. The Town Hall also houses the **Town House Museum of Lynn Life** with period rooms, historic costume, old toys and domestic paraphernalia. A short distance from the Town Hall, standing proudly by itself on the banks of the River Purfleet, is the handsome **Custom House** of 1683, designed by the celebrated local architect Henry Bell.

There's not enough space here to list all of the town's many other important buildings, but mention must be made of the **Hanseatic Warehouse** (1428), the **South Gate** (1440), the **Greenland Fishery Building** (1605), and **St George's Guildhall**, built around 1406 and reputedly the largest civic hall in England. The Hall was from time to time also used as a theatre; it's known that Shakespeare's travelling company played here, and it is considered highly likely that the Bard himself trod the boards. If true, the story would be very appropriate, since the Guildhall is now home to the **King's Lynn Arts Centre**, active all year round with events and exhibitions and since 1951 the force behind an annual Arts Festival in

July with concerts, theatre and a composer in residence. Some of the concerts are held in St Nicholas' Chapel, a medieval building whose acoustics outmatch those of many a modern concert hall.

At **Caithness Crystal Visitor Centre** (free admission), visitors can watch craftsmen at close quarters as they shape and manipulate glass into beautiful objets d'art. The centre is located on the Hardwick Industrial Estate.

Around King's Lynn

CASTLE RISING
5 miles NE of King's Lynn off the A148/A149

🏛 Castle Keep

As the bells ring for Sunday morning service at Castle Rising, a group of elderly ladies leave the mellow redbrick Bede House and walk in procession to the church. They are all dressed in long scarlet cloaks, emblazoned on the left breast with a badge of the Howard family arms. Once a year, on Founder's Day, they add to their regular Sunday costume a tall-crowned hat typical of the Jacobean period, just like those worn in stereotypical pictures of broomstick-flying witches.

These ladies are the residents of the almshouses founded by Henry Howard, Earl of Northampton in 1614, and their regular Sunday attendance at church was one of the conditions he imposed on the original 11 needy spinsters who were to enjoy his beneficence. Howard also required that each inmate of his 'Hospital of the Holy and Undivided Trinity' must also 'be able to read, if such a one may be had, single, 56 at least, no common beggar, harlot, scold, drunkard, haunter of taverns, inns or alehouses'.

The weekly tableau vivant of this

procession to the church seems completely in keeping with this picturesque village, which rates high on any 'not to be missed' list of places to visit in Norfolk. The church to which the women make their way, St Lawrence's, is an outstanding example of Norman and Early English work, even though much of it has been reconstructed. But overshadowing everything else in this pretty village is the massive **Castle Keep**, its well-preserved walls rising 50 feet high, and pierced by a single entrance. The Keep's towering presence is made even more formidable by the huge earthworks on which it stands. The castle was built in 1150, guarding what was then the sea approach to the River Ouse. (The marshy shore is now some three miles distant and still retreating.)

Despite its fortress-like appearance the castle was much more of a residential building than a defensive one. In 1331, when Edward III found it necessary to banish his ferocious French-born mother, Isabella, to some reasonably comfortable place of safety, he chose this far-from-London castle. She was to spend some 27 years here before her death in 1358. How could Edward treat his own mother in such a way? Her crime, in his view, was that the She-Wolf of France, as all her enemies, and many of her friends, called Isabella, had joined forces with her lover Mortimer against her homosexual husband Edward II (Edward's father) and later colluded in the king's grisly murder with a red-hot poker at Berkeley Castle. For three years after that loathsome assassination, Isabella and Mortimer ruled England as Regents. The moment Edward III achieved his majority, he had Mortimer hung, drawn and quartered. His mother he sent into lonely retirement at Castle Rising.

Six-and-a-half centuries later, the spacious grounds around the castle provide an appropriate backdrop for an annual display by members of the White Society. Caparisoned in colourful medieval garments, and armed with more-or-less authentic replicas of swords and halberds, these modern White Knights stage a battle for control of the castle.

TERRINGTON ST CLEMENT
6 miles W of King's Lynn off the A17

🏛 Church 🌱 African Violet Centre

Terrington St Clement is a sizable village notable for the Church of St Clement, a 14th- century Gothic masterwork, and for the **African Violet Centre**, where some quarter of a million violets are grown each year, in a wide range of colour and species. Plants from the Centre have won many awards at the Royal Chelsea Flower Show.

WALPOLE ST PETER
10 miles W of King's Lynn off the A17/A47

🏛 Church of St Peter

For many connoisseurs, Walpole's **Church of St Peter** ranks among the finest not just in Norfolk, but in the whole of England. Behind the graceful exterior of the 'Queen of the Marshlands', the highlights include the font, the broad 17th-century screen behind the nave, the chancel sanctuary and the extraordinary cobbled processional passage.

STOW BARDOLPH
8 miles S of King's Lynn off the A10

🏛 Holy Trinity Church

Holy Trinity Church at Stow Bardolph houses one of the oddest memorials in the country. Before her death in 1744, Sarah Hare,

youngest daughter of the Lord of the Manor, Sir Thomas Hare, arranged for a life-sized effigy of herself to be made in wax. It was said to be an exceptionally good likeness: if so, Sarah appears to have been a rather uncomely maiden, and afflicted with boils to boot. Her death was attributed to blood poisoning after she had pricked her finger with a needle, an act of Divine retribution, apparently, for her sin of sewing on a Sunday. Her effigy was attired in a dress she had chosen herself, placed in a windowed mahogany cabinet, and the monument set up in the Hare family's chapel, a grandiose structure that is larger than the chancel of the church itself.

DOWNHAM MARKET
10 miles S of King's Lynn off the A10/A1122

Once the site for a major horse fair, this compact little market town stands at the very edge of the Fens, with the River Great Ouse and the New Bedford Drain running side by side at its western edge. Many of its houses are built in the distinctive brick and carrstone style of the area. One of the finest examples of this traditional use of local materials can be seen at Dial House in Railway Road, built in the late 1600s.

The parish church is perched on a small hill. It's an unassuming building with a rather incongruously splendid glass chandelier from the 1730s. Another feature of the town, much loved by postcard manufacturers, is the elegant, riotously decorated cast-iron Clock Tower in the market place. This was erected in 1878 at a cost of £450. The tower's backdrop of attractive cottages provides a charming setting for a holiday snap.

Near Downham Bridge on the A1122 are located Collectors World and the Magical Dickens World. The first boasts a plethora of

Shouldham Warren

Distance: *3.1 miles (4.8 kilometres)*

Typical time: *90 mins*

Height gain: *10 metres*

Map: *Explorer 236*

Walk: *www.walkingworld.com ID:2108*

Contributor: *Joy & Charles Boldero*

ACCESS INFORMATION:

Norfolk Bus routes: Freecall 0500 626116, 9am to 5pm Monday to Friday to the village of Shouldham. You can start the walk from Point 6. However, the walk starts at the free Forestry car park at Shouldham Warren. The village of Shouldham is situated 2 miles north of the A1122 at Fincham, which is 8 miles west of Swaffham. To reach the Warren, go north up Eastgate Street out of the village and keep ahead along rough track where the road goes right.

DESCRIPTION:

The outward route is through woodland to Shouldham village and back by country lanes through the village. There is an excellent pub, The King's Arms, which has an extensive menu and is open every day. The famous October conker championships used to take place at The King's Arms. Many centuries ago, Shouldham, was famous for the healing waters of the Chalybeate spring, a natural mineral water impregnated with iron salts. Shouldham was also a popular place for its market and fair that used to be held each autumn time.

FEATURES:

Pub, Toilets, Church, Wildlife, Birds, Flowers, Great Views, Butterflies, Food Shop.

WALK DIRECTIONS:

1|From the Forestry notice board, go back along the track for a very short distance. Turn right immediately after the flat concrete with these markings on it: SU-WO-24 &6. Keep the deep ditch on the left. It is advisable in hot weather to keep dogs to the main path as adders could be in the bracken beside the path. The smell of fox is quite strong along here.

2|Go round the barrier and turn left over the wide earth bridge. Go along a tree-lined path, take either path at the fork. Cross the track and continue along the track opposite.

3|At a T-junction of tracks, turn right with a farmhouse ahead. After about 70 paces, turn left along another track.

4|At the fingerpost sign turn left along a wide grass path between fields with houses ahead. Go through a gate, continue along a narrower path, then a driveway, then a track.

5|Turn right along the village street. Opposite The Cottage at the fingerpost sign turn, left along a tarmac lane.

6|At the T-junction turn right along a lane. Turn left opposite The King's Arms in Shouldham beside the Green that has an old village pump on it (you could start the walk from here). Turn left along Eastgate Street, continue along New Road and Warren Road.

7|At the righthand bend - Spring Lane - keep straight ahead along a wide track returning to the start of the walk.

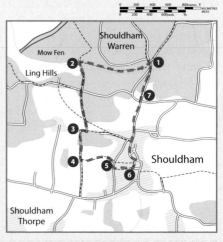

farming and household memorabilia, carts, carriages, radios, cameras, antique and collectable dolls, Armstrong Siddeley cars and much more, with rooms dedicated to Barbara Cartland, Horatio Nelson, the 1960s and m\ny others. Dickens World offers visitors a chance to step back in time into a maze of late 19th-century streets, shops, sights and sounds.

DENVER
2 miles S of Downham Market off the A10/ A1122

🏛 Denver Sluice 🏭 Denver Windmill

Denver Sluice was originally built in 1651 by the Dutch engineer, Cornelius Vermuyden, as part of a scheme to drain 20,000 acres of land owned by the Duke of Bedford. Various modifications were made to the system over the years, but the principle remains the same, and the oldest surviving sluice, built in 1834, is still in use today. Running parallel with it is the modern **Great Denver Sluice**, opened in 1964; together these two sluices control the flow of a large complex of rivers and drainage channels, and are able to divert floodwaters into the Flood Relief Channel that runs alongside the Great Ouse.

The two great drainage cuts constructed by Vermuyden are known as the Old and New Bedford rivers, and the strip of land between them, never more than 1,000 yards wide, is called the Ouse Washes. This is deliberately allowed to flood during the winter months so that the fields on either side remain dry. The drains run side by side for more than 13 miles, to Earith in Cambridgeshire, and this has become a favourite route for walkers, with a rich variety of bird, animal and insect life to be seen along the way.

Denver Windmill (see panel below), built in 1835, was put out of commission in 1941 when the sails were struck by lightning but re-opened in 2000. This wonderful working mill set on the edge of the Fens has been carefully restored. On-site attractions include a visitor centre, craft workshops, bakery and tea shop. Holiday accommodation is also available.

Denver Windmill

Denver, Downham Market, Norfolk PE38 0EG
Tel: 01366 384009
e-mail: enquiries@denvermill.plus.com
website: www.denvermill.co.uk

Built in 1835, Denver Windmill produced flour for over a hundred years until it was struck by lightening in 1941. It is now fully restored and milling flour by wind power once more. Guided tours to the top of the mill and a visitor's centre provide a fascinating insight into this process. A bakery and tearoom selling Denver Windmill flour and delicious products in which it is an ingredient are also on site as well as three craft units. Stay in the miller's house, now converted into three charming holiday cottages. School parties are made welcome with special activities. An education room is available for use.

THE SHIP INN

Brandon Creek, Downham Market, Norfolk, PE38 0PP
Tel: 01353 676228

If you are from the Ely area, the A10 usually means the road south to Cambridge. But go north, and in fifteen minutes you will reach a riverside haven where the Little and Great Ouse rivers meet, and where thirsty boatmen have stopped off for at least 350 years. With a name like the title of an adventure novel, **The Ship Inn** at Brandon Creek was CAMRA's Cambridgeshire pub of the year in 2006. The picturesque building is surrounded by benches to take advantage of its location, and leisure boats chug by or moor alongside. Inside, the hand pumps face the entrance, giving the message that this pub takes its real ale seriously. While there are several regular brews, a chalk board lists guest ales, including micro-breweries.

The well-maintained interior offers several areas, all with a different character. The railed-off sunken area of the bar is cosy and inviting, while a separate dining room makes for more formal eating, with a window bay overlooking the river offering the prime table. The Ship's menu is based on popular choices, and a board offers some daily specials - all good value and putting this towards the better end of pub food.

This is a pub for all comers, passing day-trippers, boaties, and locals alike, and children have their own menu. The Ship offers good fayre at sensible prices in very pleasant surroundings. With well-kept real ales served by polite, efficient and friendly staff, this makes for a worthwhile jaunt both for locals and those escaping the urban buzz.

HILGAY

3 miles S of Downham Market off the A10

When the Domesday Book was written, Hilgay was recorded as one of only two settlements in the Norfolk Fens. It was then an island, its few houses planted on a low hill rising from the surrounding marshland. The village is scarcely any larger today, and collectors of unusual gravestones make their way to its churchyard seeking the last resting place of George William Manby. During the Napoleonic wars, Manby invented a rocket-powered life-line that could be fired to ships in distress. His gravestone is carved with a ship, an anchor, a depiction of his rocket device and an inscription that ends with the reproachful words, 'The public should have paid this tribute'.

OXBOROUGH

10 miles E of Downham Market off the A134

🏛 Church of St John the Evangelist 🏛 Oxburgh Hall

🌿 Gooderstone Water Gardens & Nature Trail

How many hamlets in the country, one wonders, can boast two such different buildings of note as those to be seen at Oxborough? The **Church of St John the Evangelist** is remarkable for its rare brass eagle lectern of 1498, and its glorious Bedingfeld Chapel of 1525, sheltering twin monuments to Sir Edmund Bedingfeld and his wife fashioned in the then newly-popular material of terracotta.

It was Sir Edmund who built **Oxburgh Hall** (National Trust), a breathtakingly lovely moated house, of pale-rose brick and white stone. Sir Edmund's descendants still live in what a later architect, Pugin, described as 'one of the noblest specimens of domestic architecture of the 15th century.' Henry VII and his Queen, Elizabeth of York, visited in 1487 and lodged in the splendid State Apartments, which form a bridge between the lofty gatehouse towers, and ever since have been known as the King's Room and the Queen's Room. On display here is the original Charter of 1482, affixed with Edward IV's Great Seal of England, granting Sir Edmund permission to build with 'stone, lime and sand', and to fortify the building with battlements. These rooms also house some magnificent period furniture, a collection of royal letters to the Bedingfelds, and the huge Sheldon Tapestry Map of 1647 showing Oxfordshire and Berkshire.

Another more poignant tapestry, known as the Marian Needlework, was the joint handiwork of Elizabeth, Countess of Shrewsbury, and Mary, Queen of Scots, during the latter's captivity here in 1570. The Bedingfelds seemed always to draw the short straw when the Tudors needed someone to discharge an unpleasant or difficult task. It was an earlier Sir Edmund who was charged with the care of Henry VIII's discarded wife, Katherine of Aragon; Edmund's son, Sir Henry, was given the even more onerous task of looking after the King's then official bastard, the Princess Elizabeth. After Elizabeth's accession as Queen, Sir Henry presented himself at Court, no doubt with some misgivings. Elizabeth received

him civilly but, as he was leaving, tartly observed that 'if we have any prisoner whom we would have hardlie and strictly kept, we will send him to you.'

As staunch Catholics, the Bedingfelds were, for the next two-and-a-half centuries, consigned to the margins of English political life. Their estates dwindled as portions were sold to meet the punitive taxes imposed on adherents of the Old Faith. By the middle of the 20th century, the Bedingfelds long tenure of Oxburgh was drawing to a close. In 1951 the 9th Baronet, another Sir Edmund, sold Oxburgh to a builder, who promptly announced his intention of demolishing the house. Sir Edmund's mother, the Dowager Lady Sybil, was shocked by such vandalism and used her considerable powers of persuasion to raise sufficient funds to buy back the house. She then conveyed it into the safe keeping of the National Trust.

The grounds at Oxburgh provide the perfect foil for the mellow old building, reflected in its broad moat. There's a

Oxborough Hall

wonderfully formal and colourful French garden, a walled kitchen garden, and woodland walks.

Brown-signed from Oxborough, **Gooderstone Water Gardens & Nature Trail** is a unique attraction for garden lovers, naturalists, artists and photographers. The six acres of gardens include four ponds, a natural trout stream, waterways, 13 bridges, a bird hide, mature tress and shrubs, colourful borders, a nature trail, plant sales and a tea room.

Fakenham

🏛 Museum of Gas & Local History

🌱 The Natural Centre of Norfolk

Fakenham is a busy and prosperous-looking market town, famous for its National Hunt Racecourse, antique and bric-a-brac markets and auctions, and as a major agricultural centre for the region. Straddling the River Wensum, this attractive country town has a number of fine late 18th- and early 19th-century brick buildings in and around the Market Place. And it must surely be one of the few towns in England where the former gasworks (still intact) have been turned into a **Museum of Gas & Local History**, housing an impressive historical display of domestic gas appliances of every kind. Fakenham Church also has an unusual feature, a powder room - a room over the large porch, built in 1497, used for storing gunpowder. Even older than the church is the 700-year-old hunting lodge, built for the Duchy of Lancaster, which is now part of the Crown Hotel. As an antidote to the idea that Norfolk is unremittingly flat, take the B1105 north out of Fakenham and after about half a mile take the first minor road to the left. This quiet road loops over and around the rolling hills, a

10-mile drive of wonderfully soothing countryside that ends at Wells-next-the-Sea.

Southeast of Fakenham, off the A1067, **The Natural Centre of Norfolk** is home to Europe's best collection of endangered and exotic waterbirds. Over 120 species of waterfowl can be seen here in their natural surroundings, a wonderful avian refuge where you may come across anything from a scarlet ibis to the more familiar oystercatcher, along with avocets and ruff. The spacious walk-through free-flight aviaries offer close contact with shy wading birds, and in the Dulverton Aviary elegant spoonbills and bearded tits vie for your attention. There are good facilities for children and visitors with disabilities, a Bug Walk, nature trails through 200 acres of the Wensum Valley countryside, wildlife safaris, a restaurant and a shop.

Around Fakenham

THURSFORD GREEN
4 miles NE of Fakenham off the A148

🏛 The Thursford Collection

About two minutes walk from Thursford Green stands what is perhaps the most unusual museum in Norfolk, **The Thursford Collection Sight and Sound Spectacular**. George Cushing began this extraordinary collection of steam-powered traction engines, fairground organs and carousels, back in 1946 when 'one ton of tractor cost £1'. Perhaps the most astonishing exhibit is a 1931 Wurlitzer organ whose 1,339 pipes can produce an amazing repertoire of sounds - horses' hooves, fire engine sirens, claps of thunder, waves crashing on sand, and the toot-toot of an old railway engine are just some of the Wurlitzer's marvellous effects. There are regular live music shows when the Wurlitzer

---

🏠 historic building   🏛 museum and heritage   ⬚ historic site   🞄 scenic attraction   🌱 flora and fauna

displays its virtuosity. Other attractions include a steam-powered Venetian Gondola ride, shops selling a wide variety of goods, many of them locally made, and a tearoom.

A mile or so north of the Thursford museum, in the village of Hindringham, Mill Farm Rare Breeds is home to dozens of cattle, sheep, pigs, goats, ponies, poultry and waterfowl, which were once commonplace but are now very rare. These intriguing creatures have some 30 acres of lovely countryside to roam around. Children are encouraged to feed the animals and there's also an adventure playground, crazy golf course, craft and gift shop, picnic area and tearoom.

GREAT SNORING
5 miles NE of Fakenham off the A148

The names of the twin villages, Great and Little Snoring, are such a perennial source of amusement to visitors it seems almost churlish to explain that they are derived from a Saxon family called Snear. At Great Snoring the main street rises from a bridge over the River Stiffkey and climbs up to St Mary's Church.

LITTLE WALSINGHAM
5 miles N of Fakenham on the B1105

🏚 East Barsham Hall 🏛 Holy House

🏛 Shrine of Our Lady of Walsingham

🏛 Augustinian Priory 🏛 Slipper Chapel

Every year, some half a million pilgrims make their way to this little village of just over 500 souls, noted for its impressive timber-framed buildings and fine Georgian façades, to worship at the **Shrine of Our Lady of Walsingham**. In 1061 the Lady of the Manor of Walsingham, Lady Richeldis de Faverches, had a vision of the Holy Virgin in which she was instructed to build a replica of the Holy House in Nazareth, the house in which the Archangel Gabriel had

told Mary that she would be the mother of Christ. Archaeologists have located the original house erected by Lady Richeldis. It was just 13 feet by 23 feet and made of wood, later to be enclosed in stone.

These were the years of the Crusades, and the **Holy House** at Walsingham soon became a major centre of pilgrimage, because it was regarded by the pious as an authentic piece of the Holy Land. Around 1153, an **Augustinian Priory** was established to protect the shrine, now encrusted with jewels, gold and silver, and to provide accommodation for the pilgrims. The Priory is in ruins now, but the largest surviving part, a stately Gatehouse on the east side of the High Street is very impressive.

For almost 500 years, Walsingham prospered. Erasmus of Rotterdam visited in 1511 and was critical of the rampant commercialisation of the Shrine with its plethora of bogus relics and religious souvenirs for sale. He was shown a gigantic bone, 'the finger-joint of St Peter' no less, and in return for a small piece of translation was presented with a highly aromatic fragment of wood - a sliver of a bench on which the Virgin had once seated herself.

In the same year that Erasmus visited, Henry VIII also made the pilgrimage that all his royal predecessors since Richard I had undertaken. He stayed overnight at the enchanting early-Tudor mansion, **East Barsham Hall**, a glorious medley of mullioned windows, towers, turrets, and a group of 10 chimneys, each one individually carved in an amazing variety of styles. Since the King's visit, the Hall has had a succession of owners over the years, among them a Hapsburg Duke who entertained his neighbours in truly Imperial style before

B-FAIR

20a High Street, Little Walsingham, Norfolk NR22 6AA
Tel: 01328 821050
e-mail: enquiries@b-fair.co.uk website: www.b-fair.co.uk

**Fab Fairly Traded Stuff for Him for Her
for Home and Away!**

Shopping with a clear conscience is what they believe in
at **B-Fair**, a very special boutique on the main street of
the picturesque village of Little Walsingham between the
A148 and A149 near the North Norfolk coast. Owners
David Arnold and Lizzy Allen has been conscious of fair
trade buying for many years and felt that far more fair
trade goods could be offered to the public, particularly
with regard to clothing, so they created B-Fair to offer
such products for sale.

In their bright, browsable shop they sell a great
range of chic casual clothes and shoes, fun jewellery
and luxurious homewares. All the products on display
are made to last and all conform to the ethical policy,
meaning that they are either fairly traded – ensuring that
producers receive a decent living wage for the work
they do – or made from recycled/organic/natural
materials or made locally. B-Fair is open from 10am to 5pm Monday to Saturday, 11am to 5pm
Sunday and Bank Holidays.

WALSINGHAM FARMS SHOP

Guild Street, Little Walsingham, Norfolk NR22 6BU
Tel: 01328 821877
e-mail: info@walsinghamfarmsshop.co.uk
website: www.walsinghamfarmsshop.co.uk

Walsingham Farms Shop is a spectacular food and drink emporium
set in a beautiful old flint barn in the heart of the medieval
pilgrimage village of Little Walsingham. As well as offering the
best of Norfolk's cheese, dairy, eggs, pressed juices and locally
brewed beers, the shop has a butchery for truly local meat and an
open kitchen where you can watch dishes being cooked from
fresh local produce. Shop staff can also take an order over the
phone or by e-mail and have it ready to collect or deliver free
within a 5-mile radius (a boon for local holidaymakers).

Walsingham Farms Shop Partnership exists to support local
farmers as well as offering an exciting shopping experience. By
buying direct from local producers they ensure that farmers are
getting direct access to the market and customers are buying top-quality
food straight from the producer. In nearby Wells Road, the Partnership's
family-friendly Norfolk Riddle licensed restaurant (Tel: 01328 821903)
offers delicious dishes cooked from the fresh Norfolk produce sourced
through the shop, together with a traditional fish & chip shop. The
dining room is stylish and relaxed, and there's a sunny deck for alfresco
summer dining.

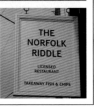

THE
NORFOLK
RIDDLE
LICENSED
RESTAURANT
TAKEAWAY FISH & CHIPS

disappearing, leaving behind some truly Imperial debts, and the brothers Gibb of the pop group the Bee Gees. The Hall is today owned by a London businessman and is not open to the public, but it stands for all to see at the entrance to the village.

After his overnight stay at East Barsham Hall, Henry VIII, like most other pilgrims, went first to the **Slipper Chapel**, a beautiful 14th-century building about a mile away in Houghton St Giles. Here he removed his shoes and completed the last stretch on foot. Despite this show of piety, some 25 years later Henry had no hesitation in closing the Priory along with all the other monastic institutions in his realm, seizing its treasures and endowments, and having its image of the Virgin publicly burnt at Chelsea.

Little Walsingham itself is an exceptionally attractive village, set in the midst of parks and woodlands, with the interesting 16th-century octagonal Clink in Common Place, used in medieval times as a lock-up for petty offenders, the scanty ruins of Walsingham's Franciscan Friary of 1347, and the former Shire Hall, which is now a museum and tourist information centre.

GREAT WALSINGHAM
5 miles N of Fakenham on the B1388

St Peter's Church

English place names observe a logic of their own, so Great Walsingham is of course smaller than Little Walsingham. The two villages are very different in atmosphere and appearance, Great Walsingham displaying the typical layout of a rural Norfolk settlement, with attractive cottages set around a green watered by the River Stiffkey, and dominated by a fine 14th-century church, **St Peter's**, noted for its superb window tracery, wondrously carved Norman

font, and perfectly preserved 15th-century carved benches.

WIGHTON
7 miles N of Fakenham on the B1105

Wighton Post Office must be one of very few in the country where you can buy a postal order and a pint at the same time. This happy state of affairs has come about because the post office desk is located in the bar of the village pub, The Carpenters Arms. The desk is open two days a week and provides all the normal post office services, apart from passports and Road Tax licences. This unusual arrangement has been featured on the TV programme *Country File*.

Just outside the village, the Wells-Walsingham Light Railway trundles its way between Little Walsingham and Wells-next-the-Sea. The longest 10¼-inch narrow-gauge steam railway in the world, it runs throughout the summer along a 20-minute scenic journey through the North Norfolk countryside.

TATTERFORD
5 miles SW of Fakenham off the A148 or A1065

Houghton Hall   Tatterford Common

This tiny village is well known to botanists for **Tatterford Common**, an unspoilt tract of rough heathland with tiny ponds, some wild apple trees and the River Tat running through it to join the River Wensum about a mile away.

About four miles west of Tatterford stands **Houghton Hall**, home of the Marquess of Cholmondely and one of Norfolk's most magnificent buildings. This glorious demi-palace was built in the Palladian style during the 1720s by Sir Robert Walpole, England's first Prime Minister. The Walpoles had been gentlemen of substance here since the 14th

HILLSIDE GALLERY & STUDIOS

*Hillside Lodge, Swaffham Road, Toftrees, Fakenham,
Norfolk NR21 7DZ
Tel: 01328 856700
e-mail: info@hillsidegallery.net
website: www.hillsidegallery.net*

The **Hillside Gallery and Studios** shows the work of
artists Debbie and Keith Osborn in the attractive
setting of their own large gardens not far from
Fakenham. Debbie, mixed media artist and designer,
spreads her talents from colourful art and textiles to exciting and
experimental modern jewellery made from beads and locally found
shells and stones, as well as womenswear and accessories. Her art
and design skills are also the basis for a range of greetings cards. Keith
is a photographer whose talents span portraiture, fine art, fashion and
commercial photography, and the gallery accepts commissions for
individual and family portraits, commercial, fashion, boudoir and
maternity photographs as well as commissions for Debbie's paintings
and textiles. The gallery's normal opening hours are 11:00 to 4.30
Tuesday to Saturday – but we are often open Sunday afternoons and
opening hours are regularly extended during the summer. Hillside
Gallery & Studios is located immediately off the A1065 Fakenham to
Swaffham road. Turn off just south of Hempton on to the minor road
signposted towards Pudding Norton. The gallery is signposted
immediately on the right. The gallery's excellent website illustrates
something of the range of Debbie's and Keith's talents.

century. With his family revenues augmented by
the considerable profits Sir Robert extracted
from his political office, he was in a position to
spend lavishly and ostentatiously on his new
house. The first step was to destroy completely
the village of Houghton (it spoilt the view), and
re-house the villagers a mile away at New
Houghton.

Although Sir Robert deliberately cultivated the
manner of a bluff, down-to-earth Norfolk
squire, the personal decisions he made regarding
the design and furnishings of the house reveal a
man of deep culture and refined tastes. It was he
who insisted that the Hall could not be built in
homely Norfolk brick, and took the expensive
decision to use the exceptionally durable stone
quarried at Aislaby in North Yorkshire and
transport it by sea from Whitby to King's Lynn.

More than two-and-a-half centuries later, the
Aislaby stone is still flawless, the only sign of its
age a slight weathering that has softened its
colour to a creamy gold.

To decorate the interior and design the
furniture, Sir Robert commissioned the versatile
William Kent. Kent was at the peak of his
powers - just look at the decoration in the Stone
Hall, the exquisite canopied bed in the Green
Velvet Bedchamber, and the finely-carved
woodwork throughout, which made impressive
use of the newly-discovered hardwood called
mahogany. And then there were the paintings, an
incomparable collection of Old Masters
personally selected by Sir Robert. Sadly, many of
them are now in the Hermitage Museum in St
Petersburg, sold by his wastrel grandson to the
Empress Catherine of Russia.

This grandson, George, 3rd Earl of Orford, succeeded to the title at the age of 21 and spent the next 40 years dissipating his enormous inheritance. When his uncle Horace (the 4th Earl, better known as Horace Walpole, novelist, MP and inveterate gossip) succeeded to the title he found 'Houghton half a ruin … the two great staircases exposed to all weathers; every room in the wings rotting with wet; the park half-covered with nettles and weeds; mortgages swallowing the estate, and a debt of above £40,000'.

Houghton's decline was arrested when the Hall passed by marriage to the Marquess of Cholmondely, Lord Great Chamberlain, in 1797. But it wasn't until 1913, when George, later the 5th Marquess, moved into the house with his new wife, Sybil Sassoon, that Houghton was fully restored to its former state of grace. The depleted collection of paintings was augmented with fine works by Sir Joshua Reynolds and others from Cholmondely Castle in Cheshire, and the Marchioness introduced new collections of exquisite French furniture and porcelain.

One of the 6th Marquess' interests was military history, and in 1928 he began the astonishing Model Soldiers Collection now on display at Houghton. More than 20,000 perfectly preserved models are deployed in meticulous reconstructions of battles such as Culloden and Waterloo, and in one exhibit, re-creating the Grand Review of the British Army in 1895, no fewer than 3,000 figures are on parade. The grounds of the estate include a 450-acre deer park, home to over 600 of the famous white fallow deer and smaller groups of exotic deer. The long-neglected kitchen garden, revived and transformed by the present Lord Cholmondeley, is a memorial to his grandmother Sybil (see above), who died in 1989. The five-acre plot, transformed into a series of outdoor rooms divided by hedges, has been named Garden of the Year by the Historic Houses Association.

EAST RAYNHAM
3 miles SW of Fakenham on the A1065

🏛 Raynham Hall

Raynham Hall is another superb Palladian mansion with a faultless pedigree – designed by Inigo Jones and with magnificent rooms created a century later by William Kent. The house is only open to the public by appointment since it is the private residence of the 7th Marquess of Townshend. It was his 18th-century ancestor, the 2nd Viscount (better known as 'Turnip' Townshend), who revolutionised English agriculture by promoting the humble turnip as an effective means of reclaiming untended land for feeding cattle in winter, and along with wheat, barley and clover, as part of the four-year rotation of crops that provided a cycle of essential nutrients for the soil. The Townshend family have owned extensive estates in this area for centuries, and in St Mary's Church there are some fine monuments to their ancestors, the oldest and most sumptuous of which commemorates Sir Roger, who died in 1493.

Swaffham

🏛 Church of St Peter & St Paul

📷 Swaffham Museum 🏛 Cockley Cley Iceni Village

Swaffham's one-time claim to be the 'Montpellier of England' was justified by the abundance of handsome Georgian houses that used to surround the large, wedge-shaped market place. A good number still survive, along with the Assembly Room of 1817 where the quality would gather for concerts, balls and soirees. The central focus of the market square is the elegant Butter Cross, presented to the

Butter Cross, Swaffham

town by the Earl of Orford in 1783. It's not a cross at all, but a classical lead-covered dome standing on eight columns and surmounted by a life-size statue of Ceres, the Roman goddess of agriculture - an appropriate symbol for this busy market town, from which 10 roads radiate out across the county.

From the market place an avenue of limes leads to the quite outstanding **Church of St Peter & St Paul**, a 15th-century masterpiece with one of the very best double hammerbeam roofs in the county, strikingly embellished with a host of angels, their wings widespread. The unknown mason who devised the church's harmonious proportions made it 51 feet wide, 51 feet high and 102 feet long. Carved on a bench-end here is a man in medieval dress accompanied by a dog on a chain. The same two figures are incorporated in the town's coat of arms, and also appear in the elegantly designed town sign just beyond the market place. The man is The Pedlar of

Swaffham, a certain John Chapman, who, according to legend, dreamed that if he made his way to London Bridge he would meet a stranger who would make him rich. The pedlar and his dog set off for London, and on the bridge he was eventually accosted by a stranger who asked him what he was doing there. John recounted his dream. Scoffingly, the stranger said 'If I were a dreamer, I should go to Swaffham. Recently I dreamt that in Swaffham lived a man named Chapman, and in his garden, buried under a tree, lay a treasure.' John hastily returned home, uprooted the only tree in his garden, and unearthed two jugs full of gold coins.

There was indeed a John Chapman who contributed generously to the building of the parish church in the late 1400s. Cynics claim that he was a wealthy merchant, and that similar tales occur in the folklore of most European countries. Whatever the truth, there's no doubt that the people of Swaffham took the story to their hearts.

John Chapman may be Swaffham's best-known character locally, but internationally the name of Howard Carter, the discoverer of Tutankhamen's tomb, is much better known. Carter, born in London in 1874, was brought up in Swaffham; his death in 1939 was attributed by the popular press to 'the Curse of Tutankhamen'. If so, it must have been an extremely sluggish curse. Some 17 years had elapsed since Carter had knelt by a dark, underground opening, swivelled his torch and found himself the first human being in centuries to gaze upon the astonishing treasures buried in the tomb of the teenage Pharaoh.

Swaffham Museum in the Town Hall is the setting for the story of the town's past. Visitors can follow Howard Carter's road to the Valley of the Kings, see the Symonds

Collection of handmade figurines, and admire the Sporle collection of locally-found artefacts. The Tourist Information Centre (01760 722255) is located in the shop area of the Museum.

Move on some 1,400 years from the death of Tutankhamen to Norfolk in the 1st century AD. Before a battle, members of the Iceni tribe, led by Boudicca, would squeeze the blue sap of the woad plant onto their faces in the hope of frightening the Roman invaders (or any other of their many enemies). At **Cockley Cley Iceni Village and Museums**, three miles southwest of Swaffham off the A1065, archaeologists have reconstructed a village of Boudicca's time, complete with wooden huts, moat, drawbridge and palisades. Reconstruction though it is, the village is remarkably effective in evoking a sense of what daily life entailed more than 1,900 years ago.

A more recent addition to Swaffham's attractions is the EcoTech Centre, opened in 1998. This environmental centre has an organic/heritage garden, a climbable wind turbine, a shop and licensed café (tel: 01760 726100 for opening times).

Around Swaffham

CASTLE ACRE
4 miles N of Swaffham off the A1065

🏛 Castle Acre Priory

Set on a hill surrounded by water meadows, Castle Acre seems still to linger in the Middle Ages. William de Warenne, William the Conqueror's son-in-law, came here very soon after the Conquest and built a Castle that was one of the first, and largest, in the country to be built by the Normans. Of that vast fortress, little remains apart from the gargantuan earthworks and a squat 13th-century gateway.

Much more has survived of **Castle Acre Priory** (see panel below), founded in 1090 and

Castle Acre Priory

Castle Acre, Norfolk PE32 2XD
Tel: 01760 755394
website: www.english-heritage.org.uk

One of the largest and best preserved monastic sites in England, the foundation of **Castle Acre Priory** in about 1090 sprang directly from a visit by William de Warenne II and his wife Gundrada to the great French monastery of Cluny. So impressed were they by its beauty and holiness that they vowed to introduce the Cluniac order of monks to England.

The Cluniac love of decoration is everywhere reflected in the extensive ruins of Castle Acre Priory, whose great 12th century church directly imitated that of Cluny itself. Its beautiful west end, standing almost to its full height, displays tiered ranks of intersecting round arches: it forms an attractive group with the late medieval porch, part timber-framed and part flintchequered, and the extremely well-preserved prior's lodging. A mansion in itself, this includes a first-floor chapel retaining traces of wall-paintings, and a private chamber with two fine oriel windows.

🎬 stories and anecdotes 🐦 famous people 🎨 art and craft 🖋 entertainment and sport 🚶 walks

set in fields beside the River Nar. Its glorious West Front gives a powerful indication of how majestic a triumph of late Norman architecture the complete Priory must have been. With five apses and twin towers, the ground plan was modelled on the Cluniac mother church in Burgundy, where William de Warenne had stayed while making a pilgrimage to Rome. Despite the Priory's great size, it appears that perhaps as few as 25 monks lived here during the Middle Ages - and in some comfort, judging by the well-preserved Prior's House, which has its own bath and built-in wash-basin. The Priory lay on the main route to the famous Shrine at Walsingham, with which it tried to compete by offering pilgrims a rival attraction in the form of an arm of St Philip.

Today, the noble ruins of the Priory are powerfully atmospheric, a brooding scene skilfully exploited by Roger Corman when he filmed here for his screen version of Edgar Allan Poe's ghostly story, *The Tomb of Ligeia*.

Castle Acre village is extremely picturesque, the first place in Norfolk to be designated a Conservation Area, in 1971. Most of the village, including the 15th-century parish church, is built in traditional flint, with a few later houses of brick blending in remarkably happily.

LITCHAM
11 miles NE of Swaffham on the B1145

🏛 Village Museum

Small though it is, this village strung alongside the infant River Nar can boast an intriguing

---

LITCHAM HALL B&B

Litcham, Kings Lynn, Norfolk PE32 2QQ
Tel: 01328 701389 Fax: 01328 701164
e-mail: hermionebirkbeck@hotmail.com

Litcham Hall is a handsome listed Georgian house built in 1781 on edge of pretty village in central Norfolk, 30 minutes from lovely north Norfolk coast. For the whole of the 19th century this was the Doctor's house in Litcham and today, over 200 years after it was built, the red-brick Hall remains at the centre of the community.

Owned by keen gardeners Hermione and John Birkbeck, the superb 3-acre garden has given the family a lot of pleasure over the 40 years since they came to Litcham Hall. Hermione invites you to come and stay with them; enjoy bed, breakfast and the garden! Swimming pool June - Sept by arrangement.

Each of the spacious, luxury en-suite bedrooms offers you an exceptional standard of comfort. Accommodation comprises 1 double en-suite, 1 twin en-suite and 1 twin with private bathroom.

Litcham is within easy reach of Sandringham, Blickling, Holkham, Houghton, Norwich, in fact anywhere in Norfolk. Norfolk is the perfect retreat to recharge the batteries and enjoy some of the hidden treasures the local area has to offer.

Village Museum, with displays of local artefacts from Roman times to the present, an extensive collection of photographs, some of which date back to 1865, and an underground lime kiln.

Dereham

🎬 St Withburga's Well 🐟 Dumpling Green

One of the most ancient towns in the county, Dereham has a recorded history stretching back to AD654 when St Withburga founded a Nunnery here. St Withburga was the daughter of King Anna of the East Angles and the sister of St Etheldreda, the abbess who founded the religious settlement at Ely. Her name lives on at **St Withburga's Well**, just west of the church. This is where she was laid to rest but, some 300 years later, the Abbot and monks of Ely

robbed her grave and ensconced the precious, fundraising relic in their own Cathedral. In the saint's desecrated grave a spring suddenly bubbled forth, its waters possessed of miraculous healing properties, and St Withburga's shrine attracted even more pilgrims than before. Some still come.

In the church of St Nicholas, the second largest in Norfolk, there are features from every century from the 12th to the 16th: a magnificent lantern tower; a lofty Bell Tower; painted roofs; and a Seven Sacrament Font. This is the largest of these notable fonts, of which only 30 have survived - 28 of them in Norfolk and Suffolk.

In the northeast transept is buried a poet, some of whose lines have become embedded in the language:

'Variety's the very spice of life,

KNIT WITS

1 Glencoe Court, Dereham, Norfolk NR19 2AX
Tel: 01362 652961
e-mail: enquiries@knitwitsdereham.co.uk
website: www.knitwitsdereham.co.uk

Knit Wits is a friendly, family run business in Dereham, the heart of Norfolk. More than just a wool shop, you will also find an impressive range of tapestries, cross stitch, quilting threads and needles, ribbons, buttons and general haberdashery. It is positively an Aladdin's Cave!

With knitting as the main focus of the shop, Fiona Joisce, the owner, aims to provide an extensive range of quality yarns, accessories and patterns from Sirdar, Stylecraft, Wendy, Robin, Patons, Rowan, Debbie Bliss, Mirasol, King Cole, Jarol and more. Knit Wits are also main agents for DMC and offer their full range of cross stitch threads and tapestry wools as well as a large selection of kits by DMC, Anchor, Maia, Margot etc. Fiona, a passionate

knitter herself, established the business with her husband in 2007. Whilst the shop is still relatively new, Knit Wits is fast building an excellent reputation for having possibly the best range of yarns in Norfolk.

Conveniently situated next to the largest free car park in town (behind the Cherry Tree Pub), you can relax and spend an enjoyable time browsing the marvellous selection on offer. Fiona is always ready with expert help and advice on knitting & related topics. Demonstrations and lessons for adult beginners are also available.

CARRICK'S AT CASTLE FARM

Castle Farm, Swanton Morley,
Norfolk, NR20 4JT
Tel: 01362 638302
e-mail: jean@castlefarm-swanton.co.uk
website: www.carricksatcastlefarm.co.uk

Set within beautiful gardens on the bank of the River Wensum where the peace and quiet is interrupted only by the birdsong, **Carrick's at Castle Farm** is a 5-star guest house located in the parish of Swanton Morley, 3 miles from the market town of Dereham.

Castle Farm has been the Carrick family home for almost 80 years, and it is from here that the farm's 720 acre arable and livestock enterprises are run.

Carrick's offers 2 ensuite and 2 with private bathrooms. Bedrooms are equipped and furnished to Tourist Board 5-star standard.

We pride ourselves on the excellence of our breakfasts and evening meals. All produce is sourced from the farm or from local growers.

Whilst Carrick's is the perfect place for peaceful relaxation, there is plenty of choice locally for the more active.

The farm has been accepted into the High Level Stewardship scheme which involves planning farming activities around the needs of biodiversity and care for the environment. One of the options we have taken up is the creation of a network of permissive footpaths around the farm, including a 2 mile river walk along the banks of the Wensum. This is one of Norfolk's most delightful walks where wild-life abounds. You may see roe deer, pheasants, hare, kingfisher and heron. You will certainly encounter rabbits and squirrels as they scatter at your approach.

Guests are encouraged to explore the farm and surrounding countryside. One of our main attractions is our 40-strong Pedigree herd of rare breed White Park cattle, which utilise the farm's water meadows and permanent pasture. Delicious meat from these cattle is available from the farm's own butchery.

Located in the heart of Norfolk, within easy reach of the county's many attractions, Carrick's is the perfect choice for the discerning business or leisure traveller. The sense of history and tradition is almost tangible as you relax beside the river, as dusk settles, watching the roach and dace rise to the may-fly.

the monarch of all I survey
God made the country
and man made the town.'

They came from the pen of William Cowper who, despite being the author of such cheery poems as *John Gilpin*, suffered grievously from depression, a condition not improved by his association with John Newton, a former slave-trader who had repented and become 'a man of gloomy piety'. The two men collaborated on a book of hymns that included such perennial favourites as *Oh! for a closer walk with God*, *Hark, my soul, it is the Lord* and *God moves in a mysterious way*. Cowper spent the last four years of his life at Dereham, veering in and out of madness. In a late-flowering romance he had married the widow Mary Unwin, but the strain of caring for the deranged poet drove her in turn to insanity and death. She, too, is buried in the church.

William Cowper died four years after Mary, in 1800. Three years later, another celebrated writer was born at the quaintly named hamlet of **Dumpling Green** on the edge of the town. George Borrow was to become one of the great English travel writers, producing books full of character and colour such as *Wild Wales* and *The Bible in Spain*. In his autobiographical novel, *Lavengro*, he begins with a warm recollection of the town where he was born: 'I love to think on thee, pretty, quiet D[ereham], thou pattern of an English market town, with thy clean but narrow streets branching out from thy modest market place, with thine old-fashioned houses, with here and there a roof of venerable thatch.' The house in which George Borrow was born, Borrow's Hall, still stands in Dumpling Green.

A much less attractive character connected with Dereham is Bishop Bonner, the enthusiastic arsonist of Protestant heretics

---

NESSA'S TACK SHOP

Pound Lane, North Tuddenham, Norfolk NR20 3DA
Tel: 01362 637101

A familiar and widely respected figure in the equestrian world, Nessa Pratt has more than 30 years' experience with horses and horse people, and 20 years in the trade. She opened **Nessa's Tack Shop** in 2005 to meet the needs of all riders, from juniors and 'happy hackers' to experienced and competition riders and to provide everything to protect and pamper their mounts.

In a purpose-built barn an impressive range of products is on display for horse and rider, with top brands at competitive prices and helpful, friendly service. She stocks everything from saddles and saddlery accessories to bridles, feed, lotions, potions, grooming kits, breeches, jodhpurs, hats, crops, rugs, stable equipment, books and equestrian-themed giftware for adults and children.

Nessa's Tack Shop is located on a mixed arable and dairy farm at North Tuddenham, on the A47 east of Dereham. This is a part of the world where riding has always been popular, and in this splendid shop riders have everything they need to pursue their chosen sport. Opening times are 9 to 5 Monday to Saturday.

---

stories and anecdotes   famous people   art and craft   entertainment and sport   walks

during the unhappy reign of Mary Tudor. He was rector of the town before being appointed Bishop of London, and he lived in the exquisite thatched terrace now called Bishop Bonner's Cottages. The exterior is ornamented with delightful pargeting, a frieze of flower and fruit designs below the eaves, a form of decoration that is very unusual in Norfolk. The cottages now house a small museum. Dereham is at one end of the Mid-Norfolk Railway, East Anglia's longest heritage railway, running through 11 miles of rural countryside linking Dereham with Wymondham. Heritage diesel services operate on most weekends during the year, with occasional steam services at peak times. Dereham station has recently been restored to its appearance in the 1950s and 1960s.

Around Dereham

GRESSENHALL
3 miles NW of Dereham off the B1146

🏛 Roots of Norfolk

The **Roots of Norfolk** collection is housed in an impressive late 18th-century former workhouse built in rose-red brick. Gressenhall Workhouse was designed to accommodate some 700 unfortunates, so it was built on a very grand scale indeed. Now one of the UK's leading rural life museums, and among Norfolk's top family attractions, there's ample room for the many exhibits illuminating the working and domestic life of Norfolk people over the past 150 years. Farming the old-fashioned way is there to be discovered on Union Farm, where heavy animals still work the fields. A stroll along the 1930s' village high street takes in the grocer's, post office and schoolroom. The surrounding 50 acres of

unspoilt countryside are perfect for walking. The site hosts numerous special events during the season, ranging from Steam Days to an international folk dance festival with more than 200 dancers taking part.

A mile or so south of Gressenhall, the tiny community of Dillington has great difficulty in getting itself noticed on even the most large-scale of maps. This hidden place is worth seeking out for Norfolk Herbs at Blackberry Farm, a specialist herb farm located in a beautiful wooded valley. Visitors are invited to browse through a vast collection of aromatic, culinary and medicinal herb plants, and to learn all about growing and using herbs.

BRISLEY
7 miles N of Dereham on the B1145

Brisley village is well known to local historians and naturalists for its huge expanse of heathland, some 170 acres of it. It's reckoned to be the best example of unspoilt common in Norfolk, and at its centre are scores of pits that were dug out in medieval times to provide clay for the wattle-and-daub houses of the period. Another feature of interest in the village is Gately Manor (private), an Elizabethan manor house standing within the remains of a medieval moat, and yet another moated house at Old Hall Farm in the southwest corner of the green.

NORTH ELMHAM
6 miles N of Dereham off the B1110

Near the village of North Elmham stand the sparse remains of a Saxon Cathedral. North Elmham was the seat of the Bishops of East Anglia until 1071, when they removed to Thetford (and then, 20 years later, to Norwich). Although there had been a cathedral here since the late 7th century, what has survived is mostly from the 11th century. Despite its grand title, the T-shaped ground plan reveals that the cathedral was no larger than a small parish church.

WATTON
10 miles SW of Dereham on the A1075

🎞 Wayland Wood

Watton's striking town sign depicts the Babes in the Wood of the famous nursery story. The story, which was already current hereabouts in the 1500s, relates that as Arthur Truelove lay dying he decided that the only hope for his two children was to leave them in the care of their uncle. Unfortunately, the uncle decided to help himself to their inheritance and paid two men to take the children into nearby Wayland Wood and kill them. In a moment of unexpected compassion, one of the men decided that he could not commit the dastardly act. He disposed of his accomplice instead, and abandoned the children in the wood to suffer whatever fate might befall them. Sadly, unlike the nursery tale in which the children find their way back home and live happily ever after, this unfortunate brother and sister perished. Their ghosts are said to wander hand-in-hand through the woods to this day.

Wayland Wood is now owned by the Norfolk Naturalist Trust, and is believed to be one of the oldest in England; Griston Hall (private), half a mile south of the wood, is a Grade II listed building, reputedly once the home of the wicked uncle in the real-life *Babes in the Wood* story.

Watton itself boasts an unusual Clock Tower, dated 1679, standing at the centre of its long main street.

THOMPSON
12 miles SW of Dereham off the A1075

This is a quiet village with a marshy man-made lake, Thompson Water, and a wild common. The Peddars Way long-distance footpath passes about a mile to the west and, about the same distance to the northeast, the Church is a splendid early 14th-century building notable for its fine carved screen and choice 17th century fittings.

ATTLEBOROUGH
12 miles S of Dereham off the A11

🎞 Church of St Mary

The greatest glory of this pleasant market town is to be found in the **Church of St Mary**. Here, a remarkable 15th century chancel screen stretches the width of the church and is beautifully embellished with the arms of the 24 bishoprics into which England was divided at that time. The screen is generally reckoned to be one of the most outstanding in the country, a remarkable survivor of the Reformation purging of such beautiful creations from churches across the land.

Collectors of curiosities will be interested in a strange memorial in the churchyard. It takes the form of a pyramid, about six feet high, and was erected in 1929 to mark the grave of a local solicitor with the rather splendid name of Melancthon William Henry Brooke, or Lawyer Brooke as he was more familiarly known. Melancthon was an amateur Egyptologist who became convinced by his studies of the Pharaohs' tombs that the only way to ensure an agreeable after-life was to be buried beneath a pyramid, precisely placed and of the correct physical dimensions. Several years before his death, he gave the most punctilious instructions as to how this assurance of his immortal existence should be constructed and located.

A few miles south of Attleborough, signposted off the A11, Snetterton Race Circuit is one of the most popular attractions in East Anglia. Highlights of the racing season include rounds of the British Superbike Championship, British Touring Car Championship and numerous classic bike and car meetings.

Thetford

🏛 Cluniac Priory 🖼 Burrell Steam Museum

🖼 Museum of Thetford Life ⛪ Boudicca's Palace

🏛 Thetford Warren Lodge 🏛 Castle

🏛 Grimes Graves 🌿 Thetford Forest

📖 Dad's Army Museum

Some 2,000 years ago, Thetford may well have been the site of **Boudicca's Palace**. In the 1980s, excavations for building development at Gallows Hill, north of the town, revealed an Iron Age enclosure. It is so extensive it may well have been the capital of the Iceni tribe which gave the Romans so much trouble. Certainly, the town's strategic location at the meeting of the Rivers Thet and Little Ouse made it an important settlement for centuries. At the time of the Domesday Book, 1086, Thetford was the sixth-largest town in the country and the seat of the Bishop of East Anglia, with its own castle, mint and pottery.

Of the **Castle**, only the 80-foot motte remains, but it's worth climbing to the top of this mighty mound for the views across the town. An early Victorian traveller described Thetford as 'An ancient and princely little town ... one of the most charming country towns in England'. Despite major development all around, the heart of the town still fits that description, with a goodly number of medieval and Georgian houses presenting an attractive medley of flint and half-timbered buildings. Perhaps the most striking is the **Ancient House Museum of**

Charles Burrell Museum

c/o Thetford Town Council, King's House, King Street, Thetford, IP24 2AP
Tel: 01842 765840
e-mail: burrell@thetfordtowncouncil.gov.uk

The Charles Burrell Museum opened in 1991 and is housed in the former Paint Shop on Minstergate in Thetford, Norfolk. The museum tells the stories of the Charles Burrell Works, the people who laboured there, and the machinery they produced. The past is captured through displays representing

different areas of the Works, such as the foundry, and the display of our collection of Burrell engines and other agricultural equipment.

The collections include a Charles Burrell and Sons Ltd steam roller and traction engine, parts of Burrell engines, factory machinery, and items linked to the Burrell Family. So, visit the Museum and step in to the world of Charles Burrell, world renowned Industrialist during the golden age of engineering and agriculture.

Thetford Life in White Hart Street, a magnificent 15th-century timber-framed house with superb carved oak ceilings. It houses the Tourist Information Centre and a museum where some of the most interesting exhibits are replicas of the Thetford Treasure, a 4th-century hoard of gold and silver jewellery discovered as recently as 1979 by an amateur archaeologist with a metal detector. The originals of these sumptuous artefacts are housed in the British Museum in London.

Even older than the Ancient House is the 12th-century **Cluniac Priory** (English Heritage), now mostly in ruins but with an impressive 14th-century gatehouse still standing. During the Middle Ages, Thetford could boast 24 churches; today, only three remain.

Thetford's industrial heritage is vividly displayed in the **Burrell Steam Museum** (see panel below), in Minstergate, which has full-size steam engines regularly in steam, re-created workshops and many examples of vintage agricultural machinery. The Museum tells the story of the Burrell Steam Company, which formed the backbone of the town's industry from the late 18th to the early 20th centuries, their sturdy machines famous around the world.

In King Street, the Thomas Paine Statue commemorates the town's most famous son, born here in 1737. The revolutionary philosopher, and author of *The Rights of Man* emigrated to America in 1774, where he helped formulate the American Bill of Rights. Paine's democratic views were so detested in

Thetford Ancient House

England that even 10 years after his death in New York, the authorities refused permission for his admirer, William Cobbett, to have the remains buried in his home country. And it wasn't until the 1950s that Thetford finally got around to erecting a statue in his honour. Ironically for such a robust democrat, his statue stands in King Street and opposite The King's House, named after James I, who was a frequent visitor here between 1608 and 1618. At the Thomas Paine Hotel in White Hart Street, the room in which it is believed that Paine was born is now the Honeymoon Suite, complete with four-poster bed. The town and many of the surrounding villages were used as locations for the much-loved, long running

stories and anecdotes   famous people   art and craft   entertainment and sport   walks

TV series *Dad's Army*, and a new attraction is the **Dad's Army Museum** in the Guildhall (tel: 01842 751975 for opening times). The Dad's Army Trail is one of five self-guided walking trails recently developed – others include the Thomas Paine Trail and the Haunted Trail.

To the west of the town stretch the 90 square miles of **Thetford Forest**, the most extensive lowland forest in Britain. The Forestry Commission began planting it in 1922, and although the woodland is largely given over to conifers, with Scots and Corsican Pine and Douglas Fir predominating, oak, sycamore and beech can also be seen throughout. There is a particularly varied trail leading from the Forestry Commission Information Centre which has detailed information about this and other walks through the area.

On the edge of the forest, about two miles west of Thetford, are the ruins of **Thetford Warren Lodge**, built around 1400. At that time a huge area here was preserved for farming rabbits, a major element of the medieval diet. The vast warren was owned by the Abbot of Thetford Priory, and it was he who built the Lodge for his gamekeeper.

Still in the forest, reached by a footpath from the village of Santon Downham, are **Grimes Graves** (English Heritage see panel below), the earliest major industrial site to be discovered in Europe. At these unique Neolithic flint mines, Stone Age labourers extracted the materials for their sharp-edged axes and knives. It's a strange experience entering these 5,000 year old shafts, which descend some 30 feet to an underground chamber. (The experience is even better if you bring your own high-powered torch - tel: 01842 810656).

Grimes Graves

Nr Thetford, Norfolk IP26 5DE
Tel: 01842 810656
website: www.english-heritage.org.uk

Descend into a prehistoric flint mine! Discover the significance of over 400 pits, forming a lunar landscape amid the unique Breckland environment, famous for its unusual wildlife. These 'Devil's Holes' long confused experts: find out about their extraordinary theories, and see finds of the mysterious objects deposited by Neolithic miners. Experience an unforgettable visit to Britain's only accessible prehistoric flint mine, dug by Stone Age miners 5,000 years ago. Descend over 10 metres to the galleries where flint was mined for tools and weapons, and wonder at the courage and ingenuity of our distant ancestors.

🏛 historic building 🏛 museum and heritage 🏛 historic site 🈺 scenic attraction 🌱 flora and fauna

Around Thetford

MUNDFORD
8 miles NW of Thetford on the A1065/A134

Mundford is a large Breckland village of flint-built cottages, set on the northern edge of Thetford Forest and with the River Wissey running by. If you ever watch TV, you've almost certainly seen Lynford Hall, a mile or so northwest of Mundford. It has provided an impressive location for scenes in *Dad's Army*, *'Allo, 'Allo', You Rang My Lord?* and *Love on a Branch Line*, as well as featuring in numerous TV commercials. The Hall is a superb Grade II listed mansion, built for the Lyne-Stevens

---

THE WHITE HART INN

7 White Hart Street, Foulden, Thetford, Norfolk IP26 5AW
Tel:01366 328638

To some it's a pub, others a 'home from home'. **The White Hart Inn** is a 19th Century traditional pub with accommodation in the heart of Foulden which is just outside Thetford, a small ancient market town filled to the brim with history and heritage sites, quiet gardens, open parkland and a relaxing riverside.

With Thetford Forest right on the doorstep, this is also the best base for discovering the wildlife and outdoor pleasures of The Brecks ... ideal for walking, cycling, riding and action-packed adventure days!

The White Hart Inn is a pub of great character, serving value for money un-pretentious pub meals and superb quality real ales from a leading Norfolk micro-brewery Buffy's Beer, as well as a good selection of wines. Excellent en-suite letting rooms with a private entrance are available. All rooms are well equipped with TVs, tea and coffee making facilities. Child friendly, dogs welcome, and a very warm welcome from the owner Victor Knight. It's the perfect place if you love walking, unwinding with traditional British food and a great bottle of wine...and not feeling guilty about it! Join in on music nights, quiz nights, and whatever else takes your fancy!

RAINBOWS RIDING SCHOOL

61 Methwold Road, Northwold, Norfolk IP26 5LN
Tel: 01366 727800

Kim Hussey opened **Rainbows Riding School** in 2007 in the village of Northwold, clearly signposted off the A134 northwest of Thetford Forest. Kim and her staff have earned a wide-ranging reputation with their expertise, friendliness and attention to individual requirements. They cater for all levels of experience and ability, and they keep a dozen horses and ponies on site. Riding lessons by the hour can be booked as late as the day before, and riding and hacking are available in the quiet, scenic countryside. Special all-day events can be arranged, including hacking picnics.

THE WEST END

43 Long Lane, Feltwell, Thetford,
Norfolk IP26 4BJ
Tel: 01842 827711

Drinkers Rejoice! **The West End** in Feltwell finally re-opened its doors in May 2008. After being closed for over seven months she's back and brimming with confidence. Since being taken over by landlady Paula Holt the pub has beaten off competition and is building a good reputation for its warm and friendly atmosphere, traditional homemade food and super selection of drinks.

Despite its traditional exterior, the interior is surprisingly modern yet cosy, and with its light, bright colours is the perfect place for an informal night out or lunch. The menu is still comfortably traditional with all the classics prepared on site and some modern dishes to tempt the adventurous. Food is served 12noon – 2pm and 6 – 9pm daily and a delicious carvery is available on Sundays from 12noon until 3pm.

And for those looking for a bit of entertainment there is a live band here at least once a month – please ring for details of the next event. The West End holds a very warm welcome to visitors and locals alike, super choice for young and old.

FINE ANTIQUE FURNITURE RESTORATION AND CONSERVATION

The Oaks, Larling, near Thetford, Norwich, Norfolk, NR16 2QS
Tel: 01953 717937
e-mail: rodlar88@btinternet.com

From high-class Antique Furniture including family heirlooms, Rod Larwood, furniture restorer and conservator, has spent his entire life working with wood, building up a rich selection of all types and ages. His business Antique Furniture Restoration and Conservation is based in Larling, near Thetford, and deals with cabinet making, veneering, gilding, marquetry, brass inlay and traditional hand polishing.

Restoring antique furniture involves making it look as good as the day it was created, and Rod loves handing over a finished piece to a delighted customer, he explains "I do get furniture which is in quite a terrible condition and it's great when a client sees it finished. They sometimes find it difficult to believe it's the same piece!"

The art of restoring a piece of furniture, from a mahogany Longcase clock to a walnut Tallboy or Tunbridge Ware box is also knowing when to stop. Rod says "It's a natural material and you want to maintain its character, you don't want to destroy its original patination". He also carries out conservation work, which means stabilizing an item so its condition does not deteriorate further. He also writes up condition reports on collections.

Rod is listed on the Conservation Register and is an accredited member of BAFRA. (British Antique Furniture Restorers Association)

family in 1885 (as a hunting-lodge, incredibly) and designed in the Jacobean Renaissance style by William Burn.

EAST HARLING
8 miles E of Thetford on the B1111

This attractive little town boasts a beautiful 15th-century church in a pastoral location beside the River Thet. Inside, a magnificent hammerbeam roof crowns the lofty nave, there's some outstanding 15th century glass and, in the Harling Chapel, the fine marble Tomb of Robert Harling. Harling was one of Henry V's knights, who met his death at the siege of Paris in 1435. Since this was long before the days of refrigeration, the knight's body was instead stewed, then stuffed into a barrel and brought back to East Harling for a ceremonious burial.

The church houses another equally sumptuous memorial, the tomb of Sir Thomas Lovell. Sculpted in alabaster, Sir Thomas is an imposing figure, clad in armour with a long sword, his head resting on a helmet, his feet on a spray of peacock's feathers. He and his wife lie beneath a wondrously ornamented canopy, decorated with multi-coloured shields and pinnacles.

BANHAM
12 miles E of Thetford on the B1114

🐾 Banham Zoo

Banham Zoo provides the opportunity to come face to face with some of the world's rarest wildlife - many of the animals who find a home here otherwise face extinction. The Zoo, with almost 1,000 animals, is particularly concerned with monkeys and apes, but in the 25 acres of landscaped gardens you'll also come across tigers, cheetahs, lemurs, birds of prey, penguins and a magnificent new giraffe enclosure. Rated among the UK's top three zoos by *Which Magazine* and voted Top Norfolk Attraction in 2007, Banham Zoo is open daily throughout the year (tel: 01953 887711).

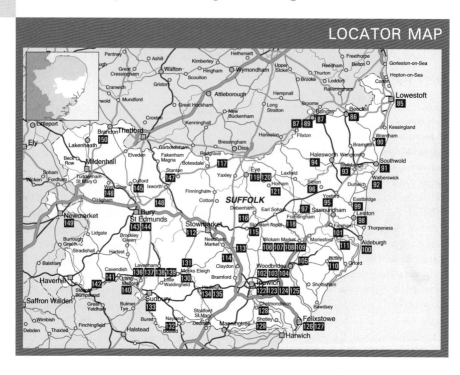

LOCATOR MAP

ADVERTISERS AND PLACES OF INTEREST

🏠 historic building 🏛 museum and heritage 🏛 historic site 🍃 scenic attraction 🌿 flora and fauna

2| Suffolk

Suffolk is a county with a wealth of attractions to delight the visitor: rural beauty, rivers and nature reserves, windmills and watermills, ancient wool towns and villages, churches hardly touched by the Victorian 'improvers', stately homes, thriving ports and holiday resorts, a conservation coastline standing defiant against the North Sea.

Suffolk is very much a maritime county, with over 50 miles of coastline. The whole coast is a conservation area, which the 50-mile Suffolk Coastal Path makes walkable

throughout. With all the miles of meandering rivers and superb stretches of coastline, it is only natural that watery pursuits are a popular pastime, and many of the local museums also have a nautical theme; the Suffolk coast has been a source of inspiration for many of the nation's most distinguished artists, writers and composers.

The sea brings its own dangers, even in human form, and it was against the threat of a Napoleonic invasion that Martello Towers were built in southeastern Suffolk, in the

🎭 stories and anecdotes 🦅 famous people 🎨 art and craft 🎟 entertainment and sport 🚶 walks

tradition of Saxon and Tudor forts and the precursors of concrete pillboxes. The marshes by the coast have traditionally been a source of reeds, the raw material for the thatch that is such a pretty sight on so many Suffolk buildings. Reed-cutting happens between December and February, the beds being drained in preparation and reflooded after the crop has been gathered. Thatching itself is a highly skilled craft, but 10 weeks of work can give a thatched roof 50 years of life.

House in the Clouds, Thorpeness

Inland Suffolk has few peers in terms of picturesque countryside and villages, and the area of central Suffolk between the heathland and the coast is a delightful place for getting away from it all to the real countryside, with unchanged ancient villages, gently flowing rivers and rich farm land. The little market towns of Stowmarket and Needham Market are full of interest, and in this part of Suffolk some of the best-preserved windmills and watermills are to be found.

Much of Suffolk's character comes from its rivers, and in the part of the county surrounding Ipswich, the Orwell and the Stour mark the boundaries of the Shotley Peninsula. The countryside here is largely unspoilt, with wide-open spaces between scattered villages.

John Constable, England's greatest landscape painter, was born at East Bergholt in 1776 and remained at heart a Suffolk man throughout his life. The Suffolk tradition of painting continues to this day, with many artists drawn particularly to Walberswick and what is known as Constable Ccountry.

Cambridgeshire, Norfolk, the A134 and the A14 frame the northern part of West Suffolk, which includes Bury St Edmunds, a pivotal player in the country's religious history, and Newmarket, one of the major centres of the horseracing world. Between and above them are picturesque villages, bustling market towns, rich farming countryside, the fens, and the expanse of sandy heath and pine forest that is Breckland. The area south and west of Bury towards the Essex border contains some of Suffolk's most attractive and peaceful countryside. The visitor will come upon a succession of picturesque villages, historic churches, remarkable stately homes, heritage centres and nature reserves. In the south, along the River Stour, stand the historic wool towns of Long Melford, Cavendish and Clare. And, of course, Sudbury, the birthplace of the painter Thomas Gainsborough, and the largest of the wool towns, still home to a number of weaving concerns.

Lowestoft

🏛 Lowestoft & East Suffolk Maritime Museum

🏛 Royal Naval Patrol Museum 🏛 Maritime Museum

🏛 War Memorial Museum 🏛 Lowestoft Museum

🏛 ISCA Maritime Museum

The most easterly town in Britain had its heyday as a major fishing port during the late 19th and early 20th centuries, when it was a mighty rival to Great Yarmouth in the herring industry. That industry has been in major decline since the First World War, but Lowestoft is still a fishing port and the trawlers continue to chug into the harbour in the early morning with the catches of the night. Guided tours of the fish market and the harbour are available.

Lowestoft is also a popular holiday resort, the star attraction being the lovely South Beach with its golden sands, safe swimming, two piers and all the expected seaside amusements and entertainments. Claremont Pier, over 600 feet in length, was built in 1902, ready to receive day-trippers on the famous Belle steamers. The buildings in this part of town were developed in mid-Victorian times by the company of Sir Samuel Morton Peto,

also responsible for Nelson's Column, the statues in the Houses of Parliament, the Reform Club and Somerleyton Hall.

At the heart of the town is the old harbour, home to the Royal Norfolk & Suffolk Yacht Club and the Lifeboat Station. Further upriver is the commercial part of the port, used chiefly by ships carrying grain and timber. The history of Lowestoft is naturally tied up with the sea, and that heritage is remembered in a number of museums in the town. Much of it is recorded in fascinating detail in the **Lowestoft & East Suffolk Maritime Museum** with model boats, fishing gear, a lifeboat cockpit, paintings and shipwrights' tools. The setting is a flint-built fisherman's cottage in Sparrow's Nest Gardens. The **Royal Naval Patrol Museum** nearby remembers the minesweeping service in models, photographs, documents and uniforms. On Heritage Quay, the *Mincarlo* is the last surviving fishing vessel built (including the engine) in Lowestoft. Visitors can tour the whole boat. The history of Lowestoft lifeboat station, one of the oldest in the UK, is one of epic rescues, great seafaring characters and pioneering developments. In 1801, its first lifeboat was built by Henry Greathead who had, in 1790, built the very first boat designed

Lowestoft Maritime Museum

Sparrows Nest Park, Whapload Road, Lowestoft, Suffolk NR32 1XG Tel: 01502 561963

Open daily from May to September, **Lowestoft Maritime Museum** specialises in the history of the Lowestoft fishing fleet, from early sail to steam and through to the modern diesel-powered vessels. Methods of fishing are recorded, including trawling and the no longer practised driftnet fishing for herring, and other displays depict the evolution of lifeboats and the town's association with the Royal Navy. A replica of the aft cabin of a steam drifter and a fine picture gallery are other attractions of this fascinating museum, where the attendants are ex-seamen and others interested in the port of Lowestoft. School parties are particularly welcome, with takeaway educational packs available, and out-of-season parties can be catered for with notice.

🎭 stories and anecdotes 🦜 famous people 🎨 art and craft 🖌 entertainment and sport 🚶 walks

for saving lives at sea. Today's state-of-the-art boathouse can be visited between 11am and 4.30pm daily. **Lowestoft Maritime Museum** (see panel on previous page), on Whapload Road, has many lifeboat-related exhibits, including the control cockpit of a Liverpool class boat. Call 01502 561963 for opening times.

England's first lighthouse was installed at Lowestoft in 1609. The present one dates from 1874.

In Sparrow's Nest Gardens is the **War Memorial Museum**, dedicated to those who served during the Second World War. There's a photographic collection chronicling the bombing of the town, aircraft models and a chapel of remembrance.

St Margaret's Church, notable for its decorated ceiling and copper-covered spire, is a memorial to seafarers, and the north aisle has panels recording the names of fishermen lost at sea from 1865 to 1923.

Lowestoft also has some interesting literary and musical connections. The Elizabethan playwright, poet and pamphleteer Thomas Nash was born here in 1567. His last work, Lenten Stuffe, was a eulogy to the herring trade and specifically to Great Yarmouth. Joseph Conrad (Jozef Teodor Konrad Korzeniowski), working as a deckhand on a British freighter bound for Constantinople, jumped ship here in 1878, speaking only a few words of the language in which he was to become one of the modern masters. The composer Benjamin Britten is associated with several places in Suffolk, but Lowestoft has the earliest claim, for it is here that he was born in 1913.

Just north of town, with access from the B1385, Pleasurewood Hill is the largest theme park in East Anglia.

Lowestoft Marina, Lowestoft

Oulton Broad, on the western edge of Lowestoft, is a major centre of amusements afloat, with boats for hire and cruises on the Waveney. It also attracts visitors to Nicholas Everitt Park to look around **Lowestoft Museum**, housed in historic Broad House. Opened by the Queen and Prince Philip in 1985, the museum displays archaeological finds from local sites, some now lost to the sea, costumes, toys, domestic bygones, civic regalia, paintings, radios and a fine collection of Lowestoft porcelain. (The porcelain industry lasted from about 1760 to 1800, using clay from the nearby Gunton Hall Estate. The soft-paste ware, resembling Bow porcelain, was usually decorated in white and blue.)

Lowestoft's **ISCA Maritime Museum** has a unique collection of ethnic working boats, including coracles, gondolas, junks, dhows, sampans and proas.

Around Lowestoft

BLUNDESTON
4 miles N of Lowestoft off the A12

Known chiefly as the village used by Charles

Dickens as the birthplace of that writer's 'favourite child', David Copperfield, the morning light shining on the sundial of Blundeston's church – which has the tallest, narrowest Saxon round tower of any in East Anglia – greeted young David as he looked out of his bedroom window in the nearby Rookery. He said of the churchyard: 'There is nothing half so green that I know anywhere, as the grass of that churchyard, nothing half so shady as its trees; nothing half so quiet as its tombstones.'

Blundeston has another notable literary connection: Blundeston Lodge was once the home of Norton Nichols, whose friend the poet Gray is reputed to have taken his inspiration for An Elegy Written in a Country Church Yard while staying there.

LOUND
5 miles N of Lowestoft off the A12

🏛 Church of St John the Baptist

Lound's parish **Church of St John the Baptist**, in the very north of the county, is sometimes known as the 'golden church'. This epithet is the result of the handiwork of designer/architect Sir Ninian Comper, seen most memorably in the gilded organ-case with two trumpeting angels, the font cover and the rood screen. The last is a very elaborate affair, with several heraldic arms displayed. The surprise package here is the modern St Christopher mural on the north wall. It includes Sir Ninian at the wheel of his Rolls-Royce – and in 1976 an aeroplane was added to the scene!

SOMERLEYTON
5 miles NW of Lowestoft on the B1074

🏛 Somerleyton Hall

Somerleyton Hall, one of the grandest and most distinctive of stately homes, is a splendid Victorian mansion built in Anglo-Italian style by Samuel Morton Peto. Its lavish architectural features are complemented by fine state rooms, magnificent wood carvings (some by Grinling Gibbons) and notable paintings. The grounds include a renowned yew-hedge maze, where people have been going round in circles since 1846, walled and sunken gardens, and a 300-foot pergola. There's also a sweet little miniature railway, and Fritton Lake Countryworld, part of the Somerleyton Estate, is a 10-minute drive away (see under Fritton in Norfolk). The Hall is open to the public on most days in summer.

Samuel Morton Peto learned his skills as a civil engineer and businessman from his uncle, and was still a young man when he added the Reform Club and Nelson's Column to his CV. The Somerleyton Hall he bought in 1843 was a Tudor and Jacobean mansion. He and his architect virtually rebuilt the place, and also built Somerleyton village, a cluster of thatched redbrick cottages. Nor was this the limit of Peto's achievements, for he ran a company that laid railways all over the world and was a Liberal MP, first for Norwich, then for Finsbury, and finally for Bristol. His company foundered in 1863 and Somerleyton Hall was sold to Sir Francis Crossley, one of three brothers who made a fortune in mass-producing carpets. Crossley's son became Baron Somerleyton in 1916, and the Baron's grandson is the present Lord Somerleyton.

HERRINGFLEET
5 miles NW of Lowestoft on the B1074

🏛 Herringfleet Windmill

Standing above the River Waveney, the parish church of St Margaret is a charming sight with its Saxon round tower, thatched roof and lovely glass. **Herringfleet Windmill** is a beautiful black-tarred smock mill in working order, the last survivor of the Broadland wind pump, whose job was to assist in draining the marshes. This example was built in 1820 and worked regularly until the 1950s. It contains a fireplace and a wooden bench, providing a modicum of comfort for a millman on a cold night shift. To arrange a visit, call 01473 583352.

BECCLES
9 miles W of Lowestoft on the A146

🏛 Church of St Michael

🏛 Church of St Margaret (Hales)

🏛 Beccles & District Museum

🏛 William Clowes Museum of Print 🏛 Roos Hall

The largest town in the Waveney district at the southernmost point of the Broads, Beccles

has, in its time, been home to Saxons and Vikings, and at one time the market here was a major supplier of herring (up to 60,000 a year) to the Abbey at Bury St Edmunds. At the height of its trading importance, Beccles must have painted a splendidly animated picture, with wherries constantly on the move transporting goods from seaports to inland towns. The same stretch of river is still alive, but now with the yachts and pleasure boats of the holidaymakers and weekenders who fill the town in summer. The regatta in July and August is a particularly busy time.

Fire, sadly such a common part of small-town history, ravaged Beccles at various times in the 16th and 17th centuries, destroying much of the old town. For that reason the dwellings extant today are largely Georgian in origin, with handsome redbrick façades. One

ONE STEP BACK

2 Exchange Square, Beccles NR34 9HL
Tel: 01502 714121

Beccles stands on the Suffolk-Norfolk border, a jewel of a town threaded onto the glistening reaches of the River Waveney. Small squares and thoroughfares, lined with independent outlets and rich in architectural merit, help give the town much of its charm.

Located in this fine old Georgian market town is a well-established retailer **'One Step Back'**. Offering a vast collection of antique and new individual pieces for both period and contemporary living. If you love the nostalgia of finding bygone treasure this store will have just the right thing, featuring top quality antique furniture, chandeliers, four-poster beds, Persian rugs, mirrors, jewellery, fine collectables and much more. Here authenticity is guaranteed and the service is second to none.

🏛 historic building 🏛 museum and heritage 🏛 historic site 🔿 scenic attraction 🌱 flora and fauna

that is not is **Roos Hall**, a gabled building dating from 1583. Just outside the town, far enough away to escape the great fire of 1586, it was built to a Dutch design, underlining the links between East Anglia and the Low Countries forged by the wool and weaving trades. Elizabeth I stayed at the Hall just after it was completed, when she visited Beccles to present the town's charter; the occasion is depicted in the town sign. One of the Hall's owners was Sir John Suckling (later to become Controller of the Household to James I), one of whose descendants was Lord Nelson. Any old Hall worth its salt has a ghost, and the Roos representative is a headless coachman who is said to appear on Christmas Eve.

The **Church of St Michael** was built in the second half of the 14th century by the Abbot of Bury. Its tower stands separate, built in the 16th century, rising almost 100 feet and containing a peal of bells. An unusual feature at the north façade is an outside pulpit taking the form of a small balcony. The priest could enter the pulpit from the church and preach to lepers, who were not allowed inside. Nelson's parents, the Reverend Edmund Nelson and Catherine Suckling, were married in St Michael's, as was the great Suffolk poet George Crabbe.

Another building with Dutch-style gables houses the **Beccles and District Museum**, whose contents include 19th-century toys and costumes, farm implements, items from the old town gaol and memorabilia from the sailing wherries, including a wealth of old photographs. Beccles, like Bungay, is an old printing town, and has the **William Clowes Museum of Print** on the site of the Newgate works of the famed printer. Here the visitor will learn about the history of printing since the 1800s, with woodcuts, books and machinery; tours of the factory are also available. A few miles northwest

of beccles, at **Hales**, **St Margaret's** is a wonderful, almost perfect little Norman church, scarcely changed since the 12th century.

BUNGAY
15 miles W of Lowestoft on the A144

🏰 Castle 🏰 Holy Trinity Church 🏛 Museum

🏛 Station 146 Tower Museum (Seething)

An ancient fortress town on the River Waveney, the river played an important part in Bungay's fortunes until well into the 18th century, with barges laden with coal, corn, malt and timber plying the route to the coast. The river is no longer navigable above Geldeston, but is a great attraction for anglers and yachtsmen.

Bungay is best known for its **Castle**, built in its original form by Hugh Bigod, 1st Earl of Norfolk, as a rival to Henry II's castle at Orford. In 1173 Hugh took the side of the rebellious sons of Henry, but this insurrection ended with the surrender of the castle to the King. Hugh was killed not long after this episode while on the Third Crusade; his son Roger inherited the title and the castle, but it was another Roger Bigod who came to Bungay in 1294 and built the round tower and mighty outer walls that stand today.

To the north of the castle are Bungay's two surviving churches of note (the Domesday Book records five). The Saxon round tower of **Holy Trinity Church** is the oldest complete structure in the town, and a brass plate on the door commemorates the church's narrow escape from the fire of 1688 that destroyed much of the town (similar disasters overtook many other towns with close-set timber-and-thatch buildings). The church of St Mary - now deconsecrated - was not so lucky, being more or less completely gutted. The tower survives to dominate the townscape, and points of interest in the church itself include a

EARSHAM STREET CAFÉ

13 Earsham Street, Bungay,
Suffolk, NR35 1AE
Tel: 01986 893103
e-mail: earshamst@aol.com

An excellent little place, **Earsham Street Café** is full of character with a cosy and friendly atmosphere. The assortment of British and Mediterranean flavours is a joy to behold, and there is a large and well thought-through wine list with House wine starting at £12.50. Well established in Bungay as a popular café, it is found in a 17th century building.

The extensive Lunch Menu suits all tastes, with a range of Starters (including rare seared tuna with Caesar style salad, smoked haddock, and toasted goats cheese & red pepper salad with olives), Light Lunches (try the deli plate for one- chorizo sausage, parma ham, anchovies, feta and avocado, or the pan fried scallops with bacon lardons and parmesan wafers), Dishes of the Day (for example slow roasted lamb with dauphinoise potato and savoy cabbage, or chilled and marinated tiger prawns with oriental noodle salad), Main Courses (many to choose from, including poached crayfish tails, crisp confit of duck with gnocchi dumplings, chorizo, wild mushrooms and spinach, and braised beef bourgignonne), as well as some scrumptious desserts, ice creams and cheeses to finish off.

The Snacks and Drinks Menu is of high quality with hot breakfasts, jacket potatoes, cakes and slices, sandwiches, and toasted sandwiches to choose from. Hot drinks, soft drinks and beers are also available throughout the day. There is also an exceptionally large wine menu, with a range of red wines, white wines, champagnes and dessert wines on offer.

Earsham Street Café has won a number of awards for it outstanding food and service, including 'Café of the Year' Les Routier UK Award Winner 2001-2004, the AA Two Rosette, was highly recommended in the Good Food Guide 2008, and has been voted by the Times as Top 10 Café- Deli in 2006 and 2007.

It is open 7 days a week, from 9.30am – 5.00pm Monday to Saturday, and from 12 - 2.30pm on Sundays. Booking is recommended to avoid disappointment. The Cakes and Slices snacks are locally produced and served after noon everyday, and all coffees are Fair Trade. Parking is available outside the café, and there's also a pay and display 5 mins walk away. Disabled access. Gift vouchers available for an original present.

woodcarving of the Resurrection presented by Rider Haggard, and a monument to General Robert Kelso, who fought in the American War of Independence.

A century before the fire, the church received a visit, during a storm, from the devilish Black Shuck, a retriever-like hound who, hot from causing severe damage at Blythburgh, raced down the nave and killed two worshippers. A weather vane in the market place puts the legend into verse:

All down the church in midst of fire
The Hellish Monster Flew
And Passing onwards to the Quire
He many people slew.

Nearby is the famous octagonal Butter Cross, rebuilt after the great fire of 1688 and topped by Justice with her scales and sword.

This building was once used as a prison, with a dungeon below.

Bungay Museum, housed in the Council offices in Broad Street, is home to an exhibition of local history including pictures, coins and photographs. North of Bungay, at Seething, is **Station 146 Tower Museum**, a restored Second World War control tower that is a memorial to the men of the USAAF 448th Bomb Group based here from 1943 to 1945. Call 01508 550288 for opening times.

EARSHAM
1 mile SW of Bungay off the A143

 Otter Trust

All Saints Church and Earsham Hall are well worth a visit, but what brings most people here is the **Otter Trust** (see panel on page 118), on the banks of the Waveney, where the

---

EARSHAM PARK FARM

Old Railway Road, Earsham, Nr Bungay,
Suffolk, NR35 2AQ
Tel: 01986 892180
e-mail: bobbie@earsham-parkfarm.co.uk
website: www.earsham-parkfarm.co.uk

Set on a hill overlooking the Waveney valley, this peaceful and spacious farmhouse has been designed with the comfort and enjoyment of guests as paramount.

All the rooms are en-suite and have very comfortable beds, proper showers/baths extensive hospitality trays, Dvd, Freeview, and very comfortable easy chairs/ sofas to relax in!

There are lots of little extras, such as a fridge for guest use, bathrobes and wineglasses in the rooms. The extensive gardens are beautiful and available for guests to use at any time.

Breakfasts are taken in the sunny dining room, using as much home produce as possible, including bread, bacon, sausages, and preserves Everything else, where possible, is sourced locally if it is not available from the farm.

For evening meals; There are several local, and very good restaurants and pubs all within 5 miles. The farm is a haven for wildlife. There are maps for guests use, if they wish to wander round the extensive network of tracks on the farm and in the surrounding countryside.

Norwich, Southwold and the coast are about half an hour away, and there are lots of other local attractions. Your hosts have an extensive knowledge of the local area.

---

 stories and anecdotes   famous people   art and craft   entertainment and sport   walks

The Otter Trust

Earsham, Bungay, Suffolk NR35 2AF
Tel: 01986 893470

The Otter Trust is the largest and oldest otter conservation organisation in the world. Its collection of otters and its breeding successes with the British otter are unique. It's highly successful reintroduction programme, using young British otters bred at its centres, has released over 100 young otters which have thrived and bred in the world so that the population has returned to normal. Three lakes are home to a wide selection of European waterfowl. The flock of free-flying Barnacle geese is probably the largest in the country. The resident birds are joined by masses of wild waterfowl, many of which spend the entire summer on the lakes with their numbers swelled in the winter by hordes of visiting migrants.

largest collection of otters in natural enclosures are bred for re-introduction into the wild. Waterfowl, herons and deer are also kept here, and there are some lovely walks by the lakes and river.

FLIXTON
2 miles SW of Bungay on the B1062

🏛 Norfolk & Suffolk Aviation Museum

Javelin, Meteor, Sea Vixen, Westland Whirlwind: names that evoke earlier days of flying, and just four of the almost 40 aircraft on show at the **Norfolk and Suffolk Aviation Museum**, on the site of a USAAF Liberator base during the Second World War. There's a lot of associated material, both civil and military, covering the period from the First World War to the present day. The site incorporates the Royal Observer Corps Museum, RAF Bomber Command Museum, the Museum and Memorial of the 446th Bomb Group – the Bungay Buckeroos – and RAF Air-Sea Rescue and Coastal Command. Exhibitions cover the story of military and civil aviation in East Anglia, and visitors can

enjoy a pleasant walk on a raised boardwalk to the River Waveney. The Museum is open Sunday to Thursday in the summer; Tuesday, Wednesday and Sunday in winter.

Flixton is named after St Flik, the first Bishop of East Anglia, who is depicted in the village sign.

MENDHAM
6 miles SW of Bungay off the A143

This pretty little village on the Waveney was the birthplace of Sir Alfred Munnings RA, who was born at Mendham Mill, where his father was the miller. Sir Alfred's painting *Charlotte and her Pony* was the inspiration for the village sign, which was unveiled by his niece Kathleen Hadingham.

CARLTON COLVILLE
3 miles SW of Lowestoft on the B1384

🏛 East Anglia Transport Museum

Many a transport enthusiast has enjoyed a grand day out at the **East Anglia Transport Museum**, where children (and grown-ups of all ages) can climb aboard to enjoy rides on buses, trams and trolleybuses (one of the resident trolleybuses was built at the Garrett Works in Leiston). The East Suffolk narrow-gauge railway (2ft) winds its way around the site behind a fleet of diesel locomotives, and there's a 1930s street with all the authentic accessories, plus lorries, vans and steamrollers.

Also in Carlton Colville is the 15th-century Church of St Peter, which incorporated parts of other buildings when restored in the 19th century. Carlton Marshes is Oulton Broad's nature reserve, with grazing marsh and fen, reached by the Waveney Way footpath.

KESSINGLAND
3 miles S of Lowestoft off the A12

🐾 Suffolk Wildlife Park

A small resort with a big history, Palaeolithic and Neolithic remains have come to light in Kessingland, and traces of an ancient forest have been unearthed on the sea bed. At the time of William the Conqueror, Kessingland prospered with its herring industry and was a major fishing port rivalled only by Dunwich. The estuary gradually silted up, sealing off the river with a shingle bank and cutting off the village's major source of wealth. The tower of the church of St Edmund reaches up almost 100 feet – not unusual on the coast - where it provides a conspicuous landmark for sailors and fishermen.

Most of Kessingland's maritime trappings have now disappeared: the lighthouse on the cliffs was scrapped 100 years ago, the lifeboat lasted until 1936 (having saved 144 lives), and one of the several former coastguard stations was purchased by the writer Rider Haggard as a holiday home.

HILL HOUSE KOI

3 Hill House Gardens, Wrentham nr Southwold,
Suffolk NR34 7JF
Tel: 01502 675569 e-mail: geoff@hillhousekoi.com
website: www.hillhousekoi.com

When Geoffrey Wilson started keeping koi in 1977, he would never have predicted that these glorious fish would one day become his livelihood. Today, with no less than 10 grand champions to his credit, Geoff travels regularly to Japan to select and purchase relatively small to medium numbers of high-grade koi to offer for sale to hobbyists at affordable prices.

Specifically, he concentrates on body shape, skin quality, bloodlines, colour and pattern when choosing which fish to bring home. He visits Japan's top breeders, as well as some lesser known ones, in both Nigata and other recognised koi producing areas such as Torazo, Dinichai, Hiroy, Muruyama, Oofuchi, Seki, Marudo, Sakai (Isawa), Shinoda, Sakuma, Hosaki and Yamazaki. This has enabled him to import high grade tosai and nisai together with specific examples of go sanke koi in sansai, yonsai and gosai.

He also specialises in pond building & Fibre glassing ponds, fitting filtration, and lacron bubble beads and all pond related items. If the time has come where you would like to see quality koi for sale that are not readily available else where at amazing value for money, then perhaps you need to visit **Hill House Koi** in Suffolk to view some truly high grade koi.

🎬 stories and anecdotes 🦜 famous people 🎨 art and craft 🎭 entertainment and sport 🚶 walks

The village's major tourist attraction is the **Suffolk Wildlife Park**, 100 acres of coastal parkland that are home to a wide range of wild animals, from aardvarks to zebras by way of bats, flamingos, meerkats and sitatunga. The flamingos have their own enclosure. The latest attractions include a re-creation of an African savannah, complete with lions, giraffes, rhinos, cheetahs, hyenas and many other African animals and birds. Burmese pythons are used for snake-handling sessions, and there are regular birds of prey flying displays. This is very much a place for all the family, and children's amenities include an adventure play area and an under-5s soft play area.

COVEHITHE
7 miles S of Lowestoft off the A12

Leave the A12 at Wrentham and head for the tiny coastal village of Covehithe, remarkable for its 'church within a church'. The massive Church of St Andrew, partly funded by the Benedictine monks at Cluniac, was left to decline after being laid waste by Dowsing's men (see page 125). The villagers could not afford a replacement on the same grand scale, so in 1672 it was decided to remove the roof and sell off some of the material. From what was left, a small new church was built within the old walls. The original tower still stands, spared by Cromwell for use as a landmark for sailors.

Southwold

A town full of character and interest for the holidaymaker and for the historian. Though

Church within a Church, Covehithe

one of the most popular resorts on the east coast, Southwold has very little of the kiss-me-quick commercialism that spoils so many seaside towns. It's practically an island, bounded by creeks and marshes, the River Blyth and the North Sea, and has managed to retain the genteel atmosphere of the 19th century. There are many attractive buildings, from pink-washed cottages to elegant Georgian town houses, some of them ranged around a series of greens that were left undeveloped to act as firebreaks after much of the town was lost in the great fire of 1659.

In a seaside town whose buildings present a wide variety of styles, shapes and sizes, William Denny's Buckenham House is among the most elegant and interesting. On the face of it a classic Georgian town house, it's actually much older, dating probably from the

THE BLACK OLIVE

80 High Street, Southwold, Suffolk, IP18 6DP
Tel: 01502 722312

Delicatessens of outstanding range and quality are places to be treasured, and the citizens of Southwold are lucky indeed to have one of the best in the **Black Olive Delicatessen**. A magnet for food-lovers not just in Southwold but for many miles around, the Black Olive is located in the busy High Street of this marvellous town. Tracy Brown took over the premises in 2005; she knows that people in this part of the world appreciate the good things in life, and her shop fully lives up to the promise of the sign above the entrance that offers 'a Taste of the World'.

As the name suggests, olives are here in abundance, with at least seven varieties ready to scoop: plain black or green, pitted or stuffed with garlic, almonds and sundried tomatoes. There are marinated artichokes and pesto, a tub of succulent peppers stuffed with feta cheese, basil-marinated sardines, anchovies, plain, with chilli, with olives (banderillas), dressed crabs, shell-on prawns, potted shrimps, lobster, scampi, cockles, mussels and samphire.

There is a vast range of cold and cured meats, salamis and sausages, and the 40+ cheeses represent England, Wales, France, Italy, Spain, Greece, Switzerland and of course local cheeses. There's freshly baked bread, locally made cakes and pastries, jams and preserves, pickles and chutneys. That should be enough to get the taste buds tingling, but the Black Olive Delicatessen has much, much more. Only a visit will bring the whole amazing range to life.

CRABAPPLE

We are in for a treat, the Black Olive Delicatessen presents **'Crabapple'** a new shop in Southwold, a fantastic greengrocers. This newly designed shop in the market place offers not only a huge range of locally grown produce but also boasts the finest florist in the area.

An allotment less than 2 miles away provides much of the UK seasonal produce; strawberries, cabbages, cauliflowers, tomatoes, salad, peas and beans. (No air miles here!).

The display of produce brims with colour and beautiful aromas, Crabapple is fast becoming a destination in its own right, offering a full range of herbs, exotic fruit & vegetables, chutneys, plants, cut flowers and squeezed to order orange juice.

The talented florist can also meet any of your bespoke floristry needs, from bouquets, weddings, sympathy tributes and special events all delivered to your door.

middle of the 16th century. Richard Buckenham, a wealthy Tudor merchant, was the man who had it built and it was truly impressive in size, as can be deduced from the dimensions of the cellar (now the Coffee House). Many fine features survive, including moulded cornices, carefully restored sash windows, Tudor brickwork and heavy timbers in the ceilings.

The town, which was granted its charter by Henry VII in 1489, once prospered, like many of its neighbours, through herring fishing, and the few remaining fishermen share the harbour on the River Blyth with pleasure craft. Also adding to the period atmosphere is the pier, damaged in a storm then restored to its original length and re-opened in 2001.

There are also bathing huts, and a brilliant white lighthouse that's over 100 years old. It stands 100 feet tall and its light can be seen 17 miles out to sea. Beneath the lighthouse there is a little Victorian pub, the **Sole Bay Inn**, whose name recalls a battle fought off Southwold in 1672 between the British and French fleets and the Dutch. This was an episode in the third Anglo-Dutch War, when the Duke of York, Lord High Admiral of England and later to be crowned James II, used Sutherland House in Southwold as his headquarters and launched his fleet (along with that of the French) from here. One distinguished victim of this battle was Edward Montagu, 1st Earl of Sandwich, great-grandfather of the man whose gambling mania did not allow him time for a formal meal. By inserting slices of meat between slices of bread, the 4th Earl ensured that his name would live on. A later Duke of York, the one who became King George VI, visited the town from 1931 to 1938 for the Duke of York's Camp, which he founded for boys from

schools and factories.

The Sole Bay Inn is one of several owned by the local brewery Adnams. One of the best known pubs is the Lord Nelson, where traces can be seen of a smugglers' passageway leading to the cliffs. Where there were smugglers, there are usually ghosts, and here it's a man in a frock coat who disappears into the cliff face.

Southwold's maritime past is recorded in the **Museum** set in a Dutch-style cottage in Victoria Street. Open daily in the summer months, it records the famous battle and also features exhibits on local archaeology, geology and natural history, and the history of the Southwold railway. The **Southwold Sailors' Reading Room** contains pictures, ship models and other items, and the main

At the Seaside, Southwold

---

attraction at Gun Hill is a set of six 18-pounder guns, captured in 1746 at the Battle of Culloden and presented to the town (hitherto more or less undefended) by the Duke of Cumberland. Another museum, probably unique of its kind, is the **Amber Museum**, which traces the history of amber through millions of years. Open 9am to 5pm (11am to 4pm Sundays and Bank Holidays).

No visitor to Southwold should leave without spending some time in the splendid **Church of St Edmund King and Martyr**, which emerged relatively unscathed from the ravages of the Commonwealth. The lovely painted roof and wide screen are the chief glories, but the slim-stemmed 15th-century pulpit and the Elizabethan Holy Table must also be seen. Inside the church there's also a splendid Jack o' the Clock – a little wooden man in War of the Roses armour, holding a bell. A rope is pulled to sound the bell to mark the start of church services.

There's some great walking in the country around Southwold, both along the coast and inland. At Wangford, a mile or so inland, is the Perpendicular Church of St Peter and St Paul, built on the site of a Benedictine priory. Even closer to Southwold is Reydon Wood Nature Reserve.

Around Southwold

WALBERSWICK
1 mile S of Southwold on the B1387

🐾 Walberswick & Westleton Heaths

Towards the end of the 16th century, a smaller church was built within the original

---

TINKERS

The Village Green, Walberswick, Suffolk IP18 6TX
Tel: 01502 722259/725407

In former builder's premises on the attractive village green at Walberswick, **Tinkers** is a browser's delight, a lovely shop where old and new and beautiful vintage items jostle for space. It is an eclectic mix carefully sourced from individual artists and craftsmen, country auctions and fairtrade and eco-friendly suppliers.

Visitors will unearth quirky collectables, vintage fabrics, china and jewellery nestling among antiques, old kitchenalia and garden tools, country painted furniture and local art, along with interesting belts, baskets and sandals for that impulse buy. Beautiful home-sewn accessories such as aprons, cushions, tea cosies and lavender bags make pretty personal treats or ideal gifts to take on a country weekend with friends. Among the suppliers are Van Den Berg (silver jewellery), Paul and Tina Crisp (driftwood art), Nettie-B (home-sewn accessories), Stardust (children's clothes) and Lunn Antiqies (nightwear).

Owner Sarah Lawrence, who has had the shop since 2005, is very much part of Walberswick life and her shop is one of the focal points of the village. The Walberswick community supply Tinkers with poetry books, cards, videos, DVDs and artwork of local interest.

📖 stories and anecdotes 🦃 famous people ✏ art and craft ✒ entertainment and sport 𝕏 walks

INTERIOR DESIGN

Tom Hart one of Suffolk's leading interior designer's heads up, the practice delivering a fresh approach to interiors for businesses and home owners.

Hart Interior Design can provide innovative design thinking, matched with a highly professional service across a range of client budgets. The studio contains one of East Anglia's premier furnishing and design product libraries including exclusive products from London, Europe and America.

Our studio is open from 11am to 4pm Monday to Friday or at weekends by appointment. To ensure we can meet your requirements we would be grateful if you could telephone us prior to travelling. If you would like a meeting in your home or other premises please call us to arrange a convenient time.

Tel: **01502 478 901**
info@hartinteriordesign.co.uk
www.hartinteriordesign.co.uk

St Andrew's, which was by then in ruins through neglect. William Dowsing, Cromwell's Parliamentary Visitor to the churches of Suffolk, was to churches what Dr Beeching was to become to railways, and at Walberswick he destroyed 40 windows and defaced all the tombs on visits during the Civil War. The churchyard is now a nature reserve. South of the village is the bird sanctuary of **Walberswick & Westleton Heaths**.

For more than two centuries, Walberswick has been a magnet for painters, with the religious ruins, the beach and the sea being favourite subjects for visiting artists. The tradition continues unabated, and many academics have also made their homes here.

BLYTHBURGH
3 miles SW of Southwold, A1095 then A12

Holy Trinity   Toby's Walks

Blythburgh's **Church of Holy Trinity** is one of the wonders of Suffolk, a stirring sight as it rises from the reed beds, visible for miles around and floodlit at night to spectacular effect. This Cathedral of the Marshes reflects the days when Blythburgh was a prosperous port with a bustling quayside wool trade. With the silting up of the river, trade rapidly fell off and the church fell into decay. In 1577 the steeple of the 14th-century tower was struck by lightning in a severe storm; it fell into the nave, shattering the font and taking two lives. The scorch marks visible to this day on the north door are said to be the claw marks of the Devil in the guise of hellhound Black Shuck, left as he sped towards Bungay to terrify the congregation of St Mary's.

Disaster struck again in 1644, when Dowsing and his men smashed windows, ornaments and statues, blasted the wooden angels in the roof with hundreds of bullets and used the nave as a stable, with tethering rings screwed into the pillars of the nave. Luckily, the bench-end carvings escaped the desecration, not being labelled idolatrous. These depict the Labours of the Months, and the Seven Deadly Sins. Blythburgh also has a Jack o' the Clock, a brother of the figure at Southwold, and the priest's chamber over the south porch has been lovingly restored complete with an altar made with wood from HMS Victory. The angels may have survived, but the font was defaced to remove the signs of the sacraments.

A mile south, at the junction of the A12 and the Walberswick road, **Toby's Walks** is an ideal place for a picnic and, like so many places in Suffolk, has its own ghost story. This concerns Tobias Gill, a dragoon drummer serving with Sir Robert Rich's troop in the army of George II. He was found drunk on heathland next to the body of a Walberswick girl named Anne Blakemore. He was accused of her murder and sentenced to death by hanging in chains. His ghost is said to haunt the heath, but this should not - and does not - deter picnicers.

The Norman Gwatkin Nature Reserve is an area of marsh and fen with two hides, walkways and a willow coppice.

WENHASTON
5 miles W of Southwold off the A12

The Church of St Peter is well worth a detour. Saxon stones are embedded in its walls, but the most remarkable feature is the Doom (Last Judgement scene), said to have been painted around 1500 by a monk from Blythburgh.

HALESWORTH

8 miles W of Southwold on the A144

🏛 Halesworth & District Museum

Granted a market in 1222, Halesworth reached the peak of its trading importance when the River Blyth was made navigable as far as the town in 1756. A stroll around the streets reveals several buildings of architectural interest. The Market Place has a handsome Elizabethan timber-framed house, but the chief attraction for the visitor is the **Halesworth and District Museum** at the railway station, in Station Road, where exhibits on local history, railway and rural life can be seen. The station's unique moveable platforms are adjacent to the museum. Local geology and archaeology includes fossils, prehistoric and medieval finds from recent excavations.

Halesworth Gallery, at Steeple End, holds a collection of contemporary paintings, sculpture and other artwork in a converted row of 17th-century almshouses.

BRAMFIELD

7 miles SW of Southwold on the A144

🏛 St Andrew's Church

The massive Norman round tower of **St Andrew's Church** is separate from the main building and was built as a defensive structure, with walls over three feet thick. Dowsing (see page 125) ran riot here in 1643, destroying 24 superstitious pictures, one crucifix, a picture of Christ and 12 angels on the roof. The most important monument is one to Sir Arthur Coke, sometime Lord Chief Justice, who died in 1629, and his wife Elizabeth. Arthur is kneeling, resplendent in full armour, while

REMNANTS

55 Thoroughfare, Halesworth IP19 8AR
Tel: 01986 874306

Exciting trimmings and fabrics used to be so hard to find, but not any more. At **Remnants**, they specialize in everything from net curtains, attention-grabbing buttons and fastenings to exquisite ribbons, lace, braid, sequins, felt, beads and much more. And are adding new items all the time.

If like owner Julie Bird, you love fashion and frippery, take a closer look, because you won't be disappointed. Because alongside haberdashery, Julie is passionate about fabrics...whether you're looking for a plain or patterned, traditional or contemporary design, Remnants has in stock metres upon metres to suit every taste and every need from clothing and curtains to upholstery. There is an excellent choice of net curtaining with 24" - 90" drop, plus Cafe net. Even if the item you require isn't in stock Julie has several sample books you can order from.

A make up service is available on all fabrics and any alterations to clothes or curtains is never too much trouble - get in touch for more details. The store is open Mon, Tues, Wed, Fri 9am – 1pm & 2pm – 4pm and Sat 9am – 1pm.

🏛 historic building 🏛 museum and heritage 🏛 historic site 🍃 scenic attraction 🌱 flora and fauna

Elizabeth is lying on her bed with a baby in her arms. This monument is the work of Nicholas Stone, the most important English mason and sculptor of his day. The Cokes at one time occupied Bramfield Hall; another family, in residence for 300 years, were the Rabetts, whose coat of arms in the church punningly depicts rabbits on its shield.

DUNWICH
5 miles S of Southwold off the B1105

🏛 Museum 🌳 Dunwich Forest

🏛 Dunwich Heath 🌳 Minsmere RSPB

Dunwich is the town that hardly exists, yet it's one of the most popular tourist spots along the Suffolk coast. Dunwich was once the capital of East Anglia, founded by the Burgundian Christian missionary St Felix and for several centuries a major trading port (wool and grain out; wine, timber and cloth in) and a centre of fishing and shipbuilding. St Felix opened a school here. Several Kings built ships here, and the town had a mint, a fishing fleet and eight churches. In 1286 a storm blocked the entrance to the harbour, and by the middle of the next century the merchant trade was lost, the fishermen and shipbuilders moved out, work ceased on defending the coastline and the end of Dunwich was in sight. (But it sent two MPs to Westminster until 1832 – one of the most notable was Sir George Downing, who established Downing College in Cambridge.) For the next 700 years the relentless forces of nature continued to take their toll, and all that remains now of ancient Dunwich are the ruins of a Norman leper chapel (in the present churchyard), the archways of a medieval friary and a buttress of one of the nine churches that once served the community.

Today's village comprises a 19th-century church and a row of Victorian cottages, one of which houses **Dunwich Museum**. Local residents set up the museum in 1972 to tell 'the amazing story of a city lost to the sea'; the historical section has displays and exhibits from Roman, Saxon and medieval times, the centrepiece being an amazing scale model showing the town and harbour as it was at the height of its prosperity in the 13th century. There are also sections devoted to natural history, social history and the arts.

Experts have calculated that the main part of old Dunwich extended up to seven miles beyond its present boundaries, and the vengeance of the sea has thrown up inevitable stories of drama and mystery. The locals say that when a storm is threatening, the sound of submerged church bells can still be heard tolling under the waves as they shift in the currents. Other tales tell of strange lights in the ruined priory and the eerie chanting of long-gone monks.

Dunwich Forest, immediately inland from the village, is one of three – the others are further south at Tunstall and Rendlesham – named by the Forestry Commission as Aldewood Forest. Work started on these in 1920 with the planting of Scots pine, Corsican pine and some Douglas fir; oak and poplar were tried but did not thrive in the sandy soil. The three forests, which between them cover nearly 9,000 acres, were almost completely

Medieval Friary, Dunwich

🎭 stories and anecdotes 🕊 famous people 🎨 art and craft ✒ entertainment and sport 🚶 walks

Dunwich, Eastbridge and Minsmere

Distance: *9.0 miles (14.4 kilometres)*
Typical time: *240 mins*
Height gain: *15 metres*
Map: *Landranger 156*
Walk: *www.walkingworld.com ID:2016*
Contributor: *Brian and Anne Sandland*

ACCESS INFORMATION:

Take the unclassified road eastwards off the A12 just northeast of Yoxford (south of the station at Darsham) 4012 6918, signposted Westleton and Dunwich. In Westleton, turn left along the B1125 signed to Blythburgh and Dunwich, then after 300 yards go right, signed for Minsmere and Dunwich. Follow signs to Dunwich Heath (right after the track to Mount Pleasant Farm on the right). Park (for a small charge) in NT car park for toilets, restaurant, shop etc. Alternative free parking is available at Dunwich Beach or Sizewell. Both have toilets and a restaurant, but will involve there-and-back extensions to the walk.

DESCRIPTION:

You have the opportunity to visit the NT property at Dunwich Heath (wheelchairs can be used over a fair proportion of the heathland and can be borrowed by private arrangement. There is also the facility to borrow or be driven in powered carriages). In addition, you can visit the ancient, formerly influential town of Dunwich (now a small village, with much of its former splendour under the sea). There is a very interesting museum and a superb and widely renowned fish restaurant there. The fish are landed on the beach within feet of the kitchen door.

There is a pub at Dunwich and another quaint old one at Eastbridge, named the Eel's Foot (see page 133). You have several opportunities to visit

the RSPB Reserve at Minsmere - an internationally famous and important site with a very wide variety of birdlife and innumerable 'twitchers'! You then walk on through the majestic woodland of Sizewell Belts and arrive close to the famous power stations. There is a visitor centre there, which is well worth a visit. Finally you have the long stretch back along the seashore or through the dunes returning to your start point.

FEATURES:

Sea, Pub, Toilets, Play Area, National Trust/NTS, Wildlife, Birds, Flowers, Great Views, Good for Wheelchairs.

WALK DIRECTIONS:

1 | The view from the NT car park where you start and end your walk. This is looking south to Sizewell and shows the final leg of the walk, back along the seashore or dunes.

2 | The car park, looking north. The cottages were previously inhabited by coastguards. Just to the left of this view are the main toilets (disabled toilets are at the cottages). Head for the toilets and go through the gap between pine trees to the right of them.

3 | Join this wide track and follow it left over the heath. (Do not take the track that rises to the right.) Continue, striaght on ignoring turns off to right and left, until you enter woodland at a stile.

4 | After the stile, continue in the same direction. At a T-junction of tracks turn left (gated path to the right). Having arrived at a narrow road, cross straight over and continue on as before, but now with fields to right and left of your track. There will be telegraph poles and wires to your right. Soon Sizewell Power Station should be visible away to the left. Enter more woodland and descend to meet another narrow road on a bend.

5 | Go straight ahead along the road (Minsmere RSPB Reserve is left). Continue to follow this road when it bears left at a house. Ignore the track off right. The house has a notice on its tall gates: Warning strange dog. It's true! There's a

🏚 historic building 🏛 museum and heritage 🏚 historic site 🐾 scenic attraction 🌿 flora and fauna

small Bedlington Terrier that can literally run up the gates! Cross the bridge over the Minsmere River, then arrive at the Eel's Foot Inn (see page 133) on your left.

6 | Carry on, still on the same road. Ignore the footpath off left, signposted Minsmere Sluice 1 and a half (unless you want to shorten the walk - in which case follow the path to the seafront and turn left). Pass the track to Lower Abbey Farm (left) and stay on the road until you reach a signposted footpath left, leading to an abandoned cottage.

7 | Take this path and when you reach the cottage, after 100 yards, turn right along a broad track between hedges. Depending on the season, the hedgerows will be covered in honeysuckle, dog roses or blackberries. Pass a farm on your right. Go gently downhill, then up again. When you reach the belt of trees on your left, look for a wide gate and stile.

8 | Cross the stile and follow the broad track through the left-hand edge of the trees, ignoring several turns off to the right. When the trees become denser on the left, you begin to descend slightly. Then at the bottom the main track bears right. Go with it: a black arrow on a post points the way.

9 | Now you will be closer to the right edge of the trees and will glimpse Sizewell Power Station over to the right. Follow the direction indicated right by two more black arrows close to each other and the power station is clearly visible, initially ahead, then as the track bears left, more to your right. Another black arrow sends you right at a fork. You have pine trees on your left and a ditch and field right. Suddenly the track veers left, away from the power station. Here you must turn off right at another black arrow.

10 | Go over two bridges and a wooden walkway.

11 | When you reach another black arrow just before the mound, which forms the boundary of the power station, go left as it indicates and follow the path through gorse to the end of the mound on your right.

12 | At the large concrete blocks (Second World War tank trap remnants) turn left along a wide grass track. The sea will now be on your right a couple of hundred yards away, beyond grass-covered dunes. You will walk parallel to it along this grass track for approximately three miles to return to the coastguard cottages, which you can see in the distance at the car park.

13 | Carry straight on!

14 | When you reach Minsmere Sluice (the point at which the shortened walk rejoins) you will also be at the SE entrance to the RSPB reserve and there will be the ruins of an ancient chapel over to your left. This is just after a metal windmill, which works incessantly at draining the marshes. Carry on as before (or turn left, if coming from Eastbridge direct). Gradually, as the huge dome of Sizewell diminishes behind, so do the coastguard cottages grow in size until you finally arrive back at the top of the final slope and at your car.

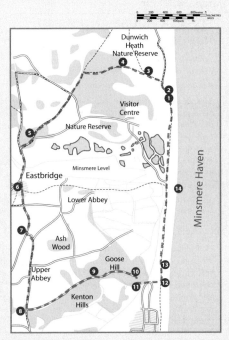

devastated in the hurricane of October 1987, Rendlesham alone losing more than a million trees. Replanting will take many years to be established.

South of the village lies **Dunwich Heath**, one of Suffolk's most important conservation areas, comprising the beach, splendid heather, a field study centre, a public hide and an information centre and restaurant in converted coastguard cottages. The heath is set within an Area of Outstanding Natural Beauty and is a designated Site of Special Scientific Interest. Around Dunwich Heath are the attractive villages of Westleton, Middleton, Theberton and Eastbridge.

In **Westleton**, the 14th century thatched church of St Peter, built by the monks of Sibton Abbey, has twice seen the collapse of its tower. The first fell down in a hurricane in 1776; its smaller wooden replacement collapsed when a

bomb fell during the Second World War. The village is also the main route of access to the RSPB-managed **Minsmere Nature Reserve**, the most important sanctuary for wading birds in eastern England. The marshland was flooded during the Second World War, and nature and this wartime emergency measure created the perfect habitat for innumerable birds. More than 100 species nest here, and a similar number of birds visit throughout the year. It is thus a birdwatcher's paradise, with many hides, and the Suffolk Coastal Path runs along the foreshore. A little way inland from Westleton lies Darsham, where another nature reserve is home to many varieties of birds and flowers.

YOXFORD

10 miles SW of Southwold on the A12

Once an important stop on the London-to-Yarmouth coaching route, Yoxford now

---

SUFFOLK HOUSE ANTIQUES

High Street, Yoxford, Suffolk IP17 3EP
Tel: 01728 668122
e-mail: andrew.singleton@suffolk-house-antiques.co.uk
website: www.suffolk-house-antiques.co.uk

Suffolk House Antiques is a dealer of 17th- and 18th-century oak and country furniture and associated works of art in Yoxford. Established more than 17 years ago by Andrew Singleton, today it is one of the country's leading dealers in early oak, walnut and country furniture, the shop boasts seven showrooms and stock stretches to more than 300 pieces. Prices range from under £100 to over £50,000.

Andrew, as a long-standing member of the British Antiques Dealers Association, has supplied pieces to many of the leading collectors of early furniture in the UK and abroad.

Most items of early furniture can be found here dressers, cupboards, chests of drawers, boxes and coffers and tables and chairs. The 'miscellaneous' collection includes stools, settles and bureaux as well as metalwork and carvings, and there is also a range of mirrors, ceramics (mostly Delftware) and tapestries. Andrew is always happy to search for particular pieces for clients. Parking is available. Open Monday, Tuesday, Thursday, Friday and Saturday 10am-1pm and 2.15pm - 5.15pm, or at other times by appointment.

🏛 historic building 🏛 museum and heritage 🏛 historic site 🌿 scenic attraction 🌱 flora and fauna

attracts visitors with its pink-washed cottages and its arts and crafts, antiques and food shops. Look for the cast-iron signpost outside the church, with hands pointing to London, Yarmouth and Framlingham set high enough to be seen by the driver of a stagecoach.

THEBERTON

12 miles SW of Southwold on the B1122

The churchyard at Theberton contains a reminder that this part of the coast was closely involved in warfare. In June 1917 a 600ft Zeppelin came in at Orford Ness and dropped bombs near Martlesham. It was shot down, and the 16 members of the crew who were killed are buried in Theberton churchyard.

SIBTON

12 miles SW of Southwold on the A1120

Two miles west of Yoxford, on the A1120, Sibton is known chiefly for its abbey (only the ruins remain), the only Cistercian house in Suffolk. The Church of St Peter is certainly not a ruin, however, and should be seen for its fine hammerbeam and collar roof.

SAXMUNDHAM

12 miles SW of Southwold off the A12

A little town that was granted its market charter in 1272. On the font of the church in Saxmundham is the carving of a woodwose - a tree spirit or green man. He and others like him have given their name to a large number of pubs in Suffolk and elsewhere. The Town Museum is a recent addition to the visitor attractions.

BRUISYARD

4 miles NW of Saxmundham off the B1119

The tiny village church sits on a hill just above a ford. The Elizabethan vestry was built with material taken from a local nunnery dissolved by Henry VIII in 1539.

PEASENHALL

6 miles NW of Saxmundham on the A1120

🏠 Woolhall

A little stream runs along the side of the main street in Peasenhall, whose buildings present several styles and ages. Most distinguished is

---

CARDINAL COTTAGE

Pory Street, Sibton, Saxmundham, Suffolk IP17 2JH
Tel: 01728 660111
e-mail: jan.belton@btinternet.com
website: www.cardinalcottageholidays.co.uk

Cardinal Cottage is a self-catering, atmospheric 16th Century beamed cottage set in the peaceful picturesque village of Sibton in rural Suffolk. The property was beautifully restored by the owners, Eric and Jan Belton, with great attention to detail and with a caring attitude for their guests'comfort and requiremets. Decorated and furnished to a high standard throughout, accomodation comprises hallway, sitting room, dining room and fully fitted kitchen on the ground floor: on the first floor there are two double bedrooms with spectacular beams, a light and airy single room and bathroom with shower, Tourist board four star rating - families and pets welcome.

🎭 stories and anecdotes   🦜 famous people   ✏ art and craft   ✒ entertainment and sport   🚶 walks

HIGH HOUSE FARM & WOODLODGE

High House Farm, Cransford, nr Woodbridge,
Suffolk IP13 9PD
Tel: 01728 663461
e-mail: info@highhousefarm.co.uk
website: www.highhousefarm.co.uk

High House Farm and **Woodlodge** provide guests with a choice of superb accommodation in an idyllic country setting off the B1119 between Saxmundham and Framlingham. Both premises stand in attractive gardens on Sarah and Tim Kindred's arable farm. High House Farm is a beautifully restored 15th century farmhouse with two bedrooms for Bed & Breakfast guests – a double with en suite shower and a family room with adjacent private bathroom. Guests can relax in a comfortable lounge, and the day starts with a generous breakfast served round a traditional farmhouse table in the large oak-beamed

dining room. Families with children are welcome, and high chairs and selection of toys and books are provided. Woodlodge was built around 1830 as a country mansion and later became two gamekeepers' cottages. As a self-catering holiday home it was renovated to offer all the modern conveniences while retaining its period appeal. Two family rooms and a twin room offer comfortable accommodation for up to eight guests, with ample living space, a fully equipped kitchen and play equipment for the youngest guests (a cot and high chair are also available). Both B&B and self-catering guests have access to paths through 18 acres of woodland, and both are ideally situated for exploring the delights of coast and countryside in the region.

the old timbered **Woolhall**, splendidly restored to its 15th-century grandeur. The oddest is certainly a hall in the style of a Swiss chalet, built for his workers by James Josiah Smyth, grandson of the founder of James Smyth & Sons. This company, renowned for its agricultural drills, was for more than two centuries the dominant industrial presence in Peasenhall. On the south side of St Michael's churchyard stands the 1805 drill-mill where James Smyth manufactured his nonpareil seed drills, one of which is on display in Stowmarket's museum.

FRISTON

3 miles SE of Saxmundham off the A1094

Friston's post mill, the tallest in England, is a prominent sight on the Aldeburgh-Snape road, moved from Woodbridge in 1812 just after its construction. It worked by wind until 1956, then by engine until 1972. St Mary's Church dates from the 11th century.

LEISTON

4 miles E of Saxmundham off the B1119

[icon] Long Shop Museum [icon] Abbey

The first **Leiston Abbey** was built on Nunsmere marshes in 1182, but in 1363 the Earl of Suffolk rebuilt it on its present site. It became one of the largest and most prestigious monasteries in the country, and its wealth probably spelled its ruin, as it fell within Henry VIII's plan for the Dissolution of the Monasteries. The ruins of the second abbey are the finest monastic ruins in this part of the county.

For 200 years the biggest name in Leiston was that of Richard Garrett, who founded

SIMPLY DELICIOUS

70 High Street, Leiston, Suffolk IP16 4BZ
Tel: 01728 833078

Simply Delicious café & deli in Leiston celebrates its 12th birthday this year, thanks to top quality products and superb customer relations. Shaun Wilson, proprietor, is a qualified chef and extremely passionate about food. Simply delicious offers a mouth-watering variety of fresh baked foods from pizza to sumptuous cakes and meals such as salads, quiches, pasta and whole food lasagnes. Shaun is always on hand baking throughout the day and while the media is guilty of exaggeration you can say without hyperbole that whenever the shop is open, Shaun is inside being kept busy.

Following your fantastic lunch, snack or afternoon tea you probably will not be able to resist the tempting range of foods available from the deil counter such as fresh coffee beans, free range meat and organic products, chutneys and a great selection of cheeses. Everything you will need to make food special again. Shaun stocks 10 cheeses 2-3 of which are locally sourced and immensely popular. These include, *Suffolk Gold* a creamy semi-hard farmhouse cheese, delicately flavoured and delicious eaten with oatcakes or an apple and *Suffolk Blue* a creamy rich blue-veined cheese, soft and luxurious – highly recommended. Remember – love food!

EELS FOOT INN

Eastbridge, Leiston, Suffolk IP16 4SN
Tel: 01728 830154
e-mail: corrinewebber@aol.com   website: www.theeelsfootinn.co.uk

Eastbridge is a village on the Suffolk coast, right next to the RSPB Minsmere Reserve. Its claim to fame is the **Eels Foot Inn**, a well-known smugglers' haunt, the Eels Foot has been here since the 1700s. The swinging sign outside shows an eel hopping across a reedy marsh river, the tip of its tail encased in a huge black boot, there are several theories as to its origin; the landlord suggests that the local eels are born with feet because of the proximity to Sizewell.

The freshwater marshes bordering the Inn afford plenty of opportunity for watching an abundance of birds and butterflies. A Bridleway leads you through scenic countryside directly to the sea, a comfortable walk of less than an hour, linking to the Suffolk Coastal Path and Dunwich to the north.

At the Eels Foot you can enjoy Adnams Cask Ales and wines or sample a glass of Suffolk Aspalls Cider. Full meals or bar snacks with a good choice of vegetarian options are available every day. The menu is simple and appetising: Suffolk ham with fried eggs and chips, and beer-battered cod. The Eels Foot has a long tradition of Folk Music and musicians still gather on a Thursday evening for a jam session. This 'Squit Night' attracts minstrels from near and far. Guitars, Banjos, Concertinas and even the Bagpipes can sometimes be enjoyed playing together in harmony! For a more Traditional Folk experience come along on the last Sunday in the month and join in the chorus of an old sea shanty or two.

The Eels Foot has six brand new en-suite bedrooms, one with wheelchair access. All rooms are comfortably furnished with TV and DVD players, coffee and tea making facilities and have views over the surrounding countryside. This is very much a place you arrive as a guest, but depart as a friend.

an engineering works here in 1778 after starting a business in Woodbridge. In the early years ploughs, threshers, seed drills and other agricultural machinery were the main products, but the company later started one of the country's first production lines for steam machines. The Garrett works are now the **Long Shop Museum**, the factory buildings having been lovingly restored, and many of the Garrett machines are now on display, including traction engines, a steam-driven tractor and a road roller; there's also a section where the workings of steam engines are explained. During the Second World War the works manufactured radar equipment and sections of Mulberry Harbours. A small area of the museum recalls the USAAF's 357th fighter group, who flew from an airfield outside Leiston during the Second World War. One of their number, a Captain Chuck Yeager, was the first man to fly faster than the speed of sound (tel: 01728 832189).

The Garrett works closed in 1980, but what could have been a disastrous unemployment situation was alleviated to some extent by the nuclear power station at Sizewell. The coast road in the centre of Leiston leads to this establishment, where visitors can take tours - on foot with access to buildings at Sizewell A - or by minibus, with a guide and videos, round Sizewell B.

ALDRINGHAM
4 miles E of Saxmundham on the B1122

🅟 Craft Market

Aldringham's church is notable for its superb 15th century font, and the village inn was once a haunt of smugglers. It now helps to refresh the visitors who flock to the Aldringham **Craft Market**, founded in 1958

and extending over three galleries, with a serious selection of arts and crafts, clothes and gifts, pottery, basketry, books and cards.

THORPENESS
6 miles E of Saxmundham on the B1353

Thorpeness is a unique seaside village with a charm all of its own. Buying up a considerable packet of land called the Sizewell estate in 1910, the architect, barrister and playwright Glencairn Stuart Ogilvie created what he hoped would be a fashionable resort with cottages, some larger houses and an atmospheric and lovely 65-acre boating and pleasure lake called the Meare, which is one metre in depth throughout and fed by the River Hundred.

The 85-foot water tower, built to aid in the lake's construction, looked out of place, so Ogilvie disguised it as a house. Known ever since as the House in the Clouds, it is now available to rent as a holiday home. The neighbouring mill, moved lock, stock and millstones from Aldringham, stopped pumping in 1940, but has been restored and now houses a visitor centre.

Every August, in the week following the Aldeburgh Carnival, a regatta is held on the Meare, culminating in a splendid fireworks show.

ALDEBURGH
6 miles SE of Saxmundham on the A1094

🏛 Moot Hall 🕭 The Benjamin Britten Connection: the Scallop Shell, the Red House
🏛 Church of St Peter & St Paul 🏛 Martello Tower
🅟 Aldeburgh Festival

And so down the coast road to Aldeburgh, another coastal town that once prospered as a port with major fishing and shipbuilding industries. Drake's Greyhound and Pelican

were built at Slaughden, now taken by the sea, and during the 16th century some 1,500 people were engaged in fishing. Both industries declined as shipbuilding moved elsewhere and the fishing boats became too large to be hauled up the shingle. Suffolk's best-known poet, George Crabbe, was born at Slaughden in 1754 and lived through the village's hard times. He reflected the melancholy of those days when he wrote of his fellow townsmen:

Here joyless roam a wild amphibious race,
With sullen woe displayed in every face;
Who far from civil arts and social fly,
And scowl at strangers with suspicious eye.

He was equally evocative concerning the sea and the river, and the following lines written about the River Alde could apply to several others in the county:

With ceaseless motion comes and goes the tide
Flowing, it fills the channel vast and wide;
Then back to sea, with strong majestic sweep
It rolls, in ebb yet terrible and deep;
Here samphire-banks and salt-wort bound the flood
There stakes and seaweed withering on the mud;
And higher up, a ridge of all things base,
Which some strong tide has rolled upon the place.

It was Crabbe who created the character of the solitary fisherman Peter Grimes, later the subject of an opera composed by another Aldeburgh resident, **Benjamin Britten**.

Aldeburgh's role gradually changed into that of a holiday resort, and the Marquess of Salisbury, visiting early in the 19th century, was one of the first to be attracted by the idea of sea-bathing without the crowds. By the middle of the century the grand houses that had sprung up were joined by smaller residences, the railway had arrived, a handsome water tower was put up (1860) and Aldeburgh prospered once more. There were even plans for a pier, and construction started in 1878, but the project proved too difficult or too expensive and was halted, the rusting girders being removed some time later.

One of the town's major benefactors was Newson Garrett, a wealthy businessman who was the first mayor under the charter of the Local Government Act of 1875. This colourful character also developed the Maltings at Snape (see under Snape), but is perhaps best remembered through his remarkable daughter, Elizabeth, who was the first woman doctor in England (having qualified in Paris at a time when women could not qualify here) and the first woman mayor (of Aldeburgh, in 1908). This lady married the shipowner James Skelton Anderson, who established the golf club in 1884.

If Crabbe were alive today he would have a rather less cantankerous opinion of his fellows, especially at carnival time on a Monday in August when the town celebrates with a colourful procession of floats and marchers, a fireworks display and numerous other events.

As for the arts, there is, of course, the **Aldeburgh Festival**, started in 1948 by Britten and others; the festival's main venue is Snape Maltings, but many performances take place in Aldeburgh itself. The **Red House**, where Britten lived from 1957 until his death in 1976, and where he composed many of his greatest works (*War Requiem, Death in Venice*), is open at certain times for guided tours. Tel:

01728 452615 for details and bookings.

The town's maritime connections remain very strong. There has been a lifeboat here since 1851, and down the years many acts of great heroism have been recorded. The very modern lifeboat station is one of the town's chief attractions for visitors, and there are regular practice launches from the shingle beach. It is recorded that in 1843 Aldeburgh had about 200 licensed fishing boats, catching sole, lobster, sprats and herring in great numbers. Just a handful of fishermen still put out to sea from the beach, selling their catch from their little wooden huts, while a thriving yacht club is the base for sailing on the Orde and, sometimes, on the sea. On the beach at the northern edge of town is a remarkable work of art – a giant steel **Scallop Shell** designed by the renowned Suffolk-born artist Maggi Hambling. It is a monument to Benjamin Britten, and the words on its rim – 'I hear those voices that will not be drowned' – are taken from Britten's opera *Peter Grimes*. The area inland from here is a nature reserve.

At the very southern tip of the town, the **Martello Tower** is one of 75 hastily built on the coast between Suffolk and Sussex against the threat of a Napoleonic invasion. This one, built with a million bricks, dates from 1814 and never saw action, although its four guns were manned until the middle of the 19th century. It serves as a reminder of the power of the sea: old pictures show it standing well back from the waves, but now the seaward side of the moat has disappeared and the shingle is constantly being shored up to protect it. Beyond it, a long strip of marsh and shingle stretches right down to the mouth of the river at Shingle Street.

Back in town there are several interesting buildings, notably the **Moot Hall** and the

🏛 historic building   🏛 museum and heritage   🏛 historic site   🦆 scenic attraction   🌿 flora and fauna

parish **Church of St Peter and St Paul**. The Moot Hall is a 16th-century timber-framed building that was built in what was once the centre of town. It hasn't moved, but the sea long ago took away several houses and streets. Inside the Hall is a museum of town history and finds from the nearby Snape burial ship. Britten set the first scene of *Peter Grimes* in the Moot Hall. A sundial on the south face of the Hall proclaims, in Latin, that it only tells the time when the sun shines.

The church, which stands above the town as a very visible landmark for mariners, contains a memorial to George Crabbe and a beautiful stained-glass window, the work of John Piper, depicting three Britten oratorios: *Curlew River, The Burning Fiery Furnace* and *The Prodigal Son*. Britten is buried in the churchyard, alongside his companion Peter

Pears and the musician Imogen Holst, daughter of Gustav Holst, sometime Director of the Aldeburgh Festival and for several years Britten's musical assistant. Elizabeth Garrett Anderson is buried in the family grave enclosed by wrought-iron railings. Part of the churchyard is set aside for the benefit of wildlife.

SNAPE

3 miles S of Saxmundham on the A1094

Snape Maltings

This 'boggy place' has a long and interesting history. In 1862 the remains of an Anglo-Saxon ship were discovered here, and since that time regular finds have been made, with some remarkable cases of almost perfect preservation. Snape, like Aldeburgh, has benefited over the years from the

Iken and Snape

Distance: *5.3 miles (8.5 kilometres)*

Typical time: *150 mins*

Height gain: *12 metres*

Map: *Explorer 212*

Walk: *www.walkingworld.com ID:640*

Contributor: *Brian and Anne Sandland*

ACCESS INFORMATION:

From Woodbridge take the A1152 eastwards. When the road forks (still on the A1152), bear left towards Snape. At Tunstall, just after the right-angled bend, turn left onto the B1069 (signposted Snape). After you pass through the northern end of the Tunstall Forest, the road from Blaxhall comes in from the left. Ignore this, but take the next turn right (to Orford/Iken). At the next left (signposted Iken 2), turn left and after 150 yards look for a picnic site sign on the left. This takes you down a narrow track to the picnic site at Iken Cliff with glorious views over the Alde. Park here.

DESCRIPTION:

Wildlife and birds abound. There is also varied plantlife. A visit to St Botolph's Church can be included and after the walk through the forest you can see the wonderful variety of attractions at Snape Maltings. These include an internationally famous concert hall, Henry Moore sculpture, galleries full of furniture, books, pictures, crafts, antiques and food. There is a restaurant and even a small garden centre.

FEATURES:

Toilets and tea and shops are only available if you include Snape Maltings. River, Church, Wildlife, Birds, Flowers, Great Views.

WALK DIRECTIONS:

1 | Head down into the right-hand corner of the picnic site.

2 | Take the footpath that leads along the Alde to Cliff Reach. Continue close to the river, finally turning away from the river to reach a road.

3 | Leave the river area by steps and walk to the road. If you want to visit the church turn left, and after 75 yards, left again (signed Iken Church). There are superb views along and across the Alde from the churchyard. Return to the point where you first joined the road then continue, rising slightly. Go left at the junction (signed to Sandy Lane). Pass a number of cottages and after the one named The Drift, where the road bends sharp left, go right along a track.

4 | Follow this signposted track. At trees on the right, bear right. Then go left, following the edge of the trees (ignore track off left through the trees) to arrive at a broad cross-track. Go slightly right, then left along another track, to continue in your original direction, this time with trees on

Iken Wood

Iken Marshes

P

Iken

Iken Heath

Iken Common

Fire Tower

Tunstall Common

Tunstall Forest

🏛 historic building   🏚 museum and heritage   🏛 historic site   🌳 scenic attraction   🐦 flora and fauna

your right. When trees on the right end, go right and then left with the track and exit carefully through bushes onto the road. Cross the road and at a broad cross-track, go right for 30 yards.

5 | Turn left at the yellow waymark. Now walk between young pine trees on either side (planted after the devastation of the hurricane of 1987). At next fork bear right along a narrower path. DO NOT follow main track with yellow waymark. After 150 yards you'll reach another wide cross-track. Cross straight over and follow the track leading straight ahead, which is now wider than the footpath you have just left. Carry on in this direction, ignoring all turns off to the right and left until you suddenly and unexpectedly come across cottages on your right (Heath Cottages). Join its drive and walk on to a junction. Take the right turn following the direction of a sign with the number 24. (Do not take the track immediately right).

6 | Despite what the map indicates here, there is no fire tower. After 100 yards or so the broad track bears right and runs straight into the distance. Leave it and take the narrower grass track, which snakes off left. A white waymark should be visible on a post at the intersection. You will soon pass through a clearing. Once again, ignore tuns off to right and left and carry on to meet a road.

7 | Turn right and follow this exceedingly pleasant, narrow metalled lane, which bisects the forest, until you reach a crossroads. Cross over and continue straight ahead until you reach the picnic place sign, pointing left to your car and the start point.

8 | If you wish to visit the Maltings, with all its attractions, descend to the bottom left of the picnic site this time. Then follow the footpath left along the Alde. To return, retrace your steps. (If you have had enough walking you could, of course take your car to the Maltings. There is ample free parking.)

philanthropy of the Garrett family, one of whose members built the primary school and set up the Maltings, centre of the Aldeburgh Music Festival.

The last 30-odd years have seen the development of the Snape Maltings Riverside Centre, a group of shops and galleries located in a complex of restored Victorian granaries and malthouses that is also the setting for the renowned Aldeburgh festival.

The Maltings began their designated task of converting grain into malt in the 1840s, and continued thus until 1965, when the pressure of modern techniques brought them to a halt. There was a real risk of the buildings being demolished, but George Gooderham, a local farmer, bought the site to expand his animal feeds business and soon saw the potential of the redundant buildings (his son Jonathan is the current owner of the site).

The Concert Hall came first, in 1967, and in 1971 the Craft Shop was established as the first conversion of the old buildings for retail premises. Conversion and expansion continue to this day, and in the numerous outlets visitors can buy anything from fudge to country-style clothing, from herbs to household furniture, silver buttons to top hats. Plants and garden accessories are also sold, and art galleries feature the work of local painters, potters and sculptors. The Centre hosts regular painting, craft and decorative art courses, and more recent expansion saw the creation of an impressive country-style store.

A short distance west of Snape, off the B1069, lies Blaxhall, famed for its growing stone. The Blaxhall Stone, which lies in the yard of Stone Farm, is reputed to have grown to its present size (five tons) from a comparative pebble the size of a football, when it first came to local attention 100 years ago. Could there be more Blarney than Blaxhall at work here?

Woodbridge

🏠 Tide Mill and Buttrum's Mill 📷 Museum

📷 Suffolk Punch Heavy Horse Museum

Udebyge, Wiebryge, Wodebryge, Wudebrige - just some of the ways of spelling this splendid old market town since it was first mentioned in writing back in AD970. As to what the name means, it could simply be 'wooden bridge' or 'bridge by the wood', but the most likely and most interesting explanation is that it is derived from Anglo-Saxon words meaning Woden's (or Odin's) town.

Standing at the head of the Deben estuary, it is a place of considerable charm with a wealth of handsome, often historic buildings

and a considerable sense of history, as both a market town and a port.

The shipbuilding and allied industries flourished here, as at most towns on the Suffolk coast, and it is recorded that both Edward III, in the 14th century, and Drake in the 16th sailed in Woodbridge ships. There's still plenty of activity on and by the river, though nowadays it is all leisure-orientated. The town's greatest benefactor was Thomas Seckford, who rebuilt the abbey, paid for the chapel in the north aisle of St Mary's Church and founded the original almshouses in Seckford Street. In 1575 he gave the town the splendid Shire Hall on Market Hill. Originally used as a corn exchange, it now houses the **Suffolk Punch Heavy Horse Museum**, with an exhibition devoted to the Suffolk Punch breed of heavy working horse, the oldest such breed in the world. The

---

JULIE PHIPPS

17 Church Street, Woodbridge, Suffolk IP12 1DS
Tel: 01394 387115
e-mail: julie@juliephipps.com
website: www.juliephipps.com

Tucked away in the splendid market town of Woodbridge, you will discover colourful and inspiring contemporary crafts and vintage homeware at **Julie Phipps**. If you just love the nostalgia of finding bygone treasures, Julie Phipps provides vintage homeware items that will bring back fond memories and make you feel good, whilst providing a unique and individual look to any décor. Whether you are a collector, enthusiast or seeking to decorate your home in an eclectic mix of past and present eras, come and visit this store to browse through the gorgeous 'delectables' on show.

Julie was once a documentary photographer but since discovering her love for crafts and glass making she has turned her passion into a successful little enterprise. Her store is filled with items from near and far-flung places, you can expect to find wonderful displays of: Welsh quilts to hand embroidered throws from Bangladesh and wooden platters from Morocco.

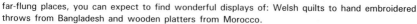

history of the breed and its rescue from near-extinction in the 1960s is covered in fascinating detail. There's also a section dealing with the other famous Suffolk breeds – the Red Poll cattle, the Suffolk sheep and the Large Black pigs. Opposite the Shire Hall is **Woodbridge Museum**, a treasure trove of information on the history of the town and its more notable residents; from here it is a short stroll down the cobbled alleyway to the magnificent parish church of St Mary, where Seckford was buried in 1587.

Seckford naturally features prominently in the museum, along with the painter Thomas

---

BEARS & STITCHES

4 Cumberland Street, Woodbridge, Suffolk IP12 4AB
Tel/Fax: 01394 388999

Pauline Backhouse, a lover of all kinds of crafts for many years, took the plunge in 1998 and turned a hobby into a successful business. In two rooms on the ground floor of a listed building, **Bears & Stitches** holds a wide-ranging and ever-changing stock of collectors' bears like Steiff, Hermann and Russ, other huggable soft toys (spot Rupert Bear and his chums), dolls house furniture and fittings and craft supplies including needlework, jewellery making, scrapbooking, card making, knitting wools and sewing threads (multiple winner of Needlework Retailer of the Year for East Anglia). Open 9.30 to 5 Monday to Saturday. A second Bears & Stitches (open Tuesday to Saturday) is in South Woodham Ferrers, Essex. Tel: 01245 328859.

FRAMES BY ROBERT

14 New Street, Woodbridge, Suffolk IP12 1DX
Tel: 01394 383467
e-mail: framesbyrobert@yahoo.co.uk

There's no doubting the warmth of the welcome extended by Robert Hewitt at his delightful artists' shop. **Frames by Robert** occupies a listed 17th century building on a corner site in the attractive and historic town of Woodbridge. Opened by Robert in 1985, it is stocked with paints,

brushes, easels, frames and everything else that an artist might require, with top brands including Windsor & Newton, Sennelier, Liquitex, Carnd'Ache, Fabriano and Aquarelle Arches. The range of products increases all the time, and if it's not on the shelves Robert will do his very best to find it. Frames by Robert also, naturally, sells frames and offers a

bespoke framing service; Robert will also undertake restoration of paintings.

Frames of Robert is open from 9.30 to 5 Monday, Tuesday, Thursday and Friday; 10 to 1.15 and 2.30 to 5 Wednesday and 9 to 4ish Saturday.

ⓕ stories and anecdotes 🕊 famous people 🎨 art and craft 🖌 entertainment and sport 🚶 walks

Churchyard, the map-maker Isaac Johnson and the poet Edward Fitzgerald. 'Old Fitz' was something of an eccentric and, for the most part, fairly reclusive. He loved Woodbridge and particularly the River Deben, where he often sailed in his little boat, *Scandal*.

Woodbridge is lucky enough to have two marvellous mills, both in working order, and both great attractions for the visitor. The **Tide Mill**, on the quayside close to the town centre, dates from the late 18th century (though the site was mentioned 600 years previously) and worked by the power of the tide until 1957. It has been meticulously restored and the waterwheel still turns, fed by a recently created pond, which replaced the original huge mill pond when it was turned into a marina. **Buttrum's Mill**, named after the last miller, is a tower mill standing just off the A12 bypass a mile west of the town centre. A marvellous sight, its six storeys make it the tallest surviving tower mill in Suffolk. There is a ground-floor display of the history and workings of the mill.

Many of the town's streets are traffic-free, so shopping is a real pleasure. If you should catch the Fitzgerald mood and feel like 'a jug of wine and a loaf of bread', Woodbridge can oblige with a good variety of pubs and restaurants.

Around Woodbridge

SUTTON HOO
1 mile E of Woodbridge off the B1083

🏛 Sutton Hoo

A mile or so east of Woodbridge on the opposite bank of the Deben is **Sutton Hoo**, sometimes known as 'page one of the history of England'. A unique and fascinating place to visit, the discovery of ship rivets in an ancient burial mound in 1939 led to one of the most amazing finds in the nation's history. This, the ship burial of an Anglo-Saxon warrior king and his most treasured possessions, had lain undisturbed for more than 1,300 years. The permanent display in the special exhibition hall reveals how Anglo-Saxon nobles lived, went to war and founded a kingdom in East Anglia. Here visitors can discover how the famous helmet and exquisite gold jewellery were made and used. A second hall houses an exhibition investigating the Anglo-Saxon thirst for imported luxuries from the Mediterranean and elsewhere. Visitors can also take the short walk to the burial mounds to see for themselves the site where the ship and treasures were found. It is now

🏛 historic building 🏛 museum and heritage 🏛 historic site 🝔 scenic attraction 🌿 flora and fauna

believed that the ship was the burial place of Raedwald, of the Wuffinga dynasty, King of East Anglia from about 610 to 625. Access to the site is on foot from the B1083. The site's extensive facilities include a restaurant, shop, children's play area and variety of walks in the surrounding countryside. There is good access for visitors with disabilities to the wholesite (tel: 01394 389700).

BROMESWELL
3 miles NE of Woodbridge off the B1084

This quiet village occupies a scenic setting. Bromeswell's church has a 12th-century archway at its entrance, a 15th-century font and an unusual Flemish well. The angels in the hammerbeam roof are plastic replicas of the originals, whose wings were clipped by Cromwell's men.

UFFORD
3 miles NE of Woodbridge off the A12

🏠 Church of the Assumption

Pride of place in a village that takes its name from Uffa (or Wuffa), the founder of the leading Anglo-Saxon dynasty, goes to the 13th-century **Church of the Assumption**. The font cover, which telescopes from five feet to 18 feet in height, is a masterpiece of craftsmanship, its elaborate carving crowned by a pelican. Many 15th-century benches have survived, but Dowsing (see page 125) smashed the organ and most of the stained glass – what's there now is mainly Victorian, some of it a copy of 15th-century work at All Souls College, Oxford.

Ufford is where the Suffolk Punch originated, Crisp's 404 being, in 1768, the progenitor of this distinguished breed of horses.

WICKHAM MARKET
5 miles N of Woodbridge off the A12

Places to see in this straggling village are the picturesque watermill by the River Deben and All Saints Church, whose 137-foot octagonal tower has a little roof to shelter the bell (see panel on page 144). At Boulge, a couple of miles southwest of Wickham Market, is the grave of Edward Fitzgerald, whose free translation of *The Rubaiyat of Omar Khayyam* is an English masterpiece. Tradition has it that on his grave is a rose bush grown from one found on Omar Khayyam's grave in Iran. Fitzgerald never left his native Suffolk in all his 74 years.

RENDLESHAM
5 miles NE of Woodbridge on the A1152

🚶 Rendlesham Forest

The Church of St Gregory the Great dates from the 14th century, but there is evidence (not physical, unfortunately) of an earlier Christian presence in the shape of Raedwald's palace. Rendlesham Hall was built in 1871 but was burnt down in 1898 and demolished in 1949. A surviving part is Woodbridge Lodge, a remarkable Gothic folly

Rendlesham Forest, part of the Forest of Aldewood, was ravaged by the great hurricane of October 1987. Seven years before that, on Christmas night, another visitation had occurred. Security guards at RAF Woodbridge, at that time a front line NATO base, spotted strange lights in the forest and went to investigate. They came upon a nine-foot high triangular object with a series of lights around it. As they approached, it did what every UFO has done and flew off before it could be definitively photographed. The next day the guards returned to the spot where it had landed

WICKHAM MARKET

Wickham Market is a bustling, thriving community close to the River Deben within the Suffolk Coastal Heritage area. It is reached either by road, turning off the A12 approximately fifteen miles north-east of Ipswich, or by rail to its station at Campsea Ashe. The centre of this large village offers free parking, a wide variety of shops with everything from flowers to food and fashion, as well as a choice of places to eat.

QUILTERS HAVEN

68 High Street, Wickham Market, IP13 0QU
Tel: 01728 746275 Fax: 01728 746314
e-mail: quilters.haven@btinternet.com   website: www.quilters-haven.co.uk

Internationally known author and teacher Karin Hellaby opened **Quilters Haven** in 1993 as a teaching centre with a shop alongside. She moved the enterprise to these handsome old High-Street premises in 1996, since when she has built up what is the largest and best stocked quilt shop in East Anglia. The stock includes thousands of fabrics, hundreds of books on patchwork, quilt making and textile crafts and a large range of haberdashery and accessories. Karin offers a mail order service and securing ordering online, and holds daily quilting and related classes in a large teaching area. Open 9am-5pm Mon - Sat.

CATHERINE HADDON

62a High Street, Wickham Market, Suffolk IP13 0QU
Tel: 01728 747102 Fax: 01728 748233
e-mail: info@catherinehaddon.co.uk website: www.catherinehaddon.co.uk

The lovely shop that carries the name of owner **Catherine Haddon** opened in 2007 and has had a very enthusiastic reception. It's full of an ever-changing collection of wonderful design accessories, lamps, pictures, mirrors, throws and of course fabrics and furniture, so a visit here is a must. Catherine also offers a full interior design service that is tailored to meet the needs of each individual client. Open10am- 4pm Thurs & Fri and 10am-1pm on Saturday, or by appointment.

VINTAGE FORTY SIX

46 High Street, Wickham Market, IP13 0QS
Tel: 01728 746642 e-mail: vintagefortysix@googlemail.com

Vintage Forty Six is an antiques and collectors' centre with 23 dealers displaying and regularly changing their antiques and good-quality collectable items. The shop incorporates Georgian china and glassware, Victorian pine, mahogany and oak furniture, Edwardian silver and jewellery Art Deco ware, studio pottery as well as art and photography. It's a place of wide appeal, to both dealers and visitors to the coastal region, and in the two spacious rooms that are made for browsing everyone should find something special and affordable. Open 10 - 4 Monday - Saturday inc bank holiday Mondays.

THE FOUR SEASONS DRESS AGENCY

70a High Street, Wickham Market, Suffolk IP13 0QU
Tel: 01728 748217

The **Four Seasons Dress Agency** sells nearly new and top-quality used ladies fashion clothes, shoes, hats, bags and jewellery on behalf of its customers. In two rooms of a handsome period building an ever-changing range is on display, with all sales on a commission basis. Items are displayed for an agreed period of time. There is also style advice and wardrobe makeovers available. A newly formed childrens agency operates within the same building offering quality clothing, toys, buggies and nursery equipment. Open 10am - 4.30pm Mon, Tues, Thurs, Fri and Sat.

and found three depressions in the ground. The UFO was apparently sighted again two days later, and security in the area was heightened. No explanation has ever been forthcoming about the incident, but interest in it continues and from time to time guided walks to the landing site are arranged.

BUTLEY

5 miles E of Woodbridge on the B1084

🏛 Butley Priory 🌳 Staverton Thicks

At the northern edge of Rendlesham Forest, the village of Butley has a splendid 14th-century gatehouse, all that remains of **Butley Priory**, an Augustinian priory founded by Ranulf de Glanville in 1171. The gatehouse is, by itself, a fairly imposing building, with some interesting flintwork on the north

façade (1320) and baronial carvings. Butley's parish church is Norman, with a 14th-century tower.

There are some splendid country walks here, notably by **Staverton Thicks**, which has a deer park and woods of oak and holly. The oldest trees date back more than 400 years. Butley Clumps is an avenue of beech trees planted in fours, with a pine tree at the centre of each clump – the technical term for such an arrangement is a quincunx.

Butley was long renowned for its oysters, and the beds have recently been revived.

CHILLESFORD

6 miles E of Woodbridge on the B1084

Brick was once big business here, and while digging for clay the locals made many finds,

---

BUTLEY POTTERY, GALLERY & BARN CAFÉ

Mill Lane, Butley, Woodbridge, Suffolk IP12 3PA
Tel: 01394 450785
e-mail: honorhussey@btconnect.com

A group of sensitively converted farm buildings incorporate **Butley Pottery**, the Barn Café and a summer Artists' Gallery. The showroom displays studio pottery, individual pieces of local Chillesford wares, sculpture in various media and Dan Hussey's unique and beautiful range of steam bent coppiced ash furniture. During the summer, there are changing exhibitions in the gallery by contemporary artists. A Self-catering unit in a charming apartment is also available here, and can be booked through www.suffolkcottageholidays.com.

The Barn Café (Tel: 01394 450800/382332) specialises in innovative cuisine, using locally produced meat and vegetables, and an abundance of fresh herbs. Unusual vegetarian creations are always appearing on the menu. Lunch bookings advisable, evening parties by arrangement. This is a delightful area of the coast, offering many hidden attractions. Cycle routes, footpaths and bird reserves abound, the river Ore and historic places such as Sutton Hoo, Orford castle and medieval woods are close by.

---

including hundreds of varieties of molluscs and the skeleton of an enormous whale. Chillesford supplies some of the clay for Aldeburgh brickworks.

ORFORD

12 miles E of Woodbridge on the B1084

🏰 Castle 🏰 St Bartholomew's Church

🦢 Orford Ness 🏛 Dunwich Underwater Studies

🦢 Havergate Island

Without doubt, one of the most charming and interesting of all the places in Suffolk, Orford has something to please everyone. The ruins of one of the most important castles in medieval England are a most impressive sight, even though the keep is all that remains of the original building commissioned by Henry II in 1165. The walls of the keep of **Orford Castle** (see panel below) are 90 feet high and 10 feet deep, and behind them are many rooms and passages in a remarkable state of preservation. A climb up the spiral staircase to the top provides splendid views over the surrounding countryside and to the sea.

St Bartholomew's Church was built at the same time, though the present church dates from the 14th century (the ruins of the original can be seen in the churchyard). A wonderful sight at night when floodlit, the church is regularly used for the performance of concerts and recitals, and many of Benjamin Britten's works were first heard here, including *Noyes Fludde* (a roundel in the floor of the west end of the nave commemorates the occasion) and the trio of oratorios *Curlew River*, *The Burning Fiery Furnace* and *The Prodigal Son*. The tower collapsed in 1830 and was not fully restored until 1962. Three bells were rescued and stood in the church until 1999, when three more bells were commissioned to give a full peal for the millennium.

These two grand buildings indicate that Orford was a very important town at one time. Indeed it was once a thriving port, but the steadily growing shingle bank of Orford Ness gradually cut it off from the sea, and down the years its appeal has changed. The sea may have gone but the river is still there, and in summer the quayside is alive with yachts and pleasure craft. On the other side of the river is **Orford Ness National Nature Reserve** (see panel above), the largest vegetated shingle spit in England and home to a variety of rare flora and fauna. The lighthouse marks the most easterly point (jointly with Lowestoft) in Britain.

Access to the spit, which is in the hands of the National Trust, is by ferry from Orford quay. From 1913 to the mid-1980s the Ness was out of bounds to the public, being used for various military purposes, including pre-war radar research under Sir Robert Watson-Watt. Boat trips also leave Orford quay for the RSPB reserve at **Havergate Island**, haunt of avocet and tern (the former returned in 1947 after being long absent).

Dunwich Underwater Studies in Front Street features exhibits on marine archaeology, coastal erosion and more, gleaned from the exploration of the ruins of the former town of Dunwich (see page 127), now largely claimed by the sea.

Back in the market square are a handsome town hall, two pubs with a fair quota of smuggling tales, an acclaimed restaurant serving Butley oysters and a smokehouse where kippers, salmon, trout, ham, sausages, chicken and even cheese and garlic are smoked over Suffolk oak.

CAMPSEA ASHE

6 miles NE of Woodbridge on the B1078

On towards Wickham Market the road passes

THE OLD STABLE

The Anchorage, Church Lane, Iken, Woodbridge,
Suffolk IP12 2ES
Tel: 01728 688263   Fax: 01728 688262
website: www.theanchorage.biz

Next to the historic thatched church in Iken, the
Old Stable is a 4-Star holiday cottage
overlooking the River Alde in a picturesque part
of the county. Owners Gunilla and John Hailes
have converted the old part-timbered coach house
and stables into self-catering accommodation
furnished to a very high standard. The ground floor
consists of a twin bedroom, shower, toilet, a
kitchen with all mod cons, a utility room and a large
living space with TV, video, DVD, radio and CD
player. Upstairs are a king-size double room and a
twin room, bathroom and toilet.

The cottage stands at the end of a long private
driveway, so peace and seclusion are guaranteed. It
is an ideal base for walking, cycling, painting,
birdwatching or just relaxing.There is a slipway to
the river for dinghy launching.

The attractive town of Woodbridge with its historic mills, the concert and crafts at Snape
Maltings, the amazing Saxon site of Sutton Hoo, the seaside town of Aldeburgh and Orford,
with its Castle, Church and nature and bird reserves, are all within easy reach.

---

through Campsea Ashe in the parish of
Campsey Ashe. The 14th-century Church of St
John the Baptist has an interesting brass showing
one of its first rectors in full priestly garb.

HOLLESLEY
5 miles SE of Woodbridge off the B1083

The Deben and the Ore almost turn this part
of Suffolk into a peninsula, and on the
seaward side lie Hollesley and Shingle Street.
The latter stands upon a shingle bank at the
entrance to the Ore and comprises a row of
little houses, a coastguard cottage and a
Martello tower. Its very isolation is an
attraction, and the sight of the sea rushing
into and out of the river is worth the journey.
The church at Hoolesley is notable for the
variety of animals and birds carved on the
pew ends. Among them is a skiapod, the best

known of which can be seen in the church at
Dennington (see page 156).

Brendan Behan did not enjoy his visit.
Brought here on a swimming outing from the
Borstal at Hollesley, he declared that the waves
had 'no limit but the rim of the world'. Looking
out to the bleak North Sea, it is easy to see
what he meant.

BAWDSEY
7 miles SE of Woodbridge on the B1083

The B1083 runs from Woodbridge through
farming country and several attractive villages
(Sutton, Shottisham, Alderton) to Bawdsey,
beyond which lie the mouth of the River
Deben, the end of the Sussex Coastal Path, and
the ferry to Felixstowe. The late-Victorian
Bawdsey Manor was taken over by the
Government and became the centre for radar

development when Orford Ness was deemed unsuitable. By the beginning of the Second World War there were two dozen secret radar stations in Britain, and radar HQ moved from Bawdsey to Dundee. The manor is now a leisure centre.

RAMSHOLT
7 miles SE of Woodbridge off the B1083

Ramsholt is a tiny community on the north bank of the Deben a little way up from Bawdsey. The pub is a popular port of call for yachtsmen, and half a mile from the quay, in quiet isolation, stands the Church of All Saints with its round tower. Road access to Ramsholt is from the B1083 just south of Shottisham.

Stowmarket

🏛 Museum of East Anglian Life

🎋 Gipping Valley Walk

The largest town in the heart of Suffolk, Stowmarket enjoyed a period of rapid growth when the River Gipping was still navigable to Ipswich and when the railway arrived. Much of

the town's history and legacy are brought vividly to life in the splendid **Museum of East Anglian Life** (see panel below), situated in the centre of town to the west of the market place (where markets are held twice a week), in a 70-acre meadowland site on the old Abbot's Hall Estate (the aisled original barn dates from the 13th century). Part of the open-air section features several historic buildings that have been moved from elsewhere in the region and carefully re-erected on site. These include an engineering workshop from the 1870s, part of a 14th-century farmhouse, a watermill from Alton and a wind pump that was rescued in a collapsed state at Minsmere in 1977. There's also a collection of working steam engines, farm animals and year-round demonstrations of all manner of local arts and crafts, from coopering to chandlery, from sheep shearing to saddlery (tel: 01449 612229). Stowmarket's Church of St Peter and St Mary acquired a new spire in 1994, replacing the 1715 version (itself a replacement), which was dismantled on safety grounds in 1975.

The town certainly merits a leisurely stroll, while for a peaceful picnic the riverbank beckons. Serious scenic walkers should make

Museum of East Anglian Life

Stowmarket, Suffolk IP14 1DL
Tel: 01449 612229 Fax: 01449 672307
website: www.eastanglianlife.org.uk

The Museum of East Anglian Life occupies a 75-acre site in the heart of Stowmarket. Its rich collections of social, rural and industrial history include a number of historic buildings such as a working watermill, a smithy, a chapel and a 13th century farmhouse. There is something for the whole family to enjoy with a variety of farm animals, adventure playground, picnic sites, café and gift shop. Throughout the year the Museum holds special events as well as demonstrations of crafts and engines in steam. The Museum is open from April to October.

🏚 historic building 🏛 museum and heritage 🏛 historic site ⌬ scenic attraction 🌱 flora and fauna

for the **Gipping Valley River Park** walk, which follows the former towpath all the way to Ipswich and incorporates a number of nature reserves.

Around Stowmarket

ELMSWELL
7 miles NW of Stowmarket off the A14

Clearly visible from the A14, the impressive church of St John the Baptist with its massive flint tower stands at the entrance to the village, facing Woolpit across the valley. A short drive north of Elmswell lies Great Ashfield, an unspoilt village whose now disused airfield played a key role in both World Wars. In the churchyard of the 13th century All Saints is a memorial to the Americans who died during the Second World War, as attested to by the commemorative altar. Some accounts say that Edmund was buried here in AD903 after dying at the hands of the Danes; a cross was put up in his memory. The cross was replaced in the 19th century and now stands in the garden of Ashfield House.

HAUGHLEY
4 miles NW of Stowmarket off the A14

🏛 Haughley Park

On the run into Stowmarket, Haughley once had the largest motte-and-bailey castle in Suffolk. All that now remains is a mound behind the church. **Haughley Park** is a handsome Jacobean redbrick manor house set in eight acres of gardens and surrounding woodland featuring ancient oaks and splendid magnolias. Woodland paths take the visitor past a half-mile stretch of rhododendrons, and in springtime the bluebells and lilies of the valley are a magical sight. The gardens are

open on Tuesdays between May and September, the house by appointment only.

HARLESTON
4 miles NW of Stowmarket off the A14

The churches of Shelland and Harleston lie in close proximity on a minor road between Woolpit and Haughley picnic site. At Shelland, the tiny Church of King Charles the Martyr is one of only four in England to be dedicated to King Charles I. The brick floor is laid in a herringbone pattern, there are high box pews and a triple-decker pulpit, but the most unusual feature is a working barrel organ dating from the early 19th century.

The Church of St Augustine at Harleston stands all alone among pine trees and is reached by a track across a field. It has a thatched roof, Early English windows and a tower with a single bell.

BUXHALL
3 miles W of Stowmarket just off the B1115

The village church here is notable for its six heavy bells, but the best-known landmark in this quiet village is undoubtedly the majestic tower mill, without sails since a gale removed them in 1929, but still standing as a silent, sturdy reminder of its working days. This is good walking country, with an ancient wood and many signposted footpaths.

NEEDHAM MARKET
4 miles SE of Stowmarket off the A14

🏛 Church of St John the Baptist

🐦 Needham Lake & Nature Reserve

A thriving village whose greatest glory is the wonderful carvings on the ceiling of the **Church of St John the Baptist**. The church's ornate double hammerbeam roof is nothing short of remarkable, especially when bathed

SHRUBLAND PARK NURSERIES

Coddenham, nr Ipswich, Suffolk IP6 9QJ
Tel: 01473 833187
e-mail: gill@shrublandparknurseries.co.uk
website: www.shrublandparknurseries.co.uk

Shrubland Park Nurseries is a family-run business situated in the heart of Suffolk, in the grand surroundings of Shrubland Park. This is not a garden centre but a 'proper' nursery, growing and selling its own plants. The owners welcome amateur and experienced gardeners alike and are always happy to give help and advice. They grow a wide range of hardy plants – Perennials, Shrubs, Climbers, Ferns and Grasses. The nursery also has one of the largest collections of Sub-Tropical, Conservatory Plants, House Plants and Succulents in Suffolk: the best selection of these more tender plants is available from early June. There are established display borders in both the glasshouse and adjacent walled garden. Shrubland Park Nurseries are open 10am to 5pm Wednesday to Sunday from Easter to the end of September. Visitors welcome at other times by appointment. These times may be subject to change, so visitors should contact the nursery to check opening times. Access to the nursery is through the main gate* opposite the Sorrel Horse Pub, about 1 mile north of Claydon, (a short distance from Junction 52 on the A14) and only 15 minutes from Ipswich town centre. (*For Sat. Nav. use IP6 0PG to get to the main gate.) The nursery also supplies plants by mail order.

in light from the strategically placed skylight. The roof is massive, as high as the walls of the church itself; the renowned authority on Suffolk churches, H Munro Cautley, described the work at Needham as 'the culminating achievement of the English carpenter'. The village also boasts some excellent examples of Tudor architecture.

The River Gipping flows to the east of the High Street and its banks provide miles of walks: the towpath is a public right of way walkable all the way from Stowmarket to Ipswich. Off the B1078 lies **Needham Lake and Nature Reserve**. The lake is a flooded gravel pit, created during the construction of the A14, and the reserve comprises a wetland area, large tracts of grassland and a small woodland known as King's Meadow.

Monthly farmers' markets are held at Alder Carr Farm, where there is also a pottery, crafts centre and farm shop.

Nearby Barking, on the B1018 south of Needham, was once more important than its neighbour, being described in 1874 as 'a pleasant village … including the hamlet of Needham Market'. This explains the fact that Barking's church is exceptionally large for a village house of worship: it was the mother church to Needham Market and was used for Needham's burials when Needham had no burial ground of its own.

BAYLHAM

7 miles SE of Stowmarket off the B1113

✦ Baylham House Rare Breeds Farm

The Roman site of Combretrovium is home to **Baylham House Rare Breeds Farm** (see panel above), where visitors can meet friendly

Baylham House Rare Breeds Farm

Mill Lane, Baylham, Suffolk IP6 8LG
Tel: 01473 830264
website: www.baylham-house-farm.co.uk

Baylham House Rare Breeds Farm is a wonderful place to take children. Previous visitors have described it as having a unique and magical quality not found elsewhere. The primary aim of the farm is to help maintain the national stock of endangered rare breed farm animals, providing the best possible care in a traditional and sympathetic way. The secondary aim is to provide people, particularly children, with an opportunity to meet healthy, contented and friendly farm animals. Four different breeds of cattle and six small flocks of rare sheep can be seen at Baylham House. The pig collection includes some very friendly Maori pigs from New Zealand called Kune Kunes and Large Blacks, one of the rarest of British pigs. The farm also keeps poultry and pygmy goats.

The farm is situated within a significant Roman site, scheduled as an Ancient Monument and includes two military forts and a large civilian settlement. Information and artefacts are displayed at the Visitors' Centre. Whilst here you can also take a walk along the lovely riverside path and spend a day in the countryside within the Gipping Valley. When you've had your fill of fresh air, you can recover with some refreshments at the Visitors' Centre, which also sells souvenirs and gifts.

farm animals and feed them with the free bag of animal food given to every child. The farm's chief concern is the survival of rare breeds, and there are breeding groups of cattle, sheep, pigs, goats and poultry.

EARL STONHAM
5 miles E of Stowmarket on the A1120

A scattered village set around three greens in farming land, Earl Stonham's Church of St Mary the Virgin boasts one of Suffolk's finest single hammerbeam roofs, and is also notable for its Bible scene murals, the 'Doom' (Last Judgement scene) over the chancel arch, and a triple hour-glass, presumably to record just how protracted were some of the sermons.

STONHAM ASPAL
6 miles E of Stowmarket on the A1120

🦉 Stonham Barns Owl Sanctuary 🦉 Redwings

On the other side of the A140 lies Stonham Aspal, where in 1962 the remains of a Roman bath-house were unearthed. The parish church has an unusual wooden top to its tower, a necessary addition to house the 10 bells that a keen campanologist insisted on installing. **Stonham Barns** is a leisure, rural pursuits and shopping complex that also houses the **Suffolk Owl Sanctuary** (open all year), home to over 60 owls and other birds of prey, and the **Redwings Horse Rescue Centre**, which opened in 2003 and provides sanctuary for over 30

🎬 stories and anecdotes 🐦 famous people 🎨 art and craft 🎭 entertainment and sport 🚶 walks

STONHAM BARNS

Pettaugh Road, Stonham Aspal,
Suffolk, IP14 6AT
Tel: 01449 711755
email: msshowground@btconnect.com
web: www.stonham-barns.com

Stonham Barns is situated between Stowmarket and Framlingham on the A1120 and is one of the most established leisure, retail and rural pursuits attractions in Suffolk. The market square boasts a number of retail shops; **The Gift Barn** is an Aladdin's cave of unusual gifts; **The Clothing Co** has ladies clothing and accessories; **Men's Gear** is a shop dedicated to men's clothing and gifts; **The Jewellery Box** has gorgeous jewellery sourced locally and from around the world; **The Kitchen Cupboard** offers locally produced foods and kitchenware and you will also see **Frankie's Hair, Beauty & Tanning Salon** where appointments are not always necessary! Don't forget your postcards can be bought and sent from our very own **Post Office**. There is a well established **Garden Centre** with a **Country Feeds** section; The **Stonham Barns Restaurant** serves delicious food 7 days a week; **Abbey Aquatics and Reptiles** specialise in rare catfish and unusual reptiles and no tourist centre is complete without an **Antiques** shop and crafts such as **Soule Pottery** and Stonham Barns is no exception.

There is so much to see and activities to keep the children busy; you can take in a show at **The Suffolk Owl Sanctuary**; play a round or two on the 9 hole **Golf Course**; you can even holiday on the complex at the **Camping and Caravan Park** and take in one of the many organised events throughout the year on **The Mid Suffolk Showground**. We even have our very own **Fishing Lakes,** where better to relax than in the heart of the Suffolk countryside where the only noise is from the dragonflies skimming across the lakes. If there is one place you must visit it is **Stonham Barns**. Open 7 days a week, 362 days a year we are waiting to give you a very warm welcome.

rescued horses, ponies and donkeys, a few of which are available for adoption (open April to end October).

MENDLESHAM
6 miles NE of Stowmarket off the A140

On the green in Old Market Street, Mendlesham, lies an enormous stone, which is said to have been used as a preaching stone, mounted by itinerant Wesleyan preachers. In the Church of St Mary there is a collection of parish armour assembled some 400 years ago, and also some fine carvings. The least hidden

local landmark is a 1,000-foot TV mast put up by the IBA in 1959.

BROCKFORD
7 miles NE of Stowmarket off the A410

🏛 Mid-Suffolk Light Railway Museum

Off the A140, a re-created Mid Suffolk Station is where visitors will find the **Mid-Suffolk Light Railway Museum**, open on summer Sundays and Bank Holidays. The museum, dedicated to preserving the memory of the railway that served the heart

MICKFIELD HOSTAS

The Poplars, Mickfield, Stowmarket, Suffolk IP14 5LH
Tel/Fax: 01449 711576
e-mail: mickfieldhostas@btconnect.com
website: www.mickfieldhostas.co.uk

Hostas are woodland plants thriving in shady, moist conditions suiting most gardens and are also happy growing in pots. They are hardy perennials emerging in the spring and dying back in the autumn. 'Forty shades of green' doesn't even approach a description of the diversity of these plants.

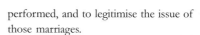

The **Mickfield Hostas** collection began with a gift from a friend in 1976. It was love at first sight and Yvonne quickly exhausted the species and cultivars available from British nurseries at the time. Happily Americans love the 'friendship plant' and are prolific breeders of new varieties to feed the addiction.

Very quickly the collection grew and now Mickfield Hostas boasts one of the largest collections of the genus in Europe. Designated as a National Collection by the National Council for the Conservation of Plants and Gardens (NCCPG) in 2007, visitors can enjoy wandering through their extensive collection of over 1800 varieties. Not only that, they can purchase from around 700 varieties they have available for sale each season. A one hectare exhibition garden is also under development and visitors are invited to see the progress when they come to the nursery, details of opening times can be found on the website.

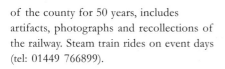

of the county for 50 years, includes artifacts, photographs and recollections of the railway. Steam train rides on event days (tel: 01449 766899).

WETHERINGSETT
7 miles NE of Stowmarket off the A410

Wetheringsett has had two well-known rectors, famous for very different reasons. Richard Hakluyt, incumbent from 1590 to 1616, is remembered for his major work *Voyages* (full title *Principal Navigation, Voyages, Traffiques and Discoveries of the English Nation*). The rector between 1883 and 1888 was a certain George Wilfrid Ellis, sometime tailor and butler, and finally a bogus clergyman. After he was unmasked as a sham, a special Act of Parliament was needed to validate the marriage ceremonies he had illegally

performed, and to legitimise the issue of those marriages.

COTTON
5 miles N of Stowmarket off the B1113

🏛 Mechanical Music Museum

South of Finningham, where Yew Tree House displays some fine pargeting, and just by Bacton, a lovely village originally built around seven greens, lies the village of Cotton, which should be visited for several reasons, one of which is to see the splendid 14th century flint church of St Andrew, impressive in its dimensions and notable for its double hammerbeam roof with carved angels.

Cotton's Mechanical Music Museum & Bygones has an extensive collection that includes gramophones, music boxes, street pianos, fairground organs and polyphons, as well as the marvellous Wurlitzer Theatre pipe organ, all playable (tel: 01449 613876).

THORNHAM MAGNA & PARVA
10 miles N of Stowmarket off the A140

🚶 Thornham Walks

The **Thornham Walks and Field Centre**, with 12 miles of walks and a herb garden and nursery, caters admirably for hikers, horticulturists and lovers of the countryside. The tiny thatched Church of St Mary at Thornham Parva houses a considerable treasure in the shape of an exquisite medieval altar painting, known as a retable, with a central panel depicting the crucifixion and four saints on each side panel. Its origins are uncertain, but it was possibly the work of the Royal Workshops at Westminster Abbey and made for Thetford Priory, or for a nearby Dominican monastery. Also to be admired is the 14th-century octagonal font and a series of fascinating wall paintings. In the churchyard is a monument to Sir Basil Spence (1907-76), architect of Coventry Cathedral.

YAXLEY
12 miles N of Stowmarket on the A140

Yaxley's Church of St Mary offers up more treasures. One is an extremely rare sexton's wheel, which hangs above the south door and was used in medieval times to select fast days in honour of the Virgin. When a pair of iron wheels were spun on their axle, strings attached to the outer wheel would catch on the inner, stopping both and indicating the chosen day. The 17th-century pulpit is one of the finest in the country, with the most glorious, sumptuous carvings. Yaxley's most

---

WORTHAM (POST OFFICE) STORES & TEA SHOP

Long Green, Wortham, Diss, Norfolk IP22 1PP
Tel: 01379 783210
e-mail: worthamstores@live.co.uk

Wortham is a typical East Anglian village with a friendly teashop, store and post office under one roof. **Wortham (Post Office) Stores & Tea Shop** are housed within two 17th century buildings. The tea shop has been well established in the area for many years.

The tea shop is a thriving place for visitors and villagers alike, whre they can enjoy a slice of freshly baked cake with a cup of tea, a hot meal or a snack. Offering a selection of refreshments, the tea shop provides the ideal environment to relax after exploring the local countryside, as a meeting point or a stop on a long journey.

There is something for everyone in Wortham Stores & Tea Shop. In addition to the fabulous food in the tea shop, the store stocks good quality local produce, including bread, cheeses, wine and local beer.

Internet access is now available in the tea shop, so you can surf the web while tasting the home-made cakes. They are so popular they don't last long!

🏛 historic building 🏛 museum and heritage 🏚 historic site 🔆 scenic attraction 🌿 flora and fauna

famous son is Sir Frederick Ashton, who is buried in the churchyard.

Framlingham

🏯 Castle 🏯 Church of St Michael

🏛 Lanman Museum

The marvellous **Castle**, brooding on a hilltop, dominates this agreeable market town, as it has since Roger Bigod, 2nd Earl of Norfolk, built it in the 12th century (his grandfather built the first a century earlier, but this wooden construction was soon demolished). The Earls and Dukes of Norfolk, the Howards, were here for many generations before moving to Arundel in 1635. The castle is in remarkably good condition, partly because it was rarely attacked – though King John put it under siege in 1215. Its most famous occupant was Mary Tudor, who was in residence when proclaimed Queen in 1553. During the reign of Elizabeth I it was used as a prison for defiant priests and, in the 17th century after being bequeathed to Pembroke College, Cambridge, it saw service as a home and school for local paupers. Nine of the castle's 13 towers are accessible - the climb up the spiral staircase and walk round the battlements are well worth the effort. On one

side the view is of the Meres, a bird sanctuary. In the north wing is the **Lanman Museum**, devoted to agricultural, craftsman's tools and domestic memorabilia.

The castle brought considerable prestige and prosperity to Framlingham, evidence of which can be found in the splendid **Church of St Michael**, which has two wonderful works of art. One is the tomb of Henry Fitzroy, bastard son of Henry VIII, beautifully adorned with scenes from Genesis and Exodus and in a superb state of repair. The other is the tomb of the 3rd Duke, with carvings of the apostles in shell niches. Also of note is the Carolean organ of 1674, a gift of Sir Robert Hitcham, to whom the Howards sold the estate. Cromwell and the Puritans were not in favour of organs in churches, so this instrument was lucky to have escaped the mass destruction of organs at the time of the Commonwealth. Sir Robert is buried in the church.

Around Framlingham

SAXTEAD GREEN

2 miles W of Framlingham off the A1120

🏯 Mill

One of the prettiest sights in Suffolk is the

🎭 stories and anecdotes 🐦 famous people 🎨 art and craft 🏛 entertainment and sport 🚶 walks

Pony and Trap, Saxtead Green

white 18th-century **Mill** that stands on the marshy green in Saxtead. This is a wonderful example of a post mill, perhaps the best in the world, dating back to 1796 and first renovated in the 19th century. Until 1947 it was a working mill and has since been kept in working order, with the sails turning even though the mill no longer grinds. In summer, visitors can climb into the buck (body) of this elegant weatherboarded construction and explore its machinery.

EARL SOHAM

3 miles W of Framlingham on the A1120

Earl Soham comprises a long, winding street that was once part of a Roman road. It lies in a valley, and on the largest of its three greens the village sign is a carved wooden statue of a falconer given as a gift by the Women's Institute in 1953. The Church of St Mary, dating from the 13th century, is well worth a visit.

DEBENHAM

6 miles W of Framlingham on the B1077

Debenham is a sizable village of architectural distinction, with a profusion of attractive timber-framed buildings dating from the 14th

to the 17th centuries. The River Deben flows beside and beneath the main street and, near one of the little bridges there is a pottery centre. St Mary's Church is unusual in having an original Saxon tower, and the roof alternates hammerbeams with crested tie beams. Just north of Debenham, off the B1077, the village of Aspall is associated with the Kitchener family. Lord Kitchener's mother, from the powerful local Chevallier family, married Henry Kitchener in 1845. Herbert, the future military hero, was born in 1850. he was proud to add the name Aspall to his titles – Viscount Kitchener of Khartoum in the Sudan, of the Vaal in South Africa and of Aspall in the county of Suffolk. The name of the village is most associated with cider, a business that started when the Chevalliers set up a cider press here.

DENNINGTON

2 miles N of Framlingham on the B1116

🏚 Church of St Mary

The pretty little village of Dennington boasts one of the oldest post offices in the country, this one having occupied the same site since 1830. The **Church of St Mary** has some very unusual features, none more so than the hanging 'pyx' canopy above the altar. A pyx served as a receptacle for the Reserved Sacrament, which would be kept under a canopy attached to weights and pulleys so that the whole thing could be lowered when the sacrament was required for the sick and the dying.

The church also has many interesting carvings, the most remarkable being that of a skiapod, a very rare representation of a mythical creature of the African desert, humanoid but with a huge boat-shaped foot with which it could cover itself and its offspring against the sun. This curious beast was 'known' to Herodotus and to Pliny, who remarked that it had 'great pertinacity in leaping'. In the chapel at the top of the south aisle stands the tomb of Lord Bardolph, who fought at Agincourt, and of his wife, their effigies carved in alabaster.

PARHAM
2 miles SE of Framlingham on the B1116

Parham Airfield

Parham Airfield is now agricultural land, but in the control tower and an adjacent hut can be found memorabilia of the 390th Bomb Group of the USAAF. Exhibits include recovered aircraft engines, parts of allied and Axis aircraft, uniforms, combat records and photographs. One of the best-known pieces is part of Joe Kennedy's Liberator bomber that exploded over Blythburgh in 1944. Also in 1944, a Flying Fortress called Glory Ann II crashed near the airfield, killing the crew. Here, too, is the Museum of the British Resistance Organisation, the only museum in the UK dedicated to the Auxiliary Units set up to counter the threat of invasion in 1940.

EASTON
5 miles S of Framlingham off the B1078

A scenic drive leads to the lovely village of Easton, one of the most colourful, flower-bedecked places in the county. A remarkable sight to the west of the village is the two-mile-long crinkle-crankle wall that surrounds Easton Park. This extraordinary type of wall, also known as a ribbon wall, weaves snake-like and is much stronger than if it were straight. This particular wall, said to be the world's longest, was built by Lord of the Manor, the Earl of Rochford, in the 1820s.

CHARSFIELD
5 miles S of Framlingham off the B1078

A minor road runs from Framlingham through picturesque Kettleburgh and Hoo to Charsfield, best known as the inspiration for Ronald Blyth's book *Akenfield*, later memorably filmed by Sir Peter Hall. A cottage garden in the village displays the Akenfield village sign and is open to visitors in the summer.

OTLEY
7 miles SW of Framlingham on the B1079

Moated Hall

The 15th-century **Moated Hall** in Otley is open to the public at certain times of the year. Standing in 10 acres of gardens that include a canal, a nuttery and a knot garden, the hall was long associated with the Gosnold family, whose coat of arms is also that of the village. The best-known member of that family was Bartholomew Gosnold, who sailed to the New World, coined the name 'Martha's Vineyard' for the island off the coast of Massachusetts, discovered Cape Cod and founded the settlement of Jamestown, Virginia. The 13th-century Church of St Mary has a remarkable baptistry font measuring six feet in length and two feet eight inches in depth. Though filled with water, the font is not used and was only discovered in 1950 when the vestry floor was raised. It may have been used for adult baptisms.

HELMINGHAM

7 miles SW of Framlingham on the B1077

Another moated hall, this one a Tudor construction, stands in Helmingham. Although the house is not open to the public, on Sundays in summer the gardens can be visited; attractions include herbaceous and spring borders, many varieties of roses, safari rides and deer, Highland cattle and Soay sheep. The Tollemache family were here for many years - one of their number founded a brewery, which, after a merger, became the Tolly Cobbold brewery, based in Ipswich.

FRAMSDEN

7 miles SW of Framlingham on the B1077

The scenery in these parts is real picture-postcard stuff, and in the village of Framsden the picture is completed by a fine post mill, built high on a hill in 1760, refitted and raised in 1836, and in use until 1934. The milling machinery is still in place and the mill is open for visits (at weekends, by appointment only).

CRETINGHAM

4 miles SW of Framlingham off the A1120

The village sign is the unusual item here, in that it has two different panels: one shows an everyday Anglo-Saxon farming scene, the other a group (of Danes?) sailing up the River Deben, with the locals fleeing. The signs are made from mosaic tiles.

BRANDESTON

3 miles SW of Framlingham off the A1120

A further mile to the east, through some charming countryside, Brandeston is another delightful spot, with a row of beautiful thatched cottages and the parish church of All Saints with its 13th-century font. The best-known vicar of Brandeston was John Lowes (1572-1646) who was accused of witchcraft by the villagers, interrogated by Witch Finder General Matthew Hopkins and hanged at Bury St Edmunds. His sad end was made even sadder by the fact that before being strung up he had to read out the burial service of a condemned witch himself, as no priest was allowed to conduct the service. Hopkins made a handsome living out of this bizarre business, preying on the superstitions of the times and using the foulest means to obtain confessions. One account of Hopkins' end is that he himself was accused of being a witch and hanged. The less satisfactory alternative is that he died of tuberculosis.

Castle and Church, Eye

Eye

🏛 Church of St Peter & St Paul

The name of this excellent little town is derived from the Saxon for an island, as Eye was once surrounded by water and marshes. The **Church of St Peter and St Paul** stands in the shadow of a mound on which a castle once stood (the remains are worth a look and the mound offers a panoramic view of the town – almost a bird's-eye view, in fact). The church's 100-foot tower was described by Pevsner as 'one of the wonders of Suffolk' and the interior is a masterpiece of restoration, with all the essential medieval features in place. The rood screen, with

---

SOULE POTTERY

23 Century Road, Eye, Suffolk IP23 7LE
Tel: 07932 633368 studio: 01379 871088
e-mail: c.soule@btinternet.com website: www.soulepottery.co.uk

Chris Soule has been a potter for 35 years and for 18 of these has been creating and manufacturing designs for leading department stores like Debenhams and Habitat. Now living in Suffolk, Chris has returned to his craft roots of making for, and selling directly to, the public. In **Soule Pottery** he uses rich earthenware glazes, exploring the role of very lively reactive glazes to provide beautiful, interesting effects. He has recently started adding lustre to some of the bolder, exciting shapes. Teapots, bowls, stain-proof mugs, vases and many other pieces can be viewed in a warm, friendly environment, and Chris is always happy to discuss special commissions. **Please phone before visiting.**

ENGLISH & CONTINENTAL ANTIQUES

1 Broad Street, Eye, Suffolk IP23 7AF
Tel/Fax: 01379 871199
e-mail: englishantiques@onetel.com
website: www.englishandcontinentalantiques.com

Situated in the pretty North Suffolk market town of Eye **English and Continental Antiques** specialises in antique furniture, art and porcelain. They also offer a "bespoke" hand made furniture service for those items hard to find!

Owner Steve Harmer has a love for early period oak and country pieces but deals across the board including burr Walnut and Georgian mahogany pieces of quality. He invites readers to view his stock on-line, and has a delivery service across the UK, even worldwide.

As well as buying and selling antique furniture there is a range of ancillary services on offer, which include restoration, upholstery and furniture logistics. Please call for a free quotation.

To compliment the fine antique furniture, you can find accessories to finish off the décor. On offer are lovely early clocks, fine porcelain, silver art and lamps. Items purchased can be delivered free of charge within East Anglia or a small fee for delivery elsewhere. A shipping facility is also available.

Please do not hesitate to call or view online, an efficient and friendly service awaits !

📖 stories and anecdotes 🐾 famous people ✐ art and craft ♫ entertainment and sport 🚶 walks

Eye

Distance: *3.5 miles (5.6 kilometres)*

Typical time: *90 mins*

Height gain: *10 metres*

Map: *Explorer 230*

Walk: *www.walkingworld.com ID:1484*

Contributor: *Joy & Charles Boldero*

ACCESS INFORMATION:

For buses, ring Travel Line 0545 583358. You can start this walk in Eye at point 7. The car park at the Pennings picnic site car park is just outside the town. This is where the walk begins. The car park is situated on a country lane south of the B1117, just east of Eye. Eye is situated on the B1077 off the A140, 4 miles southeast of Diss.

ADDITIONAL INFORMATION:

Eye Town Moor Wood has a lot of unusual features. The pond you pass has conical structures in it and beside it a lovers seat.

Eye has many beautiful buildings, one the 15th-century Guildhall by the church, which is said to be one of the finest in the county. Near the church is the old castle. The Queen's Head has an excellent menu, but does not serve food on Mondays.

At point 10 there was once a Priory, built in about 1080 by Robert Malet, Lord of Eye, in memory of his father, William, a Norman baron. There were fish ponds near by, now they are a wild life habitat, kingfishers can be seen there. To the right is the 16th century brick building that became part of a farm complex, milling, malting and brewing beer.

Opposite is the 'Abbey'. The 18th-century red brick front hides a mediaeval timber-framed building in which the Prior lived.

DESCRIPTION:

This walk is mostly across meadows, along tracks and through woodland and touches the fine old town of Eye, which has so many lovely and ancient buildings. The route uses part of the Mid-Suffolk designated paths.

FEATURES:

Lake/Loch, Pub, Toilets, Church, Castle, Wildlife, Birds, Flowers, Great Views, Butterflies, Food Shop.

WALK DIRECTIONS:

1 | From the car park turn right along the country lane.

2 | Turn right at the fingerpost and cross meadows going over stiles.

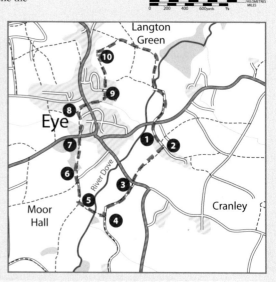

🏛 historic building 🏛 museum and heritage 🏛 historic site ⚜ scenic attraction 🌱 flora and fauna

3 | Cross the road and continue along the track opposite, Park Lane. Go under a barrier where the track becomes grassy.

4 | Turn right towards an iron bar and cross a stile to its left. Cross a meadow keeping a copse on the left. Go over a concrete humped bridge and climb a stile in the corner. Cross a second meadow and an earth bridge, then cross a third meadow to a stile ahead.

5 | After climbing this stile and crossing a bridge, turn right along a fourth meadow keeping to its left-hand side. Climb the stile and turn right along the track.

6 | At the fingerpost turn left along the field edge. This path goes into the wood. Cross the bridge and take the right fork. By the pond, ignore a path on the right. Keep along the main path to the notice board, ignoring all paths left off it.

7 | Turn right over the bridge and turn left along the gravel track. Turn right along the pavement. Turn left at the road junction. At the Town Hall turn left to the Queens Head and then turn right. By the almshouses cross the road.

8 | Turn right at the fingerpost along a driveway. The path keeps right by a stream over grass lawn. At the end turn left, then left again along a lane with houses.

9 | Cross the road and go along a signed path opposite. Keep on through a newish housing estate.

10 | Soon after house No. 3, turn right along a track; it becomes a grassy one. Climb the stile, cross a meadow and go through a gate. Turn left along the track. Climb a stile and continue along a track. Cross the road and continue along a driveway opposite. Turn right over the stile and cross a meadow. Climb a stile and go along a path under trees, then turn right along a country lane to the car park.

painted panels depicting St Edmund, St Ursula, Edward the Confessor and Henry VI, is particularly fine.

Other interesting Eye sights are the ornate redbrick Town Hall; the timbered Guildhall, with the archangel Gabriel carved on a corner post; a crinkle-crankle (serpentine) wall fronting Chandos Lodge, where Sir Frederick Ashton once lived; and a thriving theatre, one of the smallest professional theatres in the country. On the outskirts of Eye by the River Dove lies The Pennings Nature Reserve, water meadows that are home to a variety of wildlife. At Denham, a few miles east of Eye, the 95th Bomb Group Hospital and NCO's social club have been restored, with Second World War artefacts on display (tel: 01379 870514).

Around Eye

HOXNE
4 miles NE of Eye on the B1118

🎭 Goldbrook Bridge

Palaeolithic remains indicate the exceptionally long history of Hoxne (pronounced Hoxon), which stands along the banks of the River Waveney near the Norfolk border. It is best known for its links with King Edmund, who was reputedly killed here, though Bradfield St Clare and Shottisham have rival claims to this distinction. The Hoxne legend is that Edmund was betrayed to the Danes by a newlywed couple who were crossing **Goldbrook Bridge** and spotted his golden spurs reflected from his hiding place below the bridge. Edmund put a curse on all newlyweds crossing the bridge and, to this day some wedding couples take care to avoid it.

The story continues that Edmund was tied to an oak tree and killed with arrows. That same oak mysteriously fell down in 1848 while apparently in good health, and a monument at the site is a popular tourist attraction. In the church of St Peter and St Paul an oak screen (perhaps that very same oak?) depicts scenes from the martyr's life. A more cheerful event is the Harvest Breakfast on the village green that follows the annual service.

HORHAM
6 miles E of Eye on the B1117

Three distinct musical connections distinguish this dapper little village. The Norman church has had its tower strengthened for the rehanging of the peal of eight bells, which is believed to be the oldest in the world.

Benjamin Britten, later associated with the Aldeburgh Festival, lived and composed in Horham for a time, and on a famous day during the Second World War, Glenn Miller brought his band here to celebrate the 200th flying mission to set out from the American aerodrome.

WORLINGWORTH
8 miles SE of Eye off the B1118

It's well worth taking the country road to Worlingworth, a long, straggling village whose Church of St Mary has a remarkable font cover reaching up about 30 feet. It is brilliantly coloured and intricately carved, and near the top is an inscription in Greek that translates as 'wash my sin and not my body only'. Note, too, the Carolean box pews, the carved pulpit and an oil painting of

---

LOG CABIN HOLIDAYS

Athelington Hall, Horham, nr Eye, Suffolk IP21 5EJ
Tel: 01728 628233 Fax: 01728 384491
e-mail: peter@logcabinholidays.co.uk
website: www.logcabinholidays.co.uk

Log Cabin Holidays are based in picturesque rural Suffolk, with many country and coastal attractions within an easy drive. The breathtaking Suffolk Heritage Coast, which includes the lovely towns of Aldeburgh and Southwold, is only 25 minutes' drive away, and also nearby are Orford Castle, Minsmere Bird Reserve and the Sutton Hoo National trust site just outside Woodbridge.

In the grounds of Athelington Hall, Peter and Sally Havers have five immaculate two-bedroom lodges offering everything for a carefree self-catering holiday, including a fully equipped kitchen, en suite master bedroom, good-size family bathroom and a twin-bedded room. There is also a double sofa bed in the open-plan lounge. The lodges are double glazed and fully central heated, and are equipped with microwave, fridge and TV. Decking on the front of the lodge enables guests to dine outside while enjoying the sun. Within the grounds of Athelington Hall there are a number of facilities to enjoy, including a Jacuzzi hot tub, fishing in the moat, a games room and a large lawned area.

Worlingworth's Great Feast of 1810 to celebrate George III's jubilee.

LAXFIELD
12 miles E of Eye on the B1117

🏛 Heveningham Hall 🏛 Museum

Laxfield & District Museum, on the first floor of the 15th-century Guildhall, gives a fine insight into bygone ages with geology and natural history exhibits, agricultural and domestic tools, a Victorian kitchen, a village shop and a costume room. The museum is open on Saturday and Sunday afternoons in summer.

All Saints Church is distinguished by some wonderful flint 'flushwork' (stonework) on its tower, roof and nave. In the 1808 Baptist church is a plaque remembering John Noyes, burnt at the stake in 1557 for refusing to take Catholic vows. History relates that the villagers - with a single exception - dowsed their fires in protest. The one remaining fire, however, was all that was needed to light the stake.

A couple of miles east of Laxfield, **Heveningham Hall** is a fine Georgian mansion, a model of classical elegance designed by James Wyatt with lovely grounds by Capability Brown. As it runs through the grounds, the River Blyth widens into a lake.

WINGFIELD
6 miles NE of Eye off the B1118

🏛 Wingfield Old College

Wingfield Old College is one of the country's most historic seats of learning, founded in 1362 as a college for priests with a bequest from Sir John de Wingfield, Chief Staff Officer to the Black Prince. Sir John's wealth came from ransoming a French nobleman at the Battle of Poitiers in 1356.

Surrendered to Henry VIII at the time of the Dissolution, the college became a farmhouse and is now in private hands.

The Church of St Andrew was built as the collegiate church and has an extra-large chancel to accommodate the college choir. The church contains three really fine monuments: to Sir John (in stone); to Michael de la Pole, 2nd Earl of Suffolk (in wood); and to John de la Pole, Duke of Suffolk (in alabaster). Inside the church there is a 'hudd' – a shelter for the priest for use at the graveside in bad weather. On the green in the centre of the village are the imposing remains of a castle built by the 1st Earl.

FRESSINGFIELD
10 miles NE of Eye on the B1116

🏛 Ufford Hall

Fressingfield's first spiritual centre was the Church of St Peter and St Paul. It has a superb hammerbeam roof and a lovely stone bell tower that was built in the 14th century. On one of the pews the initials A P are carved. These are believed to be the work of Alice de la Pole, Duchess of Norfolk and granddaughter of Geoffrey Chaucer. Was this a work of art or a bout of vandalism brought on by a dull sermon?

Nearby **Ufford Hall** was the home of the Sancroft family, one of whom became Archbishop of Canterbury. He led the revolt of the bishops against James II and was imprisoned in the Tower of London. Released by William IV and sacked for refusing to swear the oath of allegiance, he returned home and is entombed by the south porch of the church. The village sign is a pilgrim and a donkey, recording that Fressingfield was a stopping place on the pilgrim route from Dunwich to Bury St Edmunds.

Ipswich

🏛 Christchurch Mansion   🏛 Ipswich Museum

🏛 Ipswich Transport Museum

🌱 Orwell Country Park

History highlights Ipswich as the birthplace of Cardinal Wolsey, but the story of Suffolk's county town starts very much earlier than that. It has been a port since the time of the Roman occupation, and by the 7th century the Anglo-Saxons had expanded it into the largest port in the country. King John granted a civic charter in 1200, confirming the townspeople's right to their own laws and administration, and for several centuries the town prospered as a port, exporting wool, textiles and agricultural products.

Thomas Wolsey arrived on the scene in 1475, the son of a wealthy butcher. Educated at Magdalen College, Oxford, he was ordained a priest in 1498 and rose quickly in influence, becoming chaplain to Henry VII and then Archbishop of York, a cardinal, and Lord Chancellor under Henry VIII. He was quite indispensable to the king and had charge of foreign policy as well as holding a powerful sway over judicial institutions. He also managed to amass enormous wealth, enabling him to found a grammar school in Ipswich and Cardinal's College (later Christ Church) in Oxford. Wolsey had long been hated by certain nobles for his low birth and arrogance, and they were easily able to turn Henry against him when his attempts to secure an annulment from the Pope of the king's marriage to Katherine of Aragon met with failure. Stripped of most of his offices following a charge of

KARLSSON SCANDINAVIAN DESIGN LTD
NELSON DESIGN UK

8 Tacket Street, Ipswich, Suffolk IP4 1AY
Tel: 01473 288308
e-mail: info@karlssondesign.co.uk / julia@nelsondesignuk.com
website: www.karlssondesign.co.uk / www.nelsondesignuk.com

Karlsson is a stylish shop selling passionately chosen and beautifully designed pieces. **Nelson Design UK** is an interior design consultancy, who specialise in working closely with their clients to realise their design vision. This unique design collaboration provides an oasis of inspiration from their base in Ipswich.

We all want our houses to be stylish and welcoming. It's surprising how a few bright design ideas – a change of furnishing fabrics, the addition of beautiful homewares, a well-chosen design piece – can refresh a room, and make day-to-day life a joy.

Whether you're looking for a perfect gift, iconic and bespoke furniture, stylish lighting and beautiful soft furnishings or just inspiration come and talk to us. We are confident you'll be able to find something just a little special at Karlsson Scandinavian Design Ltd. and Nelson Design UK. *Visit us and be inspired.*

🏛 historic building 🏛 museum and heritage 🏛 historic site 🝣 scenic attraction 🌱 flora and fauna

Wolseys Gate, Ipswich

grammar school - all that remains now is a red-brick gateway.

When the cloth market fell into decline in the 17th century, a respite followed in the following century, when the town was a food-distribution port during the Napoleonic Wars. At the beginning of the 19th century the risk from silting was becoming acute at a time when trade was improving and industries were springing up. The Wet Dock, constructed in 1842, solved the silting problem and, with the railway arriving shortly after, Ipswich could once more look forward to a safe future. The Victorians were responsible for considerable development: symbols of their civic pride include the handsome Old Custom House by the Wet Dock, the Town Hall, and the splendid Tolly Cobbold brewery, rebuilt at the end of the 19th century, 150 years after brewing started on the site. Victorian enterprise depleted some of the older buildings, but a number survive, notably the house where Wolsey was born, the Ancient House with its wonderful pargetting, and the fine former Tudor merchants' houses that

overstepping his authority as a legate, he was later charged with treason, but died while travelling from York to London to face the king. His death put an end to his plans for the

Christchurch Mansion

Soane Street, Ipswich, Suffolk IP4 2 BE
Tel: 01473 253246

Christchurch Mansion has excellent displays of works by Suffolk artists dating from the 17th century to the present day. It holds the most important collection outside London of paintings by Thomas Gainsborough and John Constable.

A representative selection of the Museum's fine collection of British pottery, porcelain and glassware is on display. There are superb examples of English furniture dating from the 16th to the 19th century shown in period room settings. The Suffolk Artists' Gallery shows work by Suffolk artists such as George Frost, John Moore, Alfred Munnings, F G Cotman, Philip Wilson Steer and contemporary artists as well as works by Thomas Gainsborough and John Constable.

Christchurch Mansion was the site of the Augustinian Priory of the Holy Trinity. In 1536 the Priory was suppressed and its estates seized by the Crown. Paul Withipoll, a London merchant, bought the estate and between 1548 and 1550 his son Edmund built a house on the Priory site.

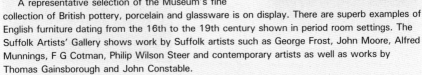

stories and anecdotes 🕮 famous people 🦚 art and craft 🖌 entertainment and sport 🎭 walks

grace the town's historic waterfront, such as Isaac Lord's and The Neptune (the latter was once home of Thomas Eldred, who circumnavigated the world with Thomas Cavendish shortly after Drake). A dozen medieval churches remain, of which St Margaret's is the finest, boasting some very splendid flintwork and a double hammerbeam roof. Another, St Stephen's, today houses the town's Tourist Information Centre.

Christchurch Mansion (see panel on page 165) is a beautiful Tudor home standing in 65 acres of attractive parkland, a short walk from the town centre. Furnished as an English country house, it contains a major collection of works by Constable and Gainsborough, as well as many other paintings, prints and sculptures by Suffolk artists from the 17th century onwards, and pottery, porcelain and fine period furniture.

Wolsey Art Gallery is a purpose-built space entered through Christchurch Mansion, which features changing displays including touring and national exhibitions.

Ipswich Museum is in a Victorian building in the High Street. Displays include a natural history gallery, a wildlife gallery complete with a model of a mammoth, a reconstruction of a Roman villa, and replicas of Sutton Hoo treasures. A recent addition is a display of elaborately carved timbers from the homes of wealthy 17th century merchants. There is also a rolling programme of exciting temporary exhibitions, events and displays.

In a former trolleybus depot on Cobham Road is **Ipswich Transport Museum**, a fascinating collection of vehicles, from

LAUREL FARM GARDEN CENTRE

Henley Road, Ipswich, Suffolk IP1 6TE
Tel/Fax: 01473 215984

Owners Samantha (Sam) and Nigel and their staff welcome everyone from beginners to seasoned gardeners at the **Laurel Farm Garden Centre**, which is located on Henley Road half a mile north of Ipswich town centre. When Sam and Nigel arrived in November 2006 they immediately immersed themselves in the Christmas rush, Nigel preparing Christmas trees and Sam, with a background in floristry, making Christmas wreaths and garlands. With that rush over, they set about refurbishing the whole place and widening its scope, with the result that it is now one of the leaders in its field in the region.

The variety of plants and gardening accessories is truly impressive: summer bedding plants, patio plants, hanging baskets (or bring your own and they'll fill it for you), vegetable and soft fruit plants, trees, shrubs, herbs, alpines, ferns, grasses, roses, climbers, lavenders, potted plants, cut flowers, bouquets.....and composts, manure, bark, topsoil and gro-bags. Also in stock are terracotta pots and troughs, oak barrels, statues, ornaments, rockery, slates, stone, pebbles, bird feeders and bird seed, bird and insect nesting boxes and a wide selection of garden furniture. This outstanding garden centre is open seven days a week.

prams to fire engines, all built or operated in the Ipswich area. Among the more unusual exhibits are a monorail for transporting spoil, a road sweeper converted from a Morris car, and the oldest trolleybus in the world - Ipswich no.2, built by Railless in 1923 (tel: 01473 715666).

Ipswich's position at the head of the River Orwell has always influenced the town's fortunes; today, a stroll along the waterfront should be included in any visit. Tudor houses and medieval churches stand alongside stylish new apartments that overlook the new marinas. An art gallery and choice of eateries enhance the experience, and there are regular pub cruises, leaving the Ipswich waterfront and travelling the Orwell (recently voted one of the prettiest rivers in England) as far as Felixstowe harbour.

On the outskirts of town, signposted from Nacton Road, is **Orwell Country Park**, a 150-acre site of wood, heath and reedbeds by the Orwell estuary. At this point the river is crossed by the imposing Orwell Bridge, a graceful construction in pre-stressed concrete that was completed in 1982 and is not far short of a mile in length. Local nature reserves have been established around Ipswich and all the way up the Gipping Valley as far as Stowmarket.

Notables from the world of the arts with Ipswich connections include Thomas Gainsborough, who got his first major commissions here to paint portraits of local people; David Garrick, the renowned actor-manager, who made his debut here in 1741 as Aboan in Thomas Southerne's *Oroonoko*; and the peripatetic Charles Dickens, who stayed

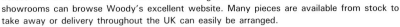

stories and anecdotes   famous people   art and craft   entertainment and sport   walks

at the Great White Horse while still a young reporter with *The Morning Chronicle*. Soon afterwards, he featured the tavern in *The Pickwick Papers* as the place where Mr Pickwick wanders inadvertently into a lady's bedroom. Sir V S Pritchett was born in Ipswich, while Enid Blyton trained as a kindergarten teacher at Ipswich High School.

Around Ipswich

BRAMFORD
1 mile NW of Ipswich off the A14

Bramford has a pretty little church, St Mary's, with a 13th-century stone screen. Elizabeth Mee, who played the church's first organ for 35 years, overcame the disability of being born blind. Bramford was once an important spot on the river route, when barges from Ipswich stopped to unload corn; the walls of the old lock are still visible. In the vicinity is Suffolk Water Park, where the lake welcomes canoeists and windsurfers.

NACTON
4 miles SE of Ipswich off the A14

🏛 Orwell Park House 🐾 Nacton Picnic Site

South of Nacton's medieval church lies **Orwell Park House**, which was built in the 18th century by Admiral Edward Vernon, sometime Member of Parliament for Ipswich. The admiral, who had won an important victory over the Spanish in the War of Jenkins Ear, was known to his men as 'Old Grog' because of his habit of wearing a cloak of coarse grogram cloth. His nickname passed into the language when he ordered that the rum ration dished out daily to sailors should be diluted with water to combat the drunkenness that was rife in the service. That was in 1740, but this allotted ration of 'grog' was officially issued to sailors right up until 1970.

George Tomline bought Orwell Park House in 1857 and made it even more splendid, adding a conservatory, a ballroom and towers. He also changed the façade along handsome Georgian lines. The house became the setting for some of the grandest shooting parties ever seen in this part of the world, and such was the power of the Tomlines that they were able to move the village away from the house to its present site.

Nacton Picnic Site in Shore Lane (signposted from the village) commands wonderful views of the Orwell and is a prime spot in winter for birdwatchers. The birds feed very well off the mud flats.

LEVINGTON
5 miles SE of Ipswich off the A14

A pretty village on the banks of the Orwell. Fisons established a factory here in 1956, and developed the now famous Levington Compost. On the foreshore below the village is an extensive marina, which has brought a bustling air to the area. The coastal footpath along the bank of the Orwell leads across the nature reserve of Trimley Marshes and on to Felixstowe.

TRIMLEY ST MARY & TRIMLEY ST MARTIN
6 miles SE of Ipswich off the A14

🐾 Trimley Marshes

Twin villages with two churches in the same churchyard, famous Trimley residents have included the Cavendish family, whose best-known member was the adventurer Thomas Cavendish. In 1590 he became the second man to sail round the world. Two years later he died while embarked on another voyage. He is depicted on the village sign. **Trimley Marshes** were created from farmland and comprise grazing marsh, reed beds and wetland that's home to an abundance of interesting plant life and many species of wildfowl, waders and migrant birds. Access is on foot from Trimley St Mary.

NEWBOURNE
7 miles E of Ipswich off the A12

A small miracle occurred here on the night of the hurricane of October 1987. One wall of the ancient St Mary's Church was blown out, and with it the stained glass, which shattered into fragments. One piece, showing the face of Christ, was found undamaged and was later incorporated into the rebuilt wall.

Two remarkable inhabitants of Newbourne were the Page brothers, who both stood over seven feet tall; they enjoyed a career touring the fairs, and are buried in Newbourne churchyard.

WALDRINGFIELD
7 miles E of Ipswich off the A12

Waldringfield lies on a particularly beautiful stretch of the Deben estuary, and the waterfront is largely given over to leisure boating and cruising. The quay was once busy with barges, many of them laden with coprolite. This fossilised dung, the forerunner of today's fertilisers, was found in great abundance in and around Waldringfield, and a number of exhausted pits can still be seen.

FELIXSTOWE
12 miles SE of Ipswich off the A14

🏛 Felixstowe Museum ⚓ Landguard Point

Until the early 17th century, Felixstowe was a little-known village - but it was the good Colonel Tomline of Orwell Park who put it on

---

THE REUNION GALLERY

36 Gainsborough Road, Felixstowe, Suffolk IP11 7HR
Tel: 01394 273366
e-mail: info@reuniongallery.co.uk
website: www.reuniongallery

School friends Pat Todd and Verena Daniels met up again years later and completed a degree in ceramics together. In 2002 they opened the **Reunion Gallery**, sharing the facilities to display and sell high-quality affordable artwork and giftware in a wide variety of media – oils, acrylic, watercolours, glass, ceramic, wood, bronze, precious metals and other natural materials. They will also undertake commissions and sourcing for individual requirements.

The Gallery is host to an ever-changing programme of exhibitions that run throughout the year. In October 'Fabric and Fibre' showcases the innovative work of Lulu Horsfield and Liz Mason. This is followed for the rest of the year by the work of owners/resident artists Pat and Verena, foremost exponents of ceramic and glassware innovation respectively. Both are members of the prestigious Suffolk Craft Society and have exhibited widely in the UK and Europe.

The gallery's Christmas Exhibition will combine the very best work by selected artists, providing customers with an excellent choice of high-quality, unique ad affordable items for gifts or personal treats. The gallery is located in the heart of Felixstowe's artists' quarter, just two minutes' walk from the main shopping street. Opening hours are 10 to 5 Tuesday to Saturday. Visit our website for an update on exhibitions and events in 2009.

🎬 stories and anecdotes 🦅 famous people 🎨 art and craft 🎭 entertainment and sport 🚶 walks

Felixstowe Museum

Viewpoint Road, Felixstowe, Suffolk IP11 7JG
Tel: 01394 674355
website: www.felixstowe.angle.uk.com

The museum is housed in the Ravelin block adjacent to Landguard
Fort. There are 12 rooms covering history of the Fort, Felixstowe
local history, Roman Felixstow, the RAF, a pleasure steamer room,
a naval room, St Audrey's Mental Hospital and the Dutch invasion
of 1667. A new room dedicated to aircraft with over 200 models
from 1913. Also a model room of over 200 aircraft and a coastal
forces 'Beehive' display.

the map by creating a port to rival its near
neighbour Harwich. He also started work on
the Ipswich-Felixstowe railway (with a stop at
Nacton for the guests of his grand parties),
and 1887 saw the completion of both
projects. Tomline also developed the resort
aspects of Felixstowe, rivalling the amenities
of Dovercourt, and by the time he died in
1887, most of his dreams had become reality.
(He was, incidentally, cremated, one of the
first in the county to be so disposed of in the
modern era.) What he didn't live to see was
the pier, opened in 1904 and still in use.

The town has suffered a number of ups and
downs since that time, but continues to thrive
as one of England's busiest ports, having been
much extended in the 1960s. The resort is
strung out around a wide, gently curving bay,
where the long seafront road is made even
prettier with trim lawns and gardens.

The Martello tower is a noted landmark, as
is the Pier, which was once long enough to
merit an electric tramway. It was shortened as
a security measure during the Second World
War. All kinds of attractions are provided for
holidaymakers, including one very unusual
one - the Felixstowe Water Clock, a curious
piece assembled from dozens of industrial
bits and pieces.

The original fishing hamlet from which the
Victorian resort was developed lies beyond a
golf course north of the town. This is
Felixstowe Ferry, a cluster of holiday homes,
an inn, a boatyard, fishing sheds and a
Martello tower. The sailing club is involved
mainly with dinghy racing, and the whole
place becomes a hive of activity during the
class meetings. A ferry takes foot passengers
(plus bicycles) across to Bawdsey.

At the southernmost tip of the peninsula is
Landguard Point, where a nature reserve
supports rare plants and migrating birds.

Just north on this shingle bank is Landguard
Fort, built in 1718 (replacing an earlier
construction) to protect Harwich harbour. It is
now home to **Felixstowe Museum** (see panel
above). The museum is actually housed in the
Ravelin Block (1878), which was used as a
mine storage depot by the army when a mine
barrier was laid across the Orwell during the
First World War. A fascinating variety of
exhibits includes local history, model aircraft
and model paddle steamers, Roman coins and
the history of the fort itself, which was the
scene of the last invasion of English soil, by
the Dutch in 1667. Beyond the fort is an
excellent viewing point for watching the
comings and goings of the ships.

FRESTON
3 miles S of Ipswich off the B1080

Freston is an ancient village on the south bank of the Orwell, worth visiting for some fine old buildings and curiosities. The most curious and best known of these buildings is the six-storey Tudor tower by the river in Freston Park (it's actually best viewed from across the river). This red-brick house, built around 1570, has just six rooms, one per storey. It might be a folly, but it was probably put up as a lookout tower to warn of enemies sailing up the river. The nicest theory is that it was built for Ellen, daughter of Lord Freston, to study a different subject each day, progressing floor by floor up the tower: charity on the ground floor, then tapestry and weaving, music, ancient languages, English literature, painting and astrology (and with Sundays off presumably). A 4,000-year-old

Freston Folly

archaeological site at Freston was revealed by aerial photography.

WOOLVERSTONE
4 miles S of Ipswich on the B1456

Dating back to the Bronze Age, Woolverstone has a large marina along the banks of the Orwell. One of the buildings in the complex is Cat House, where it is said that a stuffed white cat placed in the window would be the all-clear sign for smugglers. Woolverstone House was originally St Peter's Home for Fallen Women, run by nuns. It was designed by Sir Edwin Lutyens and has its own chapel and bell tower.

TATTINGSTONE
4 miles S of Ipswich off the A137

🏛 Tattingstone Wonder

The **Tattingstone Wonder**, visible from the A137 road between Tattingstone and Stutton, looks like a church from the front, but it isn't. It was built by Edward White, a local landowner, to provide accommodation for estate workers. He presumably preferred to look at a church from his mansion than some plain little cottages. Tattingstone lies at the western edge of Alton Water, a vast man-made lake created as a reservoir in the late 1970s. A footpath runs around the perimeter, and there's a wildlife sanctuary. On the water itself all sorts of leisure activities are on offer, including angling, sailing and windsurfing.

CHELMONDISTON
5 miles S of Ipswich on the B1456

⚓ Pin Mill

The church here is modern, but incorporates some parts of the original, which was destroyed by a flying bomb in 1944. In the same parish is the tiny riverside community of **Pin Mill**, a well-known beauty spot and sailing

HILL FARM EQUESTRIAN CENTRE

Hill Farm Lane, Chelmondiston, Suffolk IP9 1JU
Tel: 01473 780406
e-mail: meganaytonandrews@hotmail.co.uk
website: www.hfec.co.uk

Horse riding is a great outdoor activity for people of
all ages. It may seem a bit scary at first but most
horses are well trained to handle even the complete
novice. Once you get the hang of it, it can be
addictive. And it doesn't get any better than at **Hill**
Farm Equestrian Centre, situated just next to the sparkling River Orwell.
The combined experience of riding a horse and the marvellous scenery
make for a delightful day out!

Riding in England is a long-established tradition and over the years has
developed into a variety of exciting forms. You can enjoy anything from
formal riding instruction to trail riding, cross-country or the more leisurely
pursuit of trekking.

Hill Farm does it all and is especially great for children, for the youngest
children this might be their first lesson - perhaps on miniature Shetlands –
and they will love you for it! Megan Ayton-Andrews, proprietor, not only
teaches children and adults to ride she trains young riders for competition.
There is no better time or place to introduce your offspring to the delights of being confident on
horseback. Attractions such as Sutton Hoo, Orford castle and medieval woods are close by.

DEBORAH BAYNES POTTERY STUDIO

Nether Hall, Shotley, nr Ipswich, Suffolk IP9 1PW
Tel: 01473 788300 Fax: 01473 787055
e-mail: deb@deborahbaynes.co.uk
website: www.potterycourses.co.uk

Deborah Baynes has been making pots and teaching from her
studio since 1971, and she now oversees the longest established
residential studio pottery course in the UK. Each course at the
Deborah Baynes Pottery Studio begins with dinner in the oak-
beamed dining room. Excellent food and plenty of wine give students a
chance to settle in and meet their fellow potters. Some will be total
beginners, others may have more experience. The timetable follows a
similar pattern each day, starting with detailed demonstrations and
followed by tuition and making. This combination, plus practical tips
and personal attention, means that even complete beginners are soon
making successful pots.

The week-long course covers various aspects of pottery, including
hand building, decorating, glazing, throwing and the spectacular Raku
firing. With flames and smoke, food and wine and some amazing glazes
it really is the highlight of the week. On weekend and long weekend courses the emphasis is on
throwing and working on the wheel plus making spouts, lids and handles. Deborah also offers a
two-week salt-glaze master class covering everything from making to firing the massive oil-fired
kiln. Dates for this are by arrangement. Whether you are a total beginner or a complete potaholic
you are sure to have an instructive and fun time at Nether Hall.

centre. The river views are particularly lovely at this point, and it's also a favourite place for woodland and heathland walks. Pin Mill was once a major manufacturer of barges, and those imposing craft can still be seen, sharing the river with sailing boats and pleasure craft. Each year veteran barges gather for a race that starts here, at Buttermans Bay, and ends at Harwich. Arthur Ransome, author of *Swallows and Amazons*, stayed here and had boats built to his specifications. His *We Didn't Mean to Go to Sea* starts aboard a yacht mooring here.

The local hostelry is the 17th century Butt & Oyster, much visited, much painted and one of the best-known pubs in the county. To the east of the Quay is Cliff Plantation, an ancient coppiced wood of alder and oak.

STUTTON
6 miles S of Ipswich on the B1080

The elongated village of Stutton lies on the southern edge of Alton Water. The Domesday Book records six manor houses standing here, and there are still some grand properties down by the Stour. St Peter's Church is in an isolated position overlooking Holbrook Bay; a footpath from the church leads all the way along the river to Shotley Gate. A little way north, on the B1080, Holbrook is a large village with a brook at the bottom of the hill. Water from the brook once powered Alton Mill, a weatherboarded edifice on a site occupied by watermills for more than 900 years. The mill is now a restaurant.

ERWARTON
6 miles S of Ipswich off the B1456

🏠 Erwarton Hall

An impressive red-brick Jacobean gatehouse with a rounded arch, buttresses and pinnacles is part of **Erwarton Hall**, the family home of

the Calthorpes. Anne Boleyn was the niece of Philip Calthorpe, and visited as a child and as Queen. Just before her execution, Anne apparently requested that her heart be buried in the family vault at St Mary's Church. A casket in the shape of a heart was found there in 1836, but when opened contained only dust that could not be positively identified. The casket was resealed and laid in the Lady Chapel.

SHOTLEY
8 miles S of Ipswich on the B1456

Right at the end of the peninsula, with the Orwell on one side and the Stour on the other, Shotley is best known as the home of *HMS Ganges*, where generations of sailors received their training. The main feature is the 142-foot mast, up which trainees would shin at the passing-out ceremony. A small museum records the history of the establishment from 1905 to 1976, when it became a police academy. At the very tip of the peninsula is a large marina where a classic boat festival is an annual occasion.

HINTLESHAM
7 miles W of Ipswich on the A1071

Hintlesham's glory is a magnificent hall dating from the 1570s, when it was the home of the Timperley family. It was considerably altered during the 18th century, when it acquired its splendid Georgian façade. For some years the hall was owned by the celebrated chef Robert Carrier, who developed it into the county's leading restaurant. It still functions as a hotel and restaurant.

MONKS ELEIGH
16 miles W of Ipswich on the A1141

The setting of thatched cottages, a 14th-century church and a pump on the village

THE SUMMERHOUSE

Bridge Farm Barns, Monks Eleigh,
Suffolk IP7 7AY
Tel: 01449 741103
e-mail: athomeinthegarden@tiscali.co.uk
website: www.athomeinthegarden.co.uk

The **SummerHouse** is a true treasure in the
heart of Suffolk and a 'must see' on any visit to
this wonderful area. Established in 2003 by
mother and daughter team Erica Bolam and
Katie Green, this fine independent company
quickly became one of Suffolks leading suppliers in country
living style accessories. With a wealth of experience in art,
design, floristry, home styling and wildlife conservation,
Erica and Katie have created a truly unique shopping
experience at The SummerHouse.

On the Ground Floor are the Gardens and Wildlife
departments. 'Gardens' is filled with beautiful and practical
garden supplies and the fabulous centrepiece tree is always
adorned with amazing seasonal displays. 'Wildlife' holds a
very attractive and practical range of bird boxes, mammal
habitats, bug boxes, feeders, bird baths and more.

On the lower Ground Floor shoppers will find Suffolks
largest collection of stylish wrought iron garden furniture,
gazebos, arches and accessories, while a door to the back of
the barn invites you through to the amazing Conservatory
area. In here you will find a stunning display of tasteful
statuary, water features and artificial plants.

Upstairs, The SummerHouse showcase their country
living collections in 'Interiors' offering stunning designer
style from the UK and mainland Europe. Here vintage Style
and Contemporary Chic contrast and combine in a range
of lifestyle products that include occasional furniture,
table linens, mirrors, vases, candles, cushions and much
more at very affordable prices.

The Christmas displays at The SummerHouse have
been hailed as 'better than Harrods' and 'just like Narnia',
and if you are visiting Suffolk between October and
Christmas be sure to come and see the Christmas
Spectacular, it is quite unlike anything else available in the UK. The shop also hosts special
Christmas Shopping Evenings with free mulled wine and nibbles for a stress free shopping
experience. For those planning weddings, The SummerHouse has a wedding hire service where,
for that special day, you can hire decorated archways, gazebos, artificial bay trees, table centres
and more.

At The SummerHouse the ladies will gift-wrap any purchase free of charge; offer you a warm
welcome, and an unrivalled level of customer service which adds to the pleasure of a visit to
this very special place.

Situated on the Bridge Farm Barns Complex on the A1141 in the pretty village of Monks
Eleigh, The SummerHouse is Suffolks most beautiful and inspirational shop. Open from Monday
– Saturday 10am – 5pm and Sunday 11am – 5pm. Free parking and on site tea room.

🏛 historic building   🏛 museum and heritage   🏚 historic site   🍃 scenic attraction   🌿 flora and fauna

THE BILDESTON CROWN

104 High Street, Bildeston, Suffolk IP7 7EB
Tel: 01449 740510   Fax: 01449 741843
e-mail: info@thebildestoncrown.co.uk
website: www.thebildestoncrown.co.uk

Located in the heart of Suffolk's picturesque countryside, close to the historic towns of Lavenham, Bury St Edmunds and Ipswich, the **Bildeston Crown** is an original 15th century timber-framed coaching inn of wide appeal – as a place to enjoy a drink, a snack, a meal or an overnight or longer stay. The lovely old building has been imaginatively and sensitively refurbished to restore the building and cater to today's visitors without losing any of the character of its past 600 years. The two bars are ideal spots for meeting or making friends over a glass of real ale (regulars include Adnams Bitter and Greene King IPA) and when the sun shines the courtyard and garden come into their own.

Food is an integral part of the Bildeston Crown experience and Chef Chris Lee is developing an excellent reputation for an innovative style that has already gained recognition by the AA (3 Rosettes) and the Good Food Guide (joint-winner of the Up-and-Coming Chefs Award for the whole country). Chris and his team guarantee the best results by seeking out top-quality produce, sourced locally whenever possible, that includes Red Poll beef from the owners' own herd. The menus are designed to reflect the different needs and appetites of the clients. *Classics* feature regular favourites like shepherd's pie, fish & chips, rib of beef and Dover sole; *Select* is a little more adventurous and at times really quite experimental; and *Crown Tasting* provides the Bildeston Crown's ultimate dining experience with its eight-course tasting menu. There are also lunchtime sandwiches, a mid-week set lunch menu, and a Sunday lunch menu that always includes traditional roast beef.

The accommodation at this distinguished old inn is equally outstanding: each of the 12 beautifully appointed bedrooms has its own individual appeal, so that every visit brings a new experience. All the rooms have flat-screen Sky TV and wired or wireless internet access, and room service is available at all hours.

The owners of the Bildeston Crown operate two other pubs in Suffolk. The Lindsey Rose at Lindsey Tye near Ipswich (Tel: 01449 741424 web: www.thelindseyrose.co.uk) is a 15th century traditional Suffolk hall house with a warm welcome for visitors of ages and food of an exceptional standard. The Erwarton Queen at Erwarton near Ipswich (Tel: 01473 787550 web: www.erwartonqueen.com) is situated on the stunning Shotley peninsula, with glorious views of the Stour Estuary. A traditional old English pub, an ideal choice for a relaxing drink or a delicious home-cooked meal. The inn has two private dining/meeting rooms with external courtyards, one of them licensed for weddings.

green is so traditional that Monks Eleigh was regularly used on railway posters as a lure to this wonderful part of the country.

BILDESTON
14 miles W of Ipswich on the B1115

More fine old buildings here, including timber-framed cottages with overhanging upper floors. The Church of St Mary has a superb carved door and a splendid hammerbeam roof.

A tablet inside the church commemorates Captain Edward Rotherham, Commander of *The Royal Sovereign* at the Battle of Trafalgar. He died in Bildeston while staying with a friend, and is buried in the churchyard.

Constable Country

England's greatest landscape painter was born at East Bergholt in 1776 and remained at heart a Suffolk man throughout his life. His father, Golding Constable, was a wealthy man who owned both Flatford Mill and Dedham Mill, the latter on the Essex side of the Stour. The river was a major source of inspiration to the young John Constable, and his constant involvement in country matters gave him an expert knowledge of the elements and a keen eye for the details of nature. He was later to declare, 'I associate my careless boyhood with all that lies on the banks of the Stour. Those scenes made me a painter and I am grateful.'

His interest in painting developed early and was fostered by his friendship with John Dunthorne, a local plumber and amateur artist. Constable became a probationer at the Royal Academy Schools in 1799, and over the following years developed the technical skills to match his powers of observation. He painted the occasional portrait and even attempted a couple of religious works, but he concentrated almost entirely on the scenes that he knew and loved as a boy.

The most significant works of the earlier years were the numerous sketches in oil, which were forerunners of the major paintings of Constable's mature years. He had exhibited at the Royal Academy every year since 1802, but it was not until 1817 that the first of his important canvases, *Flatford Mill on the River Stour*, was hung. This was succeeded by the six large paintings that became his best-known works. These were all set on a short stretch of the Stour, and all

Boating near Flatford Mill

except *The Hay Wain* show barges at work. These broad, flat-bottomed craft were displayed in scenes remarkable for the realism of the colours, the effects of light and water and, above all, the beautiful depiction of clouds. His fellow-artist Fuseli declared that whenever he saw a Constable painting he felt the need to reach for his coat and umbrella. Though more realistic than anything that preceded them, Constable's paintings were never lacking soul, and his work was much admired by the painters of the French Romantic School.

Two quotations from the man himself reveal much about his aims and philosophy:

In a landscape I want to give one brief moment caught from fleeting time a lasting and sober existence.

'never saw any ugly thing in my life; in fact, whatever may be the shape of an object, light, shade or perspective can always make it beautiful.

At the time of his death in 1837, Constable's reputation at home was relatively modest, though he had many followers and admirers in France. Awareness and understanding of his unique talent grew only in the ensuing years, so that, today, his place as England's foremost landscape painter is rarely disputed.

Suffolk has produced many other painters of distinction. Thomas Gainsborough, born in Sudbury in 1727, was an artist of great versatility, innovative and instinctive, and equally at home with portraits and landscapes. He earned his living for a while from portrait painting in Ipswich before making a real name for himself in Bath. His relations with the Royal Academy were often stormy, however, culminating, in 1784, in a major dispute over the height at which a painting should be hung. He withdrew his intended hangings from the exhibition and never again showed at the Royal Academy.

A man of equally indomitable spirit was Sir Alfred Munnings, born at Mendham in the north of Suffolk in 1878. The last of the great sporting painters in the tradition of Stubbs and Marshall, Munnings was outspoken in his opinions on modern art. In 1949, as outgoing President of the Royal Academy, he launched an animated attack on modern art as 'silly daubs' and 'violent blows at nothing'. The occasion was broadcast on the radio; in response, many listeners complained about the 'strong language' Munnings had used. In 1956, Munnings jolted the art world again by describing that year's Summer Exhibition as 'bits of nonsense' hung on the wall.

Mary Beale, born at Barrow in 1633, was a noted portrait painter and copyist; some of her work has been attributed to Lely and Kneller, and it was rumoured that Lely was in love with her.

Philip Wilson Steer (1860-1942) was among the most distinguished of the many painters who were attracted to Walberswick. He studied in Paris and acquired the reputation of being the best of the English impressionist painters.

The Suffolk tradition of painting continues to this day, with many artists drawn to this part of the county. While nowadays crowds congregate throughout the Stour valley at summer weekends, at other times the tranquillity and loveliness are just as unmatched as they were in Constable's day.

CAPEL ST MARY
6 miles SW of Ipswich on the A12

Constable sketched here, but modern building has more or less overrun the old. A feature of the Church of St Mary is the weeing chancel -

a slight kink between the nave and the chancel that is meant to signify Christ's head leaning to the right on the cross.

BRANTHAM

8 miles SW of Ipswich on the A137

🜨 Cattawade Picnic Site

Also known as Burnt Village – possibly because it was sacked during a Danish invasion 1,000 years ago – Brantham's Church of St Michael owns one of the only two known religious paintings by Constable, Christ Blessing the Children, which he executed in the style of the American painter Benjamin West. It is kept in safety in Ipswich Museum. Just off the junction of the A137 and the B1070 is **Cattawade Picnic Site**, a small area on the edge of the Stour estuary. It's a good spot for birdwatching, and redshanks, lapwings and oystercatchers all breed on the well-known Cattawade Marshes. Fishing and canoeing are available, and there are public footpaths to Flatford Mill.

EAST BERGHOLT

8 miles SW of Ipswich on the B1070

🏛 Stour House 🜨 Flatford Mill

🜨 Willy Lot's Cottage 🏚 Bridge Cottage

🕌 St Mary's Church 🏚 Constable Country Trail

Narrow lanes lead to this picturesque and much-visited little village. The **Constable Country Trail** starts here, where the painter was born, and passes through Flatford Mill and on to Dedham in Essex. The actual house where he was born no longer stands, but the site is marked by a plaque on the fence of its

Wooden Bellcage, East Bergholt

successor, a private house called Constables. A little further along Church Street is Moss Cottage, which Constable once used as his studio. **St Mary's Church** is one of the many grand churches built with the wealth brought by the wool trade. This one should have been even grander, with a tower to rival that of Dedham across the river.

The story goes that Cardinal Wolsey pledged the money to build the tower, but fell from grace before the funds were forthcoming. The tower got no further than did his college in Ipswich, and a bellcage constructed in the churchyard as a temporary house for the bells became their permanent home, which it remains to this day. In this unique timber-framed structure the massive bells hang upside down and are rung by hand by pulling on the wooden shoulder stocks - an arduous task, as the five bells are among the heaviest in England, weighing in at over four tons.

The church is naturally something of a shrine to Constable, his family and his friends. There are memorial windows to the artist and to his beloved wife Maria Bicknell, who bore him seven children and whose early death was an enormous blow to him.

His parents, to whom he was clearly devoted, and his old friend Willy Lot, whose cottage is featured famously in *The Hay Wain*, are buried in the churchyard.

East Bergholt has an interesting mix of houses, some dating back as far as the 14th century. One of the grandest is **Stour House**, once the home of Randolph Churchill. Its gardens are open to the public, as is East Bergholt Place Garden on the B1070.

A leafy lane leads south from the village to the Stour, where two of Constable's favourite subjects, **Flatford Mill** and **Willy Lot's Cottage**, both looking much as they did when he painted them, are to be found. Neither is open to the public, and the brick watermill is run as a residential field study centre.

Nearby, **Bridge Cottage** at Flatford is a restored 16th century building housing a Constable display, a tea room and a shop. There's also a restored dry dock, and the whole area is a delight for walkers; it is easy to see how Constable drew constant inspiration from the wonderful riverside setting. Guided summer walks from the cottage, which is in the care of the National Trust, take in the sites of some of his most famous paintings (tel: 01206 298260).

NAYLAND
14 miles SW of Ipswich on the B1087

On a particularly beautiful stretch of the Stour in Dedham Vale, Nayland has charming colour-washed cottages set in narrow, winding streets, as well as two very fine 15th-century buildings in Alston Court and the Guildhall. Abels Bridge, originally built of wood in the 15th century by wealthy merchant John Abel,

divides Suffolk from Essex. In the 16th century a hump bridge replaced it, allowing barges to pass beneath. The current bridge carries the original keystone, bearing the initial A. In the Church of St James stands an altarpiece by Constable entitled *Christ Blessing the Bread and Wine*.

One mile west of Nayland, at the end of a track off the Bures road, stands the Norman Church of St Mary at Wissington. The church has a number of remarkable features, including several 13th-century wall paintings, a finely carved 12th-century doorway and a tiebeam and crown post roof.

STRATFORD ST MARY
10 miles SW of Ipswich off the A12

🏠 Ancient House　🏠 Priest's House

Another of Constable's favourite locations, Stratford St Mary is the most southerly village in Suffolk. *The Young Waltonians* and *A House in Water Lane* (the house still stands today) are the best known of his works set in this picturesque spot. The village church is typically large and imposing, with parts dating back to 1200. At the top of the village are two splendid half-timbered cottages called the **Ancient House** and the **Priest's House**. Stratford was once on the main coaching route to London, and the largest of the four pubs had stabling for 200 horses. It is claimed that Henry Williamson, author of *Tarka the Otter*, saw his first otter here.

STOKE BY NAYLAND
12 miles SW of Ipswich on the B1087

🏠 Church of St Mary

The drive from Nayland reveals quite stunning views, and the village itself has a large number of listed buildings. The magnificent **Church of St Mary**, with its 120-foot tower, dominates the

scene from its hilltop position. This church also appears in more than one Constable painting, the most famous showing the church lit up by a rainbow. William Dowsing destroyed 100 'superstitious pictures' here in his Puritan purges, but plenty of fine work is still to be seen, including several monumental brasses.

The Guildhall is another very fine building, now private residences, but in the 16th century a busy centre of trade and commerce. When the wool trade declined, so did the importance of the Guildhall, and for a time this noble building saw service as a workhouse.

The decline of the cloth trade in East Anglia had several causes. Fierce competition came from the northern and western weaving industries, which generally had easier access to water supplies for fulling; the wars on the continent of Europe led to the closure of some trading routes and markets; and East Anglia had no supplies of the coal that was used to drive the new steam-powered machinery. In some cases, as at Sudbury, weaving or silk took over as smaller industries.

POLSTEAD
11 miles SW of Ipswich off the B1068

Polstead is a very pretty village set in wooded, hilly countryside, with thatched, colour-washed cottages around the green and a wide duck pond at the bottom of the hill. Standing on a rise above the pond are Polstead Hall, a handsome Georgian mansion, and the 12th-century Church of St Mary. The church has two features not found elsewhere in Suffolk – a stone spire and the very early bricks used in its construction. The builders used not only these bricks, but also tiles and tufa, a soft, porous stone much used in Italy. In the grounds of the hall stand the remains of a Gospel Oak said to have been 1,300 years old when it collapsed in 1953. Legend has it that Saxon missionaries preached beneath it in the 7th century; an open-air service is still held here annually. The rectory is rumoured to be one of the most haunted, with phenomena including a presence in the attic and a voice calling 'John'. A former rector is said to drive around the village in a carriage drawn by a headless horse.

Polstead has two other claims to fame. One is for Polstead Blacks, a particularly tasty variety of cherry, which was cultivated in orchards around the village and used to be honoured with an annual fair. The other is much less agreeable, for it was here that the notorious Red Barn murder hit the headlines in 1827. A young girl called Maria Marten, daughter of the local molecatcher, disappeared with William Corder, a farmer's son who was the girl's lover and father of her child. It was at first thought that they had eloped, but Maria's stepmother dreamt three times that she had been murdered and buried in a red barn. A search of the barn soon revealed this to be true. Corder was tracked down to Middlesex, tried and found guilty of Maria's murder and hanged. His skin was used to bind a copy of the trial proceedings and this, together with his scalp, was put on display at Moyse's Hall in Bury St Edmunds. The incident aroused a great deal of interest; today's visitors to the village will still find reminders of the ghastly deed: the thatched cottage where Maria lived stands, in what is now called Marten's Lane, as does the farm where the murderer lived, now called Corder's Farm.

BOXFORD
12 miles W of Ipswich on the A1071

A gloriously unspoilt weaving village, surrounded by the peaceful water meadows of the River Box, Boxford's St Mary's Church

dates back to the 14th century. Its wooden north porch is one of the oldest of its kind in the country. In the church is a touching brass in memory of David Byrde, son of the rector, who died a baby in 1606. At the other end of the continuum is Elizabeth Hyam, four times a widow, who died in her 113th year.

EDWARDSTONE
14 miles W of Ipswich off the A1071

Just to the north of Boxford and close to Edwardstone Hall and the Temple Bar Gate House, Edwardstone is now a 700-acre estate originally home to the Winthrop family. Winthrop was born in Edwardstone and emigrated to the New World, eventually becoming Governor of Massachusetts.

BURES
17 miles W of Ipswich on the B1508

At this point the River Stour turns sharply to the east, creating a natural boundary between Suffolk and Essex. The little village of Bures straddles the river, lying partly in each county. Bures St Mary in Suffolk is where the church is, overlooked by houses of brick and half-timbering.

Bures wrote itself very early into the history books when on Christmas Day AD855 it is thought that Edmund the Martyr, the Saxon king, was crowned at the age of 15 in the Chapel of St Stephen. For some time after that momentous occasion, Bures was the capital seat of the East Anglian kings.

Bures also has a long connection with the Waldegrave family, possibly from as far back as Chaucer's day. One of the Waldegrave memorials shows graphically the results of a visitation by Dowsing and the Puritan iconoclasts: all the figures of the kneeling children have had their hands cut off.

Sudbury

🏛 Gainsborough's House

Sudbury is another wonderful town, the largest of the 'wool towns' and still home to a number of weaving concerns. Unlike Lavenham, Sudbury kept its industry because it was a port, and the result is a much more varied architectural picture. The surrounding countryside is some of the loveliest in Suffolk, and the River Stour is a further plus, with launch trips and fishing available.

Sudbury boasts three medieval churches, but what most visitors make a beeline for is **Gainsborough's House** in Gainsborough Street. The painter Thomas Gainsborough was born here in 1727 in the house built by his father

Salter's Hall, Sudbury

BUTLER & BROOKS

1 Friars Street, Sudbury, Suffolk CO10 2AA
Tel: 01787 374050
e-mail: Judi@butlerandbrooks.uk.com
website: www.butlerandbrooks.uk.com

Antique furniture gives any room a vintage-style look. Floral patterns on the curtains and upholstery keep things feminine, while decorative accessories add the finishing touches. Create a look you'll love with **Butler & Brooks**!

The Butler and Brooks look incorporates a stylish mix of contemporary and vintage home furnishings in line with how many people style their homes today. Continually searching for new items sourced from around the world as well as from small design houses and local designers with the aim of offering a unique mix of stylish home accessories and gifts for the home. In addition to design led classic items including collectable glassware, furniture, lighting and accessories, Butler and Brooks also love to find things that you are looking for and could even have something made specially for you that fit with both a contemporary and more traditional style. Home living...sold with love!

🏛 historic building 🏛 museum and heritage 🏛 historic site 🌿 scenic attraction 🐦 flora and fauna

John. More of the artist's work is displayed in this Georgian-fronted house than in any other gallery, and there is also assorted 18th-century memorabilia and furnishings. A changing programme of contemporary art exhibitions includes fine art, photography and sculpture, highlighting East Anglian artists in particular. A bronze statue of Gainsborough stands in the square.

About those churches: All Saints dates from the 15th century and has a glorious carved tracery pulpit and screens; 14th-century St Gregory's is notable for a wonderful medieval font; and St Peter's has some marvellous painted screen panels and a piece of 15th-century embroidered velvet.

Other buildings of interest are the Victorian Corn Exchange, now a library, Salter's Hall, a 15th-century timbered house, and the Quay Theatre, a thriving centre for the arts.

Around Sudbury

HADLEIGH
12 miles E of Sudbury on the A1071

🏛 Guildhall

The old and not-so-old blend harmoniously in a variety of architectural styles in Hadleigh. Timber-framed buildings, often with elaborate plasterwork, stand in the long main street as a reminder of the prosperity generated by the wool trade in the 14th to 16th centuries, and there are also some fine houses from the Regency and Victorian periods. The 15th-century **Guildhall** has two overhanging storeys, and together with the Deanery Tower and the church, makes for a magnificent trio of huge appeal and contrasting construction – timber for the Guildhall, brick for the tower and flint for the church.

THE SUFFOLK FLOWER COMPANY

67 High Street, Hadleigh, Suffolk IP7 5DY
Tel/Fax: 01473 827698
e-mail: sales@thesuffolkflowercompany.co.uk
website: www.thesuffolkflowercompany.co.uk

'When the Ordinary Simply Isn't Enough'

Owner Kirsty, director Justine and manager Tania believe in working with only the best quality flowers at the **Suffolk Flower Company**, which occupies a fine 16th century building on Hadleigh's main street. The ladies and their staff create what is just right for any occasion, and whether it's a single stem or a large arrangement they endeavour to provide any home or event with the 'wow' factor. Their shop is a delightful picture of brightly coloured flowers, pots, vases and other lovely things. The Suffolk Flower Company also offers a comprehensive wedding service with the emphasis once again on quality and attention to detail. They can handle anything from an intimate family affair to a formal function for hundreds, supplying anything from buttonholes and bridal bouquets to spectacular floral arches. At no 82 in the High Street (Tel: 01473 822243) is sister enterprise **Plum Green**, where Jill is the manager. From garden furniture and soft furnishings to jewellery, scented candles, bags and cards. Quality is the keynote here too, throughout a stylish range of contemporary homeware and giftware from top brands in the UK, France, Denmark and Italy.

📖 stories and anecdotes 🐦 famous people 🎨 art and craft 🍃 entertainment and sport 🚶 walks

JIM LAWRENCE TRADITIONAL IRONWORK

The Ironworks, Lady Lane Industrial Estate,
Hadleigh, Suffolk IP7 6BQ
Tel: 01473 828176 Fax: 01473 824074
e-mail: jim@jim-lawrence.co.uk
website: www.jim-lawrence.co.uk

**Beautiful Hand-Made Products
Delivered Direct to your Door**

Jim Lawrence Traditional Ironwork built up a large and loyal clientele in Stoke-by-Nayland, near Colchester, before moving a short distance into the next county and new premises in Hadleigh, just off the A1071 Sudbury-Ipswich road. The handsome, newly refurbished showrooms, with workshop attached, are stocked with products in five main categories.

Lighting
Wall lights, pendants, chandeliers, lanterns, lampshades, electrical switches and sockets and other accessories

Curtain Poles
Pole builders, curtain pole packs, bespoke poles in iron, brass and mahogany, finials, brackets and accessories

Home Furnishings
Fixtures and fittings for kitchens, bathrooms and living rooms, fireside accessories and hand-coloured engravings

Door and Window Furniture
Knobs, handles, hinges, latches and quality fittings made in-house by Jim Lawrence

Soft Furnishings
Curtains, blinds, cushions, rugs, bedding, haberdashery and a range of fabrics from embroidered silks to voile and vibrant cotton

Friendly, efficient staff welcome callers either on the phone or in person at the showrooms, which are open from 9 to 5.30 Monday to Friday and from 9 to 4 on Saturday. Everything in stock can be viewed in the showrooms or online, and clients can place their order online. If the goods are in stock they will be despatched straightaway, and if they are made to order or have to be brought into stock they will usually be sent within 14 days.
Goods can be delivered anywhere in the UK, and by special arrangement, overseas.

Guthrun, the Danish leader who was captured by Alfred and pardoned on condition that he became a Christian, made Hadleigh his HQ and lived here for 12 years. He was buried in the church, then a wooden construction but subsequently twice rebuilt. In the south chapel of the present church is a 14th-century bench-end carving depicting the legendary scene of the wolf guarding the head of St Edmund. The wolf is wearing a monk's habit, indicating a satirical sense of humour in the carpenter. Also of interest is the Clock Bell, which stands outside the tower.

A local rector and famous resident, Dr Rowland Taylor, was burnt at the stake on Aldham Common for refusing to hold a mass. A large stone, inscribed and dated 1555, marks the spot.

There are two good walks from Hadleigh, the first being along the Brett with access over medieval Toppesfield Bridge. The other is a walk along the disused railway line between Hadleigh and Raydon through peaceful, picturesque countryside.

At Raydon a few buildings survive from the Second World War base of the 353rd, 357th and 358th Fighter Groups of the USAAF.

Two miles east of Hadleigh is Wolves Wood, an RSPB reserve with woodland nature trails - and no wolves! The RSPB is continuing the traditional coppicing method of managing it, which means that the wood has a wide variety of birds, plants and animals (tel: 01473 328006 for details of guided walks and other events).

KERSEY

11 miles E of Sudbury off the A1141

🐾 Water Splash

The ultimate Suffolk picture-postcard village, Kersey boasts a wonderful collection of timbered merchants' houses and weavers'

Kersey Water Splash

cottages, paint washed and thatched. The main street has a **Water Splash**, which, along with the 700-year-old Bell Inn, has featured in many films and travelogues. The Church of St Mary, which overlooks the village from its hilltop position, is of massive proportions, testimony to the wealth that came with the wool and cloth industry. Kersey's speciality was a coarse twill broadcloth much favoured for greatcoats and army uniforms. Headless angels and mutilated carvings are reminders of the Puritans' visit to the church, though some treasures survive, including the ornate flintwork of the 15th-century south porch.

Traditional craftsmanship can still be seen in practice at the Kersey Pottery, which sells many items of stoneware plus paintings by Suffolk artists.

The Waldingfields

Distance: *3.1 miles (4.8 kilometres)*

Typical time: *60 mins*

Height gain: *15 metres*

Map: *Explorer 196*

Walk: *www.walkingworld.com ID:1876*

Contributor: *Brian and Anne Sandland*

To reach the church at Great Waldingfield, turn south east off the B1115.

DESCRIPTION:

This walk visits two churches and quaint old Suffolk villages. There are picturesque cottages and excellent paths, tracks and lanes on the way. The walk can be combined with another that starts from Great Waldingfield Church and visits Acton as well as reaching the outskirts of Little Waldingfield.

FEATURES:

Pub, Church, Wildlife, Birds, Flowers, Great Views, Butterflies, Woodland.

WALK DIRECTIONS:

1 | Starting from the church, take the road signposted No through road - Footpath to Little Waldingfield. After a descent on the track to Hole Farm, look for a signposted footpath on the right just before the farm.

2 | Turn right and before long follow a stream beside a wood (left), then take a signposted

footpath left over a bridge and through the wood.

3 | After the wood, cross a footbridge, then continue beside a very large field (on your left). When you reach a lane by the road to Archers Farm, turn left along it. Pass the church at Little Waldingfield, then turn left at the T-junction with the B1115 (past the Swan Inn).

4 | Just beyond the thatched cottage, The Grange (left), take the right hand of two signposted footpaths off left. At the far end of the field cross a footbridge, then follow signs (and a concrete roadway) around Hole Farm before reaching the lane you used at the start of your walk and ascending it to reach Great Waldingfield church again.

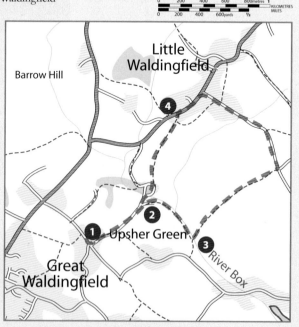

CHELSWORTH
10 miles NE of Sudbury off the A1141

Chelsworth is an unspoilt delight in the lovely valley of the River Brett, which is crossed by a little double hump-backed bridge. The timbered houses and thatched cottages look much the same as when they were built, and every year the villagers open their gardens to the public.

BRENT ELEIGH
8 miles NE of Sudbury off the A1141

The church at Brent Eleigh, on a side road off the A1141, is remarkable for a number of quite beautiful ancient wall paintings, discovered during maintenance work as recently as 1960. The most striking and moving of the paintings is one of the Crucifixion.

LAVENHAM
6 miles N of Sudbury on the A1141

🏭 Guildhall 🏛 Little Hall Museum 🏭 Priory
🏭 Church of St Peter & St Paul

An absolute gem of a town, the most complete and original of the medieval 'wool towns', with crooked timbered and whitewashed buildings lining the narrow streets. From the 14th to the 16th centuries, Lavenham flourished as one of the leading wool and cloth-making centres in the land. With the decline of that industry, however, the prosperous times soon came to an end. It is largely due to the fact that Lavenham found no replacement industry that so much of its medieval character remains: there was simply not enough money for the rebuilding and development programmes that changed many other towns, often for the worse. The

LAVENHAM OLD RECTORY

Church Street, Lavenham CO10 9SA
Tel: 01787 247572
website: www.lavenhamoldrectory.co.uk

The Old Rectory at Lavenham offers sumptuous accommodation in its three individual and impressive en-suite rooms. Situated just on the edge of this architecturally important village with its quaint medieval buildings and enjoy outstanding views of the imposing 15th century church of St Peter and St Paul The Old Rectory combines country chic style with classical Georgian décor and furnishing.

Dating back to 1720 The Old Rectory has been lovingly restored over four years by its present owners Susie and Jonathan Wright and is open to guests from the summer 2008. The grounds have been returned to their former glory including a walled vegetable garden and the house retains many of its original features.

From the moment you enter the house there is a sense of serenity and a feeling of light and space in the well-proportioned rooms. You can enjoy the expansive Thomas Gainsborough room with its country décor and triple aspect views of the gardens and the church. The John Constable room based on the Chinoserie theme of the period with its elegant furnishing and four poster bed is a superb reflection of the opulent living of the time. The De Vere room is decorated in the provencal style, again a popular theme of the Georgian times, with classically painted furniture. There is a private car park for guests.

MUNNINGS TEA ROOM & ACCOMODATION

Gabel End, 29 High Street, Lavenham, Suffolk CO10 9PT
Tel: 01787 249453
e-mail: info@munningstearoom.co.uk
website: www.munningstearoom.co.uk

Munnings is a traditional tearoom built in 1520 situated in the heart of the thriving historic village of Lavenham and decorated with a romantic Victorian flair. There are just a few tables in the beamed front room, so you may want to reserve on weekends or in high season. The beauty, elegance, and romantic charm of the Victorian Tea are a beautiful addition to modern day friendships. In the time honoured traditions of England, taking tea is now again a wonderful time to take a moment and reflect on the simple pleasures of life in the special company of friends both old and new. Unfold your fine napkin and enjoy a fresh homemade scone accompanied by a generous dollop of clotted cream, and in the true fashion of a teahouse, an assortment of finger foods, including sandwiches, homemade pastries and desserts. Opening hours are 10.00am - 6.00pm Monday to Saturday and 10.00am - 5.00pm Sunday.

Since Easter 2008, in addition to the tearoom Munnings now offers quality bed and breakfast accommodation. The accommodation comprises two double bedrooms one with private bathroom and one with a shower room. Large lounge with sky TV with private access. Lunch or afternoon tea can be booked at the tearoom.

Also available are two doubles at Munnings Barn, a 17th century barn converted in 2003 offering 4 star accommodation. Sitting in 2.5 acres with swimming pool. All rooms are en-suite. Digital TV in all rooms as well as Internet access. Situated just 10 minutes outside Lavenham, in the heart of the Suffolk countryside providing numerous tranquil walks. The Barn has excellent access to local towns of Bury St Edmunds (15mins) with its famous Cathedral Abbey gate and gardens. The Nutshell, the smallest pub in the world is worth noting, as is the famous Greene King brewery, which offers tours all year round.

And for any Horse Racing Fans! Fancy a day at the races? Transport to and from your accommodation here at the Barn or Munnings is arranged. Combined with premier enclosure badges plus a luxurious Champagne Picnic! Be sure to get some Hot Tips at Breakfast straight from the horses mouth. The shopping experience is also to be found here! So for a real taste of Suffolk, eat and sleep at Munnings!

Lavenham Guildhall

medieval street pattern still exists, complete with market place and market cross.

More than 350 of Lavenham's buildings are officially listed as being of architectural and historical interest, and none of them is finer than the **Guildhall**. This superb 16th-century timbered building was originally the meeting place of the Guild of Corpus Christi, an organisation that regulated the production of wool. It now houses exhibitions of local history and the wool trade, and has a walled garden with a special area devoted to plants used for dyes. Apart from its religious guild activities, it has served as a prison, workhouse, almshouse, wool store, nursery school, restaurant and Welcome Club for Americamn servicemen in the Second World War. **Little Hall**, is hardly less remarkable, a 15th century hall house with a superb crown post roof. It was restored by the Gayer-Anderson brothers,

ELIZABETH GASH KNITWEAR

36 Market Square, Lavenham, Suffolk CO10 9QZ
Tel: 01787 248561
e-mail: lizgashknit@tinyworld.co.uk

Elizabeth Gash Knitwear, the shop that bears the name of its owner and founder, is located in a pretty timber-framed building on Lavenham's picturesque market square. The oak-beamed interior provides a visual feast of colour, texture and pattern, and the urge to forage is almost irresistible. Most of Elizabeth's knitwear is inspired by the beautiful designs of Eastern nomadic textiles and rugs, and the range, which can be made to measure, includes knitted jackets, waistcoats, hats, bags, scarves and cushions, and each piece is infused with Elizabeth's trademark flair for colour and pattern.

Elizabeth started her knitting career with a stall in Covent Garden; as her following grew she took on some knitters and started a mail order catalogue, eventually opening her shop here in Lavenham in 2000. Her aim was to create a thriving outlet for unusual, beautiful garments made by talented designers based in the UK, among whom are Corry Marshall, Bill Baber, Sophie's Wild Woollens, The Quernstone, Terry Macey, Angelika Elsebach and the Irish company Gaeltara.

Also in stock are clothes by Flax, Noa Noa, Cut Loose, Natural Wave and Adina, all hand-picked to complement her own range, and a great selection of accessories, including bags, scarves, gloves and silver and semi-precious jewellery. Shop hours are 11 to 5 seven days a week.

CURIOSITY CORNER

1 Church Street, Lavenham, Sudbury,
Suffolk CO10 9QT
Tel: 01787 248441
e-mail: sales@curiosity-corner.com
website: www.curiosity-corner.com

Curiosity Corner is a delightful little shop situated in a lovely part of Lavenham in Suffolk, next to the Old Swan Hotel. This historic village has lots to offer and is well worth a visit, with plenty of great places to eat and drink with a wide variety of interesting shops.

Within this picturesque shop you will not only find Bears, Dolls, Gollies and other cuddlies but also a vast range of collectables and gifts including some shop exclusives.

Lavenham with its many historic timbered buildings including the Crooked house, its picturesque scenery and its locality to many other places of interest you are sure to have a good time. Although with the ever-increasing demands on everyday life, time is limited and with the ease of online shopping, products can now be available at the touch of a button. Those at Curiosity Corner have decided to be available to their customers from within their own homes. They are delighted to bring you Curiosity Corner on-line.

and has a fine collection of their furniture, pictures, sculpture and ceramics. Its small walled garden was visited in 2005 by HRH The Prince of Wales and the Duchess of Cornwall. Earlier royal visitors to the town include King Edward I (in 1275), Queen Elizabeth I (1578) and Queen Mary (1928). **The Church of St Peter and St Paul** dominates the town from its elevated position. It's a building of great distinction, perhaps the greatest of all the 'wool churches' and declared by the 19th-century architect August Pugin to be the finest example of Late Perpendicular style in the world. It was built, with generous help from wealthy local families (notably the Spryngs and the de Veres) in the late 15th and early 16th centuries to celebrate the end of the Wars of the Roses. Its flint tower is a mighty 140 feet in height, and it's

possible to climb to the top to take in the glorious views over Lavenham and the surrounding countryside. Richly carved screens and fine (Victorian) stained glass are eye-catching features within.

The Priory originated in the 13th century as a home for Benedictine monks; the beautiful timber-framed house on the site dates from about 1600. In the original hall, at the centre of the building, is an important collection of paintings and stained glass. The extensive grounds include a kitchen garden, a herb garden and a pond. The Angel Gallery on the Market Square houses exhibitions by local and national artists.

John Constable went to school in Lavenham, where one of his friends was Jane Taylor, who wrote the words to *Twinkle Twinkle Little Star.*

LONG MELFORD
2 miles N of Sudbury off the A134

🏠 Melford Hall 🏠 Holy Trinity Church
🏠 Kentwell Hall

The heart of this atmospheric wool town is its very long and, in stretches, fairly broad main street, set on an ancient Roman site in a particularly beautiful part of south Suffolk. In Roman times the Stour was a navigable river, and trade flourished. Various Roman finds have been unearthed, notably a blue glass vase that is now on display in the British Museum in London. The street is filled with antiques shops, book shops and art galleries, and is a favourite place for collectors and browsers. Some of the houses are washed in the characteristic Suffolk pink, which might originally have been achieved by mixing ox blood or sloe juice into the plaster.

Holy Trinity Church, on a 14-acre green at the north end of Hall Street, is a typically exuberant manifestation of the wealth of the wool and textile trade. It's big enough to be a cathedral, but served (and still serves) comparatively few parishioners. John Clopton, grown rich in the woollen business, was largely responsible for this magnificent Perpendicular-style edifice, which has a 180-foot nave and chancel and half timbers, flint flushwork (stonework) of the highest quality, and 100 large windows to give a marvellous sense of light and space. Medieval glass in the north aisle depicts religious scenes and the womenfolk of the Clopton family. There are many interesting monuments and brasses, and in the chantry entrance is a bas relief of the

Three Wise Men, the Virgin and Child, and St Joseph. In the Lady Chapel, reached by way of the churchyard, a children's multiplication table written on one wall is a reminder that the chapel served as the village school for a long period after the Reformation.

John Clopton's largesse is recorded rather modestly in inscriptions on the roof parapets. His tower was struck by lightning in the early 18th century; the present brick construction dates from around 1900. The detail of this great church is of endless fascination, but it's the overall impression that stays in the memory, and the sight of the building floodlit at night is truly spectacular. The distinguished 20th-century poet Edmund Blunden spent his last years in Long Melford and is buried in the churchyard. The inscription on his gravestone reads, 'I live still to love still things quiet and unconcerned.'

Melford Hall, east of town beyond an imposing 16th-century gateway, was built around 1570 by Sir William Cordell on the site of an earlier hall that served as a country retreat, before the Dissolution of the Monasteries, for the monks of St Edmundsbury Abbey. There exists an account of Cordell entertaining Queen Elizabeth I at

Melford Hall Gateway, Long Melford

Kentwell Hall

Long Melford, Suffolk CO10 9BA
Tel: 01787 310207 Fax: 01787 379318
e-mail: info@kentwell.co.uk website: www.kentwell.co.uk

Kentwell Hall, a romantic, mellow, moated redbrick Tudor
mansion in a tranquil parkland setting, has a great deal to
offer the visitor. The house was built by the Clopton
family in the first half of the 16th century with wealth
accrued from the wool trade, and the exterior has
changed little down the centuries. After the Cloptons, the
house saw a succession of owners and tenants before
being requisitioned by the Army in the Second World War.
It was in a poor state of repair when acquired by the
present owner Patrick Phillips in 1970, since when he and
his wife Judith have been lovingly restoring the house and
its gardens.

Visitors can enjoy the Tudor service rooms such as the
Great Kitchen and the Wardrobe Privy in the main house and the Bakehouse, Brewhouse
and Dairy in the separate 15th century service building. Hopper's Gothic Great Hall and
Dining Room and a series of classical 18th century rooms should also be seen, along with
the State Bedroom, the Chinese Room, the brick-paved Tudor Rose Maze Courtyard and
some very fine early heraldic stained glass. The owners have created a rare breeds farm in
the superb grounds, where other features include a restored working ice house, a rose
garden, a fern stumpery, a coppice walk, a living sundial and the largest carved tree in
England, representing the Tower of Babel.

Kentwell is famous for its recreations of Tudor domestic life and of wartime Britain,
when it saw service as a transit camp. These events take place on Bank Holidays and
selected weekends throughout the year, and in the summer a series of open-air
entertainment, from jazz to Shakespeare, is invariably well attended. The Hall was the
setting for the film version of *Toad of Toad Hall*.

the Hall in 1578, when she was welcomed by
'200 young gentlemen in white velvet, 300 in
black and 1,500 serving men'. Much of the
fine work of Sir William (whose body lies in
Holy Trinity Church) has been altered in
restoration, but the pepperpot topped towers
are original, as is the panelled banqueting hall.
The rooms are in various styles, some with
ornate walnut furniture, and there's a notable
collection of Chinese porcelain on show. Most
delightful of all is the Beatrix Potter room,
with some of her watercolours, first editions
of her books and, among the toys, the original

of Jemima Puddleduck. She was a frequent
visitor here (her cousins, the Hyde Parkers,
were, and remain, the owners), bringing small
animals to draw. The Jeremy Fisher
illustrations were mostly drawn at Melford
Hall's fishponds, and the book is dedicated to
Stephanie Hyde Parker. New attractions for
2008 are an interpretation room and craft
demonstrations. The Hall, which is a National
Trust property, stands in a lovely garden with
some distinguished clipped box hedges.
William Cordell was also responsible for the
red-brick almshouses, built in 1593 for '12

poor men', which stand near Holy Trinity. On the green near the Hall is a handsome brick conduit built to supply water to the Hall and the village along wooden pipes.

Kentwell Hall (see panel opposite) is a mellow redbrick Tudor moated mansion approached by a long avenue of limes. Its grounds include a unique Tudor rose maze, and are set out to illustrate and re-create Tudor times, with a walled garden, a bakery, a dairy and several varieties of rare-breed farm animals. The buildings include a handsome 14th-century aisle barn. The Hall was the setting for a film version of *Toad of Toad Hall* (tel: 01787 310207).

Long Melford is a great place for leisurely strolls, and for the slightly more energetic there's a scenic three-mile walk along a disused railway track and farm tracks that leads straight into Lavenham.

GLEMSFORD
5 miles NW of Cavendish on the B1065

Driving into Glemsford, the old Church of St Mary makes an impressive sight on what, for Suffolk, is quite a considerable hill. Textiles and weaving have long played a prominent part in Glemsford's history, and thread from the silk factory, which opened in

1824 and is still going strong, has been woven into dresses and robes for various members of the royal family, including the late Princess Diana's wedding dress. During the last century, several factories produced matting from coconut fibres, and in 1906 Glemsford was responsible for the largest carpet in the world, used to cover the floor at London's Olympia. To this day, one factory processes horse hair for use in judges' wigs, sporrans and busbies.

CAVENDISH
5 miles W of Sudbury on the A1092

A most attractive village, where the Romans stayed awhile - the odd remains have been unearthed - and the Saxons settled. Cavendish is splendidly traditional, with its church, thatched cottages, almshouses, and the 16th-century rectory Nether Hall, now the headquarters of Cavendish Vineyards. In the Church of St Mary, whose tower has a pointed bellcote and a room inside complete with fireplace and shuttered windows, look for the two handsome lecterns, one with a brass eagle (15th century), the other with two chained books; and for the Flemish and Italian statues. In 1381 Wat Tyler, leader of the Peasants' Revolt, was killed at Smithfield, in London, by

THE GEORGE CAVENDISH
The Green, Cavendish, Suffolk CO10 8BA
Tel: 01787 280248
e-mail: paulbaileyfox@hotmail.co.uk

Standing on the village green in Cavendish, **The George** is a much-loved local, a highly regarded dining pub and a quiet, comfortable base for Bed & Breakfast guests. Dating back to the 1600's, the pub has been smartly renovated while retaining all its traditional appeal and is in the excellent care of Paul Bailey, a talented chef and restaurateur with many years' experience. His menu, served every lunchtime and evening, tours the culinary world with dishes that run from beer-battered cod and rib-eye steaks to grey mullet with salsa verde, Cajun prawns, Chinese pork belly strips and red onion & blue cheese tart. Four en suite bedrooms provide a very pleasant base for touring an attractive part of the county.

John Cavendish, son of Sir John Cavendish, then lord of the manor and Chief Justice of England. Sir John was then hounded by the peasants, who caught him and killed him near Bury St Edmunds. He managed, en route, to hide some valuables in the belfry of St Mary's here in Cavendish, and bequeathed to the church £40, sufficient to restore the chancel. A later Cavendish – Thomas – sailed round the world in the 1580s and perished on a later voyage. In the shadow of the church, on the edge of the village green, is a cluster of immaculate thatched cottages at a spot known as Hyde Park Corner. Pink-washed and pretty as a picture, they look almost too good to be true – and they almost are, having been rebuilt twice since the Second World War due to unhappy forces that included fires and dilapidation.

CLARE

7 miles W of Sudbury on the A1092

🏛 Ancient House   🏛 Clare Castle

🏃 Clare Castle Country Park

A medieval wool town of great importance, Clare offers fine old buildings and some distinguished old ruins. Perhaps the most renowned tourist attraction is **Ancient House**, a timber-framed building dated 1473 and remarkable for its pargeting. This is the decorative treatment of external plasterwork, usually by dividing the surface into rectangles and decorating each panel. It was very much a Suffolk speciality, particularly in the 16th and 17th centuries, with some examples also being found in Cambridgeshire and Essex. The decoration could be simple brushes of a comb, scrolls or squiggles, or more elaborate, with religious motifs, guild signs or family crests. Some pargeting is incised, but the best is in relief – pressing moulds into wet plaster

or shaping it by hand. Ancient House sports some splendid entwined flowers and branches, and a representation of two figures holding a shield. The best-known workers in this unique skill had their own distinctive styles, and the expert eye could spot the particular 'trademarks' of each man (the same is the case with the master thatchers). Ancient House is now a museum, open during the summer months and housing an exhibition on local history.

Another place of historical significance is Nethergate House, once the workplace of dyers, weavers and spinners. The Swan Inn, in the High Street, has a sign that lays claim to being the oldest in the land. Ten feet in length and carved from a solid piece of wood, it portrays the arms of England and France. **Clare Castle** was a motte-and-bailey fortress

Clare Church and Ancient House

Clare Castle Country Park

Maltings Lane, Clare, Suffolk CO10 8NJ
Tel: 01787 277491

Clare Castle Country Park is open daily throughout the year and offers the visitor a variety of attractions. Within the country park can be found the remains of Clare Castle and Clare Railway Station. The former railway goods shed is now a visitor centre (open April - September). There is ample open space for picnics and games, while children can enjoy an adventure playground. Wander along the riverside path and old railway line or follow the nature and history trails to learn more about the country parks' wildlife and heritage.

that sheltered a household of 250. **Clare Castle Country Park** (see panel above), with a visitor centre in the goods shed of a disused railway line, contains the remains of the castle and the moat, the latter now a series of ponds and home to varied wild life.

At the Prior's House, the original cellar and infirmary are still in use. Established in 1248 by Augustine friars, and used by them until the Dissolution of 1538, the priory was handed back to that order in 1953 and remains their property.

A mile or so west of Clare, on the A1092, lies Stoke-by-Clare, a pretty village on one of the region's most picturesque routes. It once housed a Benedictine priory, whose remains are now in the grounds of a school. There's a fine 15th-century church and a vineyard: Boyton Vineyards at Hill Farm, Boyton End, is open early April-October for a tour, a talk and a taste.

KEDINGTON

12 miles W of Sudbury on the B1061

🏛 Church of St Peter & St Paul

Haverhill (see over page) intrudes somewhat, but the heart of the old village of Kedington gains in appeal by the presence of the River Stour. Known to many as the Cathedral of

West Suffolk, the **Church of St Peter and St Paul** is the village's chief attraction. Almost 150 feet in length, it stands on a ridge overlooking the Stour Valley. It has several interesting features, including a 15th-century font, a Saxon cross in the chancel window, a triple-decker pulpit (with a clerk's desk and a reading desk) and a sermon-timer, looking rather like a grand egg-timer. The foundations of a Roman building have been found beneath the floorboards.

The Bardiston family, one of the oldest in Suffolk, had strong links with the village and many of the family tombs are in the church. In the church grounds is a row of 10 elm trees, each, the legend says, with a knight buried beneath its roots.

Following the Stour along the B1061, the visitor will find a number of interesting little villages. In Little Wratting, Holy Trinity Church has a shingled oak-framed steeple (a feature more usually associated with Essex churches). John Sainsbury was a local resident, while in Great Wratting another magnate, W H Smith, financed the restoration of St Mary's Church in 1887. This church boasts some diverting topiary in the shape of a church, a cross and – somewhat comically - an armchair.

🎬 stories and anecdotes 🐦 famous people 🎨 art and craft 🎭 entertainment and sport 🚶 walks

HAVERHILL
14 miles W of Sudbury on the A604

🏛 Anne of Cleves House 🏛 East Town Park

Notable for its fine Victorian architecture, Haverhill also boasts one fine Tudor gem. Although many of Haverhill's buildings were destroyed by fire in 1665, the **Anne of Cleves House** was restored and is well worth a visit. Anne was the fourth wife of Henry VIII and, after a brief political marriage, she was given an allowance and spent the remainder of her days at Haverhill and Richmond. Haverhill Local History Centre, in the Town Hall, has an interesting collection of memorabilia, photographs and archive material. **East Town Park** is an attractive and relatively new country park on the east side of Haverhill.

GREAT AND LITTLE THURLOW
15 miles W of Sudbury on the B1061

Great and Little Thurlow form a continuous village on the west bank of the River Stour a few miles north of Haverhill. Largely undamaged thanks to being in a conservation area, together they boast many 17th-century cottages and a Georgian manor house. In the main street is a schoolhouse built in 1614 by Sir Stephen Soame, one-time Lord Mayor of London, whose family are commemorated in the village church.

A short distance further up the B1061 stands the village of Great Bradley, divided in two by the River Stour, which rises just outside the village boundary. Chief points of note in the tranquil parish church are a fine Norman doorway sheltering a Tudor brick porch and some beautiful stained glass, poignantly depicting a soldier in the trenches during the First World War. The three bells in the tower include one cast in the 14th century, among the oldest in Suffolk.

Bury St Edmunds

🏛 St Mary's Church 🏛 Cathedral ᛩ Art Gallery

🏛 Theatre Royal ᛩ Abbey Gardens

🏛 Moyse's Hall Museum ᛋ Nowton Park

🏛 Greene King Brewery Visitor Centre

🏛 Abbey Ruins

A gem among Suffolk towns, rich in archaeological treasures and places of religious and historical interest, Bury St Edmunds takes its name from St Edmund, who was born in Nuremberg in AD841 and came here as a teenager to become the last King of East Anglia. He was a staunch Christian, and his refusal to deny his faith caused him to be tortured and killed by the Danes in AD870. Legend has it that although his body was recovered, his head (cut off by the Danes) could not be found. His men searched for it for 40 days, then heard his voice directing them to it from the depths of a wood, where they discovered it lying protected between the paws of a wolf. The head and the body were seamlessly united and, to commemorate the wolf's deed, the crest of the town's armorial bearings depicts a wolf with a man's head.

Edmund was possibly buried first at Hoxne, the site of his murder, but when he was canonised in about AD910 his remains were moved to the monastery at Beodricsworth, which changed its name to St Edmundsbury. A shrine was built in his honour, later incorporated into the Norman Abbey Church after the monastery was granted abbey status by King Canute in 1032. The town soon became a place of pilgrimage, and for many years St Edmund was the patron saint of England, until replaced by St George. Growing rapidly around the great abbey,

St Edmundsbury Cathedral

Angel Hill, Bury St Edmunds, Suffolk IP33 1LS
Tel: 01284 754933 Fax: 01284 768655
website: www.stedscathedral.co.uk

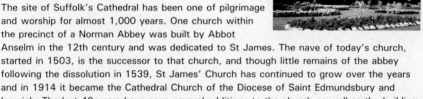

The site of Suffolk's Cathedral has been one of pilgrimage and worship for almost 1,000 years. One church within the precinct of a Norman Abbey was built by Abbot Anselm in the 12th century and was dedicated to St James. The nave of today's church, started in 1503, is the successor to that church, and though little remains of the abbey following the dissolution in 1539, St James' Church has continued to grow over the years and in 1914 it became the Cathedral Church of the Diocese of Saint Edmundsbury and Ipswich. The last 40 years have seen several additions to the church as well as the building of the Cathedral Centre, which houses the Song School, the refectory and meeting rooms. Outstanding features of the Cathedral include a magnificent hammerbeam roof and a monumental bishop's throne.

which became one of the largest and most influential in the land, Bury prospered as a centre of trade and commerce, thanks notably to the cloth industry.

The next historical landmark was reached in 1214, when on St Edmund's Feast Day the then Archbishop of Canterbury, Simon Langton, met with the Barons of England at the high altar of the Abbey and swore that they would force King John to honour the proposals of the Magna Carta. The twin elements of Edmund's canonisation and the resolution of the Barons explain the motto on the town's crest: sacrarium regis, cunabula legis – shrine of a king, cradle of the law.

Rebuilt in the 15th century, the **Abbey** was largely dismantled after its Dissolution by Henry VIII, but imposing ruins remain in the colourful Abbey Gardens beyond the splendid **Abbey Gate** and Norman Tower. **St Edmundsbury Cathedral** (see panel above) was originally the Church of St James, built in the 15th/16th centuries and accorded cathedral status (alone in Suffolk) in 1914. The original building has been much extended over the years (notably when being adapted for its

role as a cathedral) and outstanding features include a magnificent hammerbeam roof, whose 38 beams are decorated with angels bearing the emblems of St James, St Edmund

Abbey Gate, Bury St Edmunds

and St George. The monumental Bishop's throne depicts wolves guarding the crowned head of St Edmund, and there's a fascinating collection of 1,000 embroidered kneelers, several making reference to the strong links forged between Suffolk and America.

St Mary's Church, in the same complex, is well worth a visit: an equally impressive hammerbeam roof, the detached tower standing much as Abbot Anselm built it in the 12th century, and several interesting monuments, the most important commemorating Mary Tudor, sister of Henry VIII, Queen of France and Duchess of Suffolk. Her remains were moved here when the Abbey was suppressed; a window in the Lady Chapel recording this fact was the gift of Queen Victoria.

The **Abbey Gardens**, laid out in 1831, have as their central feature a great circle of flower beds following the pattern of the Royal Botanical Gardens in Brussels. Some of the original ornamental trees can still be seen, and other, later, features include an Old English rose garden, a water garden and a garden for the blind where fragrance counts for all. Ducks and geese live by the little River Lark, and there are tennis courts, putting and bowls greens, and children's play equipment. A bench in the gardens is made from the metal frame of an American Flying Fortress, commemorating US servicemen stationed hereabouts in the Second World War.

Bury is full of fine non-ecclesiastical buildings, many with Georgian frontages concealing medieval interiors. Among the most interesting are the Victorian Corn Exchange with its imposing colonnade; the

🏛 historic building   🏛 museum and heritage   🏛 historic site   🏞 scenic attraction   🌱 flora and fauna

Athenaeum, hub of social life since Regency times and scene of Charles Dickens's public readings; Cupola House, where Daniel Defoe once stayed; the Angel Hotel, where Dickens and his marvellous creation Mr Pickwick stayed; and the Nutshell, owned by Greene King Brewery and a contender for the title of the smallest pub in the country. **The Theatre Royal**, now in the care of the National Trust, was built in 1819 by William Wilkins, who was also responsible for the National Gallery in London. It staged the premiere of *Charley's Aunt*, and still operates as a working theatre.

One of Bury's oldest residents and newest attractions is the **Greene King Brewery**. Greene King beer has been brewed here in Bury since 1799; the museum's informative storyboards, artefacts, illustrations and audio displays bring the history and art of brewing to life. Brewery tours include a look round the museum and beer-tasting. The shop sells a variety of memorabilia, souvenirs, gifts and clothing – as well, of course, as bottles and cans of the frothy stuff.

Bury St Edmunds Art Gallery is housed in one of Bury's noblest buildings, built to a Robert Adam design in 1774. It has filled many roles down the years, and was rescued from decline in the 1960s to be restored to Adam's original plans. It is now one of the county's premier art galleries, with eight exhibitions each year and a thriving craft shop.

Perhaps the most fascinating building of all is **Moyse's Hall Museum**, located at one end of the Buttermarket. Built of flint and limestone about 1180, it has claims to being the oldest stone domestic building in England. Originally a rich man's residence, it later saw service as a tavern, gaol, police station and railway parcels office, but since

1899 it has been a museum, and has recently undergone total refurbishment. It houses some 10,000 items, including many important archaeological collections, from costumes, jewellery and clocks, to a 19th-century doll's house and relics of the notorious Red Barn murder. One wing contains the Suffolk Regiment collection and education room.

Outside the Spread Eagle pub on the western edge of town, is a horse trough erected to the memory of the Victorian romantic novelist Ouida (Maria Louisa Ramee, 1839-1908).

Steeped though it is in history, Bury also moves with the times, and its sporting, entertainment and leisure facilities are impressive. A mile-and-a-half outside town on the A14 (just off the East Exit) is **Nowton Park**, 172 acres of countryside landscaped in Victorian style and supporting a wealth of flora and fauna; the avenue of limes, carpeted with daffodils in the spring, is a particular delight. There's also a play area and a ranger centre.

Bury's disciplined network of streets (the layout was devised in the 11th century) provides long, alluring views. A great fire destroyed much of Bury in 1608, but it was rebuilt using traditional timber-framing techniques. Arriving here in 1698, Celia Fiennes, the inveterate traveller and architecture critic, was uncharacteristically favourable in her remarks about Cupola House, which had just been completed at the time of her visit. William Cobbett (1763-1835), a visitor when chronicling his *Rural Rides*, did not disagree with the view that Bury St Edmunds was 'the nicest town in the world' - a view that would be endorsed by many of today's inhabitants and by many of

CULFORD FARM COTTAGES

Home Farm, Culford,
nr Bury St Edmunds, Suffolk IP28 6DS
Tel/Fax: 01284 728334
e-mail: enquiries@homefarmculford.co.uk
website: www.culfordfarmcottages.co.uk

250 cares of tranquil, attractive farmland are the setting for **Culford Farm Cottages** located less than three miles from Bury St Edmunds.

Three comfortable cottages, stylishly and skilfully converted from period buildings, provide everything needed for a self-contained, stress-free self-catering holiday. Each has its own particular charm and character, and guests enjoy the shared use of a sheltered swimming pool for the summer.

The Dairy, converted from a Victorian dairy building, stands next to the owners' handsome Tudor farmhouse. It has two bedrooms, one on the ground floor, the other overlooking the sitting room. French doors lead to the enclosed garden and a hot tub.

The Smoke House, also with two bedrooms, one en suite, is a charming conversion which also has an enclosed garden and a hot tub (situated in the enclosed swimming pool garden area).

Piglet's Place, an imaginative single-storey conversion, has doors and full-length windows opening on to a quiet courtyard garden – and a hot tub. It has a double bedroom with en suite shower and two twin-bedded rooms, one with zip & link beds. This property is accessible to wheelchair users.

All the cottages have oil-fired central heating, TV with a video/DVD library, radio, hob, microwave oven, fridge-freezer, hairdryer and garden furniture. The grounds of Culford Farm Cottages offer guests the chance to stroll along the banks of the River Lark and to enjoy the fresh country air, the scenery and the varied birdlife. Charolais cattle and horses graze in the meadows. One dog is allowed in the Dairy and the Smoke House, but not in Piglet's Place. The cottages are well placed for touring the many sights of the area. The Abbey and its gardens, the Cathedral and the Theatre Royal are among the attractions in nearby Bury, and Thetford Forest, Melford Hall, West Stow Anglo-Saxon Village and Ickworth House are all within an easy drive.

the millions of visitors who have been charmed by this jewel in Suffolk's crown.

Around Bury St Edmunds

ICKLINGHAM
8 miles NW of Bury St Edmunds on the A1101

The village of Icklingham boasts not one but two churches - the parish Church of St James (mentioned in the Domesday Book) and the deconsecrated thatched-roofed All Saints, with medieval tiles on the chancels and beautiful east windows in the south aisle. At the point where the Icknield Way crosses the River Lark, Icklingham has a long history, brought to light in frequent archaeological finds, from pagan bronzes to Roman coins. The place abounds in tales of the supernatural, notably of the white rabbit who is seen at dusk in the company of a witch, causing – it is said - horses to bolt and men to die.

Just south of Icklingham, at the A1101, is Rampart Field picnic site, where pleasant walks through gorse-filled gravel workings reveal the varied plant life of a typical Breckland heath.

WEST STOW
7 miles NW of Bury St Edmunds off the A1101

🏛 Anglo-Saxon Village 🐦 Country Park

The villages of West Stow, Culford, Ingham, Timworth and Wordwell were for several centuries part of a single estate covering almost 10,000 acres. Half the estate was sold to the Forestry Commission in 1935 and was renamed the King's Forest in honour of King George V's Jubilee in that year.

An Anglo-Saxon cemetery was discovered in the village in 1849 and subsequent years have revealed traces of Roman settlements and the actual layout of the original **Anglo-Saxon Village** (see panel on page 202). A trust was established to investigate further the Anglo-Saxon way of life and their building and farming techniques. Several buildings were constructed using, as accurately as could be achieved, the tools and methods of the 5th century. The undertaking has become a major tourist attraction, with assistance from guides both human (in Anglo-Saxon costume) and in the form of taped cassettes. There are pigs and hens, growing crops, craft courses, a Saxon market at Easter, a festival in August and special events all year round. This fascinating village, which is entered through the Visitor Centre, is part of **West Stow Country Park**, a large part of which is designated a Site of Special Scientific Interest (SSSI). Over 120 species of birds and 25 species of animals have been sighted in this Breckland setting, and a well-marked five-mile nature trail links the nature reserve with the woods, a large lake and the River Lark.

HENGRAVE
3 miles NW of Bury St Edmunds on the A1101

A captivating old-world village of flint and thatch, excavations and aerial photography indicate that there has been a settlement at Hengrave since Neolithic times. The best-known building is Hengrave Hall, a rambling Tudor mansion built partly of Northamptonshire limestone and partly of yellow brick by Sir Thomas Kytson, a wool merchant. A notable visitor in the early days was Elizabeth I, who brought her court here in 1578.

Several generations of the Gage family were later the owners of Hengrave Hall - one

West Stow Anglo-Saxon Village

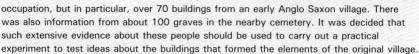

Visitor Centre, Icklingham Road, West Stow,
Bury St Edmunds, Suffolk IP28 6HG
Tel: 01284 728718 Fax: 01284 728277
website: www.stedmundsbury.gov.uk/weststow.htm

Between 1965 and 1972 the low hill by the River Lark in Suffolk was excavated to reveal several periods of occupation, but in particular, over 70 buildings from an early Anglo Saxon village. There was also information from about 100 graves in the nearby cemetery. It was decided that such extensive evidence about these people should be used to carry out a practical experiment to test ideas about the buildings that formed the elements of the original village.

Part of the Anglo Saxon Village has been reconstructed on the site where the original (inhabited from around AD420 to 650) was excavated. The reconstructions have been built over a period of more than 20 years. Each of the eight buildings is different, to test different ideas, and each has been built using the tools and techniques available to the early Anglo Saxons. Exploring the houses is an excellent way of finding out about the Anglo Saxons who lived at West Stow. Costumed "Anglo Saxons" bring the village to life at certain times, especially at Easter and during August. The new Anglo Saxon Centre is an exciting addition to the site, housing the original objects found there and at other local sites. Many of the objects have never been seen by the public before.

West Stow Anglo Saxon Village lies in the middle of a beautiful 125 acre Country Park, part of which is a Site of Special Scientific Interest. The park has a number of different habitats, including woodland, heathland, a lake and a river. There is a play area, a bird feeding area and bird hides. The Park is open daily all year, from 9am-5pm in winter, 9am-8pm in summer. Entry to the park is free.

of them, with a particular interest in horticulture, imported various kinds of plum trees from France. Most of the bundles were properly labelled with their names, but one had lost its label. When it produced its first crop of luscious green fruit, someone had the bright idea of calling it the green Gage.

The name stuck, and the descendants of these trees, planted in 1724, are still at the Hall, which is not open to the public. In the grounds stands a lovely little church with a round Saxon tower and a wealth of interesting monuments. The church was for some time a family mausoleum; restored by Sir John Wood, it became a private chapel and now hosts services of various denominations.

FLEMPTON

4 miles NW of Bury St Edmunds on the A1101

⚔ Lark Valley Park

An interesting walk from this village just north of the A1101 follows the **Lark Valley Park** through Culford Park, providing a good view of Culford Hall, which has been a school since 1935. A handsome cast-iron bridge dating from the early 19th century - and recently brought to light from amongst the reeds - crosses a lake in the park.

LACKFORD

6 miles NW of Bury St Edmunds on the A1101

More interest here for the wildlife enthusiast.

Restored gravel pits have been turned into a reserve for wildfowl and waders. Two hides are available.

EUSTON
9 miles N of Bury St Edmunds on the A1088

🏛 Euston Hall

Euston Hall, on the A1088, has been the seat of the Dukes of Grafton for 300 years. It's open to the public on Thursday afternoons and is well worth a visit, not least for its portraits of Charles II and its paintings by Van Dyck, Lely and Stubbs. In the colourful landscaped grounds is an ice-house disguised as an Italianate temple, the distinguished work of John Evelyn and William Kent.

Euston's church, in the grounds of the Hall, is the only one in the county dedicated to St Genevieve. It's also one of only two Classical designs in the county, being rebuilt in 1676 on part of the original structure. The interior is richly decorated, with a beautiful carving on the hexagonal pulpit, panelling around the walls and a carved panel of the Last Supper. Parts of this lovely wood carving are attributed by some to Grinling Gibbons. Behind the family pew is a marble memorial to Lord Arlington, who built the church.

Euston's watermill was built in the 1670s and rebuilt in 1730 as a Gothic church.

PAKENHAM
4 miles NE of Bury St Edmunds off the A143

🏛 Nether Hall 🏛 Newe House

🏭 Watermill and Windmill

On a side road just off the A143 (turn right just north of Great Barton) lies the village of Pakenham, whose long history has been unearthed in the shape of a Bronze Age barrow and kiln, and another kiln from Roman times.

Elsewhere in Pakenham are the 17th-century **Nether Hall**, from whose lake in the park the village stream flows through the fen into the millpond. **Newe House**, a handsome Jacobean building with Dutch gables and a two-storey porch, dates from the same period. The Church of St Mary has an impressive carved Perpendicular font, and in its adjacent vicarage is the famous Whistler Window - a painting by Rex Whistler of an 18th-century parish priest. The fens were an important source of reeds, and many of Pakenham's buildings show off the thatcher's art.

Pakenham's current unique claim to fame is in being the last parish in England to have a working watermill and windmill, a fact proclaimed on the village sign. The **Watermill** was built around 1814 on a site mentioned in the Domesday Book (the Roman excavations suggest that there could have been a mill here as far back as the 1st century AD). The mill, which is fed from Pakenham fen, has many interesting features, including the Blackstone oil engine, dating from around 1900, and the Tattersall Midget rollermill from 1913, a brave but ultimately unsuccessful attempt to compete with the larger roller mills in the production of flour. The mill and the neighbouring recreation park are well worth a visit.

No less remarkable is the **Windmill**, one of the most famous in Suffolk. The black-tarred tower was built in 1831 and was in regular use until the 1950s. One of the best preserved mills in the county, it survived a lightning strike in 1971. Both mills lie on the village's circular walks, and fresh flour is available from both.

IXWORTH
5 miles NE of Bury St Edmunds on the A143

Ixworth played its part as one of the Iceni tribe's major settlements, with important Roman connections and, in the 12th century,

WYKEN – THE LEAPING HARE

Wyken Vineyards, Stanton,
nr Bury St Edmunds, Suffolk IP31 2DW
Tel: 01359 250287
e-mail: info@wykenvineyards.co.uk
website: www.wykenvineyards.co.uk

Restaurant, café, country store, gardens, woodland walk - there's something for everyone at **Wyken**, which is sign posted off the A143 northeast of Bury St Edmunds. Set in beautiful Suffolk countryside, the ancient estate is mentioned in the *Doomsday Book*.

The present **Wyken Hall** is a romantic Elizabethan manor house surrounded by four acres of the 'one of the best privately owned gardens in England' (*RHS Garden Magazine '08*). In 1988 the Carlisle family planted a seven-acre vineyard on a sandy south-facing slope. This was followed by the opening of the Leaping Hare Country Store and Restaurant in a superbly converted 400 year old barn.

The wonderful **Gardens**, initiated in the 1970s by Sir Kenneth Carlisle, includes, herb, knot, rose and kitchen gardens, a copper beech maze, the dell planted with 40 silver birch, the millennium stride, a nuttery planted with English Cobs, a row of Walnut Trees leading to a Gazebo built from reclaimed farm brick and flint and wild flower meadows. The gardens are open from Easter to the end of September Sunday to Friday 2.00 pm till 6.00pm (Closed Saturdays).

The Leaping Hare Country Store is open daily from 10-00 am to 6.00 pm and sells an eclectic mix of country and garden treasures including sculpture, pottery, basket ware, clothing and design led gifts. Wyken Farmers' Market is held every Saturday from 9.00 am till 1.00 pm selling not only Wyken produce but locally reared and produced meat, fresh fish from Lowestoft, organic dairy and bread, speciality cheeses, fantastic cakes, fruit and vegetables, local honey and herbs, seasonal flowers, olive oil and other treasures.

The Leaping Hare Restaurant and Café (*Best Restaurant in Suffolk, EADT 2007 and Michelin Guide 'Bib Gourmand' 2008*) serves distinctive seasonal food that perfectly complements the estates wines and peaceful surroundings. The modern menu makes excellent use of locally sourced ingredients. Typical dishes might include venison, pheasant, fruit and vegetables from the Estate, fish and seafood from local suppliers. Lunch is served in the Restaurant from 12.00 noon to 2.00 pm daily, dinner on Friday and Saturday evenings from 7.00 pm till 9.00 pm. The café is open daily from 10.00 am serving breakfast, coffee and tea, light lunches from 12.00 noon till 4.30pm. Afternoon tea is available from 2.30pm.

🏠 historic building 🏛 museum and heritage 🏚 historic site 🏞 scenic attraction 🌿 flora and fauna

the site of an Augustinian priory. The remains of the priory were incorporated into a Georgian house known as Ixworth Abbey, which stands among trees by the River Blackbourne. The village has many 14th-century timber-framed dwellings, and the Church of St Mary dates from the same period, though with many later additions.

A variety of circular walks take in lovely parts of the village, which is also the staring point of the Miller's Trail cycle route.

A little way north of the village, on the A1088, are a nature trail and bird reserve at Ixworth Thorpe Farm. At this point a brief diversion northwards up the A1088 is very worth while.

BARDWELL
7 miles NE of Bury St Edmunds off the A1088

Bardwell offers another tower windmill. This one dates from the 1820s and was worked by wind for 100 years, then by an oil engine until 1941. It was restored in the 1980s, only to suffer severe damage in the great storm of October 1987, when its sails were torn off. Stoneground flour is still produced by an auxiliary engine.

Also in this delightful village are a 16th-century inn and the Church of St Peter and St Paul, known particularly for its medieval stained glass.

HONINGTON
7 miles NE of Bury St Edmunds on the A1088

Back on the A1088, the little village of Honington was the birthplace of the pastoral poet Robert Bloomfield (1766-1823), whose best known work is *The Farmer's Boy*. The house where he was born is now divided, one part called Bloomfield Cottage, the other Bloomfield Farmhouse. A brass plaque to his memory can be seen in All Saints Church, in the graveyard of which his parents are buried.

BARNINGHAM
8 miles NE of Bury St Edmunds on the B1111

🏃 Knettishall Heath Country Park

Near the Norfolk border, Barningham was the first home of the firm of Fisons, which started in the late 18th century. Beginning with a couple of windmills, they later installed one of the earliest steam mills in existence. The engine saw service for nearly 100 years and is now in an American museum; the mill building exists to this day, supplying animal feed.

This is marvellous walking country, and **Knettishall Heath Country Park**, on 400 acres of prime Breckland terrain, is the official starting place of the Peddars Way National Trail to Holme-next-Sea and of the Angles Way Regional Path that stretches 77 miles to Great Yarmouth by way of the Little Ouse and Waveney valleys.

STANTON
7 miles NE of Bury St Edmunds on the A143

Stanton is mentioned in the Domesday Book; before that, the Romans were here. A double ration of medieval churches - All Saints and St John the Baptist - will satisfy the ecclesiastical scholar, while for more worldly indulgences, Wyken Vineyards will have a strong appeal (see panel opposite).

WALSHAM-LE-WILLOWS
9 miles NE of Bury St Edmunds off the A143

🏛 St Mary's Church

A pretty name for a pretty village, with weatherboarded and timber-framed cottages along the willow-banked river, which flows throughout its length. **St Mary's Church** is no less pleasing to the eye, with its sturdy western tower and handsome windows in the Perpendicular style. Of particular interest inside is the superb tie and hammerbeam roof of the nave, and (unique in Suffolk, and very rare elsewhere) a tiny circular medallion, which hangs suspended from the nave wall, known as a Maiden's Garland or Virgin's Crant. These marked the pew seats of unmarried girls who had passed away, and the old custom was for the young men of the village to hang garlands of flowers from them on the anniversary of a girl's death. This particular example celebrates the virginity of one Mary Boyce, who died (so the inscription says) of a broken heart in 1685, just 20 years old. There is also a carving on the rood screen that looks rather like the face of a wolf: this may well be a reference to the benevolent creature that plays such an important role in the legend of St Edmund. A museum by the church has changing exhibitions of local history.

REDGRAVE
13 miles NE of Bury St Edmunds on the B1113

Arachnophobes beware! Redgrave and Lopham Fens form a 360-acre reserve of reed and sedge beds where one of the most interesting inhabitants is the Great Raft Spider. The village is the source of the Little Ouse and Waveney rivers, which rise on either side of the B1113 and set off on their seaward journeys in opposite directions.

THELNETHAM
12 miles NE of Bury St Edmunds off the B111

West of Redgrave between the B1113 and the B1111 lies Thelnetham, which boasts a windmill of its own. This one is a tower mill, built in 1819 to replace a post mill on the same site, and worked for 100 years. It has

now been lovingly restored. Stoneground flour is produced and sold at the mill. If you wish to visit you should set sail on a summer Sunday or Bank Holiday Monday; other times by appointment.

RICKINGHALL
12 miles NE of Bury St Edmunds on the A143

More timber-framed buildings, some thatched, are dotted along the streets of the two villages, Superior and Inferior, which follow an underground stream running right through them. Each has a church dedicated to St Mary and featuring fine flintwork and tracery. The upper church, now closed, was used as a school for London evacuees during the Second World War.

HESSETT
4 miles E of Bury St Edmunds off the A14

Dedicated to St Ethelbert, King of East Anglia, Hessett's church has many remarkable features, particularly some beautiful 16th-century glass and wall paintings, both of which somehow escaped the Puritan wave of destruction. Ethelbert was unlucky enough to get on the wrong side of the mighty Offa, King of the Mercians, and was killed by him at Hereford in AD794.

WOOLPIT
6 miles E of Bury St Edmunds on the A14

🏛 Museum 🏚 Lady's Well 🏴 Woolpit Legend

The church of St Mary the Virgin is Woolpit's crowning glory, with a marvellous porch and one of the most magnificent double hammerbeam roofs in the county.

Voted winner of Suffolk Village of the Year in 2000, the village was long famous for its brick industry, and the majority of the old buildings are faced with Woolpit Whites. This

HARVEYS GARDEN PLANTS & THE ORCHARD ROOM

Great Green, Thurston, Bury St Edmunds, Suffolk IP31 3SJ
Tel: 01359 233363
website: www.theorchardroom.co.uk
and www.harveysgardenplants.co.uk

Harveys Garden Plants is an outstanding nursery specialising in unusual perennials. Visitors to the nursery will find an abundance of rare and choice plants and enjoy four acres of developing gardens. The nursery also hosts many talks, garden courses and special events. Roger Harvey and the nursery staff are knowledgeable, friendly and approachable. Their expertise and hard work has been rewarded by winning Gold Medals at Chelsea in 2006, 2007 and 2008 and Hampton Court in 2008.

The Orchard Room is a stunning building situated within the nursery. This café/restaurant is the brainchild of Teresa Harvey and opened in 2007. It has fast gained a reputation of serving freshly prepared seasonal food in a delightful environment. Much of the food is grown at the nursery or locally sourced. For example, eggs are provided by the chickens who roam in the orchard. There is always something interesting and different on the menu; the top notch team are constantly developing innovative recipes for their customers. The air conditioned south facing room is flooded with natural light and has gorgeous views over the orchard as well as a number of flower borders. With all this combined it isn't any wonder The Orchard Room is one of three finalists in the EADT Suffolk Food and Drink Awards 2008 in the 'Best Informal Dining Venue' category – a wonderful achievement for such a young enterprise.

yellowish-white brick looked very much like more expensive stone, and for several centuries was widely exported. Some was used in the building of the Senate wing of the Capitol Building in Washington DC. Red bricks were also produced, and the village **Museum** has a permanent brick-making display and also tells the story of the evolution of the village. The Museum is open Saturday, Sunday and Bank Holiday Mondays April to September (tel: 01359 240822). Woolpit also hosts an annual music festival.

Nearby is a moated site known as **Lady's Well**, a place of pilgrimage in the Middle Ages. The water from the spring was reputed to have healing properties, most efficacious in curing eye troubles.

A favourite **Woolpit Legend** concerns the Green Children, a brother and sister with green complexions who appeared one day in a field, apparently attracted by the church bells. Though hungry, they would eat nothing until some green beans were produced. Given shelter by the lord of the manor, they learned to speak English and said that they came from a place called St Martin. The boy survived for only a short time, but the girl thrived, lost her green colour, was baptised and married a man from King's Lynn – no doubt leaving many a Suffolk man green with envy!

📻 stories and anecdotes 🐦 famous people 🎨 art and craft 🎭 entertainment and sport 🚶 walks

THE BRADFIELDS

7 miles SE of Bury St Edmunds off the A134

🌱 Bradfield Woods

The Bradfields - St George, St Clare and Combust - and Cockfield thread their way through a delightful part of the countryside and are well worth a little exploration, not only to see the picturesque villages themselves, but for a stroll in the historic **Bradfield Woods**. These woods stand on the eastern edge of the parish of Bradfield St George and have been turned into an outstanding nature reserve, tended and coppiced in the same way for more than 700 years, and home to a wide variety of flora and fauna. They once belonged to the Abbey of St Edmundsbury, and one area is still today called Monk's Park Wood.

Coppicing involves cutting a tree back down to the ground every 10 years or so. Woodlands were managed in this way to provide an annual crop of timber for local use and, after coppicing, as the root is already strongly established, regrowth is quick. Willow and hazel are the trees most commonly coppiced. Willow is often also pollarded, a less drastic form of coppicing where the trees are cut far enough from the ground to stop grazing animals having a free lunch.

Bradfield St Clare, the central of the three Bradfields, has a rival claim to that of Hoxne as the site of the martyrdom of St Edmund. The St Clare family arrived with the Normans and added their name to the village, and to the church, which was originally All Saints but was then rededicated to St Clare; it is the only church in England dedicated to her. Bradfield Combust, where the pretty River Lark rises, probably takes its curious name from the fact that the local hall was burnt to the ground during the 14th-century riots against the Abbot of St Edmundsbury's crippling tax

demands. Arthur Young (1741-1820), the noted writer on social, economic and agricultural subjects, is buried in the village churchyard.

COCKFIELD

8 miles SE of Bury St Edmunds off the A1141

Cockfield is perhaps the most widely spread village in all Suffolk, its little thatched cottages scattered around and between no fewer than nine greens. Great Green is the largest, with two football pitches and other recreation areas, while Parsonage Green has a literary connection: the Old Rectory was once home to a Dr Babbington, whose nephew Robert Louis Stephenson was a frequent visitor and who is said to have written *Treasure Island* while staying there.

Cockfield also shelters one of the last windmills to have been built in Suffolk (1891). Its working life was very short but the tower still stands, now in use as a private residence. An odd legend says that primroses will not grow in Cockfield: when the village was depopulated by the plague, primroses were thought to have caught the infection and died. A likely story!

THORPE MORIEUX

9 miles SE of Bury St Edmunds off the B1071

St Mary's Church in Thorpe Morieux is situated in as pleasant a setting as anyone could wish to find. With water meadows, ponds, a stream and a fine Tudor farmhouse to set it off, this 14th-century church presents a memorable picture of old England. Once you've looked at the church, take the time to wander round the peaceful churchyard with its profusion of springtime aconites, followed by the colourful flowering of limes and chestnuts in summer.

GREAT WELNETHAM

2 miles S of Bury St Edmunds off the A134

One of the many surviving Suffolk windmills is to be found here, just south of the village. The sails were lost in a gale 80 years ago, but the tower and a neighbouring old barn make an attractive sight.

HAWKEDON

9 miles S of Bury St Edmunds off the A143

Hawkedon is designated a place of outstanding natural beauty. Here the Church of St Mary is located atypically in the middle of the village green. The pews and intricately carved bench-ends attract the eye, along with a canopied stoup (a recess for holding holy water) and a Norman font. There is a wide variety of carved animals, many on the bench-ends but some also on the roof cornice. One of the stalls is decorated with the carving of a crane holding a stone in its claw: legend has it that if the crane were on watch and should fell asleep, the stone would drop and the noise would wake it.

WICKHAMBROOK

9 miles S of Bury St Edmunds on the B1063

Wickhambrook is a series of tiny hamlets with no fewer than 11 greens and three manor houses. The greens have unusual names - Genesis, Nunnery, Meeting, Coltsfoot - whose origins keep local historians busy. One of the two pubs has the distinction of being officially half in Wickhambrook and half in Denston.

ALPHETON

10 miles S of Bury St Edmunds on the A134

There are several points of interest in this little village straddling the main road. It was first settled in AD991 and its name means The farm of Aefflaed. That lady was the wife

of Ealdorman Beorhtnoth of Essex, who was killed resisting the Danes at the Battle of Maldon and is buried in Ely Minster.

The hall, the farm and the church stand in a quiet location away from the main road and about a mile from the village. This remoteness is not unusual: some attribute it to the villagers moving during times of plague, but the more likely explanation is simply that the scattered cottages, originally in several tiny hamlets, centred on a more convenient site than that of the church. Equally possible is that the church was located here to suit the local landed family (who desired to have the church next door to their home). The main features at the Church of St Peter and St Paul are the flintwork around the parapet, the carefully restored 15th-century porch and some traces of an ancient wall painting of St Christopher with the Christ Child. All in all, it's a typical country church of unpretentious dignity and well worth a short detour from the busy main roads.

Back in the village, two oak trees were planted and a pump installed in 1887, to commemorate Queen Victoria's 50th year on the throne. Another of the village's claims to fame is that its American airfield was used as the setting for the classic film *Twelve O'Clock High*, in which Gregory Peck memorably plays a Second World War flight commander cracking under the strain of countless missions. Incidentally, one of the reasons for constructing the A134 was to help in the development of the airfield. The A134 continues south to Long Melford. An alternative road from Bury to Long Melford is the B1066, quieter and more scenic, with a number of pleasant places to visit en route.

SHIMPLING

9 miles S of Bury St Edmunds off the B1066

Shimpling is a peaceful farming community whose church, St George's, is approached by a lime avenue. It is notable for Victorian stained glass and a Norman font, and in the churchyard is the Faint House, a small stone building where ladies overcome by the tightness of their stays could decently retreat from the service. The banker Thomas Hallifax built many of Shimpling's cottages, as well as the village school and Chadacre Hall, which Lord Iveagh later turned into an agricultural college (a role it ceased to hold in 1989 - the Hall is today again in private hands).

LAWSHALL

8 miles S of Bury St Edmunds off the A134

A spread-out village first documented in AD972 but regularly giving up evidence of earlier occupation, Lawshall was the site where a Bronze Age sword dated at around 600BC was found (the sword is now in Bury Museum). The Church of All Saints, Perpendicular with some Early English features, stands on one of the highest points in Suffolk. Next to it is Lawshall Hall, whose owners once entertained Queen Elizabeth I. Another interesting site in Lawshall is the Wishing Well, a well-cover on the green put up in memory of Charles Tyrwhitt Drake, who worked for the Royal Geographic Society and was killed in Jerusalem.

HARTEST

9 miles S of Bury St Edmunds on the B1066

🏛 Gifford's Hall   🏛 Hartest Stone

Hartest, which has a history as long as Alpheton's, celebrated its millennium in 1990 with the erection of a village sign (the hart, or stag). It's an agreeable spot in the valley, with

colour-washed houses and chestnut trees on the green. Also on the green are All Saints Church (mentioned in the Domesday Book) and a large glacial stone, the **Hartest Stone**, which was dragged by a team of 45 horses from where it was found in a field in neighbouring Somerton. From 1789 until the 1930s, Hartest staged a St George's Day Fair, an annual event celebrating King George III's recovery from one of his spells of illness. Just outside the village is **Gifford's Hall**, a smallholding that includes 14 acres of nearly 12,000 grapevines, as well as a winery producing white and rosé wines and fruit liqueurs. There are also organic vegetable gardens, wildflower meadows, black St Kilda sheep, black Berkshire pigs, goats and free-range fowl, together with a trailer ride (The Grape Express) and children's play area. The Hall is particularly famous for its sweet peas and roses, and an annual festival is held on the last weekend in June. Open from Easter to the end of October.

HORRINGER

3 miles SW of Bury St Edmunds on the A143

🏛 Ickworth House

Rejoining the A143 by Chedburgh, the motorist will soon arrive at Horringer, whose village green is dominated by the flintstone Church of St Leonard. Beside the church are the gates of one of the country's most extraordinary and fascinating houses, now run by the National Trust. **Ickworth House** was the brainchild of Frederick Augustus Hervey, the eccentric 4th Earl of Bristol and Bishop of Derry, a collector of art treasures and an inveterate traveller (witness the many Bristol Hotels scattered around Europe). His inspiration was Belle Isle, a house built on an island in Lake Windermere; the massive structure is a central rotunda linking two semi-circular wings. It was designed as a treasure house for his art collection, and work started in 1795. In 1798 Hervey was taken prisoner in Italy by Napoleonic troops and his first collection confiscated. Hervey died of stomach gout in 1803 and his son, after some hesitation, saw the work through to completion in 1829. Its chief glories are some marvellous paintings by Titian, Gainsborough, Hogarth, Velasquez, Reynolds and Kauffman, but there's a great deal more to enthral the visitor: late Regency and 18th century French furniture, a notable collection of Georgian silver, friezes and sculptures by John Flaxman, frescoes copied from wall paintings discovered at the Villa Negroni in Rome in 1777. The Italian garden, where Mediterranean species have been bred to withstand a distinctly non-Mediterranean climate, should not be missed, with its hidden glades, orangery and temple rose garden, and in the park landscaped by Capability Brown there are designated walks and cycle routes, bird hides, a deer enclosure and play areas. More recent attractions include the vineyard and plant centre. The House is open from Easter until the end of October, while the park and gardens are open throughout the year.

Arable land surrounds Horringer, with a large annual crop of sugar beet grown for processing at the factory in Bury, the largest of its kind in Europe.

Newmarket

🖼 National Horseracing Museum 🏛 Palace House

On the western edge of Suffolk, Newmarket is home to some 16,000 human and 3,000 equine inhabitants. The historic centre of British racing lives and breathes horses, with 60 training establishments, 50 stud farms, the top annual thoroughbred sales and two racecourses (the only two in Suffolk). Thousands of the population are involved in the trade, and racing art and artefacts fill the shops, galleries and museums; one of the oldest established saddlers even has a preserved horse on display - Robert the Devil, runner-up in the Derby in 1880.

History records that Queen Boudicca of the Iceni, to whom the six-mile Devil's Dyke stands as a memorial, thundered around these parts in her lethal chariot behind her shaggy-haired horses. She is said to have established the first stud here. In medieval times the chalk heathland was a popular arena for riders to display their skills. In 1605, James I paused on a journey northwards to enjoy a spot of hare coursing. He liked the place and said he would be back. By moving the royal court to his Newmarket headquarters, he began the royal patronage

National Horseracing Museum, Newmarket

National Horseracing Museum

99 High Street, Newmarket, Suffolk CB8 8JH
Tel: 01638 667333 Fax: 01638 665600
website: www.nationalstud.co.uk

"The Newmarket Experience" comprises two separate attractions: **The National Horseracing Museum** and **The National Stud**. The story of racing throughout the ages is told through the Museum's permanent collections, featuring the horses, people, events and scandals that make the sport so colourful.

Highlights include the head of Persimmon, a great Royal Derby winner in 1896; a special display about Fred Archer, the Victorian jockey who committed suicide after losing the struggle to keep his weight down; the skeleton of Eclipse, ancestor of 90 per cent of modern thoroughbreds; items associated with Red Rum, Lester Piggott, Frankie Dettori and other heroes of the Turf. In the Practical Gallery, visitors can learn everything there is to know about the horse and jockey, and experience the thrill of riding on the horse simulator. The Gallery is staffed by retired jockeys and trainers, who make the world of racing come alive. Special exhibitions have included "*Why* did you get that hat?'', a display of Gertrude Shilling's outrageous Ascot outfits. Mrs Shilling (1910-1999) was one of the most colourful and eccentric personalities ever to grace the sport.

The National Stud extends a warm welcome to all its visitors. Breeding top-class thoroughbreds, the 500-acre site has 12 yards, 9 miles of roads and tracks, 60 miles of post and rail fencing, 21 houses, a feedmill and storage for 50 tons of hay and straw - all purpose built between 1963 and 1967.

that has remained so strong throughout the years. James' son, Charles I, maintained the royal connection, but it was Charles II who really put the place on the map when he, too, moved the Royal court here in the spring and autumn of each year. He initiated the Town Plate, a race which he himself won twice as a rider and which, in a modified form, still exists.

One of the racecourses, the Rowley Mile, takes its name from Old Rowley, a favourite horse of the Merry Monarch. Here the first two classics of the season, the 1,000 and

2,000 Guineas, are run, together with important autumn events including the Cambridgeshire and the Cesarewich, valuable handicaps that always attract mammoth fields. There are some 18 race days at this track, while on the leafy July course, with its delightful garden-party atmosphere, a similar number of race days take in all the important summer fixtures.

The visitor to Newmarket can learn almost all there is to know about flat racing and racehorses by taking the grand tour of the

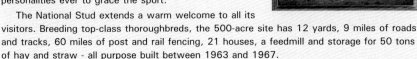

several establishments open to the public (sometimes by appointment only). The Jockey Club, which was the first governing body of the sport and, until recently, its ultimate authority, was formed in the mid-18th century and occupies an imposing building, which was restored and rebuilt in Georgian style in the 1930s. Originally a social club for rich gentlemen with an interest in the turf, it soon became the all-powerful regulator of British racing, owning all the racing and training land. When holding an enquiry, the stewards sit round a horseshoe-shaped table while the standing jockey or trainer under scrutiny faces them - on a strip of carpet by the door - hence the expression 'on the mat'.

Next to the Jockey Club building in the High Street is the **National Horseracing Museum** (see panel opposite). Opened by the Queen in 1983, its five galleries chronicle the history of the Sport of Kings from its royal beginnings through to the top trainers and jockeys of today. Visitors can ride a mechanical horse, try on racing silks, record a race commentary, ask questions and enjoy a snack in the café, whose walls are hung with murals of racing personalities. The chief treasures among the art collection are equine paintings by Alfred Munnings, while the most famous item is probably the skeleton of the mighty Eclipse, whose superiority over his contemporaries gave rise to the saying 'Eclipse first, the rest nowhere'.

A few steps away is **Palace House**, which contains the remains of Charles II's palace and which, as funds allow, has been restored over the years for use as a visitor centre and museum. In the same street is Nell Gwynn's House, which some say was connected by an underground passage beneath the street to the palace. The diarist John Evelyn spent a night in (or on?) the town during a royal visit, and declared the occasion to be 'more resembling a luxurious and abandoned rout than a Christian court'. The palace is the location for the Newmarket Tourist Information Centre.

Other must-sees on the racing enthusiast's tour are Tattersalls, where leading thoroughbred sales take place from April to December; the British Racing School, where top jockeys are taught the ropes; the 500-acre National Stud, open for tours from March till the end of September (plus autumn race days - booking essential); and the Animal Health Trust based at Lanwades Hall, where there's an informative Visitor Centre. The National Stud at one time housed no fewer than three Derby winners, Blakeney, Mill Reef, and Grundy, and is now the home in retirement of the 2004 Grand National winner, Amberleigh House.

Horses aren't all about racing, however. One type of horse you won't see in Newmarket is the wonderful Suffolk Punch, a massive yet elegant working horse, which can still be seen at work at Rede Hall Park Farm near Bury St Edmunds and at Kentwell Hall in Long Melford. All Punches descend from Crisp's horse, foaled in 1768. The Punch is part of the Hallowed Trinity of animals at the very centre of Suffolk's agricultural history; the others being the Suffolk Sheep and the Red Poll Cow. It is entirely appropriate that the last railway station to employ a horse for shunting wagons should have been at Newmarket. That hardworking one-horse-power shunter retired in 1967.

Newmarket also has things to offer the tourist outside the equine world, including the churches of St Mary and All Saints and St Agnes, and a landmark at each end of the High Street - a Memorial Fountain in honour of Sir Daniel Cooper and the Jubilee Clock Tower commemorating Queen Victoria's Golden Jubilee.

Around Newmarket

EXNING
2 miles NW of Newmarket on the A14

A pause is certainly in order at this ancient village, whether on your way from Newmarket or arriving from Cambridgeshire on the A14. Anglo-Saxons, Romans, the Iceni and the Normans were all here, and the Domesday Book records the village under the name of Esselinga. The village was stricken by plague during the Iceni occupation, so its market was moved to the next village along - thus Newmarket acquired its name.

Exning's written history begins when Henry II granted the manor to the Count of Boulogne, who divided it between four of his knights. References to them and to subsequent Lords of the Manor are to be found in the little Church of St Martin, which might well have been founded by the Burgundian Christian missionary monk St Felix in the 7th century. Water from the well used by that saint to baptise members of the Saxon royal family is still used for baptisms by the current vicar.

KENTFORD
5 miles E of Newmarket by the A14

🎞 Gypsy Boy's Grave

At the old junction of the Newmarket-Bury road stands the **Gypsy Boy's Grave**: Joseph was a shepherd boy who hanged himself after being accused of sheep-stealing.

Suicides were refused burial in a churchyard, and it was a well-established superstition that suicides be buried at a crossroads to prevent their spirits from wandering. Flowers are still sometimes laid at the Gypsy Boy's Grave, sometimes by punters hoping for good luck at Newmarket races.

MOULTON
4 miles E of Newmarket on the B1085

This most delightful village lies in wonderful countryside on chalky downland in farming country; its proximity to Newmarket is apparent from the racehorses that are often to be seen on the large green. The River Kennett flows through the green before running north to the Lark, a tributary of the Ouse. Flint walls are a feature of many of the buildings, but the main point of interest is the 15th century four-arch Packhorse Bridge on the way to the church.

DALHAM
5 miles E of Newmarket on the B1063

🏛 Dalham Hall 🎞 St Mary's Church

Eighty per cent of the buildings in Dalham are thatched (the highest proportion in Suffolk) and there are many other attractions in this pretty village. Above the village on one of the county's highest spots stands **St Mary's Church**, which dates from the 14th century. Its spire toppled over during the gales that swept the land on the night that Cromwell died, and was replaced by a tower in 1627. Sir Martin Stutteville was the leading light behind this reconstruction; an inscription at the back of the church notes that the cost was £400. That worthy man's grandfather was Thomas Stutteville, whose memorial near the altar declares that, 'he saw the New World with Francis Drake'. (Drake did not survive that

journey - his third to South America.)
Thomas' grandson died in the fullness of his
years (62 wasn't bad for those times) while
hosting a jolly evening at The Angel Hotel in
Bury St Edmunds.

Dalham Hall was constructed in the first
years of the 18th century at the order of the
Bishop of Ely, who decreed that it should be
built up until Ely Cathedral could be seen
across the fens on a clear day. That view was
sadly cut off in 1957 when a fire shortened
the hall to only two storeys high. Wellington
lived here for some years, and much later it
was bought by Cecil Rhodes, who
unfortunately died before taking up residence.
His brother Francis erected the village hall in
the adventurer's memory, and he himself is
buried in the churchyard.

All in all, Dalham is a place of charm and
interest - clearly no longer resembling the place
described in *The Times* in the 1880s as full of
ruffians and drunks, where the vicar felt
obliged to give all the village children boxing
lessons to increase their chances of survival.

MILDENHALL
8 miles NE of Newmarket off the A11

🏛 Church of St Mary 🏛 Museum

On the edge of the Fens and Breckland,
Mildenhall is a town which has many links
with the past. It was once a port for the
hinterlands of West Suffolk, though the River
Lark has long ceased to be a trade route. Most
of the town's heritage is recorded in the
excellent **Mildenhall & District Museum** in
King Street. Here will be found exhibits of
local history (including the distinguished RAF
and USAAF base), crafts and domestic skills,
the natural history of the Fens and Breckland
and, perhaps most famously, the chronicle of
the Mildenhall Treasure. This was a cache of

34 pieces of 4th-century Roman silverware -
dishes, goblets and spoons - found by a
ploughman in 1946 at Thistley Green and now
on display in the British Museum in London,
while a replica makes its home here where it
was discovered. There is evidence of much
earlier occupation than the Roman era, with
flint tools and other artefacts being
unearthed in 1988 on the site of an ancient
lake. (RAF Mildenhall is the lone air refueling
wing for the US Air Force in Europe. RAF
Lakenheath, a few miles north, is home to
one of Europe's biggest bomber fleets and
was used as a setting in the James Bond film
Tomorrow Never Dies.)

The parish of Mildenhall is the largest in
Suffolk, so it is perhaps fitting that it should
boast so magnificent a parish church as
St Mary's, built of Barnack stone; it
dominates the heart of the town and indeed
its west tower commands the flat surrounding
countryside. Above the splendid north porch
(the largest in Suffolk) are the arms of
Edward the Confessor and of St Edmund.
The chancel, dating back to the 13th century,
is a marvellous work of architecture, but pride
of place goes to the east window, divided into
seven vertical lights. Off the south aisle is the
Chapel of St Margaret, whose altar, itself
modern, contains a medieval altar stone. At
the west end, the font, dating from the 15th
century, bears the arms of Sir Henry Barton,
who was twice Lord Mayor of London and
whose tomb is located on the south side of
the tower. Above the nave and aisles is a
particularly fine hammerbeam roof whose
outstanding feature is the carved angels.
Efforts of the Puritans to destroy the angels
failed, though traces of buckshot and
arrowheads remain and have been found
embedded in the woodwork.

Brandon Country Park

Bury Road, Brandon,
Suffolk IP27 0SU
Tel: 01842 810185

For thousands of years the area where the Park is now was an open, sandy, windswept heath. Until 1942, when Lakenheath airbase was built, it was Europe's largest inland sand dune system.

Edward Bliss, a businessman, bought over a thousand hectares of the Brecks in 1820 to create a wooded park and arboretum. By the end of World War1, the park had fallen into neglect. As a result of the economic depression caused by the war, the Government was determined to become self-sufficient in timber. Thetford Forest, planted in 1927, is one of the lowland forests they created.

At the end of the last century, English Nature leased land from the Forestry Commission to return some of the commercial forestry areas to the original heathland. Brandon Park Heath, only a mile from the Visitor Centre, is the result. In just under 200 years, we've come full-circle.

When you and your family want to enjoy nature, and learn about the environment and its history, visit Brandon Country Park. At Brandon, you can stroll and picnic in the charming walled garden. You can also head further afield, following the invigorating walks and cycle trails that guide you through the arboretum, commercial forest and restored heathland.

Sir Henry North built a manor house on the north side of the church in the 17th century. His successors included a dynasty of the Bunbury family, who were Lords of the Manor from 1747 to 1933. Sir Henry Edward Bunbury was the man chosen to let Napoleon Bonaparte know of his exile to St Helena, but the best-known member of the family is Sir Thomas, who in 1780 tossed a coin with Lord Derby to see whose name should be borne by a race to be inaugurated at Epsom. Lord Derby won, but Sir Thomas had the satisfaction of winning the first running of the race with his colt, Diomed.

The other focal point in Mildenhall is the Market Place, with its 16th century timbered cross.

WORLINGTON

2 miles W of Mildenhall on the B1102

Worlington is a small village near the River Lark, known chiefly as the location of Wamil Hall, an Elizabethan mansion that stands on the riverbank. Popular lore has it that a person called Lady Rainbow haunts the place, though the spot she once favoured for appearances, a flight of stairs, was destroyed in one of the many fires the mansion has suffered.

Cricket is very much part of the village scene (there's a splendid village green), and has been since the early days of the 19th century.

BRANDON
9 miles NE of Mildenhall on the A1065

🏛 Heritage Centre 🏚 Grime's Graves 🗡 Breckland

🗡 Thetford Forest 🗡 Brandon Country Park

On the edge of **Thetford Forest** by the Little Ouse, Brandon was long ago a thriving port, but flint is what really put it on the map. The town itself is built mainly of flint, and flint was mined from early Neolithic times to make arrowheads and other implements and weapons of war. The gun flint industry brought with it substantial wealth, and a good flint-knapper could produce up to 300 gun flints in an hour. The invention of the percussion cap killed off much of the need for this type of work, however, so they turned to shaping flints for church buildings and ornamental purposes. **Brandon Heritage Centre**, in a former fire station in George Street, provides visitors with a splendid insight into this industry, while for an even more tangible feel, a visit to **Grime's Graves**, just over the Norfolk border, reveals an amazing site covering 35 acres and 300 pits (one of the shafts is open to visitors). With the close proximity of numerous warrens and their rabbit population, the fur trade also flourished here, and that, too, along with forestry, is brought to life in the Heritage Centre.

The whole of this northwestern corner of Suffolk, known as **Breckland**, offers almost unlimited opportunities for touring by car, cycling or walking. A mile south of town on the B1106 is **Brandon Country Park** (see panel opposite), a 30-acre landscaped site with a tree trail, forest walks, a walled garden and a visitor centre. There's also an orienteering route leading on into Thetford Forest, Britain's largest lowland pine forest. The High Lodge Forest Centre, near Santon Downham (off the B1107), offers many attractions, including walks, cycle trails and adventure facilities.

ELVEDEN
8 miles NE of Mildenhall on the A11

🏚 Elvedon Hall

Elveden Hall became more remarkable than its builders intended when Prince Duleep Singh, the last Maharajah of Punjab and a noted sportsman, crack shot, and the man who handed over the Koh-I-Noor diamond to Queen Victoria, arrived on the scene. Exiled to England with a handsome pension, he bought the Georgian house in 1863 and commissioned John Norton to transform it into a palace modelled on those in Lahore and Delhi. Although it is stated that in private Duleep Singh referred to Queen Victoria as 'Mrs Fagin … receiver of stolen goods', he kept close contact with the royal household and the Queen became his son's godmother. The Guinness family (Lord Iveagh) later took over the Hall and joined in the fun, adding even more exotic adornments including a replica Taj Mahal, while at the same time creating the largest arable farm in the whole of the country. In recent times, Stanley Kubrick's last film, *Eyes Wide Shut*, was shot here, as was *Tomb Raider*. The Elveden Memorial is a grand 113-foot Corinthian column erected in 1921 and dedicated to the memory of local soldiers from the three parishes of Elveden, Eriswell and Icklingham who died in action in the First World War. Their names are inscribed on the base, and a shorter list was added after the Second World War. Inside, 148 steps lead to the top, which is crowned by a mighty stone urn.

LOCATOR MAP

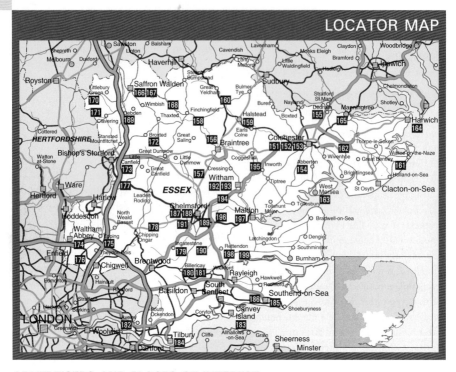

ADVERTISERS AND PLACES OF INTEREST

🏠 historic building   🏛 museum and heritage   🏚 historic site   🦋 scenic attraction   🌿 flora and fauna

3 ESSEX

Bordering the north bank of the River Thames, Essex has long been a gateway to London, and while it contains much heavy industry and urban development, it also encompasses some lovely countryside, coastal attractions and important wildlife habitats. Northeast Essex has the true feel of East Anglia, particularly around the outstanding villages of the Stour Valley - which has come to be known as Constable Country, a title it shares with neighbouring Suffolk. The inland villages and small towns here are notably historic and picturesque, offering very good touring and walking opportunities. A plethora of half-timbered medieval buildings, farms and churches mark this region out as of particular historical interest. Monuments to engineering feats past and present include Hedingham Castle, Chappel Viaduct and the Post Mill at Bocking Church Street. There are also many lovely gardens to visit, and the region's principal town, Colchester, is a mine of interesting sights and experiences.

The north Essex coast has a distinguished history and a strong maritime heritage, as exemplified in towns like Harwich, Manningtree and Mistley. Further examples are the fine Martello Towers - circular brick edifices built to provide a coastal defence against Napoleon's armies - along the Tendring coast at Walton, Clacton, Jaywick and Point Clear. The Tendring Coast contains an interesting mix of extensive tidal inlets, sandy beaches and low cliffs, and the Tendring District Council publishes a series of Tendring Trails beginning at Mistley, Manningtree, Debenham, Ardleigh and other places along the North Essex Coast.

The Stour Estuary, Hamford Water and Colne Estuary are all renowned for seabirds and other wildlife. Many areas are protected nature reserves. In the part of the county known as 'the sunshine holiday coast', resorts, both boisterous and more tranquil, dot the landscape: Clacton-on-Sea, Frinton-on-Sea and Walton-on-the-Naze offer many opportunities for relaxation and recreation.

The small northwest Essex towns of Saffron Walden, Thaxted, Great Dunmow and Stansted Mountfichet are among the most

📖 stories and anecdotes 🐿 famous people 🎭 art and craft 🖋 entertainment and sport 🚶 walks

beautiful and interesting in the nation. This area is also home to a wealth of picturesque villages boasting weatherboarded houses and pargetting. This area also retains three beautiful and historic windmills, at Stansted Mountfichet, Aythorpe Roding and Thaxted. Visitors to southwest Essex and Epping Forest will find a treasure-trove of woodland, nature reserves, superb gardens and rural delights. Epping Forest dominates much of the far western corner, but all this part of Essex is rich in countryside, forests and parks. Southwest Essex also has major attractions in Audley End House and Waltham Abbey.

The borough of Thurrock includes huge swathes of greenbelt country, and along its 18 miles of Thames frontage there are many important marshland wildlife habitats. History, too, abounds in this part of the county. Henry VIII built riverside block houses at East and West Tilbury, which later became Coalhouse Fort and Tilbury Fort. It was at West Tilbury that Queen Elizabeth I gave her most famous speech delivered to her troops, gathered to meet the threat of the Spanish Armada. At the extreme south-east of the county, Southend is a popular and friendly seaside resort with a wealth of sights and amenities. There are also smaller seaside communities that repay a visit.

The area surrounding the Rivers Blackwater and Crouch contains a wealth of ancient woodland and other natural beauties, particularly along the estuaries and the Chelmer and Blackwater Canal.

There are hundreds of acres of ancient woodland, much of it coppiced, which is the traditional woodland-management technique thatencourages a vast array of natural flora and fauna. This stretch of Essex affords some marvellous walking, cycling, birdwatching and other treats for anyone who loves the great outdoors.

The Essex-Jiangsu Culture Festival is a celebration of the 20-year link between Essex County Council and the Jiangsu Province in China. Events will take place between the summer of 2008 and March 2009, including cultural programmes, performances and exhibitions. See www.realessex.co.uk for details.

Colchester

🏰 Castle 🏛 Castle Museum

🏛 Hollytrees Museum 🏛 Natural History Museum

🏛 Tymperleys Clock Museum 🏛 St Botolph's Priory

🏛 Bourne Mill 🎨 Colchester Arts Centre

🎨 First Site 🌳 Zoo 🌳 High Woods Country Park

This ancient market town and garrison stands in the midst of rolling East Anglian countryside. Britain's oldest recorded town, it has over 2,000 years of history, much of it there to be discovered by visitors. It was first established during the 7th century BC, and to the west of town are the remains of the massive earthworks built to protect it in pre-Roman times. During the 1st century, Colchester's prime location made it an obvious target for invading Romans. The

Roman Emperor Claudius accepted the surrender of 11 British Kings in Colchester (Camolodunum). In AD60, Queen Boudicca helped to establish her place in history by taking revenge on the Romans and burning the town to the ground, before going on to destroy London and St Albans. Here in this town that was once capital of Roman Britain, Roman walls - the oldest in Britain - still surround the oldest part of town. Balkerne Gate, west gate of the original Roman town, is the largest surviving Roman gateway in the country, and remains magnificent to this day.

Today the town is presided over by its lofty town hall and enormous Victorian water tower, nicknamed Jumbo after London Zoo's first African elephant, an animal sold to P T Barnum (causing some controversy) in 1882. The tower has four massive pillars made up of one-and-a-quarter million bricks, 369 tons of stone and 142 tons of iron, all working to support the 230,000-gallon tank.

There are a number of guided town walks available, as well as bus tours. The Visitor Information Centre on Queen Street has details of the many places that are worth a visit. Market days in this thriving town are Friday and Saturday.

A good place to start any exploration of the town is **Colchester Castle** and its museum. When the Normans arrived, Colchester (a name given the town by the Saxons) was an important borough. The Normans built their castle on the foundations of the Roman temple of Claudius. Having used many of the Roman bricks in its construction, it boasts the largest Norman keep ever built in Europe - the only part still left standing. The keep houses the **Castle Museum**, one of the most exciting hands-on

Colchester Castle, Colchester

THE LEMON TREE

48 St Johns Street, Colchester,
Essex CO2 7AD
Tel: 01206 767337
Fax: 01206 765387
e-mail: pm@the-lemon-tree.com
website: www.the-lemon-tree.com

Great food and informal dining in excellent company and unique surroundings await visitors to **The Lemon Tree**, a fine bistro-style restaurant that has taken its place among the very best in the county. The restaurant encases part of Colchester's original Roman walls, providing a memorable, stunning setting for delicious meals based on premium produce. Owners Patrik and Joanna Minder and their chefs are very much committed to providing their customers with the best-quality seasonal produce, which has been sympathetically and humanely farmed wherever possible, and use commodities that have been locally produced and reared to support the local community.

The menus showcase the pick of this produce in many of their signature dishes: St Botolph's Directors sausages and mash; the marvellous Mersea oysters; Dedham Vale fillet steak or rump steak with garlic butter, slow-roasted mushrooms and chunky chips; rack of Fingringhoe lamb with a garlic & herb crust and a sweet redcurrant jus. The chefs at The Lemon Tree also take their inspiration from the world's cuisines, as shown by butternut & leek squash with toasted pumpkin seeds; tiger prawns with coconut, chilli & lime; seared king scallops with a crab, ginger & spring onion broth; tuna & sea-spiced aubergine with pak choy & crispy rice noodles; and smoked chicken & duck terrine with a Sevile orange jelly. The enjoyment level remains sky high to the end, with dessert such as iced strawberry & champagne bombe or pistachio & white chocolate cheesecake with raspberry coulis. The outstanding food is complemented by affable, efficient service and an extensive wine list from local wine merchants Lay & Wheeler.

The Lemon Tree is open at 10.30am Monday to Saturday for morning coffee, from midday to 5pm for lunch, and then until last orders 9.30am (Friday and Saturday 10pm) for a luxurious candlelit dinner. The

choice includes daily specials, great-value set price menus and the superb full à la carte menu, and the restaurant hosts regular gourmet, themed and jazz and piano evenings. Parties of up to 26 guests can be held in the amazing surroundings of the Roman Cavern, a separate dining area underneath the Roman wall – a venue like no other for a sit-down meal or champagne and canapés. For larger parties the main restaurant, with seats for up to 80, can be booked, with space for 100 more in a marquee on the terrace. Bookings can be made online, and The Lemon Tree sells hampers and gift vouchers in units from £5. For an extra special treat, The Lemon Tree offer a Gourmet Home Dining Experience, where they send along a Lemon Tree head chef to prepare in your kitchen a specially devised bespoke menu, and provide an experienced butler for your dining room to serve your guests – and the duo will even do the washing-up afterwards!

historical attractions in the country. Its fascinating collection of Iron Age, Roman and medieval relics is one of the most important in the country. There are tombstones carved in intricate detail and exquisite examples of Roman glass and jewellery. Visitors can try on Roman togas and helmets, touch some of the 2,000-year-old pottery unearthed nearby, and experience the town's murkier past by visiting the castle prisons, where witches were interrogated by the notorious Witchfinder General Matthew Hopkins. A key can be obtained at the Museum to St Martin's Church, a redundant 14th-century church with recycled Roman brickwork in its fabric. **Hollytrees Museum**, in the High Street, is located in a fine Georgian housedating back to 1718. This award-winning museum can be found on the edge of Castle Park and houses a wonderful collection of toys, costumes, curios and antiquities from the past two centuries, and a number of fine paintings including a view of Colchester by Pissarro. Also nearby, housed in the former All Saints' Church, is the **Natural History Museum**, with exhibits and many hands-on displays illustrating the natural history of Essex from the Ice Age right up to the present day.

Housed in the Minories Art Gallery, **First Site** will be a new addition to Colchester's fine choice of cultural attractions when it opens in Spring 2009. It will feature changing exhibitions of contemporary visual art. An arch in Trinity Street leads to **Tymperleys Clock Museum**, the 15th-century timber-framed home of William Gilberd, who entertained Elizabeth I with experiments in

TRADERS OF THE EAST

9 Short Wyre Street, Colchester, Essex CO1 1LN
Tel: 01206 579961
e-mail: tradersoftheeast@hotmail.co.uk

A huge and tempting window display in the red-painted shopfront gives just a hint of the colourful array of ethnic goods on sale at **Traders of the East**. The shop is located in an old timber-framed building on top of part of the town's Roman wall, in the centre of town close to the main railway station.

Owner Gill Snodgrass, who worked in a similar outlet before opening her own shop, has assembled over two floors a lovely selection of clothes, fabrics, textiles, homeware and giftware hand-picked from goods imported from India, Nepal, Tibet, Afghanistan and other Asian countries, and also from North Africa. There are clothes made in India for the Western market, semi-precious stones from India and Nepal, lapis lazuli and beautiful kelims from Afghanistan, ceramics and glass lanterns from Morocco, wall hangings, cushions, throws, lamps and lampshades, curtains, wooden ornaments, candles, incense, henna... and much, much more.

A browser's delight, with the stock constantly changing, Traders of the East is open from 10am to 5pm Tuesday to Saturday, and Sundays in December.

TOWN & COUNTRY LIGHTING

61-65 North Station Road, Colchester, Essex CO1 1RQ
Tel: 01206 572152   Fax: 01206 547163
e-mail: sales@townandcountrylighting.co.uk

Town & Country Lighting has been established for more than 30 years, trading from bright, airy premises on one of the main roads into Colchester and just two minutes' walk from Colchester's North Station.

This thriving business has been run since February 2008 by Adam and Emma, a switched-on couple who, with their staff, are ready with help and advice for all their customers. If it's one light or a thousand, this is the place to come for both trade and private customers (the former can be registered with trade terms and special offers). Town & Country Lighting is among the biggest modern lighting showrooms in Essex, with an extensive range of original, classic and contemporary lighting. Pendants, table lights, floor lamps, standard lamps, outdoor lighting for the garden, patio or porch, spotlights, picture lights, ceiling lights, chandeliers – if it goes by the name of light or lamp the chances are you'll find it here. A new shade can transform an old lamp, and here there are lampshades by the hundred on display, with access to thousands more – classic, modern or plain bizarre, and the staff can help you to find the right colour, shape, design and texture for every individual lamp. Town & Country Lighting also stocks a wide range of other things to enhance a home, including brass and wrought iron pieces, Waterford crystal, Italian glass, ceiling fans, hand-made silk shades, mirrors and occasional furniture.

They've opened a second branch of Town & Country Lighting:

9-11 Ongar Road, Brentwood, Essex CM15 9AU Tel: 01277 219889

Both premises are open from 9am to 5.30pm Monday to Saturday. There's customer parking on site at the Colchester branch, nearby parking at the Brentwood branch.

electricity. Today, this fine example of architectural splendour houses a magnificent collection of 18th- and 19th-century Colchester-made clocks. The **Colchester Arts Centre**, not far from Balkerne Gate, features a regular programme of visual arts, drama, music, poetry and dance; the Mercury Theatre is the town's premier site for stage dramas, comedies and musical theatre.

Bourne Mill, Colchester

Dutch Protestants arrived in Colchester in the 16th century, fleeing Spanish rule in the Netherlands, and revitalised the local cloth industry. The houses of these Flemish weavers in the Dutch Quarter to the west of the castle, and the Civil War scars on the walls of Siege House in East Street, bear testimony to their place in the town's history. The Dutch Quarter west of the castle remains a charming and relatively quiet corner of this bustling town.

Close to the railway station are the ruins of **St Botolph's Priory**, the oldest Augustinian priory in the country. Its remains are a potent reminder of the bitterness of Civil War times, as it was here that Royalists held out for 11 weeks during the siege of Colchester, before finally being starved into submission.

On Bourne Road, south of the town centre just off the B1025, there's a striking stepped-and-curved gabled building known as **Bourne Mill**, now owned by the National Trust. Built in 1591 from stone taken from the nearby St John's Abbeygate, this delightful, restored building near a lovely millpond was originally a fishing lodge, later converted (in the 19th century) into a mill - and still in working order.

Colchester Zoo, just off the A12 outside the town, stands in the 40-acre park of Stanway Hall, with its 16th-century mansion and church dating from the 14th century. Founded in 1963, the Zoo has a wide and exciting variety of attractions., and has gained a well-deserved reputation as one of the best in Europe. Its award-winning enclosures allow visitors to get close to the animals and provides naturalistic environments for the 170 species. There are 15 unique daily displays, including opportunities to feed an African elephant, bear, chimp or alligator, stroke a snake and watch a penguin parade. Among major new attractions are the sea lion pool with an underwater tunnel and 'Tiger Taiga' featuring the endangered Siberian tiger.

Colchester has been famous in its time for both oysters and roses. Colchester oysters are still cultivated on beds in the lower reaches of the River Colne, which skirts the northern edge of the town. A visit to the Oyster Fisheries on Mersea Island is a fascinating experience, and the tour includes complimentary fresh oysters and a glass of wine.

BUTTERFLY LODGE FARMSHOP & DAIRY

Mersea Road, Abberton, Colchester, Essex CO5 7LG
Tel: 01206 736121
e-mail: info@butterflylodge.co.uk
website: www.butterflylodge.co.uk

Butterfly Lodge Farmshop and Dairy is situated in Abberton, a beautiful rural village just five miles south of Colchester on the Mersea Road. The Farm and Dairy is run by husband and wife team, Warren and Ellie, and is respected as one of the finest producers of goats milk and goats milk products in the South-East. They were runners up 'Food Producers of Great Britian' at last year's BBC Food & Farming Awards.

As you drive up the long driveway surrounded by the forty-two acres of tranquil farmland, you may be surprised to see what appears to be quite a small farm shop by today's standards at the end, although appearances can be deceptive. The family run Farmshop has a Tardis-like quality about it. As you step in you will notice a varied selection of high quality locally sourced food and drink, local arts and crafts, a small café area and ice-cream parlour, a local post office and outside, a pleasant picnic area – it is really quite amazing.

The meat on sale is produced on the farm and reared traditionally on grass. The animals are allowed to graze freely on the chemical free land and are fed upon the highest quality cereals and hay; allowing for naturally matured meat with a fabulous taste and texture. You can purchase top quality highland/Dexter beef cuts, Shetland lamb, free range chicken, delicious Kune Kune pork, sausages and superb kid goat meat & 'Chilli Billy' Burgers, amongst the fabulous choice available.

Many people have probably not sampled goat meat, or if they have, the most likely dish to have tried this lean and tasty meat in, is a curry. Goat is widely consumed and much favoured across the world, although for some reason it is not so prevalent within the UK. Its taste can be likened to a cross between lamb and beef, so it is certainly acceptable to the palette. In addition, it is a very healthy meat, being low in cholesterol, high in iron and ounce for ounce has less fat than chicken and about the same amount of calories.

Butterfly Lodge Farm is also a large producer and supplier of fresh goat milk to the trade and public. The milk is deliciously sweet, lightly creamy and again very healthy because of the lower fat, lactose and cholesterol content. Their milk is also used to make their own 'Boudicca' soft, melt in the mouth goat's cheese, the creamy 'Monach Wyvern' semi-hard goat's cheese, as well as the highly awarded, sumptuous 'Caprilatte' goat-milk ice cream.

As well as some wonderful local condiments, oils, juices, eggs, fruit, biscuits, cakes and preserves, Butterfly Lodge has a very good and varied range of gluten free produce, which proves very popular - you can even buy gluten-free sausages! Other than the array of quality produce on sale, what really stands out about Butterfly Lodge is that it is such a warm and welcoming place to visit, take a look around, feed the animals and enjoy some wonderful home-made produce and hospitality; children just love the place and are made to feel extremely welcome.

Just north of the centre of town, **High Woods Country Park** offers 330 acres of woodland, grassland, scrub and farmland. A central lake is fed by a small tributary of the River Colne. The land originated as three ancient farms, and forms part of a Royal hunting forest. Large numbers of musket balls dating from the Civil War period have been unearthed, indicating that the woods served as a base for the Roundheads.

Around Colchester

WIVENHOE
4 miles SE of Colchester off the A133

This riverside town on the banks of the River Colne was once renowned as a smugglers' haunt, and its pretty quayside is steeped in maritime history. There are still strong connections with the sea, with boat-building having replaced fishing as the main industry. The lovely church, with its distinctive cupola atop a sturdy tower, stands on the site of the former Saxon church and retains some impressive 16th-century brasses.

The small streets lead into each other and end at the picturesque waterfront, where fishing boats and small sailing craft bob at their moorings. On the Quay visitors will find the Nottage Institute, the River Colne's nautical academy; classes here teach students about knots, skippering and even how to build a boat. It is open to visitors on Sundays in summer. The Wivenhoe Trail, by the river, is an interesting cycle track starting at the railway station and continuing along the river to Colchester Hythe. Wivenhoe Woods is dotted with grassy glades set with tables, the perfect place for a picnic.

East of the Quay, the public footpath takes visitors to the Tidal Surge Barrier, one of only two in the country. Volunteers run a ferry service operating across the River Colne between the Quay at Wivenhoe, Fingringhoe and Rowhedge. Nearby Wivenhoe Park has been the site of the campus for the University of Essex since 1962. Visitors are welcome to stroll around the grounds.

ABBERTON
3 miles S of Colchester off the B1026

🐦 Abberton Reservoir Nature Reserve

🐦 Fingringhoe Wick Nature Reserve

Two natural beauties are within reach of this village. **Abberton Reservoir Nature Reserve** is a 1,200-acre reservoir and wildlife centre, ideal for bird-watching. A site of international importance, home to goldeneye, wigeon, gadwall and shovellers, as well as a resting colony of cormorants, the site features a conservation room, shop, toilets and hides.

Four miles further east, **Fingringhoe Wick Nature Reserve** offers visitors 125 acres of woodland and lakes by the Colne estuary. Bird-watchers and nature lovers will happily explore the grassland, heathland, estuarine and freshwater habitats. Open all year round except on Mondays, the reserve hosts a full programme of events including children's activity days.

COPFORD
3½ miles SW of Colchester off the B1022

🏛 Church of St Michael & All Angels

Copford is home to the wonderful Norman **Church of St Michael and All Angels**, with its magnificent, well-restored medieval wall paintings, while Copford Green is a lovely and peaceful village. The Church of St Mary the Virgin also repays a visit.

Layer Breton

Distance: *4.0 miles (6.4 kilometres)*
Typical time: *90 mins*
Height gain: *10 metres*
Map: *Explorer 184*
Walk: *www.walkingworld.com ID:1458*
Contributor: *Brian and Anne Sandland*

ACCESS INFORMATION:

The walk starts in the car park of Layer Breton church.

ADDITIONAL INFORMATION:

Layer Marney Tower was built around 1520 for Henry VIII's Privy Seal, it is the tallest Tudor Tower and has a magnificent residence, farm and gardens attached.

DESCRIPTION:

Following field paths and country lanes this walk takes you through three small, out-of-the-way settlements, past two churches, a deer compound and a magnificent Tower.

FEATURES:

Toilets, Museum, Play Area, Church, Wildlife, Birds, Flowers, Butterflies, Good for Kids, Mostly Flat, Ancient Monument.

WALK DIRECTIONS:

1 | From Layer Breton church car park take the road south, then the first road right (signposted Layer Marney and Tiptree). Follow Shatters Road past a pond and then a junction left. Where the road goes sharp right, take a signposted footpath left.

2 | Follow the path, which bends right then follows the right hand edge of a field and heads in a dead straight line to the right of Layer Marney Tower and Church. When you reach a road go left. At the entrance to Layer Marney Tower car park go right.

3 | Pass the entrance to the Tower, then the Church (right) and continue on a broad grass track, which bends left then right (signposted) beside a deer compound, carrying on ahead when the wire fence bends left to pass through a hedge and cross a ditch by a footbridge. Continue along the right hand edge of another huge field to a gap in the

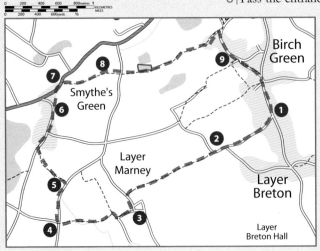

hedge (right), then pass a garage (left) and use the drive of a house to reach the road at a junction where you go right.

4 | Just after the road bends right, and before houses on the right, take a footpath left.

5 | Cross the stile and head straight across the field to a gap in the hedge between two telegraph poles. Bear half right to head for a stile next to a gate with houses beyond. At the road, go right then continue ahead (signposted Messing, Kelvedon and Colchester). Continue to a path off right through trees where the road begins a sharp left hand bend.

6 | Follow the path to the B1022 and turn right. When this road goes sharp left take a signposted footpath right (through a lay-by) to keep a hedge on your right.

7 | Continue to a stile through the hedge on the right. Cross this, turn left and carry on to another stile, which you cross to reach a road.

8 | Cross the road and take a signposted footpath over a stile. Cross a small field and another signposted stile and footbridge, and follow a clear path ahead to a track on a bend where you continue ahead passing a reservoir on your left. Ignore a track off left. Your track passes two lonely oak trees then heads towards houses. Just beyond Briar Cottage turn right on a tarmac lane past housing on both sides.

9 | You pass houses on your left and trees and a tall hedge on your right, then when you reach another road you turn right to return to the Church car park at Layer Breton.

LAYER BRETON
5½ miles SW of Colchester off the B1026

On the right side of Layer Breton Heath is Stamps and Crows, a must for gardening enthusiasts. Two-and-a-half acres of moated garden surrounding a 15th-century farmhouse. The farmhouse is not open to the public, but the gardens boast herbaceous borders, mixed shrubs, old roses and good ground cover. There is also a recently created bog garden and dovecote.

LAYER MARNEY
6 miles SW of Colchester off the B1022

🏠 Layer Marney Tower 🏠 Church of St Mary

The palace, which was planned to rival Hampton Court, was never completed, but its massive eight-storey Tudor gatehouse, known as Layer Marney Tower, is very impressive. Built between 1515 and 1525, it is one of the most striking examples of 16th-century architecture in Britain. Its magnificent four red brick towers, covered in 16th-century Italianate design, were built by Lord Marney, Henry VIII's Lord Privy Seal. As well as spectacular views from the top of the towers, they are surrounded by formal gardens designed at the turn of the century, with lovely roses, yew hedges and herbaceous borders. Also on site is a rare breeds farm, farm shop and tea room. The **Church of St Mary**, which was built behind the site of the palace, is one of the finest in the county, with a chapel with many monuments to the Marney family and a charming mural of St Christopher.

Off the B1026 a couple of miles southwest of Layer Marney is the village of Great Wigborough, which saw an early visit from a German airship. Zeppelin L33, which was hit

🎬 stories and anecdotes 🦜 famous people 🎨 art and craft 🎭 entertainment and sport 🚶 walks

Layer Marney Tower, Layer Marney

over Bromley, crashed here in September 1916; a contemporary record of the event is in St Stephen's Church, framed by aluminium taken from the wreck.

ALDHAM
4 miles W of Colchester off the A604

This picturesque village was, for a time, home to the famous Essex historian Philip Morant, who held the post of vicar here. He is buried in the local churchyard. Old Hill House in Aldham is a one-acre garden with mixed shrubs, herbaceous borders and formal herb garden for year-round interest.

CHAPPEL
5 miles W of Colchester off the A604

🏛 East Anglian Railway Museum 🏚 Chappel Viaduct

Here, on a four-acre site beside Chappel and Wakes Colne Station, is the **East Anglian Railway Museum**, a comprehensive collection spanning 150 years of railway history, with

period railway architecture, engineering and memorabilia in beautifully restored station buildings. For every railway buff, young or old, this is the place to try your hand at being a signalman and admire the handsome restored engines and carriages. There is also a delightful miniature railway. Special steam days and other events are held throughout the year. Platform One is still used by One Great Eastern services between Marks Tey and Sudbury.

The dramatic 32-arched **Chappel Viaduct** standing 75 feet above the Colne Valley, a designated European Monument, was begun in 1846 and opened in 1849.

ARDLEIGH
3 miles NE of Colchester off the A137

The westernmost village in the district known as Tendring comprises an attractive group of 16th- and 17th-century cottages grouped around the fine 15th century Butterfield Church. Spring Valley Mill, a now privately owned 18th-century timber-framed and weatherboarded edifice, was once a working watermill, later adapted to steam. Day and half-day canoeing and sailing lessons can be taken at the Ardleigh Outdoor Education Centre.

Nearby is Ardleigh Reservoir, offering up many opportunities for water sports and trout fishing.

DEDHAM
6 miles NE of Colchester off the A14

🏛 Toy Museum 🏚 Bridge Cottage
🏛 Sir Alfred Munnings Art Museum
🌱 Dedham Vale Family Farm

This is true Constable country, along the border with Suffolk, the county's prettiest area. The village has several fine old buildings, especially the 15th-century flint church, its pinnacled tower familiar from so many

🏛 historic building 🏚 museum and heritage 🏚 historic site 🔾 scenic attraction 🌱 flora and fauna

DEDHAM BOATHOUSE RESTAURANT

Mill Lane, Dedham, nr Colchester,
Essex CO7 6DH
Tel: 01206 323153   Fax: 01206 322232
e-mail: dedhamboathouse@aol.com
website: www.dedhamboathouse.com

The Boathouse in Dedham has long been known to locals and visitors as the place to hire a rowing boat or enjoy an ice cream down by the river. Those facilities still exist, but since Cameron and Claire Marshall bought the business in 2002, there have been many changes. After completing their first summer in Dedham they closed the café and turned it into the **Dedham Boathouse Restaurant**. They built a bar and a new kitchen and transformed the place into a warm, inviting and contemporary setting in which to enjoy a relaxing meal.

Cameron and his team produce a fusion of style and flavours on regularly changing menus, complemented by friendly, efficient service by Claire and her front-of-house team. The main menu is as up-to-date and appealing as the surroundings. Starters might include grilled goat's cheese, watercress and shaved fennel salad; shredded duck with sweet chilli noodles and toasted sesame seeds; and butterflied sardine fillets with gremolata, aïoli and a new potato salad. Typical main courses could be chump of lamb with braised red cabbage and rösti; fillet of cod with herb crust and dauphinoise potatoes; sea bass with coriander rice and a ginger and coconut broth; chargrilled ribeye steak; and farfalle pasta with marinated artichokes, sweet vine tomatoes and fresh basil. The enjoyment level remains sky-high to the end with St Clements mousse with mandarin jam, warm Bakewell tart or chocolate

granache cake with rum & raisin mascarpone – and superb Illy coffee to round things off. This menu is served lunchtime and evenings Tuesday to Saturday and for Sunday lunch.

A Summer Specials menu, available Tuesday to Saturday lunchtime and Tuesday to Thursday evening, includes open sandwiches and main dishes such as chicken Caesar salad or Cumberland sausage with buttered mash and red onion confit. A Taster menu in similar style operates out of season for lunch and dinner Tuesday to Thursday and lunch Friday. The superb food is complemented by wines from Old and New Worlds, with many available by the glass.

The tradition of hiring out rowing boats remains as strong as ever at Dedham Boathouse. Twenty-six clinker-built boats can be hired by the half-hour, hour or longer periods between April and September for a leisurely row along the River Stour; those feeling more energetic can head for Flatford Mill about a mile and a half away. The boats can hold four adults or two/three adults and two children (depending on age and size).

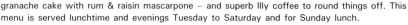

Constable paintings. There's also the school Constable went to, and good walks through the protected riverside meadows of Dedham Vale to Flatford, where **Bridge Cottage**, a restored thatched 16th-century building, houses a display about Constable, who featured this cottage in several of his paintings (his father's mill is across the river lock in Dedham).

Dedham Vale Family Farm on Mill Street is a traditional 16-acre farm boasting a comprehensive collection of British farm animals, including many different breeds of livestock such as pigs, sheep, cattle, Suffolk horses, goats and poultry. Children may enter some of the paddocks to stroke and feed the animals (bags of feed provided).

The Art & Craft Centre on Dedham's High Street is well worth a visit. Marlborough Head, a wool merchant's house dating back to 1475, is now a pub. The **Toy Museum** has a fascinating collection of dolls, teddies, toys, games, dolls' houses and other artefacts of childhoods past.

At Castle House, approximately three-quarters of a mile from the village centre on the corner of East Lane and Castle Hill, the **Sir Alfred Munnings Art Museum** is housed in the former home, studios and grounds of the famous painter, who lived here between 1898 and 1920. The museum prides itself on the diversity of paintings and

sculptures on view. The house itself is a mixture of Tudor and Georgian periods, carefully restored. Munnings' original furniture is still in place. The spacious grounds boast well-maintained gardens.

Braintree

🏛 Museum

The twin towns of Braintree and Bocking are sited at the crossroads of two Roman roads, and Braintree in particular was a Roman market town with evidence of metal industries and farming. However, it is the establishment of the wool industry in the 14th century, with many of the original timber framed buildings from this era still surviving in Bradford Street, which led to the spreading fame of the towns. Flemish weavers settled in the District bringing their weaving skills, and by the 17th century the bay cloth trade was well established. It was the sudden demise of the wool trade at the end of the 18th century that attracted the Huguenot family of Courtauld to settle in the district and establish a silk weaving industry. Courtaulds developed mechanised weaving of silk and by the 1860s employed over 3,000 local workers. The company became a worldwide success after the artificial silk industry revolutionised fashion and household textiles in the 20th century.

The **Braintree District Museum**, housed in a Victorian school on Manor Street, tells the story of the fascinating industrial heritage of the district and the Warner Textile

Flatford Birdge Cottage, Dedham

THE OLD HOUSE GUEST HOUSE

11 Bradford Street, Bocking, Braintree,
Essex CM7 9AS
Tel: 01376 550457 Fax: 01376 343863
e-mail: old_house@talk21.com
website: www.theoldhousebraintree.co.uk

The Old House Guest House is a Grade II* listed
building standing in half an acre of quiet, mature
grounds in a street of timber-framed houses. Sue and
Rob Hughes first opened their family home to Bed &
Breakfast guests in 1988, since when it has gained an
enviable reputation as a peaceful, civilised retreat for both
leisure and business guests. The oldest part of the
building dates from the 16th century, and the architectural
features of interest include fine octagonal Tudor chimneys
and handsome panelling.

   The accommodation comprises single, double, twin
and family rooms, all with central heating, television,
hairdryer, beverage tray and en-suite or private bathroom.
One room is on the ground floor and one room has a four-poster bed. The lovely panelled lounge
is a perfect spot to relax with a quiet drink, and a superb panelled Jacobean room is a popular
and characterful venue for small gatherings (up to 30). A hearty English breakfast (cooked on
the Aga) or a lighter Continental version starts the day, and packed lunches and evening meals
can be provided with a little notice.

Archive, part of the Museum's collection, is
housed in the Warner's Mills in Silks Way,
Samuel Courtauld's original Mill, which was
sold to Daniel Walters and later Warner &
Son. The Warner Textile Collection is the
second largest archive in Britain and has
examples of the many leading 19th- and
20th-century designers who worked for
the Company.

   The magnificent Town Hall Centre is one
of the many Courtauld legacies in the town. It
was built in 1928 with panelled walls, murals
by Grieffenhagen showing scenes of local
history, and a grand central tower with a
striking clock. Another fascinating reminder
of the Courtaulds' generosity is the 1930s
bronze fountain portraying a young boy with
dolphins near St Michaels Church, which
itself was founded in 1199.

A Market Charter was awarded by King
John, also in 1199, and a colourful street
market is still held to this day every
Wednesday and Saturday.

Around Braintree

FAIRSTEAD
4 miles S of Braintree off the A131

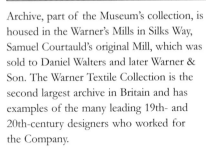 Church of St Mary & St Peter

Fairstead (or Fairsted) is an undulating parish
about three miles east of the A131, some four
miles northwest of Witham. The **Church of
St Mary and St Peter** is an ancient building
of flint, in the Norman style, consisting of
chancel, nave, north porch and a western
tower with a lofty shingled spire with four
bells, one of which dates back to before the

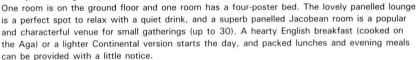
stories and anecdotes famous people art and craft entertainment and sport walks

ALLWOOD INTERIORS

Unit 3, Banters Lane Business Park, Main Street,
Great Leighs, Essex CM7 1QX
Tel: 01245 362994   Fax: 01245 362995
e-mail: soniaburdock@tiscali.co.uk

Great Leighs has been hitting the headlines in 2008 as the site of the first new racecourse in the UK for more than 80 years. But since 1992 Great Leighs has had the winner in the Bespoke Furniture Stakes in the shape of **Allwood Interiors**, founded and run by Tony and Sonia Bundock. Tony, an engineer by trade, has long had a passion for making pieces of furniture and, self-taught, has built up a fine reputation for the quality of his work. He makes his traditional hand-built furniture from oak, ash, maple, tulip and other woods both soft and hard, for the kitchen, the bedroom and the living room, fitted or freestanding, with polished, painted or distressed finish.

Tony will make home visits to take dimensions for pieces designed to individual customer's specifications, and the clients can visit the workshop to watch their pieces being made and other pieces at various stages of manufacture, as well as admiring finished pieces in the showroom. Allwood Interiors, located in a business park on the main street of Great Leighs, off the A131 between Chelmsford and Braintree, can be visited between 10am and 4pm (10am to 2pm on Sunday).

Reformation. During restoration in the late 1800s various handsome mural paintings were discovered, including, over the chancel arch, those entitled *Our Lord's Triumphal Entry into Jerusalem, The Last Supper, The Betrayal, Our Lord Being Crowned with Thorns*, and *Incidents on the way to Calvary*.

CRESSING

4 miles SE of Braintree off the B1018

🏛 Cressing Temple Barns

Cressing Temple Barns, set in the centre of an ancient farmstead, are two splendid medieval timber barns commissioned in the 12th century by the Knights Templar. They contain the timber of over 1,000 oak trees; an interpretive exhibition explains to visitors how the barns were made, as a special viewing platform brings visitors up into the roof of

the magnificent Wheat Barn for a closer look. There's also a beautiful walled garden re-creating the Tudor style, with an arbour, fount and physic garden. Special events are held throughout the year.

COGGESHALL

5 miles E of Braintree on the A120

🏛 Paycocke's House 🏛 Grange Barn

🏛 Marks Hall

This medieval hamlet, a pleasant old cloth and lace town, has some very fine timbered buildings. **Paycocke's House** on West Street, a delightful timber-framed medieval merchant's home dating from about 1500, boasts unusually rich panelling and wood carvings, and is owned by the National Trust. Inside there's a superb carved ceiling and a display of Coggeshall lace. Outdoors there's a

Paycock's House, Coggeshall

his successors to fell timber - thus his lasting legacy of avenues of mature oaks, limes and horse chestnuts, surrounded by one of the largest continuous areas of ancient woodland in the county.

The estate fell on hard times in the 19th and early 20th century, but owner Thomas Phillips Price began an association with Kew Gardens and left the estate to be held and used for 'advancement in the National interest of Agriculture, Aboriculture and Forestry'. The Thomas Phillips Price Trust was formed and registered as a charity in 1971, and a major programme of revitalisation and restoration began. The estate now flourishes with native plants and wildlife, ornamental lakes, a 17th-century walled garden, cascades, Coach House and Information Centre. This last is housed in a painstakingly refurbished 15th-century barn, and features informative displays as well as a gift shop and tea room.

Plans for the on-site arboretum were first drawn up in the late 1980s, to cover 120 acres. Still being established, it will contain a collection of trees from all over the world, laid out in geographical themes - Europe, Asia, America, and the southern hemisphere.

lovely garden. The village also has some good antique shops and a working pottery.

Located in Stoneham Street, Coggeshall Heritage Centre displays items of local interest and features changing exhibitions on themes relating to the past of this historic wool town. There's an authentic, working wool loom on site.

The National Trust also owns the restored **Coggeshall Grange Barn**, which dates from around 1140 and is the oldest surviving timber-framed barn in Europe. Built for the monks of the nearby Cistercian Abbey, it is a magnificent example of this type of architecture.

Marks Hall is an historic estate and arboretum that began life in Saxon times, and is mentioned in the Domesday Book. In the 15th century, then-owner Sir Thomas Honywood was a leading Parliamentarian who commanded the Essex Regiment during the Civil War. Local legend has it that the two artificial lakes on the grounds were dug by Parliamentary troops during the siege of Colchester in 1648. In 1758, one of his successors, General Philip Honywood, forbade (under the terms of his will) any of

FEERING
6 miles E of Braintree off the A12

Feeringbury Manor near Feering has a fine, extensive riverside garden with ponds, streams, a little waterwheel, old-fashioned plants and bog gardens, and fascinating sculpture by artist Ben Coode-Adams.

Boydells Dairy Farm

Wethersfield, Braintree, Essex CM7 4AQ
Tel: 01371 850481
e-mail: visits@boydellsdairy.co.uk
website: www.boydellsdairy.co.uk

Boydells Dairy Farm is no ordinary animal
attraction; it is a small family farm specialising
in commercial sheep milking. Visitors are given
a fun and informative guided tour based on the
normal, everyday routine of the farm, with
plenty of chance to ask questions. You will
experience lamb feeding and egg collecting;
you can watch the sheep being milked and you
might even try your hand at milking a cow!

Most farm animals can be found at Boydells
Dairy Farm – cattle, pigs, goats, ponies,
poultry, even llamas, but it is the flock of
milking sheep that is the main enterprise.

Sheep's milk (wonderful for those who suffer
from cow's milk intolerance) is used to produce
delicious cheese, yogurt and our famous
Yoggipops – a yogurt ice lolly. All of these are
for sale in the shop, together with eggs, honey, drinks and pocket money souvenirs.

Boydells Dairy Farm is between Shalford and Wethersfield on the B1053 (Saffron
Walden to Braintree road) about five miles north of Braintree.

BLAKE END

3 miles W of Braintree off the A120

🎨 Craft Centre 🌿 The Great Maze

The **Great Maze** at Blake End is one of the
most challenging in the world. Set in over 10
acres of lovely North Essex farmland, it is
grown every year from over half a million
individual maize and sunflower seeds, and is
open every summer. Continuing innovations
bring with them extra twists and turns, making
this wonderful maze, with more than five
miles of pathways, even more of a brain
teaser. A viewing platform makes it easy to
help anyone hopelessly lost! Ten per cent of
all profits go to the Essex Air Ambulance
service.

Blake House Craft Centre comprises
carefully preserved farm buildings centred
round a courtyard. One of the county's
prettiest craft centres, visitors will find a fine
array of craft shops and a restaurant serving
breakfast and morning coffee, lunch and
afternoon tea.

GREAT SALING

4 miles NW of Braintree off the A120

Saling Hall Garden is a 12-acre garden
including a walled garden dating from 1698.
The small park boasts a collection of fine
trees, and there are ponds, a water garden
and an extensive collection of unusual plants
with an emphasis on rare trees.

🏚 historic building 🏛 museum and heritage 🏛 historic site ☘ scenic attraction 🌱 flora and fauna

WETHERSFIELD

5 miles NW of Braintree on the B1053

Boydells Dairy Farm (see panel opposite) is a working farm where visitors are welcome to join in with tasks such as milking, feeding and more. A guided tour mixes fun with education, and all questions are most welcome. From bees to llamas, just about every kind of farm animal can be found here. Goat rides and donkey cart rides, a lovely picnic area and refreshments made on site, make for a most enjoyable day out. Open to the public April to September.

FINCHINGFIELD

6 miles NW of Braintree off the B1053

🏠 Church of St John the Baptist 🏠 Guildhall

This charming village is graced with thatched cottages spread generously around a sloping village green that dips to a stream and duck pond at the centre of the village. Nearby stands an attractive small 18th-century Post Mill with one pair of stones and tailpole winding. Extensively restored, visitors can climb up the first two floors.

Just up the hill, visitors will find the Norman **Church of St John the Baptist**, and the **Guildhall** (mentioned in the *Domesday*

Book), which has a small museum open on Sundays and houses a local heritage centre with displays of artwork, paintings, pottery, sewing and weaving.

Finchingfield is easily one of the most picturesque and photographed villages in Essex, it has featured in many TV programmes and is the home of the series *Lovejoy*. Here visitors will also find the privately owned Tudor stately home, Spains Hall, which has a lovely flower garden containing a huge Cedar of Lebanon planted in 1670 and an Adams sundial. Many good roses surround the kitchen garden, which contains an ancient Paulonia tree and a bougainvillea in the greenhouse. The garden is generally open on Sunday afternoons in summer.

Finchingfield also has an easily followed path along the Finchingfield Brook leading from the village to Great Bardfield.

GREAT BARDFIELD

6 miles NW of Braintree off the B1053

🏛 Museum

This old market town on a hill above the River Pant is a pleasant mixture of cottages and shops, nicely complemented by the 14th-century Church of St Mary the Virgin. Perhaps Great Bardfield's most notable feature is, however, a restored windmill that goes by the unusual name of Gibraltar.

Here in one of the prettiest villages in all of Essex, the **Great Bardfield Museum** occupies a 16th-century charity cottage and 19th-century village lockup, and features exhibits of mainly 19th- and 20th-century

Spain's Hall, Finchingfield

domestic and agricultural artefacts and some fine examples of rural crafts such as corn-dollies and straw-plaiting.

GOSFIELD
4 miles N of Braintree off the A1017

🏞 Gosfield Lake Leisure Resort

Gosfield Lake Leisure Resort, the county's largest freshwater lake, lies in the grounds of Gosfield Hall. This Tudor mansion was remodelled in the 19th century by its owner Samuel Courtauld. He also built the attractive mock-Tudor houses in the village.

Halstead

🏛 Townsford Mill

The name Halstead comes from the Anglo-Saxon for healthy place. Like Braintree and Coggeshall, Halstead was an important

weaving centre. **Townsford Mill** is certainly the most picturesque reminder of Halstead's industrial heritage. Built in the 1700s, it remains one of the most handsome buildings in a town with a number of historic buildings. This white, weatherboarded three-storey mill across the River Colne at the Causeway, was once a landmark site for the Courtauld empire, producing both the famous funerary crepe and rayon. Today, the Mill is an antiques centre, one of the largest in Essex, with thousands of items of furniture, porcelain, collectables, stamps, coins, books, dolls, postcards, costumes, paintings, glass and ceramics, old lace and clocks.

There are several historic buildings in the shopping centre of Halstead, which is part of a designated conservation area.

Though it may now seem somewhat improbable, Halstead's most famous product

MARMALADE

35 High Street, Halstead, Essex CO9 2AA
Tel: 01787 473217
e-mail: marmalademarmalade@hotmail.com

Kate Mroz always wanted her own shop and opened Marmalade in 2005. On the main street of the old weaving town of Halstead, this super shop sells seasonal ranges of women's, children's and baby clothes, along with accessories, giftware and things for the home. J J Park, Bohemia and Sara Sanskara are among the featured brands of fashionware, and among the accessories are hand-made slippers and babies' bonnets, winter hats, funky shower caps, leather belts, rings and Jonny Loves Rosie bags and jewellery. Also in stock are Orchid enamelled jewelled boxes and mirrors, magnifying glasses, photo frames, cushions, McCall candles, Gel Gems window ornaments, bookmarks, lampshades, Friendship tea bags and 100% vegetable oil soap from France. Browsers are welcome, Kate and her assistants are on hand with help and advice and this busy, friendly shop is open from 9.30am to 5pm Monday to Saturday.

Halstead is a place filled with interesting, historic buildings and needs plenty of time for a stroll. But no visit is complete without looking in at Marmalade.

Hedingham Castle

*Bayley Street, Castle Hedingham, Halstead,
Essex CO9 3DJ*
Tel: 01787 460261
website: www.hedinghamcastle.co.uk

Hedingham Castle's Norman keep, 110 feet high, was built c1140 by Aubrey de Vere and is still owned by one of his descendants, The Honourable Thomas Lindsay and his wife Virginia. There are four floors to explore, including a magnificent Banqueting Hall spanned by a remarkable 28-foot arch, one of the largest Norman arches in England. A good view of this splendid room can be obtained from the Minstrels' Gallery, built within the thickness of the 12-foot walls. A visit to the castle and its beautiful grounds is ideal for a family outing, and during the summer there are a variety of special events, which bring its colourful history alive. Come and enjoy one of our exciting Jousting Tournaments or other entertainments.

The castle and the Queen Anne house (private) are surrounded by well-kept grounds and woods. At the head of the beautiful lake is a pretty 18th-century dovecote in the Bog Garden which was planted in the 1920s and contains camellias and azaleas, water-loving plants and the huge leaves of giant gunnera. There are delightful walks around the lake and through the shady woodland under the steep ramparts of the castle defences. This Valley Walk is famous for its spectacular snowdrops in February, followed by a carpet of bluebells in May, and the castle's peaceful grounds and many fine trees are home to a large variety of birds and animals.

was once mechanical elephants. Life-sized and weighing half a ton, they were built by one W Hunwicks. Each one consisted of 9,000 parts and could carry a load of eight adults and four children at speeds of up to 12 miles per hour. Rather less unusual is the Tortoise Foundry Company, remembered for its warm tortoise stoves.

Around Halstead

CASTLE HEDINGHAM

3 miles NW of Halstead off the B1058

🏰 Castle   🚂 Colne Valley Railway Museum

🐑 Colne Valley Farm Park

This town is named after its Norman **Castle**

(see panel above), which dominates the landscape. One of England's strongest fortresses in the 11th century, even now it is impossible not to feel its power and strength. The impressive stone keep is one of the tallest in Europe, with four floors and rising over 100 feet, with 12-foot thick walls. The banqueting hall and minstrels' gallery can still be seen. It was owned by the Earls of Oxford, the powerful de Veres family, one of whom was among the barons who forced King John to accept the Magna Carta. Amongst those entertained at the castle were Henry VII and Elizabeth I.

The village itself is a maze of narrow streets radiating from Falcon Square, named after the half-timbered Falcon Inn. Attractive buildings include many Georgian and 15th-century houses comfortably vying for space, and the Church of St Nicholas, built by the de Veres, which avoided Victorian 'restoration' and is virtually completely Norman, with grand masonry and interestingly carved choir seats. There is a working pottery in St James' Street.

At the **Colne Valley Railway and Museum**, a mile of the Colne Valley and Halstead line between Castle Hedingham and Great Yeldham has been restored and now runs steam trains operated by enthusiasts. These lovingly restored Victorian railway buildings feature a collection of vintage engines and carriages; short steam train trips are available. **Colne Valley Farm Park**, set in 30 acres of traditional river meadows, is open from April to September.

The B1058 towards Sudbury, then left through Gestingthorpe and the Belchamps, makes for a pleasant excursion.

SIBLE HEDINGHAM
3 miles NW of Halstead off the A1017

Mentioned in the Domesday Book as the largest parish in England, Sible Hedingham was the birthplace of Sir John Hawkwood, one of the 14th century's most famous soldiers of fortune. He led a band of mercenaries to Italy, where he was paid to defend Florence, which is where he died. Hawkwood was buried in Florence Cathedral, where he is commemorated with a fresco by Uccello. It is thought that his body was returned to Essex and lies beneath the monument to him in Sible Hedingham's Church of St Stephen, decorated with hawks and various other beasts.

Swan Street is the main artery of this charming village, boasting several delightful

establishments devoted to providing visitors and natives of the town with places to shop, dine, enjoy a quiet drink and even stay for the night.

GESTINGTHORP
5 miles N of Halstead off the A131

🏚 Church of St Mary the Virgin

The **Church of St Mary the Virgin** in Gestingthorp is distinctive in many respects. Witness to centuries of Christian worship, the Domesday Book of 1086 tells that 'Ghestingetorp' was held by Ledmer the priest before 1066. The oldest part extant of the existing building is the blocked-up lancet window in the north wall of the chancel, which dates back to the 1200s. Apart from this, most of the chancel, nave and south aisle dates from the 14th century. The tower, constructed in about 1500, is 66 feet high. Of the six bells hung in the tower, four were cast in 1658-9 by Miles Gray, a Colchester bellfounder. The 16th century fifth and sixth bells were cast in Bury St Edmunds, and recast in 1901. The west door, set in a stepped brick arch, is the original. The unusual tracery in the East window consists of arches placed atop the apexes of the arches beneath them. The late 15th-century/early 16th-century nave roof is of the double hammer-beam type, and one of the finest in Essex. The font is late 14th century. One of the church's handsome memorials commemorates Captain L E G Oates, who died in an attempt to save the lives of his companions on an ill-fated expedition to the Antarctic in 1912.

The North Essex Coast

The Essex Sunshine Coast has 36 miles of clean, sandy beaches, including two European

ESSEX

Blue Flag beaches (Brightlingsea and Dovercourt Bay) and five Seaside award winning beaches at Clacton, Frinton, Walton, Brightlingsea and Dovercourt Bay.

Clacton-on-Sea

Jaywick Sands

Clacton is a traditional sun-and-sand family resort with a south-facing, long sandy beach, lovely gardens on the seafront and a wide variety of shops and places to explore. It also boasts a wide variety of special events and entertainments taking place throughout the year.

Settled by hunters during the Stone Age - borne witness to by the wealth of flint implements and the fossilised bones of the cave lion, straight-tusked elephant and wild ox unearthed on the Clacton foreshore and at Lion Point - the town grew over the centuries from a small village into a prosperous seaside resort in the 1800s, when the craze for the health benefits of coastal air and bathing was at its peak. The Pier was constructed in 1871; at first paddle steamers provided the only mode of transport to the resort, the railway arriving in 1882. The Pier was widened from 30 to over 300 feet in the 1930s. On the pier, apart from the traditional sideshows, big wheel, restaurants and fairground rides, there is the fascinating Seaquarium and Reptile Safari.

Amusement centres include the arcades and Clacton Pavilion. The two theatres, Princes Theatre and West Cliff, are open all year. Clacton Pavilion boasts a range of attractions, including crazy golf and dodgems. The Clifftop Public Gardens are worth a visit.

Great Clacton is the oldest part of town,

comprising an attractive grouping of shops, pubs and restaurants within the shadow of the 12th-century parish church.

A walk round the town rewards the visitor with some very handsome sights. There are three Martello Towers along this bit of the Essex coast. Just south of the town, **Jaywick Sands** is the ideal spot for a picnic by the sea, boasting one of the finest natural sandy beaches in the county.

Around Clacton-on-Sea

LITTLE CLACTON
3 miles NW of Clacton off the A133

Church of St James

Though it shares its name with its near neighbour, this is a town apart. Quiet and secluded, multiple-winner of the Best Kept Village Award, Little Clacton features a lovely Jubilee Oak, planted to celebrate Victoria's 50th year on the throne.

The fine **Church of St James** has been described as one of the most beautiful medieval churches in Essex, and sits at the heart of the village.

Oakwood Crafts Resource Centre in Little Clacton provides an environment for people with learning disabilities to learn and develop work skills, motivation, responsibility, team spirit, self-esteem and confidence through horticulture, woodwork, ceramics, crafts and catering. Set in three acres of land, it opened in 1975 and, as a horticultural centre, sells a wide range of bedding plants, shrubs and hanging baskets seasonally, along with a selection of wooden garden implements, furnishings and other items, and ceramics. Teas and coffees are available.

WEELEY

5 miles NW of Clacton off the A133

St Andrew's is the handsome parish church just south of the centre of this picturesque village. There is a lovely tree-lined path that passes Weeleyhall Wood and Weeley Lodge, with its beautifully kept gardens. Here visitors will also pass a navigational beacon that forms part of Aircraft Flight Operations for both civil and military flights.

A mile south, off the B1411, Weeley Heath is a small and attractive community boasting a lovely village green and stunning surrounding countryside.

TENDRING

7 miles NW of Clacton off the A133

This village that gives its name to both the peninsula and the district council contains the handsome Church of St Edmund with its elegant spire that can be seen for miles around. The church is dedicated to the last King of independent East Anglia, martyred by the Danes in the 9th century.

BEAUMONT-CUM-MOZE

7 miles NW of Clacton off the B114

This small village once had a quay originally constructed for loading and unloading the vessels plying the Walton backwaters. The disused Trading Quay was rebuilt in 1832 using stone from the old London Bridge. The 11th-century parish Church of St Leonard contains the grave of Viscount Byng of Vimy, one-time Governor General of Canada.

HOLLAND-ON-SEA

1½ miles NE of Clacton off the B1032

🌿 Holland Haven Country Park

This attractive community is home to

Holland Haven Country Park, 100 acres of open space near the seashore, ideal for watching the marine birds and other wildlife of the region. Throughout the area there are a number of attractive walks, which take full advantage of the varied coastal scenery.

FRINTON-ON-SEA

3 miles NE of Clacton off the B1032

Once a quiet fishing village, this town was developed as a select resort by Sir Richard Cooper, and expanded in the 1880s to the genteel family resort it is today. Situated on a long stretch of sandy beach, Frinton remains peaceful and unspoilt. The tree-lined residential avenues sweep elegantly down to the Esplanade and extensive clifftop greensward. Along its main shopping street in Connaught Avenue, the Bond Street of the East Coast, shopkeepers maintain a tradition of friendly and courteous service. Summer theatre and other open-air events take place throughout the season, and there are also some excellent tennis and golf clubs in the town. The grace and elegance of this sophisticated resort is evidenced all around, as are hints of its distinguished past: Victorian beach huts still dot the extensive beach.

The area south of Frinton Gates has a unique local character, being laid out with detached houses set along broad tree-lined avenues.

The Church of Old St Mary in the town contains some panels of stained glass in the East window designed by the Pre-Raphaelite artist Burne Jones.

A good example of 20th-century English vernacular architecture is The Homestead at the corner of Second Avenue and Holland Road, built in 1905 by C F Voysey.

PARK FRUIT FARM

Pork Lane, Great Holland, Frinton-on-Sea,
Essex CO13 0ES
Tel: 01255 674621
e-mail: s.elsworth@farmline.com
website: www.parkfruitfarm.co.uk

Park Fruit Farm and the associated shop are owned by Stephen Elsworth, whose father started the commercial side in the early 1970s and whose grandfather planted the first orchard here in 1935. The 60 acres in Great Holland, on the B1032 between Frinton and Clacton, produce an impressive 40 varieties of apples, 10 varieties of plums and damsons, and four varieties of pear, along with raspberries and blackberries.

The shop is part of the pack house and visitors can see the grader being worked and the apples being pressed for juice. As well as most of the fruit grown on the farm, the shop sells its award-winning pure, untreated apple juice, cider and cider vinegar, home-baked sweet and savoury dishes and meat, eggs, vegetables, preserves and chutneys from local farms.

Pick Your Own is available for plums between mid-July and October, and for cane fruit from August to November. Rose makes a variety of cakes with fruits from the orchard and sells them in the shop and in the tea room, where sweet and savoury snacks and hot and cold drinks are served. The shop is open Monday to Saturday from January to July, and every day from August to Christmas. It is closed during the week from Christmas to New Year.

KIRBY-LE-SOKEN

5 miles NE of Clacton off the B1034

There is a footpath in this attractive village that begins to the west of the 14th century Ship Inn and affords views of the backwaters of Hamford Water, with views of Horsey and Hedge End Islands in the middle distance.

WALTON-ON-THE-NAZE

8 miles NE of Clacton on the B1034

🏛 Old Lifeboat House Museum 🏛 The Naze

🏛 Naze Tower

Walton is all the fun of the fair. It is a cheerful, traditional resort that focuses on the pier and all its attractions, including a 10-pin bowling alley. The gardens at the seafront are colourful and the beach has good sand.

The Backwaters to the rear of Walton are made up of a series of small harbours and saltings, which lead into Harwich harbour. Walton has an outstanding sandy beach. The town's seafront was developed in 1825 and provides a fine insight into the character of an early Victorian seaside resort. The charming narrow streets of the town contain numerous shops, restaurants and pubs overlooking the second longest pier in the country. Marine Parade, originally called The Crescent, was built in 1832. The Pier, first built in 1830, was originally constructed of wood and measured 330 feet in length. It was extended to its present length of 2,610 feet in 1898.

The wind-blown expanse of **The Naze**, just north of Walton, is an extensive coastal recreation and picnic area, pleasant for walking, especially out of season when the visitor is unlikely to have to share the 150 acres, with great views out over the water. The shape of the Naze is constantly changing, eroded by wind, water and tide.

The year 1796 saw the demise of the medieval church, and somewhere beyond the 800-foot pier lies medieval Walton. The sandstone cliffs are internationally important for their shell fossil deposits. Inhabitants have been enjoying the bracing sea air at Walton since before Neolithic times: flint-shaping instruments have been found here, and the fossil teeth and the ears of sharks and whales have been discovered in the Naze's red crag cliffs. The **Naze Tower** is brick-built and octagonal in shape. Originally built as a beacon in 1720 to warn seamen of the West Rocks off-shore, it includes a roof viewing platform, an art gallery, tea rooms and a museum tel: 01255 852519. A nature trail has been created nearby, and the Essex Skipper

butterfly and Emperor moth can be seen here. The John Weston Nature Reserve provides important habitats for migrant birds.

The **Old Lifeboat House Museum** at East Terrace, in a building over 100 years old, houses an interpretive museum of local history and development, rural and maritime, covering Walton, Frinton and the Sokens.

Brightlingsea

🏚 All Saints Church 🏚 Jacobes Hall 🏛 Museum

Brightlingsea enjoys a long tradition of shipbuilding and seafaring. In 1347, 51 men and five ships were sent to the siege of Calais. Among the crew members of Sir Francis Drake's fleet, which vanquished the Spanish Armada, was one William of Brightlingsea. Brightlingsea has the distinction of being the only limb of the Cinque Ports outside Kent and Sussex.

The 13th-century **Jacobes Hall** in the town centre is one of the oldest occupied buildings in Essex. It is timber-framed with an undulating tile roof and an external staircase. Used as a meeting hall during the reign of Henry III, its name originates from its first owner, Edmund, Vicar of Brightlingsea, who was known locally as Jacob le Clerk.

All Saints Church, which occupies the highest point of the town on a hill about a mile from the centre, is mainly 13th century. Here are to be found some Roman brickwork and a frieze of ceramic tiles commemorating local residents whose lives were lost at sea. Its 97-foot tower can be seen from 17 miles out to sea. A light was once

The Marina, Walton-on-the-Naze

🏚 historic building 🏛 museum and heritage 🏚 historic site 🌳 scenic attraction 🍃 flora and fauna

placed in the tower to guide the town's fishermen home.

The Town Hard is where you can see all the waterfront comings and goings, including the activities of the Colne Smack Preservation Society, which maintains a seagoing link with the past.

Brightlingsea Museum in Duke Street offers an insight into the lives, customs and traditions of the area, housing a collection of exhibits relating to the town's maritime connections and the oyster industry.

There are plenty of superb walks along Brightlingsea Creek and the River Colne, which offer a chance to watch the birdlife on the saltings and the plethora of boats on the water. Today the town is a haven for the yachting fraternity and is the home of national and international sailing championships, with one of the best stretches of sailing on the East Coast. Day and half-day sailing and canoeing sessions are held at the Brightlingsea Outdoor Education Centre. From the new

pier visitors can board the ferry for trips to point Clear and East Mersea, providing a unique view of the Colne estuary.

Around Brightlingsea

GREAT BENTLEY
4 miles N of Brightlingsea off the A133

Reputed to have the largest village green in England, this lovely village has a number of shops, a pub with a restaurant, a beautiful church and a chapel.

ELMSTEAD MARKET
6 miles N of Brightlingsea off the A120

🌷 Beth Chatto Gardens

The Church of St Anne and St Lawrence to the north of this village has a rare carved oak, recumbent effigy of a knight in armour.

Elmstead Market is perhaps best known as the location of **Beth Chatto Gardens** (see panel below), at White Barn House,

Beth Chatto Gardens

Elmstead Market, Elmstead, Essex CO7 7DB
Tel: 01206 822007
e-mail: info@bethchatto.fsnet.co.uk website: www.bethchatto.co.uk

The Beth Chatto Gardens began in 1960. From an overgrown wasteland with poor gravel soil and boggy hollows, it has been transformed into an informal garden harmonising with rhe surrounding countryside.

In the gravel garden, areas have been filled with drought-loving plants, emulating a winding dried-up river bed. Star performers include alliums providing jewel rich colours, whilst kniphofias, verbascums and flowering grasses add strong verticals amongst the bold groupings of ballota, lavandula and santolina. The dramatic water gardens include five large ponds where, from early summer until late autumn, the impact of lush green growth is almost overpowering. Huge upturned parasols of *Gunnera tinctoria* tower above a hundred shades of green, creating a scene of harmony and tranquillity. In autumn tall grasses shimmer with ribbon-like leaves, punctuating this green landscape with their rich tones.

📖 stories and anecdotes 🦜 famous people 🎨 art and craft 🎭 entertainment and sport 🚶 walks

renowned the world over. Here visitors will find five acres of landscaped gardens including extensive water gardens, shady walks and a Mediterranean-style gravel garden where aromatic drought-loving plants thrive. The adjoining nursery contains a wide variety of plants for sale. Close by is the Rolts Nursery Butterfly Farm.

THORRINGTON
3 miles NW of Brightlingsea off the AB1027

Thorrington Tide Mill, built in the early 19th century, is the only remaining Tide Mill in Essex, and one of very few left in East Anglia. It has been fully restored, and although no longer in use, the Wheel can be run for guided groups. There is a public footpath, which runs along the creek.

China Maroc Bonsai is a specialist nursery, part of which is devoted to a peaceful Japanese garden with a waterfall and pool, where one can enjoy the tranquil atmosphere and the many fascinating outdoor bonsai. Crossing the bridge over the pool, one enters a tropical tunnel containing hundreds of indoor bonsai, many of which are imported from the hotter regions of the world, as well as bonsai and seedlings grown and cultivated on the premises.

POINT CLEAR
2 miles SE of Brightlingsea off the B1027

🏛 East Essex Aviation Society & Museum

The **East Essex Aviation Society & Museum**, located in the Martello Tower (1810) at Point Clear, not only retains its original flooring and roof, but today contains interesting displays of wartime aviation, military and naval photographs, uniforms and other memorabilia with local and US Air

Force connections. There are artefacts on show from the crash sites of wartime aircraft in the Tendring area, including the engine and fuselage section of a recovered P51D Mustang fighter as a memorial to its pilot Flight Officer Ray King of the 479th Fighter group. The museum also explores civil and military history from both World Wars. There are very good views from the tower over the Colne Estuary and Brightlingsea.

ST OSYTH
3 miles SE of Brightlingsea off the B1027

🏛 Priory

This pretty little village has a fascinating history and centres around its Norman church and the ancient ruins of **St Osyth Priory**, founded in the 12th century. The village and Priory were named by Augustinian Canons after St Osytha, martyred daughter of Frithenwald, first Christian King of the East Angles, who was beheaded by Diceian pirates in AD653. Little of the original Priory remains, except for the magnificent late 15th-century flint gatehouse, complete with battlements.

St Osyth's Priory, St Osyth

THE MERSEA DELICATESSEN

42 High Street, West Mersea, Essex CO5 8QA
Tel: 01206 384753

Mersea Island has much to attract the visitor, but for food-lovers the place to head for is the **Mersea Delicatessen** on West Mersea's High Street. Friendly owners Carol and Maureen have long been passionate about food, a passion shared by their many regular customers. They are also environmentally very aware and try to keep packaging to a minimum. Home-made pies – chicken & leek, chicken & mushroom, steak & kidney, steak & mushroom – are among the specialities, along with quiches and a range of frozen meals, including lasagne, spaghetti bolognese, sausages & mash, cottage pie and hearty casseroles.

They also stock a wide variety of delicatessen items – cooked and cured meats, cheeses, olives, pickles and chutneys. Sandwiches are made to order and there's always a selection of breads and cakes, biscuits, chocolates (Feeding Your Imagination from Devon), ice creams, jams and marmalades, coffee beans, fruit juices, wines and beers.

The Mersea Deli is open from 9am to 5pm, half day Wednesday, closed Sunday. In the same street, Mersea Island Museum tells the story of the Island's social and natural history, archaeology and the fishing industry. Mersea is a haven for birdwatchers, and most of the Island is a designated National Nature Reserve.

The village is centred on a crossroads and contains an attractive group of shops and restaurants. The Church of St Peter and St Paul in the village centre has unusual internal red brick piers and arches. The nearby creek has a small boatyard and water-skiing lake.

MERSEA ISLAND
2 miles SW of Brightlingsea off the B1025

Mersea Island Museum   Nature Reserve

Cudmore Grove Country Park

Much of this island is a **National Nature Reserve**, home to its teeming shorelife. The island is linked to the mainland by a narrow causeway, which is covered over at high tide. The towns of both East and West Mersea have excellent facilities for sailing enthusiasts. On the High Street, West Mersea, **Mersea Island Museum** has exhibits of Mersea's social and natural history, archaeology and the fishing industry, including a fisherman's cottage display. Visitors to Mersea Island Vineyard at East Mersea can take a conducted tour followed by wine tasting and a seafood platter. East Mersea is also a haven for birdwatchers. The best-known vicar of East Mersea was the Rev Sabine Baring-Gould, father of 13 children and writer of the much-loved hymn, *Onward Christian Soldiers*.

Cudmore Grove Country Park on Bromans Lane, East Mersea, boasts fine views across the Colne and Blackwater estuaries. Grassland adjoining a sandy beach, it's an ideal spot for shore walks and picnics. A pathway on the sea wall leads to a birdwatching hide.

Harwich

🏛 Maritime Museum 🏛 Lifeboat Museum

🏛 National Museum of Wireless & Television

🏛 The Redoubt

Harwich's name probably originates from the time of King Alfred, when 'hare' meant army, and 'wic' a camp. This attractive old town was built in the 13th century by the Earls of Norfolk to exploit its strategic position on the Stour and Orwell estuary; the town has an important and fascinating maritime history, the legacy of which continues into the present.

During the 14th- and 15th-century French campaigns, Harwich was an important naval base. The famous Elizabethan seafarers Hawkins, Frobisher and Drake sailed from Harwich on various expeditions; in 1561 Queen Elizabeth I visited the town, describing

it 'a pretty place and want[ing] for nothing'. Christopher Newport, leader of the *Goodspeed* expedition which founded Jamestown, Virginia, in 1607, and Christopher Jones, master of the Pilgrim ship *The Mayflower*, lived in Harwich (the latter just off the quay in King's Head Street), as did Jones' kinsman John Alden, who sailed to America in 1620. The diarist Samuel Pepys was MP for the town in the 1660s, at a time when it was the headquarters for the King's Navy. Charles II took the first pleasure cruise from Harwich's shores. Other notable visitors included Lord Nelson and Lady Hamilton, who are reputed to have stayed at The Three Cups in Church Street.

Harwich remains popular as a vantage point for watching incoming and outgoing shipping in the harbour and across the waters to Felixstowe. Nowadays, lightships, buoys and

Harwich Lifeboat Museum

Timberfields, Wellington Road, Harwich, Essex CO12 3EJ
Tel: 01255 503429
e-mail: info@harwich-society.co.uk
website: www.harwich-society.co.uk

The first lifeboat at Harwich was named the *Braybrooke* and was on station between 1821-1825. It was owned by the Essex Lifeboat Association. Following a large loss of life after the vessel *Deutschland* was lost, the Royal National Lifeboat Institute (RNLI) opened its first station in Harwich in 1876 when the lifeboat *Springwell* was put on station. *Springwell* was a 35ft 9in long, self-righting, pulling and sailing type lifeboat and cost £432.

The RNLI presence remained until 1917, the Harwich lifeboats launched 276 times and saved 333 lives. An increase in incidents resulted in the RNLI opening a lifeboat station at Harwich again in 1965 using a 16ft inflatable. The station became operational all year round the following year and the arrival of the 44ft Waveney class *Margaret Graham* in 1967 ensured the station could function in all weathers.

The Harwich Society runs a lifeboat museum in the old Victorian lifeboat shed at Timberfields. As well as numerous exhibits, the 37ft Oakley class lifeboat *Valentine Wyndham-Quin* can be seen. This lifeboat saw service at Clacton-on-Sea from 1968 to 1984. Visitors to the museum have a rare hands-on opportunity to see a lifeboat at close quarters. The Museum is open from 11am – 3pm daily from 1st May till the end of August.

miles of strong chain are stored along the front, and passengers arriving on North Sea ferries at Harwich International Port see the 90-foot high, six-sided High Lighthouse as the first landmark. Now housing the **National Museum of Wireless & Television**, it was built in 1818 along with the Low Lighthouse. When the two lighthouses were in line they could indicate a safe shipping channel into the harbour. Each had replaced earlier wooden structures, and were themselves replaced by cast iron structures (both of which still stand on the front in nearby Dovercourt) in 1863 when the shifting sandbanks altered the channel. Shipping now relies on light buoys to find its way. The Low lighthouse is now the town's **Maritime Museum**, with specialist displays on the Royal Navy and commercial shipping. Harwich is a very busy lifeboat station with about 100 call-outs a year. Many of the all-weather lifeboat calls are well out into the North Sea, while the inshore lifeboat attends the rivers and coastal areas. The **Lifeboat Museum** (see panel opposite), off Wellington Road, contains an Oakley class lifeboat and a history from 1876 of the lifeboat service in Harwich; the Ha'penny Pier Visitor Centre on the Quay has information on everything in Harwich and a small heritage exhibition. Throughout the summer, there are guided walking tours starting at the visitor centre.

The Treadwheel Crane now stands on Harwich Green, but for over 250 years it was sited in the Naval Shipyard. It is worked by two people walking in two 16-foot diameter

The Redoubt, Harwich

wheels, and is the only known British example of its kind. Amazingly, it was operational up until the 1920s. Another fascinating piece of the town's history is the Electric Palace Cinema, built in 1911 and now the oldest unaltered purpose-built cinema in Britain. It was restored by a trust and re-opened in 1981.

The importance of Harwich's port during the 19th century is confirmed by **The Redoubt**, a huge grey fort built between 1808 and 1810. Its design is an enlarged version of the Martello towers that dotted the English coast awaiting a Napoleonic invasion that never came (some of these towers, of course, still exist). Today the Harwich Society has largely restored it and opened the fort as a small museum.

The old town also contains many ancient buildings, including the Guildhall, which was rebuilt in 1769 and is located in Church Street. The Council chamber, Mayor's Parlour and other rooms may be viewed. The former gaol contains unique graffiti of ships, probably carved by prisoners, and is well worth putting aside a morning to explore (by appointment only).

Around Harwich

DOVERCOURT
1 mile S of Harwich off the A120

This residential and holiday suburb of Harwich has Market Day on Fridays. With its attractive cliffs and beach, it also boasts the Iron Lighthouse or Leading Lights located just off lower Marine Parade. The town has been settled from prehistoric times, as attested to by the late Bronze Age axe-heads found here (now in Colchester Museum). The Romans found the town a useful source of the stone Septaria, taken from the cliffs and used in building. The town that visitors see today developed primarily in Victorian times as a fashionable resort.

MISTLEY
7 miles W of Harwich off the B1352

🏛 Mistley Towers 🌱 Mistley Place Park

🎨 Mistley Quay Workshops

Here at the gateway to Constable Country, local 18th-century landowner and MP Richard Rigby had grand designs to develop Mistley into a fashionable spa to rival Harrogate and Bath, adopting the swan as its symbol. Sadly, all that remains of Rigby's ambitious scheme is the Swan Fountain, a small number of attractive Georgian houses and **Mistley Towers**, the remains of a church (otherwise demolished in 1870) designed by the flamboyant architect Robert Adams. From the waterfront, noted for its colony of swans, there are very pleasant views across the estuary to Suffolk. Mistley was once an important port and shipbuilding centre – Nelson's huge flagship *Amphian* was built here. Traditional crafts are still carried on in **Mistley Quay Workshops**, including a

pottery workshop, lute/cello maker, harpsichord maker, wood worker, bookbinder, and stained-glass window maker and restorer. There is also a tea shop on the premises (the key to Mistley Towers can be obtained from the Workshops).

Mistley Place Park Animal Rescue Centre is 25 acres of parkland affording country walks, wildlife habitats, lake, farm animals and great views across the Stour Estuary. Over 2,000 rescued animals, including rabbits, Vietnamese pigs and horses, roam freely.

MANNINGTREE
9 miles W of Harwich off the B1352

🏛 Museum 🏛 The Walls

The Walls, on the approach to Manningtree along the B1352, offer unrivalled views of the Stour estuary and the Suffolk coast, and the swans for which the area is famous. Lying on the River Stour amid beautiful rolling countryside, the scene has oft been depicted by artists over the centuries.

Back in Tudor times, Manningtree was the centre of the cloth trade, and later a port filled with barges carrying their various cargoes along the coast to London. Water still dominates today and the town is a centre of leisure sailing.

Manningtree has been a market town since 1238, and is still a busy shopping centre. It is the smallest town in Britain, and a stroll through the streets reveals the diversity of its past. There are still traditional (and mainly Georgian) restaurants, pubs and shops, as well as handcraft and specialist outlets. The views over the river are well known to birdspotters, sailors and ramblers. The town has an intriguing past - as a river crossing, market, smugglers' haven and home of Matthew

ANGEL PAVEMENT LTD

*Unit 2, Jubilee End, Dale Hall Industrial
Estate, Lawford, Manningtree,
Essex CO11 1UR
Tel: 01206 393020
e-mail: sonia@angelpavement.net
website: www.angelpavement.net*

Angel Pavement Ltd is based in a modern warehouse on the Essex/Suffolk border, in the village of Lawford, a five-minute walk from Manningtree Station and just a ten-minute drive from the A12. The main stock in trade is high-quality 19th and 20th century furnishings. The spacious, easy-to-view displays also include a wide variety of clocks, decorative items and collectables, from lighting and mirrors to costume jewellery, decorative glass, vintage perfume bottles, handbags and prints. Furniture stock includes pieces large and small, from dining chairs to wardrobes, tables, chests, cabinets, luggage racks, plant stands and much more.

Director and Company Secretary Sonia Oakden has had a passion for antiques, vintage clothing and accessories since she was a teenager, and she now shares that passion with her customers, seeking out quality items throughout the UK and beyond.

Angel Pavement offers its furniture in original, unrestored condition as well as fully restored pieces. A full furniture restoration service is available. Ashley Warren, a master of his trade with over 20 years experience, knows exactly how to bring out the best in a neglected piece of furniture. Major and minor repairs are undertaken; veneer work, marquetry and traditional methods of oil, wax and French polishing are a speciality.

At Angel Pavement they offer very competitive prices and don't expect to keep anything in stock for a long period, so on every visit the client is assured of finding something interesting and different. Their comprehensive website gives a good idea of the type of furniture and services that are on offer. Angel Pavement also regularly exhibits at major antiques fairs around the country.

Angel Pavement is open on weekdays 10am to 5pm and from 10am – 1pm on Saturday (phone first, as times can vary).

Hopkins, the reviled and self-styled
Witchfinder General who struck
terror into the local community
during the 17th century. Some of his
victims were hanged on
Manningtree's small village green.
Hopkins is buried on Mistley Heath.

It is believed that the reference in
Shakespeare's Henry IV to Falstaff
as 'that roasted Manningtree ox'
relates to the practice of roasting an
entire ox, as was done at that time at
the town's annual fair.

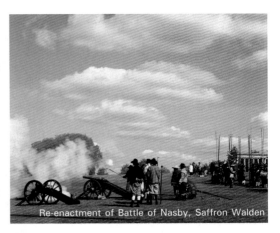
Re-enactment of Battle of Nasby, Saffron Walden

Manningtree Museum in the
High Street opened in the late 1980s and
mounts two exhibitions a year, together with
permanent photographs and pieces relating to
the heritage of Manningtree, Lawford, Mistley
and the district.

Saffron Walden

🏛 Audley End house 🏛 Museum 🏛 War Memorial
🌿 Common 🎨 Fry Public Art Gallery

Named after the Saffron crocus - grown in the
area to make dyestuffs and fulfil a variety of
other uses in the Middle Ages - Saffron
Walden has retained much of its original street
plan, as well as hundreds of fine old buildings,
many of which are timbered and have
overhanging upper floors and decorative
plastering (also known as pargeting). Gog and
Magog (or, in some versions, folk-hero Tom
Hickathrift and the Wisbech Giant) battle
forever in plaster on the gable of the Old Sun
Inn, where, legend has it, Oliver Cromwell
and General Fairfax both lodged during the
Civil War.

A typical market town, Saffron Walden's
centrepiece is its magnificent church. **Saffron**

Walden Museum first opened to the public
at its present location in 1835, and was
founded 'to gratify the inclination of all who
value natural history'. It remains faithful to
this credo, while widening the museum's scope
in the ensuing years. The museum has won
numerous awards, including joint winner of
the Museum of the Year Award for best
museum of Industrial or Social History in
1997. At this friendly, family-sized museum
visitors can try their hand at corn grinding
with a Romano-British quern, see how a
medieval timber house would have been built,
admire the displays of Native American and
West African embroidery, and come face to
face with Wallace the Lion, the museum's
faithful guardian. Over two floors, exhibits
focus on town and country (with a wealth of
wooden ploughs and other agricultural
artefacts), furniture and woodwork, costumes,
ancient Egyptian and Roman artefacts,
geology exhibits, and ceramics and glass. In
the Ages of Man gallery, the history of
northwest Essex is traced from the Ice Age to
the Middle Ages. The ruins of historic Walden
Castle are also on-site.

On the local **Common**, once known as Castle Green, is the largest surviving Turf Maze in England. Only eight ancient turf mazes survive in England: though there were many more in the Middle Ages, if they are not looked after they soon become overgrown and are lost. This one is believed to be some 800 years old.

Though many miles from the sea, it was here that Henry Winstanley - inventor, engineer and engraver, and designer of the first Eddystone Lighthouse at Plymouth - was born in 1644. He is said to have held lighthouse trials with a wooden lantern in the lavishly decorated 15th- to 16th-century church. The Lighthouse, and Winstanley with it, was swept away in a fierce storm in 1703.

The town was also famous for its resident Cockatrice, which was reputed to have hatched from a cock's egg by a toad or serpent and could, it was said, kill its victims with a glance. The Cockatrice was blamed for any inexplicable disaster in the town. Like Perseus and Medusa the Gorgon, a Cockatrice could be destroyed by making it see its own reflection, thereby turning it to stone. The Saffron Walden Cockatrice's slayer was said to be a knight in a coat of 'cristal glass'.

To the north of the town is Bridge End Garden, a wonderfully restored example of early Victorian garden, complete with a Hedge Maze (for opening times of the Maze call the TIC tel: 01799 524002). A viewing platform was reinstated in 2000 to enhance visitors' enjoyment of these lovely gardens.

Next to the gardens is the **Fry Public Art Gallery**, with a unique collection of work by 20th-century artists and designers who lived

MODISH

15 George Street, Saffron Walden, Essex CB10 1EW
Tel: 01799 528852
e-mail: sarah@modishonline.co.uk
website: www.modishonline.co.uk

A passion for gorgeous shoes and bags led Sarah Decent to share that passion by opening **Modish**, a beautiful boutique in a handsome Edwardian building. But Sarah's shoes aren't just lovely to look at; as a sample size 37 she tests each shoe personally, and if they're not comfortable they don't make it into the shop. Many of the shoes are made in Spain or Italy, and some of the most beautiful bags are in Italian leather. Behind the white-painted shopfront the well-lit display space showcases court shoes, evening shoes, day shoes, boots, pumps, trainers, sandals, both day and evening/occasion bags and fashion jewellery. The shop features both established designers and up-and-coming new talent and offers something to suit all ages and pockets with no compromise on quality and style.

Among the brand names, many of them not easily found outside London, are Ash, Audley, Blowfish, Bronx, Geox, Keds, Manas, Tamaris and Vanilla Moon (shoes) and Abro, Matt & Nat, Urban Code and Yoshi (bags). Sarah and her staff are always ready with help and advice; Modish is open from 9.30am to 5pm, Monday to Saturday.

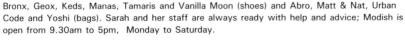

SOMETHING ELEGANT

8 Market Lane, Saffron Walden,
Essex CB10 1JZ
Tel: 01799 516669
e-mail: sales@something-elegant.co.uk
website: www.something-elegant.co.uk

Contemporary jewellery is the main stock-in-trade of **Something Elegant**, founded and owned by Richard Ketterdige. He started with a website specialising in modern silverware, and responded to the success of that enterprise by adding a retail outlet here in the lovely market town of Saffron Walden. Behind the double-fronted, double-door exterior there's plenty of space to browse at leisure among the well-lit display cabinets and choose from the impressive range of high-quality jewellery, charm jewellery and giftware for adults and children.

Generic jewellery, much of it made locally includes rings, necklaces, chokers, chains, cords, pendants, bracelets, bangles, earrings and, for men, cuff links and tie pins. Among the other featured collections are Sheila Fleet based in Orkney, Fusion from Cornwall, Ortak pens, watches by Axcent (Scandinavia) and Nooka (New York), Gallery, Rocks, Murano Glass jewellery, Fiorelli, Something Amber and children's jewellery Scribble and Little Diamonds. The shop is every day except Sunday and customers who can't get to the shop can use the website to order for themselves or for someone special a gift-wrapped present to treasure.

in and around Saffron Walden, such as Edward Bawden, Michael Rothenstein, Eric Ravilious, Kenneth Rowntree, Michael Ayrton, John Aldridge and Sheila Robinson. It also exhibits work by contemporary artists working in Essex today, demonstrating the area's continuing artistic tradition. The gallery was purpose-designed and opened in 1856 to house the collection of Francis Gibson, a Quaker banker. The gallery also houses the Lewis George Fry RBA, RWA (1860-1933) Collection, which is exhibited each summer, along with works by Robert Fry (1866-1934) and Anthony Fry.

Close to Bridge End is the **Anglo-American War Memorial** dedicated by Field Marshal the Viscount Montgomery of Alamein in 1953 to the memory of all the American flyers of the 65th Fighter Wing who lost their lives in the Second World War.

Audley End House was the home of the first Earl of Suffolk, and was at one time lived in by King Charles II. The original early 17th-century house, with its two large courtyards, had a magnificence claimed to match that of Hampton Court. Remodelled in the 18th century by Robert Adam, unfortunately the subsequent earls lacked their forebears' financial acumen, and much of the house was demolished as it fell into disrepair. Nevertheless it remains today one of England's most impressive Jacobean mansions; its distinguished stone façade set off perfectly by Capability Brown's lake. The remaining state rooms retain their palatial magnificence and the exquisite state bed in the Howard Room is hung with the original embroidered drapes. The collection of silver, the Jacobean Screen and Robert Adam's painted Drawing Room are among the many treasures. The natural history collection features more than 1,000 stuffed animals and birds. To complement this, there are paintings by Holbein, Lely and Canaletto. Fascinating introductory talks help visitors get the most from any visit to this, one of the most magnificent houses in England. This jewel also has a kitchen garden and grounds landscaped by Capability Brown, including the Temple of Concord, which Brown dedicated to George III. There is a lovely parterre, lake and Pond Garden. Circular walks help visitors make the most of all there is to see. The organic kitchen garden was recently opened to the public for the first time in 250 years. The gardens are managed by the Henry Doubleday Research Association, who grow and sell a wide range of organic produce in the shop, which also features a restaurant. The Audley End Miniature Railway (separate admission charge) is 1.5 miles long and takes visitors along Lord Braybrooke's private 10¼ inch gauge railway through the beautiful private woods of the house.

Within the rolling parkland of the grounds there are several elegant outbuildings, some of which were designed by Robert Adam. Among these are an icehouse, a circular temple and a Springwood Column (the last two can be seen from the road but are not open to the public).

Around Saffron Walden

BARTLOW
5 miles NE of Saffron Walden off the B1052

🏛 Bartlow Hills

Bartlow Hills are reputed to be the largest burial mounds in Europe dating from Roman times. Fifteen metres high, they date back to the 2nd century.

HADSTOCK
4 miles N of Saffron Walden off the B1052

As well as claiming to have the oldest church door in England, at the parish Church of St Botolph, Hadstock also has a macabre tale to tell. The church's north door was once covered with a piece of skin, now to be seen in Saffron Walden Museum. Local legend says it is a Daneskin, from a Viking flayed alive.

Lining doors with animal leather was common in the Middle Ages, and many so-called Daneskins are just that. However, the skins at Hadstock - and at Copford, in northeast Essex - are almost certainly human; the poor wretch at Hadstock undoubtedly having his hide nailed there as a warning to others. The door itself is Saxon, as are the 11th-century carvings, windows and arches, rare survivors that predate the Norman Conquest.

Linton Zoo near the village is a privately owned collection of wild animals set in 10½ acres of gardens. There is a free car park, children's play area, picnic areas and a café on site.

🏛 stories and anecdotes   🐿 famous people   🎨 art and craft   🦋 entertainment and sport   🚶 walks

BUSH FARM

Bush Road, Little Sampford, nr Saffron Walden, Essex CB10 2RY
Tel: 01799 586636
e-mail: angelabushfarm@yahoo.co.uk

Entertaining comes naturally to Angela Freeman, and as soon as she walked through the door at **Bush Farm** she knew that she was destined to share her house with Bed & Breakfast guests. Meeting, greeting and dispensing outstanding hospitality, at first part-time, soon became a full-time enterprise, and Angela welcomes many repeat visitors to her lovely 15th-century house.

The accommodation comprises three bedrooms beautifully appointed in traditional style, a double with en-suite facilities and two doubles with private bathrooms. An excellent breakfast is served in the dining room, and guests can enjoy tea and cakes in the comfortable lounge. The house has great character and atmosphere, with original exposed brickwork, oak beams and log fires that keep things cosy on cooler evenings.

The village of Little Sampford, which lies just off the B1053 southeast of Saffron Walden, is an ideal base from which to explore some of the most delightful and historic villages and towns in the region, including Thaxted, Finchingfield, Wethersfield, Radwinter and Great Bardfield, with many castles, museums and other historic buildings. It's also a great base for a walking or cycling holiday.

RADWINTER

4 miles E of Saffron Walden off the B1053

Radwinter boasts a fine church, which was largely renovated and rebuilt in the 19th century by architect Eden Nesfield and has a fine 14th-century porch. The village also has cottages and almshouses designed by Nesfield.

HEMPSTEAD

5 miles E of Saffron Walden off the B1054

The highwayman, Dick Turpin, was born here in 1705, where his parents kept an inn. The young Dick trained as a butcher in Whitechapel before turning to cattle stealing, smuggling and robbery at the head of his gang. When capture seemed imminent he fled to Yorkshire, where he continued his life of crime under the name of John Palmer. He was eventually caught while horse stealing and was

hanged in York in 1739.

Inside the 14th to 15th-century village church, an impressively life-like bust carved by Edward Marshall recalls the town's rather worthier son, William Harvey (1578-1657). Harvey was chief physician to Charles I and the discoverer of the circulation of blood, as recorded in his De Motu Cordis of 1628.

Like many other villages, Hempstead once boasted a village cockpit; its faint outline can still be traced, though the steep banks are now crowned with trees.

THAXTED

7 miles SE of Saffron Walden on the B184

🏛 Church of St John the Baptist   🏛 Guildhall

🏛 Tower Windmill

This small country town has a recorded history that dates back to before the *Domesday Book*.

Originally a Saxon settlement, it developed around a Roman road. The town's many beautiful old buildings contribute to its unique character and charm. To its credit, Thaxted has no need of artificial tourist attractions, and is today what is has been for the past 10 centuries: a thriving and beautiful town.

Thaxted has numerous attractively pargetted and timber-framed houses, and a magnificent **Guildhall**, built as a meeting-place for cutlers around 1390. The demise of the cutlery industry in this part of Essex in the 1500s led it to becoming the administrative centre of the town. Restored in Georgian times, it became the town's Grammar School, as well as remaining a centre of administration. Once more restored in 1975, it houses a permanent exhibition of old photographs and objects relating to the history of Thaxted.

The town's famous **Tower Windmill** was built in 1804 by John Webb, a local farmer. In working order until 1907, it had fallen into disuse and disrepair but has now been returned to full working order. It contains a rural life museum, well worth a visit (open 2.30pm to 5pm on Sundays and Bank Holidays from Easter to September). Close to the windmill are the town's Almshouses, which continue to provide homes for the elderly 250 years after they were built for that purpose.

The **Church of St John the Baptist** stands on a hill and soars cathedral-like over the town's streets. Begun in 1340 and completed some 170 years later, it has been described as the finest parish church in the country and, though many towns may protest long and loud at this claim, it certainly is magnificent. It was also the somewhat unlikely setting for a pitched battle in 1921.

Windmill & St Johns Church, Thaxted

The rather colourful vicar and secretary of the Church Socialist League, one Conrad Noel, hoisted the red flag of communism and the Sinn Fein flag in the church. Incensed Cambridge students tore them down and put up the Union Jack; Noel in turn ripped that down and, with his friends, slashed the tyres of the students' cars and motorbikes. A fine bronze in the church celebrates this adventurous man of the cloth.

Conrad Noel's wife is remembered for encouraging Morris dancing in the town. Today, the famous Morris Ring is held annually (in late May or early June), attracting over 300 dancers from all over the country, who dance through the streets. Dancing can also be seen around the town on most Bank Holiday Mondays, usually in the vicinity of a pub!

The composer Gustav Holst, best known for his *Planets Suite*, lived in Thaxted from 1914 to 1925, and often played the church

DEBDEN ANTIQUES

Elder Street, Debden, nr Saffron Walden,
Essex CB11 3JY
Tel: 01799 543007
e-mail: info@debden-antiques.co.uk
website: www.debden-antiques.co.uk

A stylishly converted 17th-century Essex barn is the home of **Debden Antiques & Interiors**, providing a wonderfully relaxed setting to browse the large selection of furniture and accessories for the home and garden. Furniture includes period oak, fine mahogany, Victorian pine, painted European and Chinese furniture. To compliment the antiques there is a wide selection of luxury modern accessories including lamps, candlesticks, mirrors and glass.

For those hunting for presents, there are many wonderful gifts for both young and old. Outside is the **Courtyard Garden**, filled with antique statues, urns, wrought iron furniture and ornamental stone. Visit the **Courtyard Cafe** for a relaxing drink and a bite to eat. Debden Antiques is situated between Saffron Walden and Thaxted, just follow the brown signs.

Open Tuesday to Saturday 10am - 5.30pm, Sunday & Bank Holidays 11am - 4pm.

THE CHAFF HOUSE

Ash Grove Barns, Littlebury Green,
Saffron Walden, Essex CB11 4XB
Tel/Fax: 01763 836278
e-mail: thechaffhouse@googlemail.com

For a true taste of traditional country farmhouse living, **The Chaff House** offers guests a beautifully appointed bedroom with exposed beamwork and an enormous bed. Light, bright and airy, the room is comfortably and tastefully furnished.

In addition, there are two more guest bedrooms in a separate building that also has a kitchen and can therefore be let on a self-catering basis. It is set in a courtyard with patio seating and a lovely selection of plants in pots and tubs, making for a really delightful outdoor space.

Owner Diana Duke, who lives next door, takes great pride in providing her guests with the very best – everything from the linen and towels to the excellent food is of the very highest quality. This warm, comfortable, sympathetically restored barn conversion is set in 900 acres of beautiful countryside.

Convenient for the M11, Stansted Airport and the marvellous city of Cambridge, it makes an excellent base for discovering the many sights and attractions of the region.

organ. To celebrate his connection with the town, a summer music festival attracts performers of international repute.

WIDDINGTON

4 miles S of Saffron Walden off the B1383

🌿 Mole Hall Wildlife Park

Covering over 20 acres of grounds and deer meadow, **Mole Hall Wildlife Park** offers visitors the chance to come close to a range of wild and domesticated animals. With the private fully-moated 13th-century manor house as a backdrop, the wide variety of animals in this excellent park include South American llamas, flamingos, Formosa sika deer (which are extinct in the wild), chimpanzees, muntjac, Arctic fox, wallabies, red squirrels and much more. Mole Hall is also home to two species of North American otter: short-clawed and North American. Domesticated animals such as guinea pigs,

rabbits, goats, pigs and sheep can also be seen. The Butterfly Pavilion offers a tropical experience where brilliantly coloured butterflies flit about freely. Within the tropical pavilion you can also find lovebirds and small monkeys, along with a variety of snakes, spiders and insects (safe behind glass). The pools are inhabited by goldfish, toads and terrapins among other creatures.

Widdington is also home to Priors Hall Barn, one of the finest surviving medieval 'aisled' barns in all of southeast England, and owned by English Heritage.

STANSTED MOUNTFITCHET

8 miles SW of Saffron Walden off the B1383

🏰 Castle 🏠 House on the Hill 🏚 Norman Village

Though rather close to Stansted Airport, there are plenty of reasons to visit this village. Certainly pilots approaching the airport may be surprised at the sight of a **Norman Village**,

---

WILKINSON & CO

Unit 2, Brices Yard, Butts Green, Clavering, Essex CB11 4RT
Tel: 01799 550828   Fax: 01799 550995
e-mail: sales@wilkys.co.uk
website: www.wilkys.co.uk

Wilkinson & Co is a double-fronted country store set in the Essex countryside at Butts Green, on the minor road that leads up from the B1038 at Clavering towards Langley Upper Green. Its main business is essentials for horses and riders, from feed and bedding supplies to saddles, rugs, tack, head collars, whips, gloves, boots, herbs, supplements, wormers and a wide variety of veterinary products.

Wilkinson & Co buy and sell second-hand items, including saddles and rugs, and offer a rug cleaning service. Director MarK Wilkinson and his team are on hand to provide help and advice to all their customers. They also sell food for cats, dogs, poultry and wild birds and are major stockists of electric fencing supplies, tools, locks and a variety of DIY products.

The other side of the business, in the same location, is **Ground Crew**, specialising in garden and paddock maintenance, fencing, topping, top dressing, paddock sweeping and spraying. The range of products of Wilkinson & Co can be viewed, and ordered, by consulting the excellent website.

Stansted Mountfitchet

Distance: *3.1 miles (4.8 kilometres)*

Typical time: *60 mins*

Height gain: *15 metres*

Map: *Explorer 195*

Walk: *www.walkingworld.com ID:1835*

Contributor: *Brian and Anne Sandland*

Stansted Mountfitchet is close to the M11, the A120 and Stansted Airport. To reach the car park from which the walk begins follow signs for Mountfitchet Castle - or use the train; the station is adjacent to the car park.

DESCRIPTION:

This walk starts from the car park serving the station and visitors to the castle. It takes in one of the main streets of Stansted Mountfitchet before emerging into field paths and continuing to Ugley Green (which certainly deserves a better name!) The return is on more field and farmland paths via Aubrey Buxton (which was once the pleasure park to Norman House). This delightful woodland section passes a number of small lakes before rejoining the outward route.

FEATURES:

Lake/Loch, Pub, Toilets, Play Area, Castle, Wildlife, Birds, Flowers, Great Views, Butterflies, Food Shop, Woodland.

WALK DIRECTIONS:

1|From the car park head right past the Queen's Head (left). Take a left fork (signposted Quendon and Saffron Walden), then a right

fork by the Dog and Duck and continue along Gall End. Take the path to the left of North End House.

2|Continue following the left edge of a field. Bear right, then go left through the hedge.

3|Continue on the left of another field, climbing briefly to enter and follow the right edge of another field reaching a road. Turn right, then at a signposted footpath turn left over a stile.

4|Continue in the same general direction bearing right and left through a gate.

5|Cross a track, then bear one-third right across a field. Pass through a hedge at the far side (signpost), then cross the field ahead to reach a gate. Follow the path to the right of a thatched cottage then, using its drive, arrive at a road and turn right. Bear left at a junction, then take a signposted footpath right.

6|At the far side of the first field go through a gap, then right and left through a metal hurdle barrier. Continue between a hedge left and a wire fence right, then cross a stile and

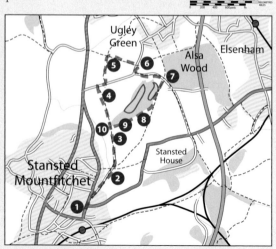

historic building   museum and heritage   historic site   scenic attraction   flora and fauna

continue ahead, ignoring a signposted footpath left and another right. Soon the path bears right and left to a narrow lane. Go right and left to reach the edge of Aubrey Buxton.

7 | Pass through the gate and follow the earth track, passing lakes on either side, ignoring turns off and bearing right, left and right again. Ignore a way out left into a field and turn right (slightly downhill).

8 | Join another path and turn left past tall willows, then clumps of bamboo (right). Cross a stream, climb slightly, then go left to leave the woodland through a wooden fence.

9 | Follow the left-hand edge of the field, left and right to a T-junction with another path.

10 | Turn left on this path (which is part of your outward route) and retrace your steps back to your car.

complete with domestic animals and the reconstructed motte-and-bailey **Mountfitchet Castle**, standing just two miles from the end of the runway. The original castle was built after 1066 by the Duke of Boulogne, a cousin of the Conqueror. Siege weapons on show include two giant catapults. Visitors can take a trip to the top of the siege tower and tiptoe into the baron's bed chamber while he sleeps!

Next door to the castle is **The House on the Hill Museum Adventure**, where there are three museums for the price of one. The Toy Museum is the largest of its kind in the world, with some 80,000 items on show, and children of every age are treated to a unique and nostalgic display.

There is every toy imaginable here, many of them now highly prized collectors' items. There is a shop selling new toys and a collectors' shop with many old toys and books to choose from. The Rock 'n' Roll, Film and Theatre Experience and the End-of-the-Pier Amuse-

ment machine displays also contribute to a grand day out here in Stansted Mountfichet.

Stansted Windmill is one of the best-preserved tower mills in the country. Dating back to 1787 and in use until 1910, most of the original machinery has survived. It is open on the first Sunday of each month from April to October; every Sunday in August, and on Bank Holiday Sundays and Mondays from 2pm to 6pm.

Great Dunmow

🏭 Great Dunmow Maltings   🚶 Flitch Way

The town is famous for the Flitch of Bacon, an ancient ceremony that dates back as far as the early 12th century. A prize of a flitch, or side, of bacon was awarded to the local man who, in the words of then-Lord Mayor Robert Fitzwalter:

'does not repent of his marriage nor quarrel, differ or dispute with his wife within a year and a day after the marriage.'

Amidst great ceremony, the winning couple would be seated and presented with their prize. The first recorded winner was Richard Wright in 1445, the last (genuine) in 1751 were Thomas and Anne Shakeshaft. The custom had lapsed on the Dissolution of the Monasteries, was briefly revived in the 18th century, and became established again after 1885. Trials to test the truth are all in good fun, and carried out every leap year. The successful couple are carried through the streets on chairs and then presented with the Flitch. The 'bacon chair' can be seen in Little Dunmow parish church.

Other places of historical interest include the parish church of St Mary at Church End, Great Dunmow, dating back to 1322. The Clock House, a private residence built in 1589, was the home of St Anne Line, martyred for sheltering a Jesuit priest. The **Great Dunmow Maltings**, opened to the public in 2000 after restoration costing £750,000, is the most complete example of a medieval timber-framed building of its type in the United Kingdom, and a focal point for local history in the shape of Great Dunmow Museum, with changing displays illustrating the history of the town from Roman times to the present day. H G Wells lived at Brick House in Great Dunmow, overlooking the Doctor's Pond, where in 1784 Lionel Lukin is reputed to have tested the first unsinkable lifeboat.

The **Flitch Way** is a 15-mile country walk along the former Bishop's Stortford-to-Braintree railway, taking in Victorian stations, impressive views, and a wealth of woodland wildlife.

Around Great Dunmow

CHICKNEY
6 miles NW of Great Dunmow off the B1051

Here can be found the rustic and remote little Saxon Church of St Mary's, with 1,000 years of history. Delightfully unspoilt inside, it retains its 14th-century tower with pyramid spire. Craftsmanship on display includes the rare pre-Reformation altar.

BROXTED
6 miles NW of Great Dunmow off the B1051

🏛 Parish Church

✎ Church Hall Farm Antique & Craft Centre

The parish **Church of St Mary the Virgin** here in the handsome village of Broxted has

---

THE GRANARY

Moor End Farm, Broxted, nr Great Dunmow, Essex CM6 2EL
Tel: 01371 870821 Fax: 01371 870170
e-mail: moorendfarm@btconnect.com
website: www.moorendfarm.com

Dating from Victorian times, **The Granary** at Moor End Farm has been sympathetically converted into spacious, comfortable self-catering cottages. They have all been tastefully furnished and decorated. The Arches and The Willows, which sleep four, have a double and twin bedroom and a bathroom upstairs, while the open plan downstairs floor has dining, sitting and fully-fitted kitchen areas. The Dairy is similar but slightly larger, it sleeps six and has two en-suite bathrooms.

There are also two smaller cottages, The Byre and The Stable. These are one bedroom and sleep two, but are just as comfortable and well fitted out.

All the cottages surround a quiet courtyard and there is ample parking. Behind them is a large communal garden with tables and chairs. There is a barbeque available if required.

Moor End is a 420-acre arable farm, which has been in the Burton family since 1935. In an area of Special Landscape Value, the farm is at the centre of an extensive network of paths and trails. It provides an ideal base for exploring East Anglia.

🏛 historic building 🏛 museum and heritage 🏛 historic site ⌬ scenic attraction ⚘ flora and fauna

two remarkably lovely stained glass windows commemorating the captivity and release of John McCarthy and the other Beirut hostages, dedicated in January 1993. Though just a few minutes' drive from Stansted Airport off the M11, it is a welcoming haven of rural tranquillity.

Church Hall Farm Antique and Craft Centre in Broxted is housed in a magnificent Grade II listed barn flanked by a willow-lined pond with its own resident ducks! The building itself is a miracle of medieval craftsmanship, located just a few yards from Broxted parish church.

LITTLE EASTON
2 miles NW of Great Dunmow off the B184

🏛 Church

The charming 12th-century **Church** in this small village is rich in historic features. Its Maynard Chapel features some outstanding marble monuments of the family that gives the chapel its name, as well as some famous brasses. The church's oldest treasures are, however, a well-preserved and priceless 12th-century wall painting and several 15th-century frescoes. Two more recent additions, a pair of stained glass windows, were unveiled in 1990. The Window of the Crusaders and the Window of Friendship and Peace are a lasting memorial to the American 386th Bomb Group. Known as The Marauders, they were stationed nearby for 13 months during the Second World War and lost over 200 of their number in battle overseas during that short time.

Little Easton Manor boasts extensive gardens, lakes and fountains. The ancient Barn Theatre at Little Easton Manor is one of the finest and oldest tithe barns in the country, with magnificent oak timbers and an ancient tiled roof. Host to performances by many of

the most distinguished names over the years - including Ellen Terry, Hermione Baddeley, Charlie Chaplin, George Formby and many others - the sympathetic restoration of the facilities has meant its continued use as a setting for special events. Both the Barn Theatre and the Turkey Barn within the grounds are available for private hire. Day-ticket angling can also be arranged.

GREAT EASTON
3 miles NW of Great Dunmow off the B184

Great Easton boasts a wealth of cottages and farmhouses with ornamental plasterwork, clustered Tudor chimneys and half-timbering. Great Easton's well-known and very popular Green Man pub occupies a handsome building dating back to the 15th century.

TAKELEY
4 miles W of Great Dunmow off the A120

The village is built on the line of the old Roman Stane Street. There are plenty of pretty 17th-century timbered houses and barns to be seen in the village, and the church still has many of its original Norman features along with some Roman masonry. Rather unusually, it has a modern font that is surrounded by a six-foot-high medieval cover.

HATFIELD BROAD OAK
3 miles SW of Great Dunmow off the B184

🌲 Hatfield Forest

This very pretty village has many notable buildings for visitors to enjoy, including a church dating from Norman times, some delightful 18th-century almshouses and several distinctive Georgian houses.

Nearby **Hatfield Forest** is a rare surviving example of a medieval Royal hunting forest. It has wonderful 400-year-old pollarded trees,

THE LION & LAMB

Stortford Road, Little Canfield, nr Takeley, Dunmow, Essex Cm6 1SR
Tel: 01279 870257
Fax: 01279 870423
email: mike@lionandlamb.co.uk
website: www.lionandlamb.co.uk

Hospitality is in generous supply at **The Lion & Lamb**, which stands on the B1256 (previously the A120) at Little Canfield. The new A120 has taken much of the passing traffic away, giving this picture-postcard inn a much more tranquil feel. It is run by Mike Shields, whose belief in traditional pub values has made the place such a success. The immaculate interior – a further tribute to Mike and his staff – has a delightfully old-world appeal, with masses of oak beams, open fires, red brick features and rustic furniture.

In this cosy, inviting atmosphere, a good selection of real ales are kept in perfect condition, and an outstanding selection of wines from around the world can be enjoyed on their own or with a meal. An excellent chef sets the standard for cooking hereabouts, and his menus, which are available all day long, highlight prime produce, much of it local. Salads and quiches provide wholesome light meals, and other choices run from pasta to daily fish specials, meat dishes both plain and sauced, and the popular Sunday roasts. The restaurant is divided into intimate areas, and a self-contained room with access to the garden is an ideal venue for a private party. The inn has a large car park, and there are plenty of seats in the beer garden for fair-weather sipping. Mike has recently acquired a nearby house offering Bed & Breakfast accommodation 1½ miles from Stansted Airport. The White House, at Smiths Green, Dunmow Road, Takeley, has three available rooms, with another 10 planned. The White House has now been awarded AA 4 Gold Stars Highly Commended.

Open 7 days a week 10.00am to 5.30pm. Getting to the Lion & Lamb is very simple, leave the new A120 Stanstead Airport to Braintree road at Dunmow West junction, and drive for about a mile on the B1256 towards Takeley. The inn is on your right.

🏚 historic building 🏛 museum and heritage 🏛 historic site 🌄 scenic attraction 🌱 flora and fauna

two lakes (fishing for pike, tench, roach, rudd, perch and carp) and an 18th-century shell house built as a rustic grotto. Guided tours can be arranged. Once covering a great deal more land, the remaining 400 hectares are now protected by the National Trust and offer splendid woodland walks along with good chases and rides.

AYTHORPE RODING
4 miles SW of Great Dunmow off the B184

Aythorpe Roding Windmill is the largest remaining post mill in Essex. Four storeys high, it was built around 1760 and remained in use up until 1935. It was fitted in the 1800s with a fantail which kept the sails pointing into the wind. It is open to the public on the last Sunday of each month from April to September, 2-5 p.m.

PLESHEY
5 miles SE of Great Dunmow off the A130

Pleshey, midway between Chelmsford and Great Dunmow, is surrounded by a mile-long earthen rampart protecting the remains of its castle, of which only the motte with its moat and two baileys survive. There are good views from the mound, which – although only 60 feet high – is one of the highest points in Essex. The village is truly delightful, with a number of thatched cottages, and the area is excellent for walkers and ramblers.

Waltham Abbey

- Waltham Abbey & Lee Navigation Canal
- Epping Forest District Museum
- Royal Gunpowder Mills & Dragonfly Sanctuary
- Myddleton House Gardens
- Lee Valley Regional Park

The town of Waltham began as a small Roman settlement on the site of the present-day Market Square. The early Saxon kings maintained a hunting lodge here; a town formed round this, and the first church was built in the 6th century. By the 8th, during the reign of Cnut, the town had a stone minster church with a great stone crucifix that had been brought from Somerset, were it had been found buried in land owned by Tovi, a trusted servant of the king. This cross became the focus of pilgrims seeking healing. One of those cured of a serious illness, Harold Godwinsson, built a new church, the third on the site, which was dedicated in 1060 - and it was this self-same Harold who became King and was killed at the battle of Hastings six years later. Harold's body was brought back to Waltham to be buried in his church. The church that exists today was built in the first quarter of the 12th century. It was once three times its present length, and incorporated an Augustinian Abbey, built in 1177 by Henry II. The town became known as **Waltham Abbey**, as the Abbey was one of the largest in the country and the last to be the victim of Henry VIII's Dissolution of the Monasteries in 1540.

The Abbey's Crypt Centre houses an interesting exhibition explaining the history of both the Abbey and the town, highlighting the religious significance of the site. Some visible remains of the Augustinian Abbey include the chapter house and precinct walls, and cloister entry and gateway in the surrounding Abbey Gardens. The Abbey Gardens are also host to a Sensory Trail exploring the highlights of hundreds of years of the site's history; there's also a delightful Rose Garden.

Along the Cornhill Stream, crossed by the impressive stone bridge, the town's **Dragonfly Sanctuary** is home to over half the native British species of dragonflies and damselflies. It is noted as the best single site for seeing these species in Greater London, Essex and Hertfordshire.

A Tudor timber-framed house forms part of the **Epping Forest District Museum** in Sun Street. The wide range of displays includes exhibits covering the history of the Epping Forest District from the Stone Age to the present day. Tudor and Victorian times are particularly well represented, with some magnificent oak panelling dating from the reign of Henry VIII, and re-creations of Victorian rooms and shops. There is also an archaeological display and temporary exhibitions covering such subjects as contemporary arts and crafts. The museum has several hands-on displays that help to bring history to life, and features special events and adult workshops throughout the year.

Sun Street, the town's main thoroughfare, is pedestrianised. It contains many buildings from the 16th century onwards. The Greenwich Meridian (0 degrees longitude) runs through the street, marked out on the pavement and through the Abbey Gardens.

In spite of its proximity to London and more recent development, the town retains a peaceful, traditional character, with its timber-framed buildings and small traditional market, which has been held here since the early 12th century (now every Tuesday and Saturday – there is also a Farmers' Market held every third Thursday of the month, when farm-fresh produce is offered for sale). The whole of the town centre has been designated a conservation area. The Market Square boasts many fine and interesting buildings such as the Lych-gate and The Welsh Harp, dating from the 17th and 16th centuries respectively.

The Town Hall offers a fine example of Art

Waltham Abbey

Nouveau design, and houses the Waltham Abbey Town Council Offices and Epping Forest District Council Information Desk. The Tourist Information Centre is in Highbridge Street, opposite the entrance to the Abbey Church.

To the west of town, the **Lee Navigation Canal** offers opportunities for anglers, walkers, birdwatching and pleasure craft. Once used for transporting corn and other commercial goods to the growing City of London, and having associations with the town's important gunpowder industry for centuries, the canal remains a vital part of town life.

Gunpowder production became established in Waltham as early as the 1660s; by the 19th century the **Royal Gunpowder Mills** (see panel opposite) employed 500 workers, and production did not cease until 1943, after which time the factory became a research facility. In the spring of 2000, however, all this changed and the site was opened to the public for the first time. Of the 175 acres the site occupies, approximately 80 have been designated a Site of Special Scientific Interest, as the ecology of the site offers a rare opportunity for study. With two-thirds of the site a Scheduled Ancient Monument, there are some 21 listed buildings to be found here, some of which date from the Napoleonic Wars. The site also contains some of the finest examples of industrial archaeology in the world. Regular events and activities include costumed living history. Call 01992 707370 for opening times.

Lee Valley Regional Park is a leisure area stretching for 26 miles along the River Lea (sometimes also spelled Lee) from East India Dock Basin, on the north bank of the River Thames in East London, to Hertfordshire. There's a range of facilities ideal for anglers, walkers and birdwatchers. The Lee Valley is an important area of high biodiversity, sustaining a large range of wildlife and birds. Two hundred species of birds, including internationally important populations of Gadwall and Shoveler ducks, can be seen each year on the wetlands and water bodies along the Lea.

Lee Valley Park Farms, along Stubbins Hall Lane, boasts two farms on site: Hayes Hill and Holyfield Hall. At Hayes Hill Farm, visitors can interact with the animals, visit the children's adventure playground and enjoy a picnic. This traditional farm also boasts old-fashioned tools and equipment, an exhibition in the medieval barn and occasional craft demonstrations. The entry fee to Hayes Hill Farm also covers a visit to Holyfield Hall

Royal Gunpowder Mills

Beaulieu Drive, Waltham Abbey, Essex EN9 1JY
Tel: 01992 707370 Fax: 01992 707372
website: www.royalgunpowdermills.com

The **Royal Gunpowder Mills** in Waltham Abbey is open to the general public thanks to funding from the Heritage Lottery Fund and Ministry of Defence. This secret site, which was home to gunpowder and explosive production and research for more than three centuries, has been developed to offer visitors a truly unique day out.

Gunpowder production began at Waltham Abbey in the mid 1660s on the site of a late medieval fulling mill. The gunpowder mills remained in private hands until 1787, when they were purchased by the crown. From this date, the Royal Gunpowder Mills developed into the pre-eminent powder works in Britain and one of the most important in Europe.

Set in 175 acres of natural parkland, and boasting 21 important historic buildings, the regenerated site will offer visitors a unique mixture of fascinating history, exciting science and beautiful surroundings. Approximately 70 acres of the site, containing some of the oldest buildings and much of the canal network, will be open for visitors to explore freely. The remaining area of the site, including the largest heronry in Essex, has been designated as a Site of Special Scientific Interest and will be accessible to the public by way of special guided tours. Open April to September.

stories and anecdotes 🐦 famous people 🎨 art and craft 🖋 entertainment and sport 🚶 walks

Emperor Dragonfly,
Andy McGeeney

Lee Valley Regional Park, Waltham Abbey

famous plantsman who created them - EA Bowles, the greatest amateur gardener of his time. Breathtaking colours and interesting plantings - such as the National Collection of award-winning bearded iris, the Tulip Terrace and the Lunatic Asylum (home to unusual plants) - are offset by a beautiful carp lake, two conservatories and a rock garden.

Around Waltham Abbey

EPPING
4 miles E of Waltham Abbey off the B182

Just off the B1391, on the outskirts of Epping town centre towards Waltham Abbey, this town's handsome St John's Church was designed over 100 years ago by G F Bodley.

LOUGHTON
5 miles SE of Waltham Abbey off the A121

⚘ Epping Forest

Corbett Theatre in Rectory Lane in Loughton is a beautiful Grade I listed converted medieval tithe barn, where classical, modern and musical theatre productions are performed. The theatre is set in a five-acre site with lovely gardens.

Loughton borders **Epping Forest**, a magnificent and expansive tract of ancient hornbeam coppice, mainly tucked between the M25 and London. There are miles of leafy walks and rides (horses can be hired locally), with some rough grazing and occasional distant views. Epping Forest Visitor Centre: 020 8508 0028; e-mail: epping.forest@cityoflondon.co.uk

Farm, a working farm and dairy where visitors can see milking and learn about modern farming methods. Seasonal events such as sheep-shearing and harvesting are held, and there's an attractive farm tea room and a toy shop. A farm trail is another of the site's attractions, offering wonderful views of the Valley, an expanse of open countryside dotted with lakes and wildflower meadows attracting a wide range of wildlife including otters, bats, dragonfly, kingfisher, great-crested grebe and little-ringed plover. The area is ideal for walking or fishing, and the bird hides are open to all at weekends; permits available for daily access. Guided tours by arrangement. The Visitor Information centre is also here. At the southern end of Lee Valley Park, The House Mill, one of two tidal mills still standing at this site, has been restored by the River Lea Tidal Mill Trust. It was built in 1776 in the Dutch style, and was used to grind grain for gin distilling.

Myddleton House Gardens within Lee Valley Park is the place to see the work of the

ARTFUL EXPERIENCE CREATIVE CAFÉ

26 Lindsey Street, Epping, Essex CM16 6RD
Tel: 01992 517749

A wealth of fun is guaranteed for visitors to Artful Experience Creative Cafe!

While young children play in the play area provided, carers can enjoy light snacks and beverages. Or take the opportunity to develop your creative side and create unique masterpieces to give to friends or keep for yourself.

This popular venture in the heart of Epping, owned by June Hooke, has a wide selection of bisque pottery, wooden items and silk ties to paint. There are also soft toys and cards to make.

Artful Experience is open from 10am to 6pm Monday to Saturday and 11am to 4pm on Bank Holidays.

A creative after-school club operates on Tuesday, Wednesday and Thursday. Service includes collection from school, drinks, snacks and a structured creative activity and evening meal.

Workshops and events are held throughout the year. Please call for further information.

ABRIDGE
7 miles SE of Waltham Abbey off the A113

The BBC Essex Garden at Crowther Nurseries, Ongar Road, is a working garden consisting of a vegetable plot, two small greenhouses, lawns and herbaceous and shrub borders. Sheila Chapman, clematis expert, is also on site, as the garden boasts 600 varieties of clematis. The garden is also home to a range of farmyard animals which visitors are welcome to see and interact with, and there's a delightful tea shop filled with homemade cakes.

CHIGWELL
8 miles SE of Waltham Abbey off the A113

🌿 Hainault Forest Country Park

Hainault Forest Country Park is an ancient woodland covering 600 acres, with a lake and rare breeds farm, managed by the London Borough of Redbridge and the Woodland Trust for Essex County Council.

Hainault Forest Country Park, Chigwell

📖 stories and anecdotes 🐦 famous people 🎨 art and craft 🎭 entertainment and sport 🚶 walks

Queen Elizabeth's Hunting Lodge

Rangers Road, Chingford, Essex E4 7RH
Tel: 02085296681

Queen Elizabeth's Hunting Lodge was originally called the Great Standing. It was built in 1543 for Henry VIII and was used as a grandstand to watch the hunting of deer or possibly to shoot from.

CHINGFORD
6 miles S of Waltham Abbey off the A11

🏛 Queen Elizabeth Hunting Lodge

Queen Elizabeth Hunting Lodge (see panel above) in Rangers Road, Chingford, is a timber-framed hunting grandstand first built for Henry VIII. This unique Tudor-era survivor boasts exceptional carpentry, and is situated in a beautiful part of Epping Forest with ancient oaks and fine views. At one time the Lodge was the destination for hundreds of day-trippers who came by bus from the East End and other parts of London to spend a day enjoying the open spaces and the fresh air.

BROXBOURNE
5 miles N of Waltham Abbey off the A10

At Broxbourne Old Mill and Millpool, the remains of the old watermill can be seen, the waterwheel of which has been restored to working order.

HODDESDON
6 miles N of Waltham Abbey off the A10

🏛 Rye House Gatehouse

Rye House Gatehouse in Rye Road was built by Sir Andre Ogard, a Danish nobleman, in 1443. It is a moated building and a fine example of early English brickwork. Now restored, visitors can climb up to the battlements. A permanent exhibition covers

the architecture and history of the Rye House Plot to assassinate Charles II in 1683. Guided tours by prior arrangement. The building lies adjacent to a Royal Society for the Protection of Birds reserve. Other features include an information centre, shop, and circular walks around the site.

HARLOW
10 miles NE of Waltham Abbey on the A414

🏛 Museum 🌱 Gibberd Garden

🎨 Gibberd Collection

🌱 Parndon Wood Nature Reserve

The New Town of Harlow sometimes gets short shrift, but it is in fact a lively and vibrant place with a great deal more than excellent shopping facilities. There are some very good museums and several sites of historic interest. The **Gibberd Collection** in Harlow Town Hall offers a delightful collection of British watercolours featuring works by Elizabeth Blackadder, Sutherland, Frink, Nash and Sir Frederick Gibberd, Harlow's master planner and the founder of the collection.

The **Museum of Harlow** occupies a Georgian manor house set in picturesque gardens, which includes a lovely pond and is home to several species of butterfly. The museum has extensive and important Roman, post-medieval and early 20th-century collections, as well as a full programme of

FRIARS FARM

Hatfield Heath, Bishop's Stortford, Hertfordshire CM22 7AP
Tel: 01279 730244 Fax: 01279 730244
e-mail: enquires@friarsfarmbedandbreakfast.co.uk
website: www.friarsfarmbedandbreakfast.co.uk

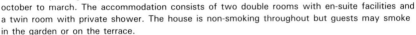

Friars Farm is a working arable farm offering bed & breakfast lodgings, with a warmth & friendliness that can't be matched. The ivy clad 19th century farmhouse has been home to the Hockley family for five generations and is situated on a quiet country lane just outside Hatfield Heath equi-distant from Bishop's Stortford and Harlow with stunning views over farmland yet convenient for Stansted Airport.

Countryside and fresh air enthusiasts will relish the numerous footpaths throughout the surrounding farmland or can cycle through the country lanes. Take time to explore the wealth of beautiful places in this area with its ancient market towns, medieval churches and castles. Browse in specialist antique shops, craft and garden centres. A peaceful ambience pervades this award winning Victorian house with an attractive open log fireplace where guests can warm themselves from october to march. The accommodation consists of two double rooms with en-suite facilities and a twin room with private shower. The house is non-smoking throughout but guests may smoke in the garden or on the terrace.

When your thoughts turn to food you can be sure of finding a delightful country pub, tea room (you can enjoy the home-made fare, or can savour from a wide range of excellent restaurants for that special occasion. Come and experience the peace, tranquillity and fresh air of this corner of Essex and Hertfordshire.

temporary exhibitions. It also incorporates the Mark Hall Cycle Museum and Gardens, a unique collection of cycles and cycling accessories illustrating the history of the bicycle from 1818 to the present day, including one made of plastic, one that folds, and one where the seat tips forward and throws its rider over the handlebars if the brakes are applied too hard.

Gibberd Garden, on the eastern outskirts of Harlow in Marsh Lane, Gilden Way, is well worth a visit, reflecting as it does the taste of Sir Frederick Gibberd, the famous architect. This seven-acre garden was designed by Sir Frederick on the side of a small valley, with terraces, wild garden, landscaped vistas, pools and streams and some 80 sculptures. Marsh Lane is a turning off the B183.

Harlow Study and Visitors Centre in

Netteswellbury Farm is set in a medieval tithe barn and 13th-century church. The site has displays outlining the story of Harlow New Town.

Parndon Wood Nature Reserve, Parndon Wood Road, recorded as a woodland for at least 900 years, is a haven for flora, fungi, birds, mini-beasts, small mammals and deer. Visitors can follow the guided trail around the wood and use the observation hides and the fully accessible conservation centre. With over 50 acres of oak and hornbeam woodland, this is a beautiful, peaceful place to wander (tel: 01279 430005). Other nature reserves in and around the town, each with its own appeal, include Parndon Moat Marsh, Maymeads Marsh, Marshgate Springs and Hawkenbury Meadow.

stories and anecdotes famous people art and craft entertainment and sport walks

CHIPPING ONGAR

8 miles SE of Harlow on the A414

🏛 Church of St Martin of Tours

🏛 Epping Ongar Railway Volunteer Society

Today firmly gripped in the commuter belt of London, Chipping Ongar began as a Saxon market town protected beneath the walls of a Norman castle. The motte and bailey were built by Richard de Lucy in 1155. Indeed, the town's name comes from 'cheaping', meaning market. Only the mound and moat of the castle remain, but the contemporary **Church of St Martin of Tours** still stands. Built in 1080, it has fine Norman flint walls and an anchorite's recess. There are several other interesting buildings in the town, some dating from Elizabethan times. Station House, on the High Street, is the headquarters of the **Epping Ongar Railway Volunteer Society**. It runs a heritage railway on the five-mile journey between Ongar and Coopersale over the former end of the London Transport Central Line. Original Great Eastern stations; heritage diesel trains (tel: 01277 365200).

Explorer David Livingstone was a pupil pastor of the town's 19th century United Reform Church, and lived in what are now called Livingstone Cottages before his missionary work in Africa began.

BOBBINGWORTH

2 miles NW of Chipping Ongar off the A414

Blake Hall Gardens at Bobbingworth near Chipping Ongar incorporate a Tropical House, an Ice House, bog garden, wild gardens, herbaceous borders, rose garden, sunken garden, duck pond and an ornamental wood. The south wing of Blake Hall itself houses the Airscene Aviation Museum run by local RAF enthusiasts.

FYFIELD

2 miles N of Chipping Ongar off the B184

🏛 Fyfield Hall

The name 'Fyfield' means five river meadows. Originally a Saxon enclave, the village church of St Nicholas is Norman. There's a beautiful mill house with flood gates in the village. **Fyfield Hall**, opposite the church, is said to be the oldest inhabited timber frame building in England (it dates from AD870).

HIGH LAVER

3 miles N of Chipping Ongar off the B184

The philosopher John Locke (1632-1704) is buried in the churchyard of All Saints, and an inscription that he himself wrote is set in the inner south wall.

WILLINGALE

3 miles NE of Chipping Ongar off the B184

St Christopher's and St Andrew's, churches of the respective parishes of Willingale Doe and Willingale Spain, stand side by side in the same churchyard in the heart of this lovely village. St Andrew's is the older, dating back to the 12th century; it is protected by the Churches Conservation Trust.

BEAUCHAMP RODING

3 miles NE of Chipping Ongar off the B184

One of the eight Rodings, it was at Beauchamp Roding that a local farm labourer, Isaac Mead, worked and saved enough to become a farmer himself in 1882. To show his gratitude to the land that made him his fortune, he had a corner of the field consecrated as an eternal resting place for himself and his family. Their graves can still be seen in the undergrowth.

Beauchamp's Church of St Botolph stands alone in the fields, marked by a tall 15th-century tower and reached by a track off the

THE MALTINGS RECLAMATION

The Maltings, Chelmsford Road (A414),
Norton Heath, nr Ongar, Essex CM4 0LN
e-mail: themaltingsreclamation@hotmail.com
website: www.maltingsreclamation.com

East of Ongar on the A414 Chelmsford road, **The
Maltings Reclamation** is a leading dealer in
architectural antiques and period fixtures and
fittings. Owner Chris Hussey had been involved in
reclamation and roofing supplies for 30 years when
he saw the chance to branch out on his own; he
bought The Maltings, an extensive acreage of buildings and grounds
that includes a two-acre lake with carp fishing.

Chris and his team are on hand with a warm welcome, help and
advice for customers who can spend many hours browsing through
the vast array of reclaimed goods, curios, collectables and objects
large and small for the house and garden that fill an interesting
building – worth a visit in its own right with some splendid original
oak and elm beams – and an extensive outdoor space.

The stock includes beams, flooring and floorboards, York stone,
bricks, setts, flagstones, fireplaces and fireside accessories, slates,
railings, lamp posts, cast-iron tables, chairs and baths, urns,
planters, statuary, stone seats, fountains, columns, garden
ornaments and much, much more. The goods on display change
constantly, so every visit to this intriguing place will unearth something interesting – practical,
decorative and very often both.

B184. Inside, the raised pews at the west end
have clever space-saving wooden steps, pulled
out of slots by means of iron rings.

GOOD EASTER AND HIGH EASTER
5 miles NE of Chipping Ongar off the B184

A quiet farming village, now in the commuter
belt for London, Good Easter's claim to fame
is the making of a world-record daisy chain
(6,980 feet 7 inches) in 1985. The village's
interesting name is probably derived from
'Easter', the Old English for 'sheepfolds' and
'Good' from a Saxon lady named Godiva.

Close to Good Easter, and thus named
because it stands on higher ground than its
neighbour, High Easter is a quiet and very
picturesque village not far from the impressive
Aythorpe Post Mill.

KELVEDON HATCH
4 miles S of Chipping Ongar off the A128

🏠 Nuclear Bunker

An unremarkable 1950s bungalow in the rural
Essex village of Kelvedon Hatch is the
deceptively simple exterior for the **Kelvedon
Hatch Nuclear Bunker**.

In 1952, 40,000 tons of concrete were used
to create a base some 80 feet underground for
up to 600 top government and civilian
personnel in the event of nuclear war. Visitors
can pass through blast doors made of tank
metal to explore room after room to see
communications equipment, a BBC studio, sick
bay, massive kitchens and dormitories, power
and filtration plant, government administration
room and the scientists' room, where nuclear

fall-out patterns would have been measured (tel: 01277 364883).

GREENSTED
1½ miles SW of Chipping Ongar off the A414

🏛 St Andrew's Church

St Andrew's Church in Greensted is said to be the world's oldest wooden church, dating from the 9th to the 11th centuries, with a later Tudor chancel. It is famous as the only surviving example of a Saxon log church extant in the world, built from split oak logs held together with dowells. Over the centuries the church has been enlarged and restored; later additions include the simple weatherboarded tower, Norman flint walls, the Tudor tiled roof, Victorian stone coping, porch and stained glass

St Andrew's Church, Greensted

windows. The body of King Edmund (later canonised a saint) is believed to have rested here in 1013.

The village also has associations with the Tolpuddle Martyrs - six Dorset farm labourers who were taken to court on a legal technicality because they agitated for better conditions and wages, and formed a Trade Union. After their conviction in 1834 they were condemned to transportation to Australia for seven years. There was a public outcry for their release, and their sentences were commuted in 1837. Unable to return to Dorset, they were granted tenancies in Greensted and High Laver.

One of the martyrs, James Brine, of New House Farm (now Tudor Cottage, on Greensted Green), married Elizabeth Standfield, daughter of one of his fellow victims - the record of their marriage in 1839 can be seen in the parish register.

NORTH WEALD
3 miles W of Chipping Ongar off the A414

🏛 Airfield Museum

North Weald Airfield Museum and Memorial at Ad Astra House, Hurricane Way, North Weald Bassett is a small, meticulously detailed House of Memories displaying the history of the famous airfield and all who served at RAF North Weald from 1916 to 1964. Collections of photos and artefacts such as uniforms and the detailed records of all flying operations are on display. There is also a video exhibit recounting a day-to-day account of North Weald history. Guided tours of the airfield can be arranged for large groups.

Brentwood

🏛 Cathedral 🏛 Museum

🌿 Thorndon Country Park

Brentwood is a very pleasant shopping and entertainment centre, with quite a distinguished past. It was on the old pilgrim and coaching routes to and from London.

Brentwood Cathedral on Ingrave Road was built in 1991. This classically-styled church incorporates the original Victorian church that stood on this spot. It was designed by the much-admired architect Quinlan Terry, with roundels by Raphael Maklouf (who also created the relief of the Queen's head used on current coins).

Brentwood Centre on Doddinghurst Road is one of the top entertainment venues in the UK, with an extensive programme of concerts, shows, bands and top comedy names. Sport and fitness facilities include pool, health suite and sunbeds.

Brentwood Museum at Cemetery Lode in Lorne Road, in the Warley Hill area of

Brentwood, is a small and picturesque cottage museum concentrating on local and social interests during the late 19th and early 20th centuries. It is set in an attractive disused cemetery, which is in itself of unique interest and is open on the first Sunday of every month from 2.30pm to 4.30pm and throughout the summer months.

Thorndon Country Park boasts historic parkland, lakes and woods. The site, formerly a Royal deer park, also features a wildlife exhibition and attractive gift shop. Fishing is also available.

Around Brentwood

MOUNTNESSING
6 miles SE of Chipping Ongar off the A12

This village has a beautifully restored early 19th-century windmill as its main landmark, though the isolated church also has a massive beamed belfry. Mountnessing Post Mill in Roman Road is open to the public. This traditional weatherboarded post mill was built

Ingatestone Hall

Ingatestone, Essex CM4 9NR
Tel: 01277 353010 Fax: 01245 248979

Ingatestone Hall is a 16th-century mansion and grounds, built by Sir William Petre, Secretary of State to four Tudor monarchs, and still occupied by his descendants. The house substantially retains its original form and appearance (including two priests' hiding places) and contains furniture, pictures and family memorabilia accumulated over the centuries.

A programme of special events is available on request and there is a gift shop and a tea room in the grounds. A picnic area is sited in Car Park Meadow. The house and/or grounds are available to hire for a variety of events including fairs, exhibitions, concerts, lectures and location filming. Open Saturday, Sunday and Bank Holiday afternoons from Easter to the end of September, plus Wednesdays, Thursdays and Fridays in the school summer holidays.

📖 stories and anecdotes 🐦 famous people 🎨 art and craft 🏃 entertainment and sport 🥾 walks

BARLEYLANDS FARM

Barleylands Road, Billericay, Essex CM11 2UD
Tel: 01268 290229 Fax: 01268 290222
e-mail: info@barleylands.co.uk

There's plenty to see and do for all the family at **Barleylands Farm**, which combines a Farm Centre, Craft Village and Showground.

In the farm centre, children can explore the bale maze and adventure playground, bounce on the giant bouncy pillow, play in the sandpit, race their parents in the dinocar paddock and meet the friendly farm animals, including sheep, lambs, pigs, goats, donkeys, ponies and furry friends in the pets corner. Other amusements include a tractor and trailer ride and a trip on the miniature train. The latest attraction is the new Discovery Centre, with exhibitions themed around the past, present and future.

Beyond Barleylands Central Station is the Craft Village, home to over 60 fantastic craft shops including glasswork, pottery, painting, textiles, paper crafts, homeopathy, toys, dancing lessons, photography, cake making, dress hire, bridge playing, hairdressing, a tea room and a restaurant. The showground is home to the Essex Country Show and numerous other events, including farmers' markets and car boot sales. Activities, tours and workshops linked to the National Curriculum are held throughout the year. Call 01268 290213 for more information on educational visits.

BILLERICAY COOKSHOP

100 High Street, Billericay, Essex CM12 9BY
Tel: 01277 633403
Website: www.billericaycookshop.co.uk

If you're bored with the monotony of cloned shops in cloned high streets offering the same products in exactly the same way then you need to visit **The Billericay Cookshop** and its sister shop The Emporium. Together the two outlets offer West End Wow with Country Charm.

The Cookshop offers an incredible choice of cookware and tableware to suit every taste and every pocket from a potato peeler to the latest food processor. Whether you're a gourmet cook or just looking for something to serve the take away on, you will find it here - and if you can't, please ask, and we will endeavor to track it down for you.

Moving away from the kitchen, The Emporium is an opportunity to add a little something to the rest of the home whether it's the bedroom, bathroom, lounge or even the garden. You will find towels, bed linens and table linens, vases and candles. We also have a seductive selection of perfumeries and glamorous gifts for ladies and men.

We are passionate about our products and our customer service is paramount. We offer carry to car, free home delivery in the local area and provide a wedding and gift list service. We are lucky and proud to have been voted Britain's Best Cookshop and Britain's Best New Retailer in the 2006 national Retail Awards. Come and see what you think!

in 1807 and restored to working order in 1983. Visitors can see the huge wooden and iron gears; a pair of stones have been opened up for viewing.

INGATESTONE
6 miles E of Chipping Ongar off the B1002

🏛 Ingatestone Hall

Ingatestone Hall (see panel on page 275) on Hall Lane is a 16th-century mansion set in 11 acres of grounds. It was built by Sir William Petre, Secretary of State to four monarchs, whose family continue to reside here. Open to the public in summer, the Hall contains family portraits, furniture and memorabilia accumulated over the centuries. Guided tours by prior arrangement.

BILLERICAY
6 miles E of Brentwood off the A129

🏛 Chantry House   🏠 Barleylands Farm

🌲 Norsey Wood

There was a settlement here as far back as the Bronze Age, though there is to date no conclusive explanation of Billericay's name. There is no question about the attraction of the High Street, though, with its timber weatherboarding and Georgian brick buildings. The **Chantry House**, built in 1510, was the home of Christopher Martin, treasurer to the Pilgrim Fathers.

The Peasants' Revolt of 1381 saw the massacre of hundreds of rebels just northeast of the town, at **Norsey Wood**. Today, this area of ancient woodland is a country park, managed by coppicing (the traditional way of ensuring the timber supply), which also encourages plant- and birdlife.

Barleylands Farm (see panel opposite) and Visitors' Centre features a glass-blowing studio, blacksmith's and other craft shops, a wealth of farm animals, chick hatchery, duck pond and one of the largest collections of vintage farm machinery in the country, together with a play area, picnic area and, on Sunday afternoons, a steam railway.

STOCK
6 miles NE of Brentwood off the B1007

Stock boasts a fine early 19th-century tower windmill on five floors, with superb late 19th-century machinery that has been restored to working order. Stock's delightful church has a traditional Essex-style wooden belfry and spire, lending character to this pleasant village of well-kept houses.

GREAT WARLEY
1 mile S of Brentwood on the B186

Warley Place was formerly home to one of the most famous women gardeners, Ellen Willmott, who died in 1934. She introduced to Warley - and to Britain - many exotic plants. A trail takes visitors through what is now Warley Place Nature Reserve, with 16 acres of what was once domesticated garden but has now reverted to woodland. A fascinating selection of trees, shrubs and wildlife make this well worth a visit.

SOUTH WEALD
2 miles W of Brentwood off the A12

🐑 Old Macdonald's Educational Farm Park

🐑 Weald Country Park

This very attractive village has, at its outskirts, **Weald Country Park**, a former estate with medieval deer park, partially landscaped in the 1700s. Featuring lake and woodland, visitors' centre, landscapes exhibition and gift shop, with facilities for fishing and horse-riding, there are guided events and activities programmes held throughout the year.

Another good day out in the open air can be had at **Old Macdonald's Educational Farm Park**, where visitors can see the largest selection of pure-bred British farm animals and poultry in the southeast of England. Specialising in native rare-breeds, with nine breeds of pig, 23 of sheep, six of cattle, 30 of poultry and 30 of rabbit to see and learn about, as well as shire horses, deer, owls, otters, goats, ferrets, red squirrels and much more. The farm boasts informative breed labelling and excellent facilities.

GRAYS
4 miles E of Brentwood off the M25

🏛 Thurrock Museum

Thurrock Museum is in the Thameside Complex in Grays. It collects, conserves and displays items of archaeology and local history from prehistoric times to the end of the 20th century. The archaeological items include flint and metal tools of people who lived in prehistoric Thurrock and pottery, jewellery and coins from the Roman and Saxon period.

WEST THURROCK
1½ miles SW of Grays off the A13

Immortalised by the film *Four Weddings and a Funeral*, little St Clement's Church occupies a striking location and is one of a number of picturesque ancient churches in the borough. Although this 12th century church is now deconsecrated, it was in its day a stopping point for pilgrims; visitors can see the remains of its original round tower. There is also a mass grave to the boys of the reformatory ship *Cornwall* who were drowned in an accident off Purfleet.

Arena Essex Raceway is the chief venue for motorsports in the area. Regular 'banger

racing' takes place at the track in West Thurrock, near Lakeside Shopping Centre and Retail Park. The Centre attracts many millions of visitors a year, and boasts over 300 shops, a food court and multiplex cinema. The Retail Park features more shops, as well as restaurants, a cinema, a leisure bingo complex and a watersports centre at the lake.

PURFLEET
3 miles W of Grays off the M25/A13

🏛 Heritage Military Centre

Fans of Bram Stoker's novel *Dracula* will know that the famous vampire buys a house called Carfax in Purfleet. The town's esteemed Royal Hotel, by the Thames, is said to have played host to Edward VII, while still Prince of Wales in the 1880s and 1890s, at which time the hotel was called Wingrove's. The Purfleet **Heritage and Military Centre** is a heritage and military museum featuring displays of many items of interest and memorabilia in the setting of the No 5 Gunpowder Magazine on Centurion Way. This remaining magazine was built in the 1770s for testing and issuing gun powder to the army and navy.

Purfleet Conservation Area includes several buildings that were part of a planned village built by the one-time owners of the chalk quarry, the Whitbread family.

AVELEY
3 miles NW of Grays off the M25/A13

🌿 Mardyke Valley

Mardyke Valley is an important wildlife corridor running from Ship Lane in Aveley to Orsett Fen. Many pleasant views can be had along the seven-mile stretch of footpaths and bridleways. Davy Down within Mardyke Valley consists of riverside meadows, ponds and wetland. The Visitors Centre is in the well-preserved water pumping station on the B186 near South Ockendon. Aveley's 12th-century St Michael's Church features many Flemish brasses and other items of historical interest.

SOUTH OCKENDON
3 miles N of Grays off the A13/A1306

🌱 Belhus Woods Country Park

🌱 Grangewater Country Park

Belhus Woods Country Park (see panel below) covers approximately 250 acres and contains an interesting variety of habitats, including woodland, two lakes and the remains of a pond designed by 'Capability' Brown. The Visitors Centre to this superb park can be found at the main entrance off Romford Road. Belhus Park Golf Course is a well-established 18-hole course set within this beautiful parkland.

Grangewaters Country Park, also in South Ockendon, has two lakes. Managed by Thurrock Environmental and Outdoor Education Centre, it offers watersports such as windsurfing, sailing and canoeing, as well as off-road biking, climbing and other outdoor pursuits. Brannetts Wood is one of the oldest

Belhus Wood Country Park

Romford Road, Aveley, Essex RM15 4XJ
Tel: 01708 865628

Belhus Woods Country Park has a diverse landscape of woodlands, grasslands and lakes. You can fish, play games, fly kites, have a picnic or ride your horse here. You may prefer to just sit by tranquil waters feeding the birds or, in spring, to quietly wander through a woodland carpet of bluebells.

The estate was once owned by the Barrett-Lennard family. Capability Brown and Richard Woods laid out an 18th-century park for Lord Dacre over earlier more formal gardens. The Shrubbery and Long Pond were created by Woods in 1770 and are now cut by the M25.

A stench pipe disguised as a Tudor chimney, also survives in the south of the Park. The ancient woodlands have changed little in shape and size since their mapping in 1777 by Chapman and Andre, although there has been significant extra planting since. The woodlands are home to rich communities of wildlife. An observant birdwatcher may see green, greater or lesser spotted woodpeckers and numerous creepy crawlies can be spotted by an enthusiastic child. The Ranger Service manages the woods according to their timber content and wildlife value. Timber from Running Water Wood is used for thatching and hurdle making, with the hazel plots cut on a regular eight year cycle. This traditional management practice, called coppicing, benefits the wildlife by increasing light penetration allowing seeds to germinate and plants to thrive. You can now experience the splendour of plants, once common in traditional coppiced woodlands, such as early purple orchids and graceful ragged robins in a sea of bluebells.

The Visitor Centre has a shop and education facilities where light refreshments, gifts and information can be obtained. The Essex Ranger Service also offers guided walks, volunteer tasks, assisted school visits and a variety of events throughout the year.

recorded ancient woodlands in South Essex.
It can be reached from the Mardyke Way, or
from South Road here in South Ockendon.

The village Church of St Nicholas has
one of only six round church towers in
Essex. This one was built in the 13th
century and used to have a spire, which was
sadly destroyed by lightning in the 17th
century.

HORNDON-ON-THE-HILL
6 miles NE of Grays off the B1007/A13

🌿 Langdon Hills

Listed in the Domesday Book as
Horninduna, a name which also appears on a
Saxon coin of Edward the Confessor, it is
said to have once been the site of a Royal
Anglo-Saxon mint. The town's 16th-century
Woolmarket indicates the importance of the
wool trade to the region, and is one of the
area's historical treasures. The upper room
served as Horndon's manor courtroom, while
the lower, open area was used for trading in
woollen cloth.

The main entrance and Visitors Centre for
**Langdon Hills Conservation Centre and
Nature Reserve** are located off the Lower
Dunton Road north of Horndon-on-the-Hill.
A bridleway and footpaths lead visitors to
meadows, a pond and outstanding ancient
woods. Also within the reserve is the
Plotlands Museum, housed in an original
1930s plotland bungalow known as the Haven.

LINFORD
3 miles NE of Grays off the A13/A1013

🏛 Walton Hall Museum

Walton Hall Museum on Walton Hall Road
has a large collection of historic farm
machinery in a 17th-century barn. It affords
visitors the opportunity to watch traditional

Walton Hall Museum, Linford

craftsmen, such as a blacksmith,
saddlemaker, printer and wheelwright,
together with a printing shop, baker's, dairy
and nursery.

STANFORD-LE-HOPE
4 miles NE of Grays off the A1014

🌿 Stanford Marshes

Stanford Marshes cover an area to the south
of Stanford-le-Hope, next to the Thames. The
Marshes are home to a variety of wildlife and
are an ideal location for birdwatching. Grove
House Wood in Stanford-le-Hope is a nature
reserve managed by Essex Wildlife Trust and
the local Girl Guides. A footpath here leads to
reed beds, a pond and a brook as well as an
area of woodland.

The graveyard of St Margaret's Church has
an unusual half-barrelled tomb, of one James
Adams (d. 1765), that is decorated with
gruesome stone-carved symbols of death.

CORRINGHAM
7 miles NE of Grays off the A13/A1014

🌿 Langdon Hills Country Park

Corringham has a picturesque cluster of
timber-framed houses in the old village,
leading up to its medieval church, which
retains some Saxon and Norman features.
Langdon Hills Country Park north of

Corringham is 400 acres of ancient woodland and meadows. It has many rare trees and spectacular views of the Essex countryside.

CANVEY ISLAND
10 miles NE of Grays off the A130

📷 Dutch Cottage Museum

📷 Castle Point Transport Museum

Canvey Island is a peaceful and picturesque stretch of land overlooking the Thames estuary with views to neighbouring Kent. The island boasts two unusual museums. **Dutch Cottage Museum** (see panel below) is an early 17th-century eight-sided cottage built by one of Vermuyden's Dutch workmen and boasting many traditional Flemish features. **Castle Point Transport Museum** is housed in a 1930s bus garage. It contains an interesting collection of Eastern National buses and coaches and various other commercial vehicles mainly from the period 1944 to 1981. The Canvey Miniature Railway

Dutch Cottage Museum

Canvey Road, Canvey Island,
Essex SS7 3PB
Tel: 01268 794005

The Dutch Cottage Museum is housed in an ancient dwelling, which dates from 1618. It was most probably used as a workman's cottage at the time when it was decided to reclaim land from the sea and to unite the five islands of Canvey into one island.

Cornelius Vermuyden was the Dutch engineer invited to take charge of this work in the time of James I, and he brought over many Dutch workmen who laboured under his direction, and for his services he was later knighted. You can see a copy of his portrait in the living room of the cottage.

The Dutchmen were not paid but they received one acre out of every three they reclaimed. There are still families on the Island who have Dutch surnames and are probably descendants of the original Dutchmen.

At first the cottage had a floor of beaten earth and shells, but successive generations have improved it, for there are five separate layers to the present floor. This is why the ceiling of the living room is so low, the most recent of rough brick. These floor bricks are of a different size from the bricks of today, thus showing that they must be of great age.

At some period a kitchen was added to the original structure and the cottage was inhabited until it was made into a Museum. The door and window frames are replicas of the originals and the building is decorated in colours known to have been used by the original Dutch reclaimers. Many of the beams are the original ones but have had to be supported by steel plates on either side. The fireplace was bricked round at some unknown date.

The New Exhibition Hall was provided by the (then) Canvey Council to house the many exhibits that could no longer find a place in the cottage. Here you will find a fine collection of corn dollies from Essex and many other counties; embanking tools, which were used in the old days for keeping the sea-walls and ditches in good order, and equipment brought from the old smithy in the Long Road.

📷 stories and anecdotes 🕊 famous people 🎨 art and craft ✐ entertainment and sport 🚶 walks

at the Waterside Farm Centre has two steam miniature railways guaranteed to delight the child in all of us. The Island's most famous son is Dean Macey, the recently retired world-class decathlete.

WEST TILBURY
3 miles E of Grays off the A1089

West Tilbury was the site chosen for the Camp Royal in 1588, to prepare for the threatened Spanish invasion. Queen Elizabeth I visited the army here, and made her famous speech,

'I know I have the body but of a weak and feeble woman: but I have the heart and stomach of a king, and a king of England too.'

Hidden away in rural tranquillity over-looking the Thames estuary, West Tilbury remains unspoilt in spite of its proximity to busy, industrial Tilbury. The former local church (now a private dwelling) in this quaint little village is a nautical landmark used for navigation. The list of Rectors of the church, dating from 1279-1978, when the church was disestablished, can be seen in The King's Head Pub.

EAST TILBURY
5 miles E of Grays off the A13

🏛 Thamesside Aviation Museum 🏛 Coalhouse Fort

Coalhouse Fort is considered to be one of the best surviving examples of a Victorian Casement fortress in the country. As such it is a protected Scheduled Ancient Monument. Built between 1861 and 1874 as a first line of defence to protect the Thames area against invasion, it stands on the site of other defensive works and fortifications dating back to around 1400. Even before the Middle Ages, this was an important site.

Part of the construction work on the Fort

was overseen by Gordon of Khartoum. It was constructed to be a dedicated Artillery casement fortress, which meant that the guns were housed in large vaulted rooms with armour-plated frontages. Beneath these rooms lies an extensive magazine tunnel system to service the artillery.

Over the years many alterations were made to the Fort to accommodate new artillery. The Fort was manned during both World Wars, and is now owned by Thurrock Borough Council and administered by The Coalhouse Fort Project, a registered charity run entirely by volunteers. Open to the public, it contains reconstructions of period guns and other displays, and also houses the **Thameside Aviation Museum**, with a large collection of local finds and other aviation material. In the two parade grounds visitors will find various artillery pieces and military vehicles. One recent addition to the many pieces of historical military equipment is a Bofor Anti-Aircraft Gun of the Second World War. The site also offers visitors the chance to handle period equipment or try on a period uniform.

During the year the Fort hosts a range of shows, including an historic artillery rally when various big guns are fired by crews in the uniforms of the period, including a Second World War crew firing a 1940 25pdr field gun. A guided tour (included in the price of admission) allows visitors to see the magazine tunnels beneath the gun casements and offer a feel for the work and conditions of a Victorian gunner. The tour also takes in the roof of the Fort, from which you will be able to judge for yourself the value of a fortification at this point along the Thames. The view from here is outstanding, taking in the two sister forts in Kent and, on a clear day, Southend.

The Fort is set in a lovely riverside park with

walks and a children's play area, as well as other items of military history including a Quick Fire Battery and Minefield Control box. You can also follow the old railway tracks from the Fort to the side of the old jetty, where many of the armaments and supplies for the fort were shipped in.

It is possible that East Tilbury's St Catherine's Church occupies the site of one of the first Christian monasteries in the 7th century. Its half-built tower was constructed by the First World War Garrison of Coalhouse Fort.

The Bata Estate is a conservation area of architectural and historical interest. Established in 1933, the British Bata Shoe Company was the creation of Czech-born Thomas Bata, who also developed a housing estate for his workforce. This range of uniform flat-roofed houses can still be seen on site.

TILBURY
3 miles SE of Grays off the A1089

🏚 Tilbury Fort

Tilbury Fort (see panel below) is a well-preserved and unusual 17th-century structure with double moat. The largest and best

example of military engineering in England at that time, the fort also affords tremendous views of the Thames estuary. The most violent episode in the fort's history occurred in 1776, during a particularly vociferous cricket match that left three people dead. For a small fee visitors to the fort can fire a 1943 3.7mm anti-aircraft gun - a prospect most children and many adults find irresistible! Owned by English Heritage, the site was used as a military Block House during the reign of Henry VIII and was rebuilt in the 17th century. It remains one of Britain's finest examples of a star-shaped bastion fortress. Extensions were made in the 18th and 19th centuries, and the Fort was still being used in the Second World War.

Tilbury Festival is held every year in July in the field near the fort, and features arena events, craft and food stalls, and living history re-enactments. Tilbury Energy and Environment Centre at Tilbury Power Station provides a nature reserve and study centre for schools and community education. There is a flat two-mile nature trail leading to and from the Centre.

Tilbury Fort

Tilbury, Essex RM18 7NR
Tel: 01375 858489

Ever wanted to fire a real anti-aircraft gun? Come to Tilbury Fort and you can. Discover the history of this most impressive of English artillery forts, from Henry VIII's time right up to World War II. Walk through Charles II's imposing Water Gate, noticing the mighty gun emplacements that protected London against attack by warships. Tour the ramparts and inspect the guns, while enjoying the panoramic views across the Thames, near the place where Queen Elizabeth I made her famous Armada Speech.

The audio tour leads you round the site step by step. In the museum and exhibition housed in the East Gunpowder Magazine, you can follow the fortunes of Tilbury, from the creation of its first fortifications in the 16th century, to the two World Wars.

Southend-on-Sea

🏛 Central Museum 🏛 Prittlewell Pirory Museum

🏚 Saxon Cemetery 🏚 Pier & Museum

🎨 Beecroft Art Gallery 🌿 Sealife Adventure

🐚 Kursaal

To be beside the seaside at Southend-on-Sea means that there is always plenty to do and see, with many events throughout the year to ensure its continuing appeal and popularity. The town is one of the best loved and friendliest resorts in Britain, featuring the very best ingredients for a day or a break at the seaside. With seven miles of beaches and a European Blue Flag Award, this treasure trove boasts Adventure Island theme park, Cliffs Pavilion (the largest purpose-built performing arts venue in Essex), a distinguished art gallery and several interesting museums.

Southend Pier and Museum brings to life the fascinating past of the longest Pleasure Pier in the world. The Pier itself (Pier of the Year 2007) is 1.33 miles long; visitors can either enjoy a leisurely walk along its length or take advantage of the regular train service that plies up and down the pier. One of the trains is named after Sir John Betjeman, a frequent visitor to the town; he once said, (perhaps

Sealife Adventure, Southend-on-Sea

underestimating the town's many other attractions): 'The Pier is Southend, Southend is the Pier'. **Beecroft Art Gallery** boasts the work of four centuries of artistic endeavour, with some 2,000 works including those by Lear, Molenaer, Seago and Constable.

Sealife Adventure employs the most

BISHOP BROTHERS

172 London Road, Southend-on-Sea, Essex SS1 1PH
Tel/Fax: 01702 330336
e-mail: S.Bishop53@googlemail.com
website: www.bishop-brothers.com

Quality, consistency and attention to detail have long been hallmarks of **Bishop Brothers**, silversmiths and jewellers occupying characterful premises on London Road (A13) just west of its junction with the A127. Satisfied customers from all over the world are a justifiable source of pride to the owner, who specialise in antique repairs, rings, bracelets, brooches, antique jewellery and top-quality models and pieces in silver, gold and platinum. in the workshop he creates commissioned pieces after discussion and exchange of ideas with clients. the workshop is open 10am - 6pm Monday to Friday.

🏚 historic building 🏛 museum and heritage 🏚 historic site 🌀 scenic attraction 🌿 flora and fauna

advanced technology to bring visitors incredibly close to the wonders of British marine life, offering fun ways of exploring life under the waves, with concave bubble windows helping to make it seem that you're actually part of the sea-creatures' environment. Another exhibit features a walk-through tunnel along a reconstructed seabed. The Shark Exhibition is not to be missed.

A floral trail guided tour around the parks and gardens will reveal why Southend has won the Britain in Bloom Awards every year since 1993, as well as medals at the Chelsea Flower Show.

The **Kursaal** on the Eastern Esplanade is an indoor entertainment complex, one of the largest in the country, with indoor bowling, a casino, snooker and pool and theme restaurants.

Boat trips in summer include occasional outings on a vintage paddle steamer.

In Victoria Avenue, the **Southend Central Museum, Planetarium and Discovery Centre** has displays of archaeology, wildlife and local history. The only planetarium in Essex provides a striking illusion of the night sky, and there's an exciting new hands-on Discovery centre (tel: 01702 434449).

Prittlewell Priory Museum, slightly north of Southend town centre in Priory Park, is a well-preserved 12th-century Cluniac Priory set in lovely grounds and housing collections of the Priory's history, natural history and the Caten collection of radios and communications equipment. Southend's award-winning coastline supports a number of important habitats, and the foreshore is an international SSSI (Site of Special Scientific Interest).

Long before the name of Southend existed, Prittlewell was established as a Saxon settlement between 500 and 850, and the first signs of its Saxon past were unearthed in 1923. By far the most important discovery came in 2004, when a wood-lined chamber in a Saxon Cemetery came to light filled with gold and bronze ornaments, glass vessels, weapons and other treasures. The chief archaeologist at English Heritage described the find as 'a discovery of international importance which stunningly illuminates the rich and complex world of the so-called Dark Ages'. Many of the finds are on display in the British Museum, but there are plans to bring them to a special site in Southend.

Around Southend-on-Sea

LEIGH-ON-SEA
2 miles W of Southend off the A13

Leigh-on-Sea has a character quite different

Sunrise, Leigh-on-Sea

OLD LEIGH STUDIOS

61 High Street, The Old Town, Leigh-on-Sea,
Essex SS9 2EP
Tel: 01702 470490
websites: www.richardbaxter.com or www.sheila-appleton.co.uk

With splendid views of the Thames estuary and just 5 minutes stroll from Leigh-on-Sea railway station, you will find **Old Leigh Studios** run by three talented artists - Sheila Appleton, Richard Baxter and Kate Baxter. All the paintings and ceramics displayed in this stylish, well-lit gallery are created in the artists' studios and working pottery behind. Enjoy browsing through Sheila's paintings depicting the familiar buildings, boats and characters of this charming fishing village in works brimming with colour and life. Sheila has painted Leigh for many years and is equally at home using watercolours, oils and acrylics. She delights in making people smile with her humorous comments on life and has appeared on radio and television.

Richard Baxter shares the larger studio with wife Kate where he makes all his unique pottery. Whilst he sells in many galleries and is a well-known British potter, this is the best place to see the full breadth of his output, from stylishly functional terracotta to beautifully glazed fluid porcelain bowls and ceramic designs inspired by the waves on the sea.

Kate's distinctive and collectable ceramics and paintings take you to a colourful world of coral reefs, lost cities and enchanted forests. She decorates tile panels to enhance any kitchen or bathroom. You will receive a warm welcome at this friendly gallery and find beautiful art to suit every taste and pocket. Open 11am–5pm Tuesday to Sunday.

from Southend, being more intimate and serene, with wood-clad buildings and shrimp boats in the working harbour. The shellfish stall on the harbourside is justly famous. The Leigh Heritage Centre, housed in an ancient former smithy in the waterside High Street of the Old Town, is now home to historical artefacts and a photographic display of the history of Leigh-on-Sea.

The unspoilt fishing village of Old Leigh has a long and distinguished history. It is picturesque, with seafront houses and narrow winding alleys. It has also earned its place in history: the pilgrim ship *The Mayflower*

restocked here en route to the New World of America back in the mid-17th century, and the Dunkirk rescue embarked from here, as commemorated by plaques, flags and a memorial at St Clements Church.

ROCHFORD
3 miles N of Southend off the B1013

The Old House, at 17 South Street, is an elegant, lovingly restored house originally built in 1270. The twisting corridors and handsome rooms of this fine structure offer a glimpse into the past; the building now houses some District Council offices, and is said to be haunted.

HADLEIGH
5 miles NW of Southend off the A13

🏰 Castle ⚹ Country Park

Hadleigh Castle, built originally for Edward III, is owned by English Heritage and once belonged to Anne of Cleves, Katherine of Aragon and Katherine Parr. The ruins were also immortalised in a painting by Constable. The remains of this once impressive castle can still be seen. The curtain walls towers, which survive almost to their full height, overlook the Essex marshes and the Thames estuary.

    Hadleigh Castle Country Park offers a variety of woodland and coastal walks in grounds overlooking the Thames estuary. A Guided Events programme runs throughout the year.

HOCKLEY
6 miles NW of Southend off the A129

🌿 Hockley Woods

Hockley Woods is a 280-acre ancient woodland, managed for the benefit of wildlife and for the public. Traditional coppice management encourages a diverse array of flora and fauna, including the nationally rare Heath Fritillary butterfly.

    Volpaia in Woodlands Road is a lily specialist's small but beautiful woodside garden, with rare collected species and own-bred hybrid lilies, shade-loving shrubs and plants for sale.

RAYLEIGH
6 miles NW of Southend off the A1016

Dutch Cottage at Crown Hill in Rayleigh is a tiny traditional Flemish eight-sided cottage based on a 17th-century design created by Dutch settlers.

    Rayleigh Mount is a prominent landmark in this part of the county. Once a motte-and-bailey castle built in the 11th century, it was abandoned some 200 years later. Rayleigh Windmill, in Bellingham Lane close to Rayleigh Mount, was built around 1809; the tower mill houses a fascinating collection of bygones mostly used in and around Rayleigh. Refreshments are available from the coffee shop adjacent to the Mill.

HULLBRIDGE
8 miles NW of Southend off the A132

Jakapeni Rare Breed Farm at Burlington Gardens in Hullbridge is a pleasant smallholding set in 30 acres of rolling countryside. Specialising in sheep and pigs, with other pets and wildlife, there's also a fishing lake, country walk and pets corner. Snacks and light refreshments are available from the café, and there's an attractive shop.

Hadleigh Castle, Hadleigh

HATTERS

Moulsham Mill, Parkway, Chelmsford, Essex CM2 7PX
Tel: 01245 351121
website: www.hattershathire.co.uk

Hats in all sizes, for all ages and all occasions, are the stock in trade of **Hatters**, which is located in a fine old mill building not far from the Cathedral in Chelmsford.

The shop is owned and run by Monica Smith, who was so used to seeing ladies wearing the 'wrong' hats that she decided to do something about it by opening Hatters. Monica and her staff offer a friendly, personal service in a pleasant, relaxed atmosphere, and the shop is filled almost from floor to ceiling with hats for sale and hire for the races, weddings, formal events and other occasions that call for something a little bit special.

Designers usually in stock include Peter Bettley, Mad Hatters, Classics, Nigel Raymond, Victoria Ann among many others. Monica also offers a premier design service, with colour specifications to go with a special outfit.

In addition to the lovely hats, Hatters keeps a range of complementary accessories, including comfortable, stylish shoes, gloves, scarves and jewellery. The shop is open Monday to Friday (not Tuesday) from 10am to 4pm and Saturday from 10am to 1pm. Clients should book an appointment if possible before a visit.

BLUE LAWN & EDIBLE

17-19 Baddow Road, Chelmsford, Essex CM2 0BX
Tel/Fax: 01245 250083
e-mail: claremoore3@btinternet.com
website: www.bluelawn.co.uk

Next to the Odeon cinema in the centre of town, **Blue Lawn & Edible** are cool, stylish, contemporary retreats from the hustle and bustle of the outside world. Behind its cream exterior with top-to-windows, Blue Lawn is a womenswear boutique that brings the sophistication of London stores to the area, with a feel that reflects owner Clare Moore's ethic of timeless, effortless style.

Aimed at stylish individuals whose aspirations reach far beyond a High Street wardrobe, Blue Lawn's three floors stock more than 50 European brands, including mainline collections from Vivienne Westwood, Chloë, Belstaff and John Rocha, along with shoes, jewellery and other accessories.

Its neighbour, Edible, is an attractive store with long windows in its duck-egg blue exterior that look in on the lifestyle and culinary treats within. On the ground floor is a modern café/coffee bar surrounded by beautiful homeware and giftware from France, Italy and Belgium. Upstairs is an apartment-style space with a long central table where shoppers can relax, chat, read or work surrounded by travel art and photography.

 historic building   museum and heritage   historic site   scenic attraction   flora and fauna

Chelmsford

🏛 Cathedral 🏛 Museum

Roman workmen cutting the great road linking London with Colchester built a fort at what is today called Chelmsford. Then called Caesaromagus, it stands at the confluence of the Rivers Chelmer and Can. The town has always been an important market centre and is now the bustling county town of Essex. It is also directly descended from a new town planned by the Bishop of London in 1199. At its centre are the principal inn, the Royal Saracen's Head, and the elegant Shire Hall of 1791. Three plaques situated high up on the eastern face of the Hall overlooking the High Street represent Wisdom, Justice and Mercy. The building now houses the town magistrates court.

Christianity came to Essex with the Romans and again, later, with St Cedd (AD654); in 1914 the diocese of Chelmsford was created. **Chelmsford Cathedral** in New Street dates from the 15th century and is built on the site of a church constructed 800 years ago. The cathedral is noted for the harmony and unity of its perpendicular architecture. It was John Johnson, the distinguished local architect who designed both the Shire Hall and the 18th-century Stone Bridge over the River Can and who also rebuilt the Parish Church of St Mary when most of its 15th-century tower fell down. The church became a cathedral when the new diocese of Chelmsford was created. Since then it has been enlarged and re-organised inside. The cathedral boasts memorial windows dedicated to the USAAF airmen who were based in Essex between 1942 and 1945.

The Marconi Company, pioneers in the manufacture of wireless equipment, set up the first radio company in the world here in the town, in 1899. Exhibits of those pioneering days of wireless can be seen in the **Chelmsford Museum** in Oaklands Park, Moulsham Street, as can interesting displays of Roman remains and local history. Fine and decorative arts (ceramics, costume, glass), coins, natural history (live beehive, animals, geological exhibits) rub shoulders with displays exploring the history of the distinguished Essex Regiment. The museum is set in a lovely park complete with children's play area.

Also in the town, at Parkway, is Moulsham Mill Business & Craft Centre, set in an early 18th-century water mill that has been renovated and now houses a variety of craft workshops and businesses. Crafts featured include jewellery, pottery, flowers, lace-making, dolls' houses and bears, and decoupage work. There is a charming picnic area nearby, and a good café.

Three modern technologies - electrical engineering, radio, and ball and roller bearings - began in Chelmsford. At the Engine House Project at Sandford Mill Waterworks, museum collections from the town's unique industrial story provide extra fun and a fascinating insight into the science of everyday things.

Around Chelmsford

GREAT BADDOW
1 mile S of Chelmsford off the A12/A130

Baddow Antiques Centre at The Bringy, Church Street, is one of the leading antiques centres in Essex. Here, 20 dealers offer a wide selection of silver, porcelain, glass, furniture, paintings and collectibles. There is also a

DESIGN COTTAGE

37 Beehive Lane, Great Baddow, nr Chelmsford, Essex CM2 9TQ
Tel: 01245 287435 Fax: 01245 355211
e-mail: chrissytodd@hotmail.co.uk
website: www.lomas-pigeon.co.uk

Chris Todd has been involved in interior design for 20 years, during which time she has built a far-reaching reputation with her unerring eye for design, colour and quality. A warm welcome and friendly, personal service are bywords at **Design Cottage**, where curtains, blinds, fabrics and wallpapers are the main areas of the business.

As well as selling goods from the shop they offer a complete service that can start with a visit to the customer's home with fabric and wallpaper books to choose the design and colour, to take measurements and to work out an estimate, and ends with the fitting of the curtains and blinds on poles and tracks (all the fittings and accessories included). Specialised offerings include tented ceilings and fabric-panelled walls.

The shop stocks fabrics and wallpapers from leading manufacturers such as Colefax & Fowler, Jane Churchill, Nina Campbell, Harlequin, Mulberry and Romo. It's always a pleasure to visit Design Cottage, which is located in Great Baddow, just ten minutes' drive from the centre of Chelmsford. The shop is open from 10am to 4pm Monday to Friday (closed Wednesday) and from 9am to 12noon on Saturday, otherwise by appointment – it's best to call before setting out.

---

collection of 300 Victorian brass and iron bedsteads on display.

SANDON

2 miles SE of Chelmsford off the A414

The village green here in Sandon has produced a notable Spanish oak tree, the biggest in the country, planted in the centre of the village green. This oak tree is remarkable, not so much for its height, as for the tremendous horizontal spread of its branches. Around the green are a fine church and a number of attractive old houses, some dating back to the 16th century when Henry VIII's Lord Chancellor, Cardinal Wolsey, was Lord of the Manor of Sandon.

SOUTH HANNINGFIELD

6 miles S of Chelmsford off the A130

The placid waters of nearby **Hanningfield**

Reservoir (see panel opposite) were created by damming Sandford Brook, and transformed the scattered rural settlement of Hanningfield into a lakeside village. Now on the shores of the lake, the 12th-century village church's belfry has been a local landmark in the flat Essex countryside for centuries. Some of the timbers in the belfry are said to have come from Spanish galleons, wrecked in the aftermath of Sir Francis Drake's defeat of the Armada.

The Visitor Centre at the Reservoir overlooks the 870-acre reservoir and the gateway to the 100-acre woodland beyond. The Centre also offers refreshments, a gift shop and toilet.

HIGHWOOD

3 miles SW of Chelmsford off the A414

🏛 Hylands House

Hylands House was built in 1728, a beautiful

🏛 historic building 🏛 museum and heritage 🏛 historic site ⌕ scenic attraction 🌱 flora and fauna

HANNINGFIELD RESERVOIR

Tel: 0870 2403549

website: www.eswater.co.uk

Hanningfield Reservoir, owned by Essex & Suffolk Water is the second largest in the country and is primarily an essential water source for homes and businesses in Essex. The reservoir, set in the picturesque part of Essex is a great place for a day out for all the family including anglers, walkers and wildlife enthusiasts.

The reservoir is one of the premier fisheries in the UK, you can enjoy some outstanding trout fishing by either bank or boat, set in a picturesque part of Essex.

The fishery stocks the highest quality of fin perfect trout throughout the season. Day permits and season permits are available along with fishing lessons for those who are new to the sport. It's a wonderful haven for nature, and is renowned for its nationally important populations of wildfowl, which can be viewed from the reservoir's four birdwatching hides.

The Essex Wildlife Trust visitor centre is set within a Site of Special Scientific Interest (SSSI) and in the shop you will find an extensive range of fishing tackle, clothing and gifts.

Located on the lakeside with spectacular views over the reservoir, Café On The Water is open all year round, serving hot and cold meals, snacks and beverages for all the family, with fantastic views across the water. For further information on Hanningfield Reservoir call 0870 240 3549 or visit www.eswater.co.uk.

neo-Classical Grade II listed villa set in over 500 acres of parkland landscaped by Repton. Pre-booked guided tours of the house and gardens are available (tel 01245 605500). The house is host to many events. Hylands Park features lawns, rhododendron bushes, woodland paths, ornamental ponds and Pleasure Gardens adjacent to the house.

WRITTLE

2 miles W of Chelmsford off the A414

From a tucked-away corner of St John's Green in this village came Britain's first regular broadcasting service; an experimental 15-minute programme beamed out nightly by Marconi's engineers. Opposite the Green, the Cock & Bell is reputed to be haunted by a young woman who committed suicide on the railway. Further along this street is the Wheatsheaf, one of the smallest pubs in the country.

Writtle's parish Church of St John features a cross of charred timbers, a reminder of the fire that gutted the chancel in 1974. Ducks swim on the pond of the larger and quite idyllic main village green, which is surrounded by lovely Tudor and Georgian houses.

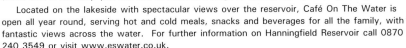
stories and anecdotes 🐦 famous people 🎨 art and craft 🏃 entertainment and sport 🚶 walks

BYGONES OF WRITTLE

44 The Green, Writtle, nr Chelmsford, Essex CM1 3DU
Tel: 01245 421127
e-mail: sue@bygonesofwrittle.co.uk website: www.bygonesofwrittle.co.uk

Writtle is one of the most attractive villages in the land, with a lovely variety of Tudor and Georgian properties surrounding the picturesque village green and duck pond. Chelmsford is almost on the doorstep, but Writtle has managed to retain its rural charm and character. History has touched this delightful place down the years – Robert the Bruce was born here in 1274, and it was from a little hut in Lawford Lane that Britain's first regular broadcasting service was transmitted by Marconi's engineers (the little hut is now in the Chelmsford Science and Industry Museum at Sandford Mill). That was then and now is now, but one of the village's most appealing places to visit goes by the name of Bygones.

Bygones of Writtle is a splendid shop located in a 17th-century building overlooking the village green at the front, and a courtyard and walled garden at the back that now boasts a vast array of home-grown vegetables. Behind the Old Curiosity Shop frontage, the beautiful interior is an Aladdin's cave of splendid gifts for all occasions. Everything on display is chosen by owners Sue Field and Cindy Fisher for being just that little bit extra special. There are also further finds to be made in the Antiques Barn. Sue and Cindy are great supporters of local talent, which is in plentiful supply in and around Writtle, and a wide variety of local crafts and paintings can always be found at Bygones.

Every visit is guaranteed to uncover new delights, and when inspiration for a present runs out, gift vouchers come to the rescue. At the back of the shop, leading to the courtyard and large walled garden, is a delightful tea room serving scrumptious home-baked cakes and delicious authentic cream teas and speciality coffees. There are high chairs and the premises are wheelchair accessible. Bygones is open from 10am to 5 pm Tuesday through to Saturday.

OLIVERS NURSERIES

Maldon Road, Witham, Essex CM8 3HY
Tel: 01376 513239 Fax: 01376 510728
website: www.oliversnurseries.co.uk

'Think Plants Think Olivers'

That's the motto of **Olivers Nurseries**, a
working nursery, plant and garden centre
and farm shop located on the B1018 south
of Witham and just a short drive from the
main A12. It was started on a small scale by

current owner Charles Willett's father in 1949, and Charles
spent some years selling on a limited seasonal basis before
opening the full enterprise in 2002, since when it has
expanded into a friendly and welcoming Garden Centre.

The extensive stock of plants includes fruit trees,
ornamental trees, shrubs, climbers, alpines and conifers,
roses, ferns and grasses, seeds and bulbs. In spring and
early summer they specialise in supplying a large variety of
bedding plants, many of them home-grown, and ready
planted hanging baskets. In the summer they grow
strawberries, raspberries, gooseberries and other soft fruit
on the nursery, with Pick Your Own available.

In the run-up to Christmas they sell a selection of real
Christmas trees and decorative holly wreaths, and the
Christmas Craft Fayre, held on the second weekend in
December, is a popular annual occasion. There is easy
access to all areas of the Garden Centre and ample parking.

Once inside, visitors will find everything to satisfy their
gardening needs: gardening tools, trellis, stakes, netting and
mesh, terracotta and glazed pots, bird food and feeders,
fertilizers and pest control to name but a few.

Oriental Waters and Floral Expressions are two
enterprises to be found within Oliver Nurseries. Oriental
Waters stocks pre-formed ponds, pond-liners, pumps,
filters and coldwater fish, while in the Floral Area they
create lovely fresh flower displays and sell dried and silk
flowers, baskets and oases for customers to make their
own flower arrangements; there are also houseplants,
cacti, ceramic pots and vases. The Farm Shop is stocked
with prime meat and dairy products, fruit and vegetables,
pickles and preserves, cakes, books, cards and gifts. Due
to open towards the end of 2008 at this enterprising
establishment is a Coffee Shop with home baking,
sandwiches, hot and cold snacks and, in the summer,
strawberry cream teas with home-grown fruit from their
own 'pick-your-own' fruit crops, grown just 100 yards
away in the field.

Qualified, experienced staff are always on hand to give
assistance at Olivers, which is open from 9am to 5pm
Monday to Saturday and from 10am to 4pm on Sunday.

WITHAM

6 miles NE of Chelmsford off the A12/B1018

🏛 Dorothy L Sayers Centre

The River Brain flows through this delightful town; a continuous walk has been created along its length for a distance of about three miles. The settlement dates back to at least the 10th century; remains of a Roman temple have been found at Ivy Chimneys, off Hatfield Road. Blackwater Lane leads to Whetmead, a nature reserve of 25 acres between the rivers Blackwater and Brain.

The **Dorothy L Sayers Centre** in Newland Street houses a collection of books by and about Sayers, the theologian, Dante scholar and novelist/creator of the Lord Peter Wimsey mysteries, who lived in Witham for many years.

MELLONS FABRICS

80 High Street, Witham, Essex CM8 1AH
Tel: 01376 512008
e-mail: mellonsltd@btconnect.com   website: www.mellonsltd.co.uk

Mellons Fabrics... a coordinated approach for people who love their home! If you're looking for a fabulous range of soft furnishings, including luxury bespoke curtains and blinds – look no further! For over 40 years, Mellons Fabrics have been offering their expertise and experience to customers to help them develop their ideas and fuel their imagination. The highly experienced and friendly staff will visit your home to measure and estimate how much fabric you need, while giving advice on choosing fabrics, trimmings, blinds, pole and traces to suit your particular requirements, including making-up and fitting if you wish.

UPSONS FARM SALES

Ivy Barns Farm, Hatfield Peverel,
nr Chelmsford, Essex CM3 2JH
Tel: 01245 380274 Fax: 01245 380155
website: www.upsonsfarm.co.uk

John Upson, who runs **Upsons Farm**, has been in farming all his life and took over the business his father started some 40 years ago. The farm, which used to concentrate on growing vegetable crops for seed, is now given over to selling home-grown and locally sourced vegetables and other prime produce. The sales area is a modern brick and timber barn purpose-built for displaying and selling a wide range of foodstuffs and other goods. Besides the vegetables and fruit, the shop sells free-range eggs from the farm's own hens, dairy products, Maldon salt, chutneys, pickles, Tiptree jams, marmalade and honey, plus apple juice produced by John's cousin David. Also on sale are live hens, hen houses, poultry accessories and feed for horses, livestock and birds. A warm, welcoming team makes shopping a real pleasure, and the farm has ample parking. Shop hours are 9am to 6pm, Sunday 9am to midday.

Ivy Barns Farm is located close to the village green at Hatfield Peverel, a short drive from the A12 between Chelmsford and Witham (leave at J20a or 20b).

🏛 historic building 🏛 museum and heritage 🏛 historic site 🍃 scenic attraction 🌿 flora and fauna

LITTLE BRAXTED
6 miles NE of Chelmsford off the A12/ B1018

Little Braxted has been voted the best-kept village on a regular basis since 1973. St Mary's chapel was built in 1888, and can accommodate only 12 people at a time. Services are held every Wednesday. The village church of St Nicholas is mentioned in the Domesday Book, and is famous for its murals.

TIPTREE
11 miles NE of Chelmsford on the B1023

As all true jam-lovers will know, Tiptree is famed as the home of the Wilkin & Son Ltd jam factory, a Victorian establishment that now boasts a fascinating visitors centre in the grounds of the original factory.

KELVEDON
11 miles NE of Chelmsford off the A12

🏛 Museum

This village alongside the River Blackwater houses the **Feering and Kelvedon Museum**, which is dedicated to manorial history and houses artefacts from the Roman settlement of Canonium, agricultural tools through the ages and other interesting exhibits.

LITTLE BADDOW
5 miles E of Chelmsford off the A414

Blakes Wood is a designated Site of Special Scientific Interest, an ancient woodland of

---

KELVEDON CLOCKS

2 High Street, Kelvedon, nr Colchester, Essex CO5 9AG
Tel: 01376 573434
e-mail: chrislpapworth@btconnect.com
website: www.kelvedonclocks.co.uk

Kelvedon Clocks Ltd is a traditional clockmakers shop specialising in antique clocks and watches. Owner Chris Papworth has wide contacts throughout the trade and all the major antique fairs; he monitors auctions and has runners who buy for him on the Continent, which enables him to offer one of the best selections of antique clocks and watches in the country. As Chris says, a well-chosen antique clock will add the finishing touch to any home – a school clock for the kitchen, a bracket clock, a French mantle clock or one of the many wall clocks in the lounge or sitting room. A fine small longcase/ grandfather clock will fit even a modern hall. The sight and sound of an antique clock not only makes a house a home but becomes part of the family – perhaps for generations to come. All the clocks are genuine, easily managed and come with advice to help their owners enjoy them. Chris, with over 45 years' experience, is a member of the British Watch & Clockmakers Guild, the British Horological Institute and the Essex Antique Dealers Association. Kelvedon Clocks is housed in part of what was the White Hart Inn, dating back to the late 1500s and Grade II listed. The shop is open from 9am to 5pm Tuesday, Wednesday and Thursday and from 10am to 5pm on Saturday; other times by appointment.

---

hornbeam and sweet chestnut renowned for its bluebells. There is a good circular way-marked one-and-a-half mile walk.

Cruising along the Chelmer and Blackwater Canal provides the visitor with a unique view of this part of rural Essex.

DANBURY
5 miles E of Chelmsford off the A414

🌿 Common 🌿 Country Park

This village is said to take its name from the Danes who invaded this part of the country in the Dark Ages. In the fine church, under a rare 13th-century carved effigy, a crusader knight was found when the tomb was opened in 1779, perfectly preserved in the pickle that

filled his coffin. Fine carving is also a feature of the bench ends; the oldest among them have inspired modern craftsmen to continue the same style of carving on all the pews. In 1402, 'the devil appeared in the likeness of Firor Minor, who entered the church, raged insolently to the great terror of the parishioners ... the top of the steeple was broken down and half the chancel scattered abroad.' And, in 1941, another harbinger of disaster, a 500lb German bomb, reduced the east end to ruins.

At **Danbury Common**, acres of gorse flower in a blaze of golden colour for much of the year. Along with Lingwood Common, Danbury Common is at the highest point of

Danbury Country Park

Danbury, Chelmsford, Essex CM3 4AN
Tel: 01245 222350
website: www.essex.gov.uk/countryparks

Created in 1088, the park has had a long and interesting history. The formal garden is separated from the rest of the park by two ha-has. These structures stopped the deer and domestic animals that roamed the park from reaching the gardens, without spoiling the view from the house. The Park has changed much during its history. The estate has been referred to as Danbury Palace since the Ecclesiastical Commission bought it in 1845 for the Bishops of Rochester and, at other times, St Albans. The Park's character changed dramatically in the following years as nearly 1,000 trees were felled and the high brick wall was built along the north side of the palace garden. Essex County Council purchased half of the Norman deer park and Palace buildings after World War Two, this has been divided into three different parts, one of which is the Country Park.

Much of the site is covered by ancient woodland, boasting impressive specimens of beech, oak and even wild service trees: a rare native tree only found in ancient woods and hedgerows. The woods abound with wildlife, from the secretive mole and stealthy fox, to the majestic badger and shy muntjac deer. Rare insects hide in the crevices of the ancient oaks while a myriad of birds sing among their branches. Spring and summer see the woodland come alive with flowers like bluebells, foxgloves and Townhall clock. In autumn, all manner of fungi explode silently from soil, log and trunk, filling the woods with their gaudy colours and pungent smells.

the gravel ridge between Maldon and Chelmsford. There is evidence here of Napoleonic defences and old reservoirs. Circular nature trails make exploring the area easily accessible. To the west, **Danbury Country Park** (see panel opposite) offers another pleasant stretch of open country, boasting woodland, a lake and ornamental gardens. Guide available by appointment.

St Giles Leper Hospital, Maldon

WOODHAM WALTER
6 miles E of Chelmsford off the B1010

Woodham Walter is a small village that lies two-and-a-half miles west of the ancient market town and coastal port of Maldon. It is rumoured that Henry VIII hunted in Woodham Walter during his reign. During the troubled times after Henry's death, Mary Tudor was concealed in Woodham Walter Hall, from whence she was planning to escape from England in 1550. The church in Woodham, St Michael's, was consecrated in April 1564 and is said to be one of the oldest still standing in the world.

MALDON
10 miles E of Chelmsford on the A414

🏛 Museums 🏛 Heritage Centre

Maldon's High Street has existed since medieval times, and the alleys and mews leading from it are full of intriguing shops, welcoming old inns and good places to eat. One of the most distinctive features of the High Street is the Moot Hall. Built in the 14th century for the D'Arcy family, this building passed into the hands of the town corporation

and was the seat of power in Maldon for over 400 years. The original brick spiral staircase (the best-preserved of its kind in England) and the 18th-century courtroom are of particular interest. Guided tours are available on Saturdays in summer and by appointment with Maldon Town Council (01621 857373) at other times.

A colourful appliqued embroidery made to commemorate the 1,000th anniversary of the crucial Battle of Maldon (see Northey Island on page 299) is on display at the **Maeldune Heritage Centre** (see panel on page 298) Maeldune being the Saxon name for Maldon. The 42ft embroidery was designed by Humphrey Spender. The Centre is housed in the Grade I listed St Peter's Building, erected in the 17th century by a local benefactor when the nave of the church that had once stood on this site collapsed. It can be found at the junction of the High Street and the steep and architecturally interesting Market Hill. The benefactor, one Thomas Plume, erected the building to house his collection of 6,000 books and a school; The Plume Library in St Peter's Building is open to the public.

A few minutes' walk down one of the small

Maeldune Heritage Centre

St Peters Church, Market Hall, Maldon,
Essex CM9 5PZ
Tel: 01621 851628

The Maeldune Centre has its origins in a
turbulent period of English History over 1,000
years ago when the fate of Anglo-Saxon England
lay in the balance under the onslaught of the
Danish invaders. In AD991, Earldorman
Byrthnoth fought a ferocious battle at Maldon in
an attempt to save his fellow countrymen from
the Danes.

Although he was defeated and killed, his
heroism lives on in a famous Anglo-Saxon poem
and also in the Maldon Embroidery, which was created some thousand years later to
celebrate this battle. Housed in the Maeldune Centre, the 42ft long embroidery depicts the
history of Maldon, in stunning colour and detail. It has been justly praised nationally and has
been exhibited at Olympia and featured on television.

Artefacts from an important Roman-British site, excavated at Heybridge near Maldon,
are also on display. A recent acquisition is a photographic archive compiled by the Maldon
Society. Nearly 3,000 photographs from 19th and 20th century Maldon and District can be
seen on computer from which prints can be made available. Additionally, there are
exhibitions of work by local artists that are changed ever month.

roads leading from the High Street brings you
to the waterfront, where the old wharves and
quays are still active. Moored at Hythe Quay are
several Thames sailing barges, all over 100
years old and still boasting their traditional
rigging and distinctive tan sails. The barges and
quay are overlooked by two pubs, the Queen's
Head and the Jolly Sailor. Maldon, famous for
its sea salt, is the only place in England still
making salt from sea water. Salt production in
Maldon dates from Roman times and, from its
current premises on the waterfront, has
continued uninterrupted since 1882.

Promenade Park lies adjacent to Hythe Quay.
This attractive park next to the River
Blackwater opened in 1885, and the
Edwardian-style gardens include an ornamental
lake with an amphitheatre that provides a

unique setting for outdoor arts and drama
productions. Children's attractions include a
water splash park, galleon ship and sandy play
area, and also in the park are a picnic site,
amusement centre, tennis courts and mini-golf.
A varied programme of events takes place in
the park throughout the year, including the Mad
Maldon Mud Race and the RNLI Rowing Race,
both held annually over the Christmas and New
Year holidays.

Housed in what was originally the park-
keeper's lodge, by the park gates, **Maldon
District Museum** looks back on the
colourful history of the town through
permanent and changing displays of exhibits
and objects associated with the area and the
people of Maldon. Closed November to
March (tel: 01621 842688). On Station Road,

the **Combined Military Services Museum** has collections of British military artifacts including items of national importance such as the only surviving MK2 'Cockle' Canoe as used in the Cockleshell Heroes raid(tel: 01621 841826).

Ruins are all that remain of the St Giles the Leper Hospital, founded by King Henry II in the 12th century. As with all monastic buildings, it fell into disuse after Henry VIII's Dissolution of the Monasteries, though it retained its roof and was used as a barn until the late 19th century. Many other buildings in the town, almost as old, fortunately remain - including two fine churches.

TOLLESBURY
9 miles NE of Maldon on the B1023

Located at the mouth of the River Blackwater is the marshland village of Tollesbury. Tollesbury Marina has been designed as a family leisure centre for the crews and passengers of visiting yachts. The Marina, with its tennis courts, heated covered swimming pool, bar and restaurant is ideally located for exploring the Blackwater and the neighbouring estuaries of the Crouch, Colne, Stour and Orwell. Guests arriving by land are welcome to use some Cruising Club facilities. Tollesbury Wick is a 600-acre nature reserve owned and managed by the Essex Wildlife Trust.

LANGFORD
2 miles NW of Maldon off the B1019

🏛 Museum of Power

The **Museum of Power**, Hatfield Road, covers all aspects of power, from domestic batteries to the massive machines that powered British industry. It includes the steam-powered pumping-station machinery of the redundant waterworks in which the museum is housed; other attractions include household bygones, an Edwardian workshop, miniature steam railway rides, a model village, tea room and riverside nature trail (tel: 01621 843183).

NORTHEY ISLAND
1 mile SE of Maldon off the B1018

🐦 Northey Island

Northey Island, comprising mainly salt-marsh, is owned by the National Trust. Access to this nature reserve is on foot via a causeway passable at low tide. It is a Site of Special Scientific Interest, an important stopover for wintering birds.

The sea walls of the Island make for an interesting walk, and were used as the camp base for the Viking army in AD991, when Byrhtnoth led the Saxons against the invading army. A fierce three-day battle took place, with Byrhtnoth's head eventually being cut off and the Viking warriors retreating despite their victory, leaving the English King, Ethelred the Unready, to pay an annual tribute, danegold, to the Danes to prevent further incursions.

HEYBRIDGE BASIN
2 miles E of Maldon off the B1026

Here the Chelmer and Blackwater Canal meets the tidal estuary. The busy sea lock and the activities of crafts of all sizes provide an endlessly changing scene. A café and a shop selling local crafts occupy an old chandlery, and two pleasant inns overlook the water.

PURLEIGH
3 miles SW of Maldon on the B1010

The first recorded vineyard in Purleigh was planted in the early 12th century, only 400

FB ANTIQUES

Rawlings Farm Buildings, Unit 7,
Main Road, Rettendon Common,
Chelmsford, Essex CM3 8DY
Tel: 01245 401210
e-mail: info@fgbantiques.co.uk
website: www.fgbantiques.com

FB Antiques (established 1960) proudly bears the initials of its owner and founder Fred Bruschweiler, who has been in the antiques business for more than 50 years. After spending many years buying furniture and antiques in East Germany, he sold to the trade and the export market from his headquarters in Rayleigh. He was the first to export furniture to Australia and other far-flung places.

Now based in renovated farm buildings at Rettendon Common, FB Antiques is undoubtedly one of the most exciting sources of high-quality antique and revival furniture. It is the largest stockist in Essex, selling to the trade, the export market, the interior design market and the general public and further building up its extensive home and international clientele.

The two large warehouses are filled with a vast selection of the finest furniture (with the emphasis on the 18th century) for every room in the house, in oak, mahogany and walnut and a variety of other woods, along with an extensive range of home furnishings. The craftsmen employed at FB Antiques are masters of their trade, and visitors to the showroom will always find help and advice on hand. They offer a complete packing and shipping service and are always ready to buy quality antique furniture.

FB Antiques is a member of LAPADA, the largest and most prestigious associaton of professional art and antiques dealers in the United Kingdom. Among the many outstanding

pieces handled by the company are bars of distinction and character made by craftsmen with the emphasis firmly on quality and authenticity. Suitable for hotels, restaurants and clubs, they would also be a stunning feature in a grand private house. Built in oak or mahogany, with an authentic old, rustic look, they can be built to individual requirements; they feature superb carving, tiles, ornate mirrors and stained-glass ceilings and canopies.

The showrooms, which can be visited between 10am and 5pm (11am to 2pm Saturday and Sunday), are located between the A12 and Rettendon Roundabout on the old A130 at Rettendon Common; between the Baddow Antiques Centre on the old A130 and Battlesbridge. Clients who are unable to visit the showroom in person can browse the virtual showroom on the excellent and comprehensive website.

🏛 historic building   🏠 museum and heritage   🏚 historic site   ♨ scenic attraction   🌿 flora and fauna

yards from the site of New Hall Vineyards in Chelmsford Road. It covered three acres of land next to Purleigh Church, where first US President George Washington's great-great-grandfather was the rector - until the time he was removed from this office for sampling too much of the local brew! Purleigh Vineyard became Crown property in 1163; subsequently the wines produced were taken each year to London to be presented to the monarch.

RETTENDON
6 miles SW of Maldon off the A130

🌱 RHS Garden

Highlights at the **Royal Horticultural Society Garden at Hyde Hall** include a 1,600 square metre Dry Garden with hundreds of species that show the fantastic range and style of plants that can be grown to cope with drought and exposure to high light levels; colour-themed herbaceous borders, an Australian & New Zealand garden; a rose garden; themed vegetable plots; and the Robinson Garden showcasing plants that love cool, shady, damp conditions. Meals and snacks are available in the attractive thatched barn; there is also a plant centre, and fine views can be had from this attractively landscaped hilltop garden.

SOUTH WOODHAM FERRERS
5 miles SW of Maldon off the B1012

The empty marshland of the Crouch estuary, a yachtsman's paradise, was chosen by Essex County Council as the site for one of its most attractive new town schemes. At its centre, this successful 20th-century new town boasts a traditional market square surrounded by pleasant arcades and terraces built in the old Essex style with brick, tile and weatherboard.

Marsh Farm Country Park in South Woodham Ferrers (see panel on page 302), is a working farm and country park adjoining the River Crouch. Sheep, pigs, cattle and hens roam; visitors can also partake of the adventure play area, farm trail, visitors centre, gift shop and tea rooms. Guided tours are available by prior arrangement. Special events are held throughout the year.

BATTLESBRIDGE
7 miles SW of Maldon off the A132

Battlesbridge Antiques Centre at Hawk Hill in Battlesbridge is the largest in Essex. Housed in five period buildings, more than 70 dealers display and sell their wares. The heart of the Centre is Cromwell House, its ground floor dedicated to specialist dealers with individual units. They will advise, value and give an expert opinion free of charge. They offer a wide variety of old and interesting pieces and collectables.

The Centre's Haybarn Cottages were constructed as dwellings, while, alongside, The Bridgebarn began life as a barn with thatched roof and dates from the 19th century, at which time there were lime kilns nearby. It was converted to its present tiled roof in the 1930s. The building retains some fine oak beamwork, and houses a small 'penny arcade' with working model roundabout, fortune teller, and What The Butler Saw machine as well as a large collection of antiques for sale.

The Old Granary is nestled on the riverbank and houses five floors of dealers selling collectables, reproductions, antiques and crafts, including specialists in old phones, clocks, furniture, cigarette cards, jewellery, fireplaces, interior design, dried flowers and much more. There are superb

Marsh Farm Country Park

Marsh Farm Road, South Woodham Ferrers, Chelmsford, Essex CM3 5WP
Tel: 01245 321552

Marsh Farm Country Park overlooks the River Crouch and is surrounded by its creeks on three sides. The Park is a SSSI (Site of Special Scientific Interest), as it is a good example of Essex grazing marshes, carrying such rare plants as sea barley and grass vetchling. It is also internationally important as an over-wintering site for brent geese. Over 150 species of bird have been seen around the Park. Every winter the marshes are invaded by droves of wildfowl, making Marsh Farm a popular birdwatching spot.

Marsh Farm Country Park has been many things during its history. Iron age settlers were attracted here by a river rich for fishing, hunting and salt. There is evidence of salt making scattered across the site in the form of saltpans and 'red hills': saltwater was evaporated by the sun or by using very hot stones, which left a red earth deposit. The sea salt left behind was a highly valued commodity. Over 300 years ago, the marshes were drained. A sea wall was built by the Dutch, transforming tidal creeks into the grazing marshes we see at Marsh Farm today.

In dry weather the sea wall offers a wide, level path; however, during the winter months it becomes very muddy. The Open Farm is fully accessible for wheelchairs.

views from the top floor of the River Crouch and surrounding area, to be enjoyed as you take tea in the top-floor coffee shop.

This superb location is also the site of a Classic Motor Cycle Museum, with displays evoking the history of motorcycling through the ages and some interesting memorabilia. Open on Sundays or by appointment. Three classic vehicle events are held annually.

MUNDON

3 miles SE of Maldon off the B1018

Mundon and the surrounding area boast some excellent walking. St Peter's Way, a long-distance path from Ongar to St Peter's Chapel, Bradwell-on-Sea, leads through the village and past the disused Church of St Mary. This 14th-century church is maintained by the Friends of Friendless Churches and is

🏠 historic building 🏛 museum and heritage 🏚 historic site ♔ scenic attraction 🌱 flora and fauna

open to the public. Tolstoy is known to have visited the village.

ALTHORNE
6 miles SE of Maldon on the B1012

🏛 Church of St Andrew

The **Church of St Andrew**, some 600 years old, has a fine flint-and-stone tower, built in the perpendicular style. Inside the church there's a 15th-century font, which retains its original carvings of saints and angels. A brass plaque dated 1508 records that William Hyklott 'Paide for the werkemanship of the wall'; an inscription over the west door remembers John Wylson and John Hyll, who probably paid for the tower.

To the south, where Station Road meets Burnham Road, stands the village's War Memorial. This solid structure of beams and tiles lends dignity and honour to the tragic roll-call of names listed on it.

To the north of the village is the golden-thatched and white-walled Huntsman and Hounds, an alehouse since around 1700.

STEEPLE AND ST LAWRENCE
8 miles SE of Maldon off the B1021

Public footpaths lead down to the water from the village of Steeple; the houses of St Lawrence stand close to the water. Several sailing clubs and some waterside caravan and camping parks ensure that there is plenty of activity on the adjacent stretch of the River Blackwater. The St Lawrence Rural Discovery Church, on high ground further inland, overlooks the villages and the River Blackwater to the north; it also offers views over the River Crouch to the south. Exhibitions with local themes are held in the church during the summer months.

BRADWELL-ON-SEA/BRADWELL WATERSIDE
12 miles E of Maldon off the B1021

🏛 St Peter's on the Wall 🦐 Dengie Peninsula

A visit to Bradwell-on-Sea (the name derives from the Saxon words brad pall, meaning 'broad wall') is well worth the long drive for its sense of being right out on the edge of things – the timeless emptiness is if anything exaggerated by the distant views of buildings across the water on Mersea Island and the bulk of the nearby (now decommissioned) nuclear power station. A walk eastwards along the old Roman road across the marshes takes you to the site of their fort, 'Othona', on which the visitors of today will find the chapel of **St Peter's on the Wall**, built by St Cedd and his followers in AD654 using rubble from the ruined fort. In the 14th century the chapel was abandoned as a place of worship, and over the following centuries used at various times as a barn and a shipping beacon. Restored and re-consecrated in 1920, it is well worth the half-mile walk from the car park to reach it. It is the site of a pilgrimage each July.

There is an unusual war memorial marking the site of the Bradwell Bay Secret Airfield, used during the Second World War for aircraft unable to return to their original base.

Bradwell Lodge, in the village centre, is a part-Tudor former rectory that has known some famous visitors. Gainsborough, the Suffolk artist, used rooms as a studio, while the Irish writer Erskine Childers, who was shot by the Irish Free State in 1920 because he fought for the IRA, wrote *The Riddle of the Sands* here.

At Bradwell Waterside, a large marina has berths for 300 boats. The now-

St Peter's on the Wall, Bradwell-on-Sea

decommissioned nuclear power station has a waymarked nature trail.

To the south of the village lie the remote marshes of the **Dengie Peninsula**, parts of which are important nature reserves. The salty tang of sea air, brought inland on easterly winds, gives an exhilarating flavour to the marshlands. Like the Cambridgeshire and Lincolnshire fens, this once-waterlogged corner of Essex was reclaimed from the sea by 17th-century Dutch engineers. The views across the marshes take in great sweeps of countryside inhabited only by wildfowl and seabirds.

BURNHAM-ON-CROUCH
12 miles SE of Maldon on the B1012

St Mary's Church   Museum

Mangapps Railway Museum

Burnham-on-Crouch is attractively old-fashioned, and probably best known as a

yachting venue. It is lively in summer, especially at the end of August when the town hosts one of England's premier regattas, Burnham Week. This week of racing and shore events attracts many visiting craft and landlubbers alike. In winter many yachts are left to ride at anchor offshore, and the sound of the wind in their rigging is ever-present.

Behind the brightly coloured cottages along the Quay lies the High Street and the rest of the town, its streets lined with a delightful assortment of old cottages and Victorian and Georgian houses and shops.

In past times, working boats thronged the estuary where yachts now ply to and fro. Seafarers still come ashore to buy provisions, following a tradition that goes back to medieval times when Burnham was the market centre for the isolated inhabitants of Wallasea and Foulness Islands in the estuary. A ferry still links Burnham with Wallasea at

historic building   museum and heritage   historic site   scenic attraction   flora and fauna

weekends during the summer, and a programme of boat trips to see the seals on Foulness Sands operates from Burnham Quay.

Near the Yacht Harbour, west of the town and accessible along the sea wall path, is the Riverside Park. Also alongside the river can be found the Millfield Recreation Ground and a sports centre.

Burnham-on-Crouch & District Museum on The Quay features agricultural, maritime and social history exhibits relating to the Dengie Hundred. There is also a small archaeological collection. Special exhibitions are mounted periodically.

Mangapps Railway Museum on the edge of town offers an extensive collection of railway relics of all kinds, including steam and diesel locos, carriages and wagons, relocated railway buildings, one of the largest collections of signalling equipment open to the public, a complete country station and items of East Anglian railway history. Train rides on a one-mile stretch of track are available at selected times (tel: 01621 784898).

St Mary's Church is constructed of Kentish ragstone that was transported to Burnham by sea. Construction was begun in the 12th century and was completed in the 14th, but since that time the nucleus of the town has moved closer to the waterfront. The arches and pillars are particularly fine examples of medieval craftsmanship, hence the church being known as The Cathedral of the Dengie.

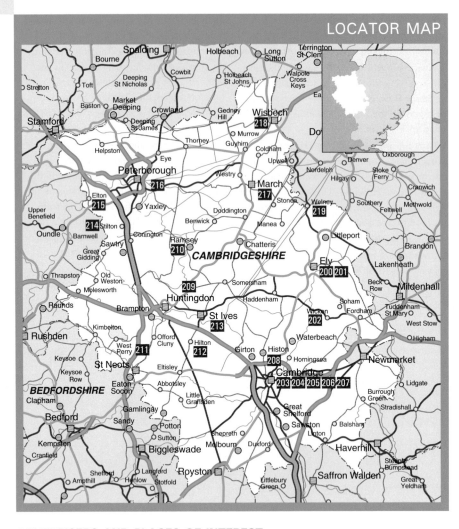

LOCATOR MAP

ADVERTISERS AND PLACES OF INTEREST

🏚 historic building   🏛 museum and heritage   🏛 historic site   ♌ scenic attraction   🌱 flora and fauna

4 Cambridgeshire

Extending over much of the county from the Wash, the flat fields of the Fens are like a breath of fresh air, far removed from the hustle and bustle of modern life. These fields contain some of the richest soil in England, and villages such as Fordham and small towns like Ely rise out of the landscape on low hills. Before the Fens were drained, this was a land of mist, marshes and bogs, of small islands inhabited by independent folk, their livelihood the fish and waterfowl of this eerie, watery place. The region is full of legends of web-footed people, ghosts and witchcraft. Today's landscape is the result of human ingenuity, with its constant desire to tame the wilderness and create farmland. This fascinating story spans the centuries from the earliest Roman and Anglo-Saxon times, when the first embankments and drains were constructed to lessen the frequency of flooding. Throughout the Middle Ages large areas were reclaimed, with much of the work being undertaken by the monasteries. The first straight cut bypassed the Great Ouse, allowing the water to run out to sea more quickly. After the Civil War, the New Bedford River was cut parallel

to the first. These two still provide the basic drainage for much of Fenland. The significant influence of the Dutch lives on in some of the architecture and place names of the Fens. Over the years it became necessary to pump rainwater from the fields up into the rivers and, as in the Netherlands, windmills took on this task. They could not always cope with the height of the lift required, but fortunately the steam engine came along, to be replaced eventually by the electric pumps that can raise thousands of gallons of water a second to protect the land from the ever-present threat of rain and tide. The Fens offer unlimited opportunities for exploring on foot, by car, bicycle or by boat. Anglers are well catered for, and visitors with an interest in wildlife will be in their element.

Southeastern Cambridgeshire covers the area around the city of Cambridge and is rich in history, with a host of archaeological sites and monuments to visit, as well as many important museums. The area is fairly flat, so it makes for great walking and cycling tours, and offers a surprising variety of landscapes. The Romans planted vines here and, to this

🎬 stories and anecdotes 🐦 famous people ✍ art and craft 🍂 entertainment and sport 🚶 walks

day, the region is one of the main producers of British wines. At the heart of it all is Cambridge itself, one of the leading academic centres in the world and a city that deserves plenty of time to explore - on foot, by bicycle or by the gentler, more romantic option of a punt.

Christchurch College, City of Cambridge

The old county of Huntingdonshire is the heartland of the rural heritage of Cambridgeshire. Here, the home of Oliver Cromwell beckons with a wealth of history and pleasing landscapes. Many motorists follow the Cromwell Trail, which guides tourists around the legacy of buildings and places in the area associated with the man. The natural start of the Trail is Huntingdon itself, where Cromwell was born the son of a country gentleman. Other main stopping places are covered in this chapter.

The Ouse Valley Way (26 miles long) follows the course of the Great Ouse through pretty villages and a variety of natural attractions. A gentle cruise along this area can fill a lazy day to perfection, but for those who prefer something more energetic on the water there are excellent, versatile facilities at Grafham Water. The Nene-Ouse Navigation Link, part of the Fenland Waterway, provides the opportunity for a relaxed look at a lovely part of the region. It travels from Stanground Lock near Peterborough to a lock at the small village of Salters Lode in the east, and the 28-mile journey passes through several Fenland towns and a rich variety of wildlife habitats.

Ely

🏛 Cathedral 🏛 Oliver Cromwell's House

🏛 Ely Museum 🏛 The Stained Glass Museum

Ely is the jewel in the crown of the Fens, in whose history the majestic **Cathedral** and the Fens themselves have played major roles. The Fens' influence is apparent even in the name: Ely was once known as Elge or Elig ('eel island') because of the large number of eels that lived in the surrounding fenland. Ely owes its existence to St Etheldreda, Queen of Northumbria, who in AD673 founded a monastery on the 'Isle of Ely', where she remained as abbess until her death in AD679. It was not until 1081 that work started on the present Cathedral, and in 1189 this remarkable example of Romanesque architecture was completed. The most outstanding feature in terms of both scale and beauty is the Octagon, built to replace the original Norman tower, which collapsed in 1322.

Alan of Walsingham was the inspired architect of this massive work, which took 30 years to complete and whose framework weighs an estimated 400 tons. Many other notable components include the 14th century Lady Chapel, the largest in England, the Prior's Door, the painted nave ceiling and St Ovin's cross, the only piece of Saxon stonework in the building.

The Cathedral is set within the walls of the monastery, and many of the ancient buildings still stand as a tribute to the incredible skill and craftsmanship of their designers and builders. Particularly worth visiting among these are the monastic buildings in the College, the Great Hall and Queens Hall.

Just beside the Cathedral is the Almonry, in whose 12th century vaulted undercroft visitors can take coffee, lunch or tea - outside in the garden if the weather permits. Two other attractions that should not be missed are a place where visitors can make their own rubbings from replica brasses, and **The Stained Glass Museum** (see panel below). The latter, housed in the south Triforium of the Cathedral, is the only museum of stained glass in the country and contains over 100 original panels from every period, tracing the

CAMBRIDGESHIRE

The Stained Glass Museum

The South Triforium, Ely Cathedral, Ely,
Cambridgeshire CB7 4DL
Tel: 01353 660347 Fax: 01353 665025
website: www.stainedglassmuseum.com

This unique museum offers an insight into the long story of stained glass. For at least 1,300 years the art has been practised in Britain. The Main Gallery is located on the upper level of the Cathedral accessed by a spiral staircase. It contains displays of stained glass windows, ranging over eight centuries, in specially illuminated cases. A touch-screen virtual visit is available on the ground floor

There is a range of gifts, cards and books relating to stained glass and also work by local glass artists in the museum shop. Friends of the Museum support the work done here in various ways, and also have a wide programme of events and visits to do with stained glass and art in a wider context.

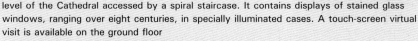

🎬 stories and anecdotes 🕊 famous people 🎨 art and craft 🖉 entertainment and sport 🚶 walks

The Old Palace, Ely

Information Centre is itself a tourist attraction, since it is part of a pretty black-and-white timbered building that was once **Oliver Cromwell's House**. It is the only remaining house, apart from Hampton Court, where Oliver Cromwell and his family are known to have lived; parts of it date back to the 13th century, and its varied history includes periods when it was used as a public house and, more recently, a vicarage. 2008 marks the 350th anniversary of Oliver Cromwell's death, the house has been refurbished and a number of special events were planned throughout the year. There are eight period rooms, including a re-creation of the room where he died, a permanent Civil War exhibition and a presentation on the life and times of Cromwell. The last room on a tour of the

complete history of stained glass.

The Old Palace, the official residence of the Bishops of Ely until 1940, is now a hospice. It is fronted by two towers, and notable features inside include the Georgian sitting room and the Bishop's private chapel. In the garden is a giant plane tree - claimed to be the oldest in Europe. The Tourist

Ely Museum at the Old Gaol

The Old Gaol, Market Street, Ely, Cambridgeshire CB7 4LS
Tel: 01353 666655

Ely Museum is housed in one of the oldest buildings in Ely, dating from the 13th century. It has been a private house, a tavern, a registry office and the Bishops' Gaol. Sensitively renovated in 1997, much of the building's history can still be seen, including prisoners' graffiti, hidden doorways and original planking on the walls. The displays include fossils from marine dinosaurs, prehistoric tools and weapons, Roman pottery and Anglo Saxon jewellery. An archive film shows methods of farming in the past, and the Debtors and Condemned Cells show visitors what the Bishops' Gaol was really like.

Ely Museum has a level front entrance, an adapted toilet and a stairlift to the upper floor. There are chairs throughout the Museum for visitors. Quiz sheets are free to children, there is a Teacher's Resource Pack, and many objects that can be touched. Guided tours are available by appointment. There are visitors' toilets and a nappy changing unit. The gift shop sells many items from the Robert Opie range as well as local history publications, and work by local artists and crafts people. Special events and exhibitions are held throughout the year, including finds identification afternoons, living history days and a programme of talks.

🏛 historic building   🏛 museum and heritage   🏛 historic site   🗘 scenic attraction   🌱 flora and fauna

house is the Tithe Office, where visitors can watch a presentation telling the 'Story of the Fens'.

The Old Gaol, in Market Street, houses **Ely Museum** (see panel opposite), with nine galleries telling the Ely story from the Ice Age to modern times. The tableaux of the condemned and debtors' cells are particularly fascinating and poignant.

Ely is not just the past, and its fine architecture and sense of history blend well with the bustle of the streets and shops and the riverside. That bustle is at its most fervent on Thursdays, when the largest general market in the area is held. Every Saturday there's a craft and collectables market, and on the second and fourth Saturdays of the month Ely hosts a Farmers' Market.

At Babylon Gallery on Ely's Waterside, in a converted 18th-century brewery warehouse, visitors will find an exciting collection of contemporary arts and crafts, in a programme of changing local and international exhibitions.

Around Ely

PRICKWILLOW
4 miles NE of Ely on the B1382

🏛 Museum

On the village's main street is the **Prickwillow Drainage Engine Museum**, which houses a unique collection of large engines associated with the drainage of the Fens. The site had been in continuous use as a pumping station since 1831, and apart from the engines there are displays charting the history of Fens drainage, the effects on land levels and the workings of the modern drainage system.

LITTLEPORT
6 miles N of Ely on the A10

🏛 St George's Church

St George's Church, with its very tall 15th-century tower, is a notable landmark here in Littleport. Of particular interest are two stained-glass windows depicting St George slaying the dragon. Littleport was the scene of riots in 1861, when labourers from Ely and Littleport, faced with unemployment or low wages and soaring food prices, attacked houses and people in this area, causing several deaths. Five of the rioters were hanged then buried in a common grave at St Mary's Church. A plaque commemorating the event is attached to a wall at the back of the church.

LITTLE DOWNHAM
3 miles N of Ely off the A10

Little Downham's Church of St Leonard shows the change from Norman to Gothic in church building at the turn of the 13th century. The oldest parts are the Norman tower and the elaborately carved south door. Interior treasures include what is probably the largest royal coat of arms in the country. At the other end of the village are the remains (mainly the gatehouse and kitchen) of a 15th-century palace built by a Bishop of Ely. The property is in private hands and part of it is an antiques centre.

COVENEY
3 miles W of Ely off the A10

🏛 Church of St Peter-ad-Vincula

A Fenland hamlet on the Bedford Level just above West Fen, Coveney's **Church of St Peter-ad-Vincula** has several interesting features, including a colourful German screen dating from around 1500 and a painted

Wardy Hill

Distance: *5.5 miles (8.8 kilometres)*
Typical time: *120 mins*
Height gain: *0 metres*
Map: *Explorer 228*
Walk: *www.walkingworld.com ID:1170*
Contributor: *Joy & Charles Boldero*

ACCESS INFORMATION:

For information about bus routes ring 0870 608 2608. There is parking on the very wide grass verge at By-way sign on the edge of Wardy Hill village, by Beumont Farm fence line. Wardy Hill is situated on a minor road off the A142 4 miles west of Ely.

ADDITIONAL INFORMATION:

Wardy Hill is set on an island above the fens, on what is known as the Isle of Ely. Wardy Hill means 'lookout'. In centuries past this was to watch for cattle raiders coming across the fens. It is thought it was a Bronze Age settlement as shields and swords have been found here.

The New Bedford River, or Hundred-Foot Drain as it is also called, was built after the Old Bedford River, built by the Dutchman Vermuydrn in the 1600s, was found to be inadequate. The land between the two rivers is a flood plain and part of the RSPB famous Welney Washes. To the left on the horizon Ely Cathedral can be seen.

The Three Pickerels pub at Mepal has an excellent menu. It is closed on Monday lunch times. Open all day on Sundays.

DESCRIPTION:

This walk runs beside the New Bedford River to Mepal, then returns by tracks and footpaths that can be muddy after heavy rain and country lanes.

FEATURES:

River, Pub, Toilets, Wildlife, Birds, Flowers, Great Views, Butterflies.

WALK DIRECTIONS:

1 | Go westwards through the village, ignoring all footpaths off the country lane. Continue along Jerusalem Drove to left-hand bend.

2 | At bridleway sign go right along track passing Toll Cottage. Climb stile and cross to next one and climb it, going up the bank.

3 | Turn left along river bank. Much further along go down bank to metal gate and climb stile. Continue along the track. Climb stile.

4 | Turn right along road in Mepal, then almost immediately left to pub. Retrace steps to junction and turn right along pavement.

5 | Cross road by right-hand bend and turn left along New Road. At end, go around gate and cross field. Climb stile, cross second field, climb stile.

6 | Turn left along track, then almost immediately right. Cross field and slippery bridge.

7 | Turn right along track. Cross road and continue along the track opposite. Cross track and continue straight along track. At fork either path can be used.

8 | Turn left at cross tracks.

9 | At T junction of tracks turn right.

10 | Turn left along country lane back to start of walk.

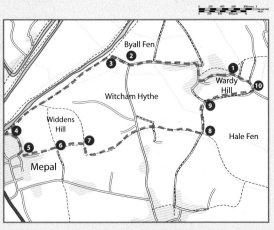

Danish pulpit. Unusual figures on the bench ends and a fine brass chandelier add to the opulent feel of this atmospheric little church.

SUTTON
6 miles W of Ely off the A142

A very splendid 'pepperpot' tower with octagons, pinnacles and spire tops marks out Sutton's grand church of St Andrew. Inside, take time to look at the 15th-century font and a fine modern stained-glass window.

The reconstruction of the church was largely the work of two Bishops of Ely, whose arms appear on the roof bosses. One of the Bishops was Thomas Arundel, appointed at the age of 21.

A mile further west, there's a great family attraction in the Mepal Outdoor Centre, an outdoor leisure centre with a children's playpark, an adventure play area and boat hire.

HADDENHAM
5 miles SW of Ely on the A1123

🏚 Great Mill

More industrial splendour: Haddenham **Great Mill**, built in 1803 for a certain Daniel Cockle, is a glorious sight, and one definitely not to be missed. It has four sails and three sets of grinding stones, one of which is working. The mill last worked commercially in 1946 and was restored between 1992 and 1998. Open on the first Sunday of each month and by appointment.

Other places of interest in and around Haddenham, which lies on the highest ridge (120ft) in the Isle of Ely, include Holy Trinity Church and Porch House, a typical Elizabethan long house.

STRETHAM
5 miles S of Ely off A10/A1123

🏚 Stretham Old Engine

The **Stretham Old Engine**, a fine example of a land-drainage steam engine, is housed in a restored, tall-chimneyed brick engine house. Dating from 1831, it is one of 90 steam pumping engines installed throughout the Fens to replace some 800 windmills. It is the last to survive, having worked until 1925 and still under restoration. During the great floods of 1919 it really earned its keep by working non-stop for 47 days and nights.

This unique insight into Fenland history and industrial archaeology is open to the public on summer weekends, and on certain dates the engine and its wooden scoop-wheel are rotated (by electricity, alas!). The adjacent Stoker's Cottage contains four plainly appointed rooms with period furniture and old photographs of fen drainage down the years.

Downfield Windmill, six miles southeast of Ely on the A142 bypass, was built in 1726 as a smock mill, destroyed by gales and rebuilt in 1890 as an octagonal tower mill. It still grinds corn and produces a range of flours and breads for sale (open Sundays and Bank Holidays).

Stretham Old Engine, Ely

WICKEN
9 miles S of Ely off the A1123

🏛 St Lawrence's Church 🐦 Wicken Fen

Owned by the National Trust, **Wicken Fen** (see panel above) is the oldest nature reserve in the country, celebrating its centenary in 1999. Its 600 acres of wetland habitats are famous for their rich plant, insect and bird life, and a delight for both naturalists and ramblers. Features include boardwalk, adventurer's and nature trails, hides and watchtowers, wild ponies, a cottage with 1930s furnishings, a working wind pump (the oldest in the country), a visitor centre and a shop. Open daily, dawn to dusk.

St Lawrence's Church is well worth a visit, small and secluded among trees. In the churchyard are buried several members of the Cromwell family, including Henry and his grandson Oliver (not the Roundhead leader). One of Roundhead Cromwell's many nicknames was 'Lord of the Fens': he defended the rights of the Fenmen against those who wanted to drain the land without providing adequate compensation.

Wicken Windmill is a fine and impressive smock windmill restored back to working order. One of only four smock windmills making flour in the UK, it is open the first weekend of every month and every Bank Holiday (except Christmas and Good Friday) from 11am until 5pm, and also over the National Mills Weekend, the second week in May.

ISLEHAM
10 miles SE of Ely off the B1104

The remains of a Benedictine priory with a lovely Norman chapel under the care of English Heritage, are a great draw here in Isleham. Also well worth a visit is the Church of St Andrew, a 14th-century cruciform building entered by a very fine lychgate. The 17th-century eagle lectern is the original of a similar lectern in Ely Cathedral.

SNAILWELL
12 miles SE of Ely off the A142

Snailwell's pretty, mainly 14th-century Church of St Peter on the banks of the River Snail boasts a 13th-century chancel, a hammerbeam and tie beam nave roof, a 600-year-old font, pews with poppy heads and two medieval oak screens. The Norman round tower is unusual for Cambridgeshire.

TYLERS FARM SHOP

Hall Farm, 71 Church Road, Wicken, nr Ely, Cambridgeshire CB7 6XT
Tel/Fax: 01353 721029

Bob and Christine Tyler have owned and run **Tylers Farm Shop** for more than 20 years, building a far-reaching reputation for quality and service. Their bright, spotless shop is filled with top-notch local produce, from cuts and joints of pork, beef and lamb, hand-made sausages and burgers, bacon, cooked and cured meats, pork pies, poultry, eggs, milk, butter, cheese, bread, biscuits, preserves, honey and locally-milled flour, sold in three varieties. Barbecue packs are available to order. The shop, which stands opposite St Lawrence's Church, is open from 9am to 5.30pm Wednesday to Friday, 8am to 1pm on Saturday.

🏛 historic building 🏛 museum and heritage 🏚 historic site 🍃 scenic attraction 🐦 flora and fauna

Cambridge

🏛 The Colleges 🏛 University Library

🏛 The Churches 🏛 Bridge of Sighs

🏛 Mathematical Bridge 🏛 Fitzwilliam Museum

🏛 Museum of Zoology

🏛 Museums of Archaelology & Anthropology

🏛 Museum of Technology 🏛 Whipple Museum

🏛 Museum of Earth Sciences

🏛 Scott Polar Research Institute

🏛 Cambridge & County Folk Museum

🌱 University Botanic Gardens ⚗ Kettle's Yard

There are nearly 30 Cambridges spread around the globe, but this, the original, is the one that the whole world knows as one of the leading university cities. Cambridge was an important town many centuries before the scholars arrived, standing at the point where

forest met fen, at the lowest fording point of the river. The Romans took over a site previously settled by an Iron Age Belgic tribe, to be followed in turn by the Saxons and the Normans.

Soon after the Norman Conquest, William I built a wooden motte-and-bailey castle; Edward I built a stone replacement: a mound still marks the spot. The town flourished as a market and river trading centre, and in 1209 a group of students fleeing the Oxford riots arrived.

The first of the **Colleges** was Peterhouse, founded by the Bishop of Ely in 1284, followed in the next century by Clare, Pembroke, Gonville & Caius, Trinity Hall and Corpus Christi. The total is now more than 30; the most distinctive of the modern colleges is Robinson College, built in striking post-modern style in 1977; it has the look of

GWEN RAVERAT, CAMBRIDGE & THE DARWINS

Broughton House, 98 King Street, Cambridge, Cambridgeshire CB1 1LN
Tel: 01223 314960
e-mail: bhgallery@btconnect.com
website: www.broughtonhousegallery.co.uk

Gwen Raverat, granddaughter of Charles Darwin, friend of Rupert Brooke, Virginia Woolf and others of the Bloomsbury Group, wrote the classic *Period Piece*, a memoir of a Cambridge childhood, set in her home Newnham Grange, now part of Darwin College. She had become the leading wood engraver of her generation. Her work varied from freestanding prints of Cambridge and France, to illustrations to books such as *The Cambridge Book of Poetry for Children*.

The archive of all the prints made by her during her lifetime (mostly for sale), plus all the books written about her (also for sale), and greeting card reproductions of some of her work are housed in **Broughton House** in King Street. Give us a ring or e-mail us to come and browse and enjoy our walled garden. Wheelchairs and children welcome. Pay and Display parking.

Fishing at Grantchester (1930)

The Olive Pickers (1922)

a fortress, its concrete structure covered with a 'skin' of a million and a quarter hand-made red Dorset bricks. It was the gift of the self-made millionaire engineer and racehorse owner David Robinson. All the colleges are well worth a visit, but places that simply must not be missed include King's College Chapel with its breathtaking fan vaulting, glorious stained glass and Peter Paul Rubens' Adoration of the Magi; Pepys Library, including his diaries, in Magdalene College; and Trinity's wonderful Great Court. A trip by punt along the 'Backs' of the Cam brings a unique view of many of the colleges and passes under six bridges, including the **Bridge of Sighs** (St John's) and the extraordinary wooden **Mathematical Bridge** at Queens.

Cambridge has nurtured more Nobel Prize winners than most countries - 32 from Trinity alone - and the list of celebrated alumni covers every sphere of human endeavour and achievement: Byron, Tennyson, Milton and Wordsworth; Marlowe and Bacon; Samuel Pepys; Sir Isaac Newton and Charles Darwin; Charles Babbage, Bertrand Russell and Ludwig Wittgenstein; actors Sir Ian McKellen, Sir Derek Jacobi and Stephen Fry; Lord Burghley; Harold Abrahams, who ran for England in the Olympics; and Burgess, Maclean, Philby and Blunt, who spied for Russia. The 'Cambridge Mafia' was the title given to a group of senior Conservatives at Cambridge together in the early 1960. Their number included Ken Clarke, John Gummer, Norman Lamont, Peter Lilley and Michael Howard, all in John Major's 1992 cabinet, Norman Fowler and Leon Brittan. Pembroke College, the third oldest, produced an impressive array of comedy stars and

SANDRA JANE

46-48 King Street, Cambridge, Cambridgeshire CB1 1LN
Tel: 01223 323211   Fax: 01223 507095
e-mail: contact@sandrajane.co.uk   website: www.sandrajane.co.uk

Sandra Jane is a high-quality interior design store in the heart of Cambridge. Large windows in the Grade II listed building give a glimpse of the array of decorative and practical items for the home on display over its two floors. Opened by Sandy Turkentine in 1998, the family-run business is filled with things that make a house a home, and a home individual and special.

The stock includes fabrics, wallpaper and trimmings from over 40 top designers, sample books, cushions, throws, furniture (inside and outside), curtain poles and tracks, mirrors and lighting ranging from small bedside lamps to floor-standing lamps and chandeliers. There's

  also a great selection of jewellery, along with clothes, pottery, vases and smaller items as diverse as photo frames, reading glasses and bath oils.

The goods come from well-known brands as well as lesser-known sources from all over the world, and the stock is constantly changing. Services offered at Sandra Jane include curtain- and blind-making and wedding lists. Store hours are 9.30am to 5.30pm Monday to Saturday.

🏛 historic building 🏛 museum and heritage 🏛 historic site ⚜ scenic attraction 🌱 flora and fauna

Kettle's Yard House

Castle Street, Cambridge, Cambridgeshire CB3 0AQ
Tel: 01223 352124
website: www.kettlesyard.co.uk
e-mail: mail@kettlesyard.cam.ac.uk

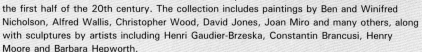

For 16 years, **Kettle's Yard** was the home of Jim Ede, a former curator at the Tate Gallery, London, and his wife, Helen. It houses Ede's collection of art, mostly of the first half of the 20th century. The collection includes paintings by Ben and Winifred Nicholson, Alfred Wallis, Christopher Wood, David Jones, Joan Miro and many others, along with sculptures by artists including Henri Gaudier-Brzeska, Constantin Brancusi, Henry Moore and Barbara Hepworth.

Paintings and sculptures are interlaced with furniture, glass, ceramics and natural objects. Ede's vision of Kettle's Yard was of a place that was not *"an art gallery or museum, nor ... simply a collection of works of art reflecting my taste or the taste of a given period. It is, rather, a continuing way of life from these last fifty years, in which stray objects, stones, glass, pictures, sculpture, in light and in space, have been used to make manifest the underlying stability ... "*

Each afternoon (apart from Mondays) visitors can ring the bell and ask to look around.

writers, including Peter Cook, Eric Idle, Clive James, Bill Oddie and Tim Brooke-Taylor. The best way to see the Colleges is on an official TourCambridge guided tour (book on 0871 226 8006 or at the TIC). There are also open-top bus tours round the city and 'chauffeured' punt tours on the River Cam.

The Colleges apart, Cambridge is packed with interest for the visitor, with a wealth of grand buildings both religious and secular, and some of the country's leading museums, many of them run by the University. The **Fitzwilliam Museum** is renowned for its art collection, which includes works by Titian, Rembrandt, Gainsborough, Hogarth, Turner, Renoir, Picasso and Cezanne, and for its antiquities from Egypt, Greece and Rome. **Kettle's Yard** (see panel above) has a permanent display of 20th-century art in a house maintained just as it was when the Ede family donated it, with the collection, to the University in 1967. The **Museum of**

Classical Archaeology has 500 plaster casts of Greek and Roman statues, and the **University Museum of Archaeology and Anthropology** covers worldwide prehistoric archaeology with special displays relating to Oceania and to the Cambridge area. The **Museum of Technology**, housed in a Victorian sewage pumping station, features an impressive collection of steam, gas and electric pumping engines and examples great and small of local industrial technology. Anyone with an interest in fossils should make tracks to the **Sedgwick Museum of Earth Sciences**, while in the same street (Downing) the **Museum of Zoology** offers a comprehensive and spectacular survey of the animal kingdom. The **Whipple Museum of the History of Science** tells about science through instruments; the **Scott Polar Research Institute** has fascinating, often poignant exhibits relating to Arctic and Antarctic

Punting on River Cam, Cambridge

exploration; and the **University Botanic Garden** (see panel below) boasts a plant collection (more than 8,000 species) that rivals those of Kew Gardens and Edinburgh. The 40-acre site includes the National Collections of species tulips, fritillaries and hardy geraniums.

The work and life of the people of Cambridge and the surrounding area are the subjects of the **Cambridge and County Folk Museum**, housed in a 16th century building that for 300 years was the White Horse Inn. It traces the everyday lives of the local people from 1700 onwards, with sections

Cambridge University Botanic Garden

Cory Lodge, Bateman Street, Cambridge, Cambridgeshire CB2 1JF
Tel: 01223 336265
website: www.botanic.cam.ac.uk

Opened in 1846 by Professor John Henslow, Charles Darwin's teacher and mentor, this heritage-listed **Botanic Garden** displays over 8,000 plant species, including important collections of species tulips, geraniums, lavenders and fritillaries, as well as the finest arboretum in the East of England.

The majestic Main Walk of towering evergreens forms the backbone of the superb 19th century Garden that also boasts the flamboyant Glasshouses of tropical and desert plants, and the Rock Garden, which displays the alpine plants of every continent geographically and affords a wonderful vantage point over the Lake. The Woodland Garden is a stunning mix of mature trees and rich herbaceous underplanting, whilst the extraordinary, unique Systematic Beds, designed in 1845, display over 95 families of hardy herbaceous plants.

The 20th century Garden reflects the horticultural and scientific developments of the time: the British Wild Plants collection is unparalleled; the Dry Garden is an on-going experiment to create a gorgeous garden that can survive the dry Cambridge climate without any watering; the Genetics Garden tells the story of the sweet pea experiments undertaken here by William Bateson in the 1900s, which led to the modern science of genetics; the ancestry of the modern rose is unravelled in the Rose Garden and the Winter Garden is an inspirational lesson in achieving colour, beauty and scent in the winter months.

🏠 historic building 📷 museum and heritage 🏛 historic site ⌕ scenic attraction 🌿 flora and fauna

Visit our ARK shops in Cambridge

2 floors, Just of Market Square

2 St Mary's Passage, Cambridge CB2 3PQ
Tel: 01223 363372

4 floors, parking in front of shop

9 Norfolk Street, Cambridge CB1 2LD
Tel: 01223 307676

website: www.arkcambridge.co.uk

Our shops are open 7 days a week plus Bank Holidays

devoted to crafts and trades, town & gown, witchbottles, skating, and eels. One of the city's greatest treasures is the **University Library**, one of the world's great research libraries with six million books, one million maps and 350,000 manuscripts.

Cambridge also has many fine **Churches**, some of them used by the colleges before they built their own chapels. Among the most notable are St Mary the Less, originally dedicated to St Peter (from which nearby Peterhouse College gets its name); St Benet's (its 11th-century tower is the oldest in the county); St Mary the Great, the 'University Church', a marvellous example of Late Perpendicular Gothic; Our Lady & the English Martyrs; Holy Trinity, known for its connections with the Evangelical movement, and St Peter Castle Hill. This last is one of the smallest churches in the country, with a

nave measuring just 25 feet by 16 feet. Originally much larger, the church was largely demolished in 1781 and rebuilt in its present diminished state using the old materials, including flint rubble and Roman bricks. The Church of the Holy Sepulchre, always known as the Round Church, is one of only five surviving circular churches in England.

Around Cambridge

GIRTON
3 miles NW of Cambridge off the A14

The first Cambridge college for women was founded in 1869 in Hitchin, by Emily Davies. It moved here to Girton in 1873, to be 'near enough for male lecturers to visit but far enough away to discourage male students from

🎭 stories and anecdotes 🦜 famous people 🎨 art and craft ✏ entertainment and sport 🚶 walks

DAISY CHAIN

2 High Street, Histon, Cambridgeshire CB24 9LG
Tel: 01223 232121
e-mail: gifts@daisychainhiston.co.uk
website: www.daisychainhiston.co.uk

Daisy Chain is a delightful shop selling a tempting array of gifts, cards, jewellery and accessories that are very much out of the ordinary. The spacious shop is perfect for browsing among the innovative range of products - selected to suit every budget and occasion. Other products include household accessories, children's clothing, baby gifts and personalised items. This wonderful variety is regularly updated and stock is purchased in small quantities to maintain a diverse assortment. The owners invite you to get away from the stresses and strains of city shopping and wander around Daisy Chain's fascinating array of colours and aromas.

doing the same'. The problem went away when Girton became a mixed College in 1983.

RAMPTON
6 miles NW of Cambridge off the B1049

🏛 Giant's Hill

A charming village in its own right, with a tree-fringed village green, Rampton is also the site of one of the many archaeological sites in the area. This is **Giant's Hill**, a motte castle with part of an earlier medieval settlement.

MILTON
3 miles N of Cambridge off the A10

🏃 Milton Country Park

Milton Country Park offers fine walking and exploring among acres of parkland, lakes and woods. There's a visitor centre, a picnic area and a place serving light refreshments.

WATERBEACH
6 miles NE of Cambridge on the A10

🏛 Denny Abbey 🏛 Farmland Museum

Denny Abbey, easily accessible on the A10, is an English Heritage Grade I listed Abbey with ancient earthworks. On the same site, and run as a joint attraction, is the **Farmland Museum**. The history of Denny Abbey runs

from the 12th century, when it was a Benedictine monastery. It was later home to the Knights Templar, Franciscan nuns of the Poor Clares order and the Countess of Pembroke, and from the 16th century was a farmhouse. The old farm buildings have been splendidly renovated and converted to tell the story of village life and Cambridgeshire farming up to modern times. The museum is ideal for family outings, with plenty of hands-on activities for children and a play area, gift shop and weekend tearoom.

LODE
6 miles NE of Cambridge on the B1102

🏛 Anglesey Abbey

Anglesey Abbey dates from 1600 and was built on the site of an Augustinian priory, but the house and the 100-acre garden came together as a unit thanks to the vision of the 1st Lord Fairhaven. His mother was American, his father English, and when he left the Abbey to the National Trust in the 1960s he wanted the house and garden to be kept to 'represent an age and way of life that is quickly passing'. The garden, created in its present form from 1926, is a wonderful place for a stroll, with 98 acres of landscaped gardens including wide grassy walks, open

Anglesey Abbey, Lode

churchyard and two fine old windmills. The churches of St Mary and St Cyriac stand side by side, a remarkable and dramatic sight in the steeply rising churchyard. St Mary's became the parish church, but St Cyriac's has the ring of six bells in its handsome octagonal bell tower. One of the mills, a restored 1850s tower mill, still produces flour and can be visited by appointment.

At Swaffham Bulbeck, a little way to the south, stands another church of St Mary, with a 13th-century tower and 14th-century arcades and chancel. Look for the fascinating carvings on the wooden benches and a 15th-century cedarwood chest decorated with biblical scenes.

lawns, a riverside walk and one of the finest collections of garden statuary in the country. Lode Mill is a working watermill that runs on the first and third Saturdays of each month. There's also a plant centre, shop and restaurant. In the house itself is Lord Fairhaven's magnificent collection of paintings (a seascape by Gainsborough, landscapes by Claude Lorraine), sumptuous furnishings, tapestries, Ming porcelain and clocks.

BOTTISHAM
5 miles E of Cambridge on the A1303

🏠 Holy Trinity Church

John Betjeman ventured that Bottisham's **Holy Trinity Church** was 'perhaps the best in the county', so time should certainly be made for a visit. Among the many interesting features are the 13th-century porch, an 18th-century monument to Sir Roger Jenyns and some exceptionally fine modern woodwork in Georgian style.

SWAFFHAM PRIOR
8 miles NE of Cambridge on the B1102

Swaffham Prior gives double value to the visitor, with two churches in the same

REACH
8 miles NE of Cambridge off the A4280

The charming village of Reach is home to the oldest fair in England, which celebrated its 800th anniversary on 1st May, 2000.

BURWELL
10 miles NE of Cambridge on the B1102

🏠 Church of St Mary 🏛 Museum 🏰 Devil's Dyke

Burwell is a village of many attractions with a history going back to Saxon times. **Burwell Museum** reflects many aspects of a village on the edge of the Fens up to the middle of the 20th century: a general store, model farm, local industries and children's toys are among the displays.

Next to the museum is the famous Stephens Windmill, built in 1820 and extensively restored.

🎬 stories and anecdotes 🐦 famous people 🎨 art and craft 🖊 entertainment and sport 🚶 walks

The man who designed parts of King's College Chapel, Reginald Ely, is thought to have been responsible for the beautiful **St Mary's Church**, which is built of locally quarried clunch stone and is one of the finest examples of the Perpendicular style. Notable internal features include a 15th-century font, a medieval wall painting of St Christopher, and roof carvings of elephants, while in the churchyard, a gravestone marks the terrible night in 1727 when 78 Burwell folk died in a barn fire while watching a travelling Punch & Judy show.

Behind the church are the remains of Burwell Castle, started in the 12th century but never properly completed.

The **Devil's Dyke** runs through Burwell on its path from Reach to Woodditton. This amazing dyke, 30 yards wide, was built, it is thought, to halt Danish invaders.

LINTON
10 miles SE of Cambridge on the B1052

🏛 Bartlow Hills 🐾 Zoo

The village is best known for its zoo, but visitors will also find many handsome old buildings and the church of St Mary the Virgin, built mainly in Early English style.

A world of wildlife set in 16 acres of spectacular gardens, **Linton Zoo** is a major wildlife breeding centre and part of the inter-zoo breeding programme for endangered species. Collections include wild

cats, birds, snakes and insects. For children there is a play area and, in summer, pony rides and a bouncy castle.

Chilford Hall Vineyard, on the B1052 between Linton and Balsham, comprises 18 acres of vines, with tours and wine-tastings available. Some two miles further off the A1307, **Bartlow Hills** are the site of the largest Roman burial site to be unearthed in Europe.

DUXFORD
8 miles S of Cambridge off A505 by J10 of the M11

📷 Duxford Aviation Museum 🏛 St John's Church

Part of the Imperial War Museum, **Duxford Aviation Museum** is Europe's premier aviation heritage complex, with an outstanding collection of 200 historic aircraft, more than 60 of which are in airworthy condition. First World War bi-planes join with the Lancaster, Concorde, Gulf War jets and the SR-71 Blackbird spyplane in this extraordinary collection, which is located on a former key Battle of Britain airfield.

Imperial War Museum, Duxford

The American Air Museum, where many of the aircraft are suspended as if in flight, is part of this terrific place, and the centrepiece of this part of the complex is a B-29A Suprefortress, the only example of its kind outside the United States. Major air shows take place several times a year, and among the permanent features are a reconstructed wartime operations room, a hands-on exhibition for children, and a dramatic land warfare hall with tanks, military vehicles and artillery. Everyone should take time to see this marvellous show - and it should be much more than a flying visit! But it can actually be just that, as Classic Wings offer visitors the chance to fly over Duxford in an elegant 1930s de Havilland Rapide. Next to the green, the Church of St John features many striking wall paintings and some exquisite carvings.

At nearby Hinxton, a few miles further south, is another mill: a 17th-century water mill that is grinding once more.

SHEPRETH

8 miles S of Cambridge off the A10

🐦 Nature Reserve   🐦 Wildlife Park

🐦 Docwra's Manor

A paradise for lovers of nature and gardens and a great starting point for country walks, **Shepreth L Moor Nature Reserve** is an L-shaped area of wet meadowland - now a rarity - that is home to birds and many rare plants. The nearby Shepreth **Wildlife Park** is a haven in natural surroundings to a wide variety of animals, which visitors can touch and feed. The 18th-century **Docwra's Manor** is a series of enclosed gardens with multifarious plants that is worth a visit at any time of year. Fowlmere, on the other side of the A10, is another important nature reserve, with hides and trails for the serious bird-watcher.

GRANTCHESTER

2 miles SW of Cambridge off the A603

🐦 Paradise Nature Reserve   🍵 The Orchard

A pleasant walk by the Cam, or a leisurely punt on it, brings visitors from the bustle of Cambridge to the famous village of Grantchester, where Rupert Brooke lived and Byron swam. The walk passes through **Paradise Nature Reserve**.

Rupert Brooke, who spent two happy years at Grantchester, immortalised afternoon tea at **The Orchard** and wrote of his love of the place in a poem while staying in Berlin.

> *God! I will pack, and take a train,*
> *And get me to England once again!*
> *For England's the one land I know,*
> *Where men with splendid hearts may go;*
> *And Cambridgeshire, of all England,*
> *The shire for men who understand;*
> *And of that district I prefer*
> *The lovely hamlet of Grantchester.*

And of the afternoon tea experience:

> *Stands the church clock at ten to three*
> *And is there honey still for tea?*

The Orchard, first planted in 1868, became a tea garden by chance in 1897 when a group of Cambridge students asked the owner, a Mrs Stevenson, if she could serve them tea under the trees in the orchard rather than on the front lawn. So started a great tradition that continues to this day. Brooke died at sea in 1915 on his way to the Dardanelles and is buried on the island of Scyros.

Time should also be allowed in Grantchester for a look at the Church of St Andrew and St Mary, in which the remains of a Norman church have been incorporated into the 1870s main structure.

BARTON
3 miles SW of Cambridge off the A603

Looking south from this pleasant village you can see the impressive array of radio telescopes that are part of Cambridge University's Mullard Radio Astronomy Observatory.

ARRINGTON
11 miles SW of Cambridge off the A603

🏛 Wimpole Hall   🌱 Wimpole Home Farm

🏃 Wimpole Park

Arrington's 18th-century **Wimpole Hall**, bequeathed to the National Trust by Elsie Bambridge, a daughter of Rudyard Kipling, is probably the most spectacular country mansion in the whole county, and certainly the largest 18th-century country house in Cambridgeshire. The lovely interiors are the work of several celebrated architects, and there's a fine collection of furniture and pictures. The magnificent, formally laid-out grounds include a Victorian parterre, a rose garden and a walled garden.

Landscaped **Wimpole Park**, with hills, woodland, lakes and a Chinese bridge, provides miles of wonderful walking and is perfect for anything from a gentle stroll to a strenuous hike.

A brilliant attraction for all the family is **Wimpole Home Farm**, a working farm that is the largest rare breeds centre in East Anglia. The animals include Bagot goats, Tamworth pigs, Soay sheep and Longhorn cattle, and there's also a pets corner, mini pedal tractors and a horse-drawn wagon ride. Children will happily spend hours with the animals or in the adventure playground.

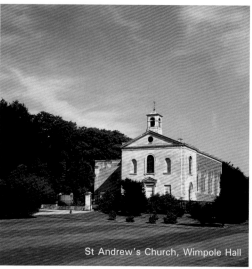
St Andrew's Church, Wimpole Hall

CAXTON
6 miles W of Cambridge off the A12198/A428

Caxton is home to Britain's oldest surviving post mill, and at Little Gransden, a couple of miles further southwest on the B1046, another venerable mill has been restored. A scheduled ancient monument, it dates from the early 17th century and was worked well into the early years of the 20th century.

MADINGLEY
4 miles W of Cambridge on the A428

🏛 American Cemetery

The **American Cemetery** is one of the loveliest, most peaceful and most moving places in the region, a place of pilgrimage for the families of the American servicemen who operated from the many wartime bases in the county. The cemetery commemorates 3,811 dead and 5,125 missing in action in the Second World War.

🏛 historic building 🏛 museum and heritage 🏚 historic site ⚜ scenic attraction 🌱 flora and fauna

Madingley Hall is a Tudor mansion set in a Capability Brown garden. It was leased in 1861 by Queen Victoria and Prince Albert for the use of their son the Prince of Wales during his brief spell as an undergraduate. The Hall was acquired by Cambridge University in 1948.

Huntingdon

🏠 Hinchingbrooke House 📷 Cromwell Museum

🚶 Spring Common 🌳 Hinchingbrooke Country Park

⛪ All Saints Church ⛪ St Mary's Church

The former county town of Huntingdonshire is an ancient place first settled by the Romans. It boasts many grand Georgian buildings, including the handsome three-storeyed Town Hall.

Oliver Cromwell was born in Huntingdon in 1599 and attended Huntingdon Grammar School. The schoolhouse was originally part of the Hospital of St John the Baptist, founded during the reign of Henry II by David, Earl of Huntingdon. Samuel Pepys was also a pupil here.

Cromwell was MP for Huntingdon in the Parliament of 1629, was made a JP in 1630 and moved to St Ives in the following year. Rising to power as an extremely able military commander in the Civil War, he raised troops from the region and made his headquarters in the Falcon Inn.

Appointed Lord Protector in 1653, Cromwell was ruler of the country until his death in 1658. The school he attended is now the **Cromwell Museum**, located on Huntingdon High Street, housing the only public collection relating specifically to him, with exhibits that reflect many aspects of his political, social and religious life. The museum's exhibits include an extensive collection of Cromwell family portraits and personal objects, among them a hat and seal, contemporary coins and medals, an impressive Florentine cabinet - the gift of the Grand Duke of Tuscany - and a surgeon's chest made by Kolb of Augsburg. This fine collection helps visitors interpret the life and legacy of Cromwell and the Republican movement.

All Saints Church, opposite the Cromwell Museum, displays many architectural styles, from medieval to Victorian. One of the two surviving parish churches of Huntingdon, All Saints was considered to be the church of the Hinchingbrooke part of the Cromwell family, though no memorials survive to attest to this. The Cromwell family burial vault is contained within the church, however, and it is here that Oliver's father Robert and his grandfather Sir Henry are buried. The church has a fine chancel roof, a very lovely organ chamber, a truly impressive stained-glass window and the font in which Cromwell was baptised - the old font from the destroyed St John's Church, discovered in a local garden in 1927.

Huntingdon's other church, **St Mary's**, dates from Norman times, but was almost completely rebuilt in the 1400s. It boasts a fine Perpendicular west tower, which partially collapsed in 1607. The damage was extensive, and the tower was not completely repaired until 1621. Oliver Cromwell's father, Robert, contributed to the cost of the repairs, as recorded on the stone plaque fixed to the east wall of the nave, north of the chancel arch.

Cowper House (No 29 High Street) has an impressive early 18th-century frontage. A plaque commemorates the fact that the poet William Cowper (pronounced 'Cooper') lived here between 1765 and 1767.

Among Huntingdon's many fine former

coaching inns is The George Hotel. Although badly damaged by fire in 1865, the north and west wings of the 17th-century courtyard remain intact, as does its very rare wooden gallery. The inn was one of the most famous of all the posting houses on the old Great North Run. It is reputed that Dick Turpin used one of the rooms here. The medieval courtyard, gallery and open staircase are the scene of annual productions of Shakespeare.

Along the south side of the Market Square, the Falcon Inn dates back in parts to the 1500s. Oliver Cromwell is said to have used this as his headquarters during the Civil War. In October 2008 Huntingdon celebrated 50 years of success for the motor company of Lola, which has won races in Formula One, Champ Cars and IndyCars. Many of the 4,000

cars produced by Lola joined a parade on October 12th.

About half a mile southwest of town stands **Hinchingbrooke House**, which today is a school but has its origins in the Middle Ages when it was a nunnery (ghostly nuns are said to haunt the building to this day). The remains of the Benedictine nunnery can still be seen. It was given to the Cromwell family by Henry VIII in 1538. Converted by the Cromwell family in the 16th century and later extended by the Earls of Sandwich, today's visitors can see examples of every period of English architecture from the 12th to early 20th centuries. King James I was a regular visitor, and Oliver Cromwell spent part of his childhood here. The 1st Earl of Sandwich was a central figure in the Civil War and subsequent

JOHNSON'S OF OLD HURST

Church Farm, Church St, Old Hurst, Huntingdon, Cambridgeshire, PE28 3AF
Tel: 01487 824658

Johnson's of Old Hurst is a paradise of quality and service. At Johnson's they have been producing meat for over 100 years and their animals are still reared in the traditional manner. They have their own butchery on the farm and you can be assured that they are fanatical about the quality of preparation and trimming. You would need to go a long way to find anyone else with such an intimate knowledge of the meat they were preparing. Available are home and local farm reared beef, pork, lamb, poultry, game, venison and ostrich.

The farm makes for a great day out, many of the animals are on view to the public, there is an animal corner where children are encouraged to mix with the livestock, and as of autumn 2008, you can enjoy a traditional afternoon tea in the new tearoom and gardens.

What's more, this traditional farm is not afraid to pilot a truly unique venture in the UK, establishing a fully working crocodile farm. Andy Johnson has several crocodiles for breeding stock, including one that is 9ft long! Crocodile can be eaten as a meat steak or even spare ribs; 'It's white, low fat meat with the grain of fish. Some people say it is similar to chicken, but it's not, it tastes of crocodile,' says Andy. A new crocodile enclosure should be completed in 2009 and this will put the crocodiles on view for the public for the first time. Watch this space!

▥ historic building ▣ museum and heritage ▥ historic site ⊕ scenic attraction ♣ flora and fauna

Restoration, while the 4th Earl (inventor of the lunchtime favourite that bears his name) was one of the most flamboyant politicians of the 18th century. The house is open for guided tours, including lovely cream teas served in the Tudor kitchens.

Hinchingbrooke Country Park covers 180 acres of grassy meadows, mature woodland, ponds and lakes. There is a wide variety of wildlife including woodpeckers, herons, kestrels, butterflies and foxes. The network of paths makes exploring the park easy, and battery-powered wheelchairs are provided for less able visitors. The Visitors' Centre serves refreshments at peak times.

Half a mile north, **Spring Common** offers another chance to enjoy some marvellous Cambridgeshire countryside. Covering 13 acres, its name comes from the natural spring that runs constantly and has long been a gathering place. The town developed around, rather than within, this area of rural tranquillity, which boasts a range of diverse habitats including marsh, grassland, scrub and streams. Plant life abounds, providing food and shelter for a variety of animals, amphibians, birds and invertebrates.

Ramsey Abbey, Ramsey

Around Huntingdon

HARTFORD
½ mile N of Huntington off the B1514

At just half a mile from Hartford Marina, this lovely village offers plenty of excellent riverside walks.

WARBOYS
7 miles NE of Huntingdon off the B1040

An interesting walk from Warboys to Ramsey takes in a wealth of history and pretty scenery. St Mary Magdalene's Church has a tall, very splendid tower.

RAMSEY
9 miles NE of Huntingdon on the B1040

🏛 Abbey 🏛 Rural Museum
🏛 Church of St Thomas à Becket of Canterbury

A pleasant market town with a broad main street down which a river once ran, Ramsey is home to the medieval Ramsey Abbey, founded in AD969 by Earl Ailwyn as a Benedictine monastery. The **Abbey** became one of the most important in England in the 12th and 13th centuries, and as it prospered, so did Ramsey, so that by the 13th century it had become a town with a weekly market and an annual three-day festival at the time of the feast of St Benedict. After the Dissolution of the Monasteries in 1539, the Abbey and its lands were sold to Sir Richard Williams, great-grandfather of Oliver Cromwell. Most of the buildings were then

🎬 stories and anecdotes 🐦 famous people ✂ art and craft ✐ entertainment and sport 🚶 walks

Ramsey Rural Museum

The Woodyard, Wood Lane, Ramsey, Huntingdon,
Cambridgeshire PE26 2XD
Tel: 01487 815715

The museum is housed in 17th-century farm buildings
and is set in open countryside on the edge of a friendly
market town. So why not step back in time and find out
how life was lived in small fenland community.

Find out how your medicines would have been prepared in the chemists shop and how
shoes would have been repaired in the clothes shop. How would you have managed in the
war? Would you have liked to wear a gas mask? Step inside some Victorian Rooms and find
out how mothers managed without running water or electricity.

What sort of job would your father have had? Perhaps he would have worked on a farm,
cut peat or dug ditches. Would he have been a blacksmith or a thatcher?

Researching your family history? The local family history archive includes: monumental
inscriptions, photographs, census returns, maps, births, deaths, marriages, documents and
land deeds. Microfiche readers and a photocopying service are available

demolished, the stones being used to build
Caius, King's and Trinity Colleges at
Cambridge, the towers of Ramsey,
Godmanchester and Holywell churches, the
gate at Hinchingbrooke House and several
local properties. In 1938 the house was
converted for use as a school, which it
remains to this day.

To the northwest are the ruins of the once
magnificent stone gatehouse of the late 15th
century - only the porter's lodge remains, but
inside can be seen an unusual, large carved
effigy made of Purbeck marble and dating back
to the 14th century. It is said to represent Earl
Ailwyn, founder of the Abbey. The gatehouse,
now in the care of the National Trust, can be
visited daily from April to October.

The **Church of St Thomas à Becket of
Canterbury** forms an impressive vista at the
end of the High Street. Dating back to about
1180, it is thought to have been built as a
hospital or guesthouse for the Abbey. It was
converted to a church to accommodate the

many pilgrims who flocked to Ramsey in the
13th century. The church has what is reputed
to be the finest nave in Huntingdonshire,
dating back to the 12th century and consisting
of seven bays. The church's other treasure is a
15th-century carved oak lectern, thought to
have come from the Abbey.

Most of **Ramsey Rural Museum** (see
panel above) is housed in an 18th-century
farm building and several barns set in open
countryside. Among the many fascinating
things to see here are a Victorian home and
school, a village store, and restored farm
equipment, machinery, carts and wagons. The
wealth of traditional implements used by local
craftsmen such as the farrier, wheelwright,
thatcher, dairyman, animal husbandman and
cobbler offer an insight into bygone days.

The unusual Ramsey War Memorial is a
listed Grade II memorial consisting of a fine
bronze statue of St George slaying the dragon
atop a tall, octagonal pillar crafted of
Portland stone.

🏛 historic building 🏛 museum and heritage 🏛 historic site 🍃 scenic attraction 🌱 flora and fauna

UPWOOD
8 miles NE of Huntingdon off the B1040

🐦 Woodwalton Fen 🐦 The Great Fen Project

🐦 Holme Fen National Nature Reserve

Upwood is a pleasant, scattered village in a very tranquil and picturesque setting. **Woodwalton Fen** nature reserve, reached from Chapel Road, covers 208 hectares and comprises wildflower meadows, reed beds and woodland and hosts a vast range of wildlife, including almost half of Britain's dragonfly species. It is at the southern end of **The Great Fen Project**, which will connect with **Holme Fen National Nature Reserve** to create a 3,700 hectare wetland between Huntingdon and Peterborough. It will provide a haven for wildlife and a massive green space for people, creating new opportunities for recreation, education and business. Follow progress on the website: www.greatfen.org.uk.

SAWTRY
8 miles NW of Huntingdon on the A1

The main point of interest here has no point! All Saints Church, built in 1880, lacks both tower and steeple, and is topped instead by a bellcote. Inside the church are marvellous brasses and pieces from ancient Sawtry Abbey.

Just south of Sawtry, Aversley Wood is a conservation area with abundant birdlife and plants.

HAMERTON
9 miles NW of Huntingdon off the A1

🐦 Zoological Park

Hamerton **Zoological Park** has hundreds of animals from tortoises to tigers. Specially designed enclosures make for unrivalled views of the animals, and the park features meerkats, marmosets and mongooses, lemurs, gibbons,

possums and sloths, snakes and even creepy-crawlies such as cockroaches.

STILTON
12 miles NW of Huntingdon off the A1

Stilton has an interesting high street with many fine buildings, and is a good choice for the hungry or thirsty visitor, as it has been since the heyday of horse-drawn travel. Journeys were a little more dangerous then, and Dick Turpin is said to have hidden at the Bell Inn.

ELLINGTON
4 miles W of Huntingdon off the A14

Ellington is a quiet village just south of the A14 and about a mile north of Grafham Water. Both Cromwell and Pepys visited, having relatives living in the village, and it was in Ellington that Pepys' sister Paulina found a husband, much to the relief of the diarist, who had written: 'We must find her one, for she grows old and ugly.' All Saints Church is magnificent, like so many in the area, and among its many fine features are the 15th-century oak roof and the rich carvings in the nave and the aisles. The church and its tower were built independently.

WOOLLEY
5 miles W of Huntingdon off the A1/A14

This quiet and secluded hamlet attracts a broad spectrum of visitors including anglers, golfers, walkers and riders, drawn by its lush and picturesque beauty and rural tranquillity.

SPALDWICK
6 miles W of Huntingdon off the A14

A sizable village that was once the site of the Bishop of Lincoln's manor house, Spaldwick boasts the grand church of St James, which dates from the 12th century and has seen restoration in most centuries, including the 20th, when the spire had to be partly rebuilt after being struck by lightning. Two miles further west, Catworth is another charming village, regularly voted Best Kept Village in Cambridgeshire and well worth exploring.

BARHAM
6 miles W of Huntingdon off the A1/A14

This delightful hamlet boasts 12 houses, 30 people and an ancient church with box pews, surrounded by undulating farmland. Nearby attractions include angling and sailing on Grafham Water, go-karting at Kimbolton and National Hunt racing at Huntingdon.

KEYSTON
12 miles W of Huntingdon off the A14

🏛 Church of St John the Baptist

A delightful village with a pedigree that can be traced back to the days of the Vikings, Keyston has major attractions both sacred and secular: the **Church of St John the Baptist** is impressive in its almost cathedral-like proportions, with one of the most magnificent spires in the whole county, while The Pheasant is a well-known and very distinguished pub-restaurant.

BRAMPTON
2 miles SW of Huntingdon off the A1

Brampton is where Huntingdon Racecourse is situated. An average of 18 meetings (all jumping) are scheduled every year; in November, the Grade II Peterborough Chase is the feature race.

Brampton's less speculative attractions include the 13th-century church of St Mary, and Pepys House, the home of Samuel's uncle, who was a cousin of Lord Sandwich and who got Samuel his job at the Admiralty.

GRAFHAM
5 miles SW of Huntingdon on the B661

🌱 🏕 Grafham Water

Created in the mid-1960s as a reservoir, **Grafham Water** offers a wide range of outdoor activities for visitors of all ages, with 1,500 acres of beautiful countryside, including the lake itself. The 10-mile perimeter track is great for jogging or cycling, and there's excellent sailing, windsurfing and fly-fishing.

The area is a Site of Special Scientific Interest, and an ample nature reserve at the western edge is run jointly by Anglian Water and the Wildlife Trust. There are nature trails, information boards, a wildlife garden and a dragonfly pond. Many species of waterfowl stay here at various times of the year, and bird-watchers have the use of six hides, three of them accessible to wheelchairs. An exhibition centre has displays and video presentations of the reservoir's history, a gift shop and a café.

KIMBOLTON
8 miles SW of Huntingdon on the B645

🏛 Castle

History aplenty here, and a lengthy pause is in order to look at all the interesting buildings. St Andrew's Church would head the list were it not for **Kimbolton Castle**, which, along with its gatehouse, dominates the village. Parts of the original Tudor building are still to be seen, but the appearance of the castle today owes much to the major remodelling carried out by Vanbrugh and Nicholas Hawksmoor in the first decade of the 18th century. The gatehouse was added by Robert Adam in 1764. Henry VIII's first wife, Katherine of Aragon, spent the last 18 months of her life imprisoned here, where she died in 1536. The castle is now a school, but can be visited on certain days in the summer (don't miss the Pellegrini murals).

BUCKDEN

4 miles SW of Huntingdon on the A1

🏛 Buckden Towers

This historic village was an important coaching stop on the old Great North Road. It is known particularly as the site of **Buckden Towers**, the great palace built for the Bishops of Lincoln. In the splendid grounds are the 15th-century gatehouse and the tower where Henry VIII imprisoned his first wife, Katherine of Aragon, in 1533 (open only on certain days of the year).

LITTLE PAXTON

8 Miles SW of Huntingdon off the A1

🐦 Paxton Pits Nature Reserve

Fewer than three miles north of St Neots at Little Paxton, is **Paxton Pits Nature Reserve**. Created alongside gravel workings, the Reserve attracts thousands of water birds, which visitors can observe from hides. The wealth of wildlife means that the area is

Buckden Towers, Buckden

an SSSI (Site of Special Scientific Interest) and ensures a plethora of colour and activity all year round. The site also features nature trails and a visitors' centre. It has

Paxton Pits Nature Reserve

High Street, Little Paxton, Huntingdon, Cambridgeshire, PE10 6ET
Tel: 01480 406795

At **Paxton Pits Nature Reserve** you can enjoy peaceful and gentle strolls as well as longer walks through 75 hectares of lakes, meadow, grassland, scrub and woodland. As well as the Heron and Meadow Trails, the River Trail, and some of the Permissive paths surrounding Paxton Pits are also waymarded. The permissive paths are not part of the reserve but the landowners have given permission for them to be used.

🎬 stories and anecdotes 🐦 famous people 🎨 art and craft 🎭 entertainment and sport 🚶 walks

thousands of visiting waterfowl, including one of the largest colonies of cormorants, and is particularly noted for its wintering wildfowl, nightingales in late spring and kingfishers. There are about four miles of walks, some suitable for wheelchairs. Spring and summer also bring a feast of wild flowers, butterflies and dragonflies.

St Neots Museum, St Neots

Just north again is the Great Paxton church, originally a Saxon Minster.

ST NEOTS

10 miles SW of Huntingdon off the A1

🏛 Church of St Mary the Virgin 🏛 Museum

🏛 Market Square

St Neots dates back to the founding of a Saxon Priory, built on the outskirts of Eynesbury in AD974. Partially destroyed by the Danes in 1010, it was re-established as a Benedictine Priory in about 1081 by St Anselm, Abbot of Bec and later Archbishop of Canterbury. For the next two centuries the Priory flourished. Charters were granted by Henry I to hold fairs and markets. The first bridge over the Great Ouse, comprising 73 timber arches, was built in 1180. The name of the town comes from the Cornish saint whose remains were interred in the Priory some time before the Norman Conquest. With the Dissolution of the Monasteries, the Priory was demolished. In the early 17th century, the old bridge was replaced by a stone one. This was then the site of a battle between the Royalists and Roundheads in 1648 - an event sometimes re-enacted by Sealed Knot societies.

St Neots repays a visit on foot, since there are many interesting sites and old buildings tucked away. The famous **Market Square** is one of the largest and most ancient in the country. A market has been held here every Thursday since the 12th century. In the centre of the square is the Day Column, a cast-iron structure erected in 1822 by John Day, a local brewer, to enhance the square and to provide lighting. The magnificent parish **Church of St Mary the Virgin**, Eynesbury, is a very fine edifice, known locally as the Cathedral of Huntingdonshire. It is an outstanding example of Late Medieval architecture. The gracious interior complements the 130-foot Somerset-style tower, with a finely carved oak altar, excellent Victorian stained-glass and a Holdich organ, built in 1855. James Toller, known as the 'Eynesbury Giant', was reputed to be 8ft 6in tall when he died in 1818 at the age of 20. He was buried beneath the font to avoid the attention of body-snatchers.

St Neots Museum - opened in 1995 - tells the story of the town and the surrounding area. Housed in the former magistrates' court and police station, it still has the original cells. Eye-catching displays trace local history from prehistoric times to the present day. Open Tuesday to Saturday.

🏛 historic building 🏛 museum and heritage 🏛 historic site 🜨 scenic attraction 🦋 flora and fauna

BUSHMEAD

12 Miles SW of Huntingdon off the B660

The remains of Bushmead Abbey, once a thriving Augustinian community, are well worth a visit. The garden setting is delightful, and the surviving artefacts include some interesting stained-glass. Open weekends in July and August.

GODMANCHESTER

2 miles SE of Huntingdon off the A1

🏛 Island Hall 🐾 Wood Green Animal Shellter

🐾 Port Holme Meadow

Godmanchester is linked to Huntingdon by a 14th-century bridge across the River Ouse. It was a Roman settlement and one that continued in importance down the years, as the number of handsome buildings testifies. One such is **Island Hall**, a mid-18th-century mansion built for John Jackson, the Receiver General for Huntingdon; it contains many interesting pieces. This family home has lovely Georgian rooms, with fine period detail and fascinating possessions relating to the owners' ancestors since their first occupation of the house in 1800. The tranquil riverside setting and formal gardens add to the peace and splendour - the house takes its name from the ornamental island that forms part of the grounds. Octavia Hill was sometimes a guest, and wrote effusively to her sister that Island Hall was 'the loveliest, dearest old house, I never was in such a one before.' Open only to pre-booked groups.

Wood Green Animal Shelter at Kings Bush Farm, Godmanchester is a purpose-built, 50-acre centre open to the public all year round. Cats, dogs, horses, donkeys, farm animals, guinea pigs, rabbits, llamas, wildfowl and pot-bellied pigs are among the many creatures for visitors to see, and there is a specially adapted nature trail and restaurant.

St Mary's Church is Perpendicular in style, though not totally in age, as the tower is a 17th century replacement of the 13th century original. A footpath leads from the famous Chinese Bridge (1827) to **Port Holme Meadow**, at 225 acres one of the largest in England and the site of Roman remains. It is a Site of Special Scientific Interest, with a huge diversity of botanical and bird species. Huntingdon racecourse was once situated here, and it was a training airfield during the

---

MONACH FARM RIDING STABLES

The Green, Hilton, Huntingdon, Cambridgeshire PE28 9NB
Tel: 01480 830426
e-mail: emy2@dialstart.net website: www.monachfarm.co.uk

An ABRS Approved yard, Pony Club Centre and NVQ outreach centre. It offers adult restart classes, takes children from 4 years of age and provides group and private tuition for all abilities. In the school holidays it offers a range of activity days. Wildlife walks and nature trails available on the farm's own land. Based on a working livestock farm with cattle, sheep, pigs and goats, as well as a Farm Shop selling traditional meat and Caprilatte ice cream.

MONACH FARM

Set on the picturesque village green, with one of only three turf mazes in the country and just a 20-minute drive from Cambridge city centre, Monach Farm is a unique rural experience.

🎭 stories and anecdotes 🦜 famous people 🎨 art and craft 🎟 entertainment and sport 🚶 walks

First World War. Another site of considerable natural activity is Godmanchester Pits, accessed along the Ouse Valley Way and home to a great diversity of flora and fauna.

PAPWORTH EVERARD
6 miles SE of Huntingdon on the A1198

One of the most recent of the region's churches, St Peter's dates mainly from the mid-19th century. Neighbouring Papworth St Agnes has an older church in St John's, though parts of that, too, are Victorian. Just up the road at Hilton is the famous Hilton Turf Maze, cut in 1660 to a popular medieval design.

BOXWORTH
7 miles SE of Huntingdon off the A14

🌱 Overhall Grove

A village almost equidistant from Huntingdon and Cambridge, and a pleasant base for touring the area, Boxworth's Church of St Peter is unusual in being constructed of pebble rubble.

A mile south of Boxworth is **Overhall Grove**, one of the largest elm woods in the country and home to a variety of wildlife.

The Great Ouse Valley

HEMINGFORD ABBOTS
3 miles SE of Huntingdon off the A14

🏚 Hemingford Grey Manor

Once part of the Ramsey Abbey Estate,

The Manor at Hemingford Grey, Hemingford Abbots

Hemingford Abbots is set around the 13th-century church of St Margaret, along the banks of the Great Ouse. Opportunities for angling and boating facilities, including rowing boats for hire, as well as swimming, country walks, golf and a recreation centre are all within a couple of miles. The village hosts a flower festival every two years.

Just to the east is Hemingford Grey, with its church on the banks of the Ouse. The **Manor at Hemingford Grey** is reputedly the oldest continuously inhabited house in England, built around 1130. Visits (by appointment only) will reveal all the treasures in the house and garden.

FENSTANTON
7 miles SE of Huntingdon off the A14 bypass

🏚 'Capability' Brown

Lancelot **'Capability' Brown** (1716-1783) was Lord of the Manor at Fenstanton from 1768, and served for a time as High Sheriff of Huntingdonshire. Born in Northumberland, Brown started his working life as a gardener's boy before moving on to Stowe, where he worked under William Kent.

🏚 historic building 🏛 museum and heritage 🏚 historic site ☘ scenic attraction 🌱 flora and fauna

When Kent died, Brown set up as a garden designer and soon became the leading landscape artist in England, known for the natural, unplanned appearance of his designs. His nickname arose from his habit of remarking, when surveying new projects, that the place had 'capabilities'. Brown, his wife and his son are buried in the medieval church. His grave is inscribed with a eulogy by the poet and landscape gardener William Mason. Any visit here should also take in the 17th-century manor house and the red-brick Clock Tower.

HOUGHTON
5 miles E of Huntingdon on the A1123

🏚 Houghton Mill

Houghton is a popular tourist destination thanks to its proximity to **Houghton Mill** and opportunities for riverside walks, as well as its charming thatched buildings and shops. Milling takes place on Sundays and Bank Holiday Mondays. Houghton Meadows is a Site of Special Scientific Interest, with an abundance of hay meadow species. One of the most popular walks in the whole area links Houghton with St Ives.

ST IVES
6 miles E of Huntingdon off the A1123

🏛 Norris Museum   🌱 Wilthorn Meadow

🌱 Holt Island Nature Reserve

This is an ancient town on the banks of the Great Ouse that once held a huge annual fair. The town's motto is 'sudore non sopore', meaning 'by work, not sleep' – a pun on Slepe, the town's original name. Its present name remembers St Ivo, said to be a Persian bishop who came here in the Dark Ages to spread a little light.

In the Middle Ages, kings bought cloth for their households at the village's great wool fairs and markets, and a market is still held here every Monday. The Bank Holiday Monday markets are particularly lively affairs, and the Michaelmas fair fills the town centre for three days.

Seagoing barges once navigated up to the famous six-arched bridge that was built in the 15th century and has a most unusual two-storey chapel in its middle. Oliver Cromwell lived in St Ives in the 1630s; Frederick Pomeroy's statue of him on Market Hill, with its splendid hat, is one of the village's most familiar landmarks. It was made in bronze with a Portland stone base, and was erected in 1901. It was originally designed for Huntingdon, but they wouldn't accept it! The Victoria Memorial marked the Queen's Diamond Jubilee in 1897, but it wasn't put up until 1902. The inscription on the side says that it was unveiled on June 26th, the day of Edward VII's coronation – but it wasn't. The coronation

St Ives Bridge & Chantry, St Ives

🎞 stories and anecdotes   🦅 famous people   🎨 art and craft   🎭 entertainment and sport   🚶 walks

DOLLS HOUSE NUMBER NINE

The Coach House, 9 The Broadway, St Ives,
Cambridgeshire PE27 5BX
Tel/Fax: 01480 464684
e-mail: dollshousenumber9@btinternet.com
website: www.dollshousenumbernine.co.uk

Established in 1990 as a model railway specialist, **Dolls House Number Nine** has expanded to include dolls' houses and miniatures, teddies, gollies, Scalextric sets and Airfix kits. In the Grade II listed building, the well laid-out displays include a wide range of hand-built MDF and birch ply houses, room boxes and conservatories. Houses can be made to order to specific designs. The shop can supply all dolls' house and miniature needs including furniture, wallpaper, carpeting, flooring, gardens, ponds, flowers, food and lighting. The shop is open from 9.15am to 5pm (by appointment only Thursday and Sunday).

was postponed because the king was ill, and the Memorial was unveiled a few days later, but no one got round to changing the inscription.

The beautiful parish church in its churchyard beside the river is well worth a visit. The quayside provides a tranquil mooring for holidaymakers and there are wonderful walks by the riverside.

Clive Sinclair developed his tiny TVs and pocket calculators in the town; another famous son of St Ives was the great Victorian rower John Goldie, whose name is remembered each year by the second Cambridge boat in the Boat Race.

The **Norris Museum**, in a delightful setting by the river, tells the story of Huntingdonshire for the past 175 million years or so, with everything from fossils, mammoth tusks and models of the great historic reptiles, through to flint tools, Roman artefacts and Civil War armour as well as lace-making and ice-skating displays, and contemporary works of art. A truly fascinating place that is open throughout the year, admission is free. Exhibitions include

a life-size replica of a 160-million-year-old ichthyosaur. There are remains of woolly mammoths from the Ice Age, tools and pottery from the Stone Age to Roman times, and relics from the medieval castles and abbeys. Also on show are toys and models made by prisoners of the Napoleonic Wars.

Just outside St Ives are **Wilthorn Meadow**, a Site of Natural History Interest where Canada geese are often to be seen, and **Holt Island Nature Reserve**, where high-quality willow is being grown to reintroduce the traditional craft of basket-making. Allow some time for spotting the butterflies, dragonflies and kingfishers.

BLUNTISHAM
3 miles NE of St Ives on the A1123

There's an impressive church here in Bluntisham, with a unique 14th-century chancel that ends in three sides. The rector here at one time was the father of Dorothy L Sayers (creator of nobleman sleuth Lord Peter Wimsey) and Dorothy once lived in the large Georgian rectory on the main road.

EARITH

4 miles E of St Ives on the A1123

🐦 Ouse Washes

The **Ouse Washes**, a special protection area, runs northeast from the village to Earith Pits, a well-known habitat for birds and crawling creatures; some of the pits are used for fishing. The Washes are a wetland of major international importance supporting such birds as ruffs, Bewick and Whooper swans, and hen harriers. The average bird population is around 20,000. Some of the meadows flood in winter, and ice-skating is popular when the temperature really drops. There's a great tradition of ice-skating in the Fens, and Fenmen were the national champions until the 1930s.

SOMERSHAM

4 miles NE of St Ives on the B1040/B1060

🐦 Raptor Foundation

The **Raptor Foundation** is located here, a major attraction where owls and other birds of prey find refuge. There are regular flying displays and falconry shows. Somersham

Peterborough Cathedral, Peterborough

once had a palace for the Bishops of Ely, and its splendid church of St John would have done them proud.

Peterborough

🏛 Cathedral 🏛 Museum 🏛 Railworld

🏛 Nene Valley Railway

🎨 Thorpe Meadows Sculpture Park

The second city of Cambridgeshire has a long and interesting history that can be traced back to the Bronze Age, as can be seen in the archaeological site at Flag Fen. Although a cathedral city, it is also a New Town (designated in 1967), so modern development and expansion have vastly increased its facilities, while retaining the quality of its historic heart.

Peterborough's crowning glory is, of course, the Norman **Cathedral**, built in the 12th and 13th centuries on a site that has seen Christian worship since AD655. Henry VIII made the church a cathedral, and his first queen, Katherine of Aragon, is buried here, as for a while was Mary Queen of Scots after her execution at Fotheringay. Features to note are the huge (85-foot) arches of the West Front, the unique painted wooden nave ceiling, some exquisite late 15th-century fan vaulting, and the tomb of Katherine.

Though the best-known of the city's landmarks, the Cathedral is by no means the only one. The Peterborough **Museum and Art Gallery** covers

PLANTATION

Oundle Road, Polebrook, Peterborough, PE8 5LQ
Tel 01832 274755   www.plantation.co.uk
e-mail: info@plantation.co.uk

Plantation is a new, independent plant centre located just outside the beautiful and historic market town of Oundle. It was purpose-built in 2006 and grows a broad range of plants and trees on its four acre site. With its all-wooden shop and inspirational plant displays it offers a refreshing and different experience for both keen gardeners, looking for specific plants, and new gardeners who want help and ideas in developing their garden.

Other products include pots and containers, topiary, hedging, grow your own kits, composts, seeds and organic pest controls. Plantation also offers garden consultation and encourages customers to bring along photos or drawings and will help in advising on suitable plants for space and use. Open days are held regularly with special events and courses running throughout the year. Please look at the website for details or call ahead.

In the shop you will find garden related gifts and tools. Refreshments and cream teas are available seasonally. Oundle hosts an international music festival, Festival of Literature and Farmers' Market and has a wide range of independent shops and activities. It is well worth a visit any time.

---

all aspects of the history of Peterborough from the Jurassic period to Victorian times.

There are twin attractions for railway enthusiasts in the shape of **Railworld**, a hands-on exhibition open daily dealing with modern rail travel, and the wonderful **Nene Valley Railway**, which operates 15-mile steam-hauled trips between Peterborough and its HQ and museum at Wansford. A feature on the main railway line at Peterborough is the historic Iron Bridge, part of the old Great Northern Railway and still virtually as built by Lewis Cubitt in 1852.

Just outside the city, by the river Nene, is **Thorpe Meadows Sculpture Park**, one of several open spaces in and around the city with absorbing collections of modern sculpture.

Around Peterborough

ELTON

6 miles SW of Peterborough on the B671

🏛 Elton Hall

Elton is a lovely village on the river Nene, with stone-built houses and thatched roofs. **Elton Hall** (see panel opposite) is a mixture of styles, with a 15th-century tower and chapel, with a major Gothic influence. The grandeur is slightly deceptive, as some of the battlements and turrets were built of wood to save money. The hall's sumptuous rooms are filled with art treasures (Gainsborough, Reynolds, Constable) and the library has a wonderful collection of antique tomes.

Elton Hall and Gardens

Nr Peterborough, Cambridgeshire PE8 6SH
Tel: 01832 280468
e-mail: office@eltonhall.com website: www.eltonhall.com

Elton Hall is an extraordinary, romantic, part Gothic house that has been in the Proby family since 1660. It lies at the heart of a 3,800-acre Estate made up of a mixture of property including farms, houses and cottages, commercial property and woodland. The Estate straddles the Cambridgeshire and Northamptonshire borders and is well located for access from the East and West along the A14 and A47 and is 86 miles north of London, just off the A1.

The Hall is a mixture of styles. The garden or south front incorporates the 15th century tower and chapel, which were built at the time of Henry VII. In the 17th century, a new wing was added to the west.

The garden you see today was laid out in 1913 with the construction of the paths, the lawns, the lily pond, the well-head and the rose garden wall. By 1980 a large part of the Edwardian garden had fallen into disrepair and since the early 1980s there has been a major restoration programme. The rose garden has been replanted and a new sunken garden, a shrub garden and an arboretum created.

The Gothic orangery was built to celebrate the Millennium and a Gothic arbour was completed to mark the Jubilee celebrations.

LONGTHORPE
2 miles W of Peterborough off the A47

🏛 Longthorpe Tower

Longthorpe Tower, part of a fortified manor house, is graced by some of the very finest 14th-century domestic wall paintings in Europe, featuring scenes both sacred and secular: the Nativity, the Wheel of Life, King David, the Labours of the Months. The paintings were discovered during renovations after the Second World War.

THORNHAUGH
8 miles NW of Peterborough off the A1/A47

🌱 Sacrewell Farm

Hidden away in a quiet valley is **Sacrewell**

Farm and Country Centre, whose centrepiece is a working watermill. All kinds of farming equipment are on display, and there's a collection of farm animals, along with gardens, nature trails and general interest trails, play areas, a gift shop and a restaurant serving light refreshments.

BURGHLEY
14 miles NW of Peterborough off the A1

🏛 Burghley House

The largest and grandest house of the Elizabethan Age, **Burghley House** presents a dazzling spectacle with its domed towers, walls of cream coloured stone, and acres of windows. Clear glass was still ruinously

🎬 stories and anecdotes 🦜 famous people 🎨 art and craft 🎭 entertainment and sport 🚶 walks

expensive in the 1560s, so Elizabethan grandees like Cecil flaunted their wealth by having windows that stretched almost from floor to ceiling. Burghley House also displays the Elizabethan obsession with symmetry - every tower, dome, pilaster and pinnacle has a corresponding partner.

Contemporaries called Burghley a 'prodigy house', a title shared at that time with only one other stately home in England - Longleat in Wiltshire. Both houses were indeed prodigious in size and in cost. At Burghley, Cecil commissioned the most celebrated interior decorator of the age, Antonio Verrio, to create rooms of unparalleled splendour. In his Heaven Room, Verrio excelled even himself, populating the lofty walls and ceiling with a dynamic gallery of mythological figures.

The 18 State Rooms at Burghley house a vast treasury of great works of art. The walls are crowded with 17th-century Italian paintings and Japanese ceramics, and rare examples of European porcelain grace every table, alcove and mantelpiece; the wood carvings of Grinling Gibbons and his followers add dignity to almost every room. Also on display are four magnificent state beds along with important tapestries and textiles.

In the 18th century, Cecil's descendants commissioned the ubiquitous Capability Brown to landscape the 160 acres of parkland surrounding the house. These enchanting grounds are open to visitors and are also home to a large herd of fallow deer, first established in Cecil's time. Brown also designed the elegant Orangery, which is now a licensed restaurant overlooking rose beds and gardens.

A more recent addition to Burghley's attractions is the Sculpture Garden. Twelve acres of scrub woodland have been reclaimed and planted with specimen trees and shrubs, and now provide a sylvan setting for a number of dramatic artworks by contemporary sculptors.

Throughout the summer season, Burghley hosts a series of events of which the best known, the Burghley Horse Trials, takes place at the end of August.

PEAKIRK
7 miles N of Peterborough off the A15

A charming little village, somewhat off the beaten track, Peakirk boasts a village church of Norman origin that is the only one in the country dedicated to St Pega, the remains of whose hermit cell can still be seen.

CROWLAND
10 miles NE of Peterborough off the A1073

🏠 Trinity Bridge 🏛 Abbey

It is hard to imagine that this whole area was once entirely wetland and marshland, dotted with inhospitable islands. Crowland was one such island, then known as Croyland; back in the 7th century, a small church and hermitage was established, which was later to become one of the nation's most important monasteries. The town's impressive parish church was just part of the great edifice thatonce stood on the site. A wonderful exhibition can be found in the **Abbey** at Crowland, open all year round. The remains cover a third of the Abbey's original extent.

Crowland's second gem is the unique **Trinity Bridge** - set in the centre of town on dry land. Erected in the 14th century, it has three arches built over one over-arching structure. Before the draining of the Fens, Trinity Bridge crossed the point where the River Welland divided into two streams.

Crowland Abbey, Crowland

the 19th century by the Dukes of Bedford. The main innovation was a 10,000-gallon water tank that supplied the whole village; other villages had to use unfiltered river water. Open Easter to the end of September.

FLAG FEN

2 miles E of Peterborough signposted from the A47 and A1139

🏛 Bronze Age Centre

Flag Fen **Bronze Age Centre** (see panel on page 342) comprises massive 3,000-year-old timbers that were part of a major settlement and have been preserved in peaty mud. The site includes a Roman road with its original surface, the oldest wheel in England, re-creations of a Bronze Age settlement, a museum of artefacts, rare breed animals, and a visitor centre with a shop and restaurant. Ongoing excavations, open to the public, make this one of the most important and exciting sites of its kind.

THORNEY

8 miles E of Peterborough on the A47

🏛 Abbey 🏛 Heritage Museum

Thorney Abbey, the Church of St Mary and St Botolph, is still a dominating presence, even though what now stands is but a small part of what was once one of the greatest of the Benedictine abbeys. Gravestones in the churchyard are evidence of a Huguenot colony that settled here after fleeing France in the wake of the St Bartholomew's Day massacre of 1572 to settle the drained fenland at the request of Oliver Cromwell.

The Thorney **Heritage Museum** is a small, independently-run museum of great fascination, describing the development of the village from a Saxon monastery, via Benedictine Abbey to a model village built in

WHITTLESEY

5 miles E of Peterborough off the A605

🏛 Museum 🎭 Straw Bear Procession

The market town of Whittlesey lies close to the western edge of the Fens and is part of one of the last tracts to be drained. Brick-making was a local speciality, and 180-foot brick chimneys stand as a reminder of that once-flourishing industry. The church of St Andrew is mainly 14th century, with a 16th-century tower; the chancel, chancel chapels and naves still have their original roofs.

A walk around this charming town reveals an interesting variety of buildings: brick, of course, and also some stone, thatch on timber frames, and rare thatched mud boundary walls.

The **Whittlesey Museum**, housed in the grand 19th-century Town Hall in Market

---

🎭 stories and anecdotes 🐦 famous people 🎨 art and craft 🚲 entertainment and sport 🚶 walks

Flag Fen Bronze Age Centre

The Droveway, Northey Road,
Peterborough, Cambridgeshire PE6 7QJ
Tel: 91733 313414 Fax: 01733 349957
e-mail: office@flagfen.co.uk
website: www.flagfen.com

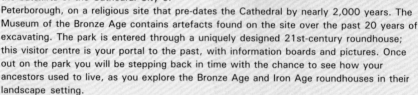

Flag Fen is one of Europe's most important Bronze Age sites; this archaeological jewel is situated on the outskirts of the Cathedral City of Peterborough, on a religious site that pre-dates the Cathedral by nearly 2,000 years. The Museum of the Bronze Age contains artefacts found on the site over the past 20 years of excavating. The park is entered through a uniquely designed 21st-century roundhouse; this visitor centre is your portal to the past, with information boards and pictures. Once out on the park you will be stepping back in time with the chance to see how your ancestors used to live, as you explore the Bronze Age and Iron Age roundhouses in their landscape setting.

The Preservation Hall contains undercover archaeology, along with a 60-metre mural depicting life in the Bronze Age in the Fens. During the summer months, archaeologists can often be seen at work, uncovering Peterborough's past.

Workshops and Lectures are among our full programme of events, which include Sword and Bronze Casting, Flint Knapping, Theatre in the Park, and our Annual big event, which attracts visitors from across the country. If you would like details please contact us.

Street, features an archive of displays on local archaeology, agriculture, geology, brick-making and more. Reconstructions include a 1950s corner shop and post office, blacksmith's forge and wheelwright's bench.

A highlight of Whittlesey's year is the **Straw Bear Procession** that is part of a four-day January festival. A man clad in a suit of straw dances and prances through the streets, calling at houses and pubs to entertain the townspeople. The origins are obscure: perhaps it stems from pagan times when corn gods were invoked to produce a good harvest; perhaps it is linked with the wicker idols used by the Druids; perhaps it derives from the performing bears that toured the villages until the 17th century. What is certain is that at the end of the jollities the straw suit is ceremoniously burned.

Whittlesey was the birthplace of the writer L P Hartley (*The Go-Between*) and of General Sir Harry Smith, hero of many 19th-century campaigns in India. He died in 1860, and the south chapel off St Mary's Church (note the beautiful spire) was restored and named after him.

MARCH
14 miles E of Peterborough off the A141

🏚 St Wendreda's Church　🏛 Museum

🏊 Nene-Ouse Navigation Link

March once occupied the second-largest 'island' in the great level of Fens. As the land was drained the town grew as a trading and religious centre, and in more recent times as a market town and major railway hub. **March and District Museum**, in the High Street, tells the story of the people and the history of

FOX NARROWBOATS

10 Marina Drive, March, Cambridgeshire PE15 0AU
Tel: 01354 652770
e-mail: reception@foxboats.co.uk
website: www.foxboats.co.uk

There can be few more relaxing ways to take a break from the daily routine than on a comfortable narrowboat, and the family business of **Fox Narrowboats** is among the leaders in its sphere. They built their first narrowboat in 1973 and four years later became hire fleet operators. In 1981 the business moved to a purpose-built marina with a capacity that has risen from 50 to 200 moorings. The Fox narrowboats, developed over 35 years, are solidly built and easy to control, with optimum use made of space. The exteriors are regularly maintained and painted in a stylish colour scheme. They are all Quality in Tourism 5-Star graded.

March and the surrounding area, and includes a working forge and a reconstruction of a turn-of-the-century house.

The uniquely dedicated **Church of St Wendreda**, at Town End, is notable for its magnificent timber roof, a double hammerbeam with 120 carved angels, a fine font and some impressive gargoyles. John Betjeman declared the church to be 'worth cycling 40 miles into a headwind to see'.

The **Nene-Ouse Navigation Link** runs through the town, affording many attractive riverside walks and, just outside the town off the B1099, Dunhams Wood comprises four acres of woodland. The site contains an enormous variety of trees, along with sculptures and a miniature railway.

STONEA
3 miles SE of March off the B1098

🏛 Stonea Camp

Stonea Camp is the lowest hill fort in Britain. Built in the Iron Age, it proved unsuccessful against the Romans. A listed ancient monument whose banks and ditches were restored after excavations in 1991, the site is also an increasingly important habitat for wildlife.

CHATTERIS
8 miles S of March off the A141

🏛 Museum

A friendly little market town, where the Chatteris **Museum and Council Chamber** features a series of interesting displays on Fenland life and the development of the town. Themes include education, agriculture, transport and local trades, along with temporary exhibitions and local photographs, all housed in five galleries.

The church of St Peter and St Paul has some 14th-century features but is mostly more modern in appearance, having been substantially restored in 1909.

Wisbech

🏛 Peckover House

🏛 Octavia Hill's Birthplace House

🏛 Elgoods Brewery 🏛 Wisbech & Fenland Museum

♔ Angles Theatre

One of the largest of the Fenland towns, a port in medieval times and still enjoying shipping trade with Europe, Wisbech is at the centre of a thriving agricultural region. The

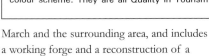

🎬 stories and anecdotes 🐦 famous people ♔ art and craft 🖋 entertainment and sport 🏃 walks

Wisbech

Distance: *3.1 miles (4.8 kilometres)*

Typical time: *120 mins*

Height gain: *5 metres*

Map: *Explorer 235*

Walk: *www.walkingworld.com ID:739*

Contributor: *Joy & Charles Boldero*

Bus service: ring the Tourist Information Centre in Wisbech on 01945 583263. There are several free car parks in the town. The walk starts from the large Love Lane car park off Alexandria Road, near the church.

DESCRIPTION:

Wisbech is an ancient port and has many historic buildings. There is a fine brass on the floor of St Peter and St Paul's Church of Thomas de Braustone, Constable of Wisbech Castle in the 1400s.

The Norman Castle was replaced by a Bishop's Palace in 1478, and in the 17th century this was replaced by a mansion house built for John Thurloe, who was Oliver Cromwell's Secretary of State. Later, this was replaced by the Georgian Crescent in 1816. Along New Inn Yard on the left is one of the oldest timber-framed buildings in the town.

Along South Brink on the left is the house where Octavia Hill was born, now a museum. She was one of the founder members of the National Trust. Along North Brink there are many old historic houses including the 18th-century Peckover House, owned by the NT. Elgood's Brewery has a museum; the brewery has functioned for the past 200 years. The Wisbech and Fenland Museum has many interesting items including the manuscript of *Great Expectations* by Charles Dickens.

FEATURES:

River, Pub, Toilets, Museum, Church, Castle, Stately Home, National Trust/NTS. Good for wheelchairs.

WALK DIRECTIONS:

1 | Turn right into Love Lane, going towards the church. At the church turn right, then left along the street that leads to the Market Place. Turn left into Market Street.

2 | At the T-junction, turn left around The Crescent. Turn right along High Street, then left along the alley, New Inn Yard. Turn left along River Nene Quay to the statue. Cross the road and continue along Post Office Lane, crossing the road to the car park. Cross the car park, keeping to the right-hand side. Turn right from the car park, then left along Somers Road and continue along Coal Wharf Road.

3 | Turn right at T-junction along South Brink with the river on the left. Cross road at traffic-lights, turn left along North Brink. Cross two roads. At Elgood's Brewery retrace your steps, crossing one road.

4 | Turn left along Chapel Road. Turn right up Exchange Square, then left at road, left again along Old Market. Cross the road and continue along North Street. Go over the river bridge and keep right beside it for a short distance.

5 | Cross the road and turn left signed Pedestrian Zone. Cross School Lane and turn right along Scrimshire's Passage. Turn left along Hall Street. Turn right by Boots the Chemist, cross the market square and go along Market Street opposite.

6 | Turn left, then left again going down steps. Turn right into Love Lane which leads to the car park.

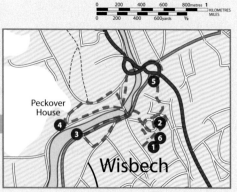

Georgian houses beside River Nene, Wisbech

overmantels, and ornate plaster decorations. At the back of the house is a beautiful walled garden with summer houses and an orangery with 300-year-old orange trees.

No 8 South Brink is the birthplace of Octavia Hill (1838-1912), co-founder of the National Trust and a tireless worker for the cause of the poor, particularly in the sphere of housing. The house is now **Octavia Hill's Birthplace House**, a museum with displays and exhibits commemorating her work.

18th century in particular saw the building of rows of handsome houses, notably in North Brink and South Brink, which face each other across the river. The finest of all the properties is undoubtedly **Peckover House**, built in 1722 and bought at the end of the 18th century by Jonathan Peckover, a member of the Quaker banking family. The family gave the building to the National Trust in 1948. Behind its elegant façade are splendid panelled rooms, Georgian fireplaces with richly carved

More Georgian splendour is evident in the area where the Norman castle once stood. The castle was replaced by a bishop's palace in 1478, and in the 17th century by a mansion built for Cromwell's Secretary of State, John Thurloe. Local builder Joseph Medworth built the present Regency villa in 1816; of the Thurloe mansion, only the gate piers remain.

The **Wisbech and Fenland Museum** is one of the oldest purpose-built museums in

📖 stories and anecdotes 🐦 famous people ✿ art and craft 🎭 entertainment and sport 🚶 walks

the country, and in charming Victorian surroundings visitors can view displays of porcelain, coins, rare geological specimens, Egyptian tomb treasures and several items of national importance, including the manuscript of Charles Dickens' *Great Expectations*, Napoleon's Sèvres breakfast set captured at Waterloo, and an ivory chess set that belonged to Louis XIV.

Wisbech is the stage for East Anglia's premier Church Flower Festival, with flowers in four churches, strawberry teas, crafts, bric-a-brac, plants and a parade of floats. The event takes place at the beginning of July. The most important of the churches is the Church of St Peter and St Paul, with two naves under one roof and an independent tower with a peal of 10 bells. Note the royal arms of James I and, in the north chancel, a mosaic by Salviati of Leonardo's Last Supper.

Another sight to see in Wisbech is **Elgoods Brewery** on the banks of the River Nene. Visitors can watch traditional brewing methods using original open copper vessels, before sampling a selection of Elgood's wide range of prize-winning real ales in the Visitors Centre bar. Behind the brewery is a four-acre garden incorporating specimen trees about 200 years old, herbaceous borders, a lake, rockery,

water features and lawns leading to a maze planted with thuja and laurel. Also well worth a look is the impressive 68-foot limestone memorial to Thomas Clarkson, one of the earliest leaders of the abolitionist movement. He was born in Wisbech, son of the headmaster of the Grammar School. The monument, which towers over Bridge Street, was designed by Sir George Gilbert Scott in Gothic style. Clarkson's tireless efforts in the campaign against slavery were finally recognized nationally in 1997, 150 years after his death, when a plaque was laid in his memory in Westminster Abbey.

Still a lively commercial port, Wisbech boasts a restored Marina and new facilities for small craft that include floating pontoons with berths for 75 yachts. River trips are available from the yacht harbour.

Elgoods Brewery and Gardens, Wisbech

Angles Theatre – one of the oldest working theatres in Britain – is a vibrant centre for the arts, located in a Georgian building with a history stretching back over 200 years. Some of the best talent in the nation, from poets and musicians to dance, comedy and theatrical troupes come to perform in the intimate 112-seat auditorium.

Wisbech's Lilian Ream Photographic Gallery is named after a daughter of Wisbech born in the late 19th century who, at the time of her death in 1961, had amassed a collection of over 1,000 photographs of Wisbech people, places and events, making for a unique and fascinating insight into the history and culture of the town. The gallery is housed in the Tourist Information Centre in Bridge Street.

The Fens Around Wisbech

WEST WALTON AND WALTON HIGHWAY

3 miles NE of Wisbech off the A47/B198

🏛 Fenland & West Norfolk Aviation Museum

Several attractions can be found here, notably the Church of St Mary the Virgin in West Walton with its magnificent 13th-century detached tower that dominates the landscape. Walton Highway is home to the **Fenland and West Norfolk Aviation Museum**, whose exhibits include Rolls-Royce Merlin engines, a Lightning jet, a Vampire, crashed aircraft, a Jumbo jet cockpit simulator, uniforms and

The Wildfowl & Wetlands Trust

Hundred Foot Bank, Welney, Wisbech, Cambridgeshire PE14 9TN
Tel/Fax: 01353 860711
e-mail: welney@wwt.org.uk
website: wwt.org.uk

The Wildfowl & Wetland Trust Welney is a wetland paradise of international importance with something to offer whatever the season. In winter, enjoy the magic of hundreds of Whooper and Bewick's Swans accompanied by flocks of thousands of ducks. During the day, carpets of Wigeon graze this precious wetland, while flocks of Pintail, Teal, Gadwall and Shoveler dabble in the pools and lagoons. Late afternoon is a special time as flocks of swans flight-in to claim their night roosting sites. Summer brings an atmosphere of peace and tranquillity broken only by the piping calls of waders, drumming Snipe and the chatter of warblers. Lush meadows are bordered by a dazzling display of Purple Loosestrife, Great Willowherb and Marsh Woundwort.

Visitors can stroll along the boardwalks through rustling reedbeds, and spend a while pond-dipping for water beasts. The Visitor Centre houses displays, educational facilities and a well-stocked gift shop. WWT Welney also runs a packed programme of special events throughout the year.

🎬 stories and anecdotes 🦢 famous people 🖌 art and craft 🎭 entertainment and sport 🚶 walks

memorabilia. The museum is open weekends during the summer.

LEVERINGTON
1 mile NW of Wisbech off the A1101

The tower and spire of the Church of St Leonard date from the 13th and 14th centuries. The most exceptional feature of an exceptionally interesting church is the 15th-century stained-glass Jesse window in the north aisle. There are many fine memorials in the churchyard. Oliver Goldsmith wrote *She Stoops to Conquer* while staying in Leverington.

PARSON DROVE
6 miles W of Wisbech on the B1169

Samuel Pepys visited Parson Drove in 1663. He stayed at the village's Swan Inn, and mentions it in his diaries, though he was not complimentary. Parson Drove is most certainly not the 'heathen place' once described by Pepys!

It was a centre of the woad industry until 1914, when the last remaining woad mill was demolished.

The Parson Drove Visitors' Centre is set in the old Victorian lock-up on the village green, a building with an unusual 170-year history. Photographs and documents trace the story of this lovely Fens village. The Church of St John the Baptist has many treasures, including delightful carved medieval faces and large clear windows with medieval glass in the tracery.

WELNEY
12 miles S of Wisbech off the A1101

🐦 Wildfowl & Wetlands Trust

The **Wildfowl & Wetlands Trust** (see panel on page 347) in Welney is a nature reserve that attracts large numbers of swans and ducks in winter. Special floodlit 'swan evenings' are held, and there is also a wide range of wild plants and butterflies to be enjoyed.

🏛 historic building 🏛 museum and heritage 🏛 historic site ⌘ scenic attraction 🐦 flora and fauna

Cambridgeshire

CAMBRIDGE

*Wheeler Street, Cambridge,
Cambridgeshire CB2 3QB
e-mail: tourism@cambridge.gov.uk
Tel: 0906 586 2526*

ELY

*Oliver Cromwell's House, 29 St Mary's
Street, Ely, Cambridgeshire CB7 4HF
e-mail: tic@eastcambs.gov.uk
Tel: 01353 662062*

PETERBOROUGH

*3-5 Minster Precincts, Peterborough,
Cambridgeshire PE1 1XS
e-mail: tic@peterborough.gov.uk
Tel: 01733 452336*

ST NEOTS

*The Old Court, 8 New Street,
St Neots, Cambridgeshire PE19 1AE
e-mail: stneots.tic@huntsdc.gov.uk
Tel: 01480 388788*

WISBECH

*2-3 Bridge Street, Wisbech,
Cambridgeshire PE13 1EW
e-mail: tourism@fenland.gov.uk
Tel: 01945 583263*

Essex

BRAINTREE

*Town Hall Centre, Market Square,
Braintree, Essex CM7 3YG
e-mail: tic@braintree.gov.uk
Tel: 01376 550066*

CLACTON-ON-SEA

*Town Hall, Station Road,
Clacton-on-Sea, Essex CO15 1SE
e-mail: emorgan@tendringdc.gov.uk
Tel: 01255 686633*

COLCHESTER

*Tymperleys Clock Museum, Trinity
Street, Colchester, Essex CO1 1JN
e-mail: vic@colchester.gov.uk
Tel: 01206 282920*

HARWICH

*Iconfield Park, Parkeston, Harwich,
Essex CO12 4EN
e-mail: harwichtic@btconnect.com
Tel: 01255 506139*

MALDON

*Coach Lane, Maldon,
Essex CM9 4UH
e-mail: tic@maldon.gov.uk
Tel: 01621 856503*

SAFFRON WALDEN

*1 Market Place, Market Square,
Saffron Walden, Essex CB10 1HR
e-mail: tourism@uttlesford.gov.uk
Tel: 01799 510444*

SOUTHEND-ON-SEA

*Pier Entrance, Western Esplanade,
Southend-on-Sea, Essex SS1 1EE
e-mail: vic@southend.gov.uk
Tel: 01702 215620*

WALTHAM ABBEY

*2 Highbridge Street, Waltham Abbey,
Essex EN9 1DG
e-mail: tic@walthamabbey.org.uk
Tel: 01992 652295*

Norfolk

AYLSHAM

*Bure Valley Railway Station, Tourist
Information Centre, Norwich Road,
Aylsham, Norfolk NR11 6BW
e-mail: aylsham.tic@broadland.gov.uk
Tel: 01263 733903*

BURNHAM DEEPDALE

*Deepdale Farm, Burnham Deepdale,
Norfolk PE31 8DD
e-mail: info@deepdalefarm.co.uk
Tel: 01485 210256*

CROMER

*Prince of Wales Road, Cromer,
Norfolk NR27 9HS
e-mail: cromerinfo@north-
norfolk.gov.uk
Tel: 0871 200 3071*

DISS

*Meres Mouth, Mere Street, Diss,
Norfolk IP22 3AG
e-mail: dtic@s-norfolk.gov.uk
Tel: 01379 650523*

DOWNHAM MARKET

*The Priory Centre, 78 Priory Road,
Downham Market,
Norfolk PE38 9JS
e-mail: downham-market.tic@west-
norfolk.gov.uk
Tel: 01366 383287*

GREAT YARMOUTH

*25 Marine Parade, Great Yarmouth,
Norfolk NR30 2EN
e-mail: tourism@great-yarmouth.gov.uk
Tel: 01493 846345*

HOLT

*3 Pound House, Market Place, Holt,
Norfolk NR25 6BW
e-mail: holtinfo@north-norfolk.gov.uk
Tel: 0871 200 3071*

HOVETON

*Station Road, Hoveton,
Norfolk NR12 8UR
e-mail: hovetoninfo@broads-
authority.gov.uk
Tel: 01603 782281*

TOURIST INFORMATION CENTRES

HUNSTANTON
Town Hall, The Green, Hunstanton,
Norfolk PE36 6BQ
e-mail: hunstanton.tic@west-
norfolk.gov.uk
Tel: 01485 532610

KING'S LYNN
The Custom House, Purfleet Quay,
King's Lynn, Norfolk PE30 1HP
e-mail: kings-lynn.tic@west-
norfolk.gov.uk
Tel: 01553 763044

NORWICH
The Forum, Millennium Plain,
Norwich, Norfolk NR2 1TF
e-mail: tourism@norwich.gov.uk
Tel: 01603 727927

SHERINGHAM
Station Approach, Sheringham,
Norfolk NR26 8RA
e-mail: sheringhaminfo@north-
norfolk.gov.uk
Tel: 0871 200 3071

SWAFFHAM
Town Hall, London Street, Swaffham
Norfolk, PE37 7DQ
e-mail: swaffham@eetb.info
Tel: 01760 722255

WELLS-NEXT-THE-SEA
Staithe Street, Wells-next-the-Sea,
Norfolk NR23 1AN
e-mail: wellstic@north-norfolk.gov.uk
Tel: 0871 200 3071

WYMONDHAM
Market Cross, Market Place,
Wymondham, Norfolk NR18 0AX
e-mail: wymondhamtic@btconnect.com
Tel: 01953 604721

Suffolk

ALDEBURGH
152 High Street, Aldeburgh,
Suffolk IP15 5AQ
e-mail: atic@suffolkcoastal.gov.uk
Tel: 01728 453637

BECCLES
The Quay, Fen Lane, Beccles,
Suffolk NR34 9BH
e-mail: becclesinfo@broads-
authority.gov.uk
Tel: 01502 713196

BURY ST EDMUNDS
6 Angel Hill, Bury St Edmunds,
Suffolk IP33 1UZ
e-mail: tic@stedsbc.gov.uk
Tel: 01284 764667

FELIXSTOWE
91 Undercliff Road West, Felixstowe,
Suffolk IP11 2AF
e-mail: ftic@suffolkcoastal.gov.uk
Tel: 01394 276770

FLATFORD
Flatford Lane, Flatford, East Bergholt,
Suffolk CO7 6UL
e-mail: flatfordvic@babergh.gov.uk
Tel: 01206 299460

LAVENHAM
Lady Street, Lavenham,
Suffolk CO10 9RA
e-mail: lavenhamtic@babergh.gov.uk
Tel: 01787 248207

LOWESTOFT
East Point Pavilion, Royal Plain,
Lowestoft, Suffolk NR33 0AP
e-mail: touristinfo@waveney.gov.uk
Tel: 01502 533600

NEWMARKET
Palace House, Palace Street,
Newmarket, Suffolk CB8 8EP
e-mail: tic.newmarket@forest-
heath.gov.uk
Tel: 01638 667200

SOUTHWOLD
69 High Street, Southwold,
Suffolk IP18 6DS
e-mail: southwold.tic@waveney.gov.uk
Tel: 01502 724729

STOWMARKET
Wilkes Way, Stowmarket,
Suffolk IP14 1DE
e-mail: tic@midsuffolk.gov.uk
Tel: 01449 676800

SUDBURY
Town Hall, Market Hill, Sudbury,
Suffolk CO10 1TL
e-mail: sudburytic@babergh.gov.uk
Tel: 01787 881320

WOODBRIDGE
Station Buildings, Woodbridge,
Suffolk IP12 4AJ
e-mail: wtic@suffolkcoastal.gov.uk
Tel: 01394 382240

INDEX OF ADVERTISERS

INDEX OF ADVERTISERS

INDEX OF ADVERTISERS

INDEX OF ADVERTISERS

INDEX OF WALKS

Looking for more walks?

The walks in this book have been gleaned from Britain's largest online walking guide, to be found at *www.walkingworld.com*.

The site contains over 2000 walks from all over England, Scotland and Wales so there are plenty more to choose from in this book's region as well as further afield - ideal if you are taking a short break as you can plan your walks in advance. There are walks of every length and type to suit all tastes.

Want more detail for the walks in this book? Next to every walk in this book you will see a Walk ID. You can enter this ID number on Walkingworld's 'Find a Walk' page and you will be taken straight to the details of that walk.

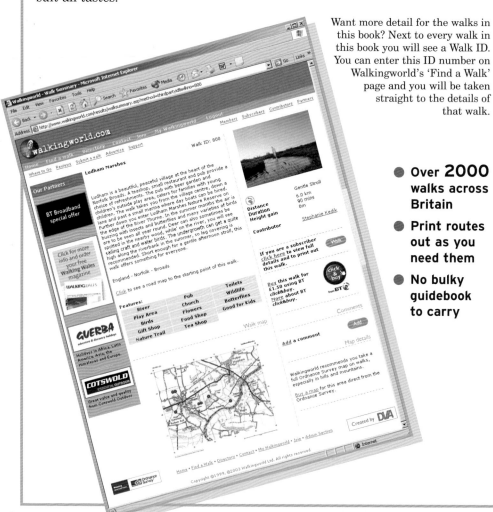

- Over **2000** walks across Britain
- Print routes out as you need them
- No bulky guidebook to carry

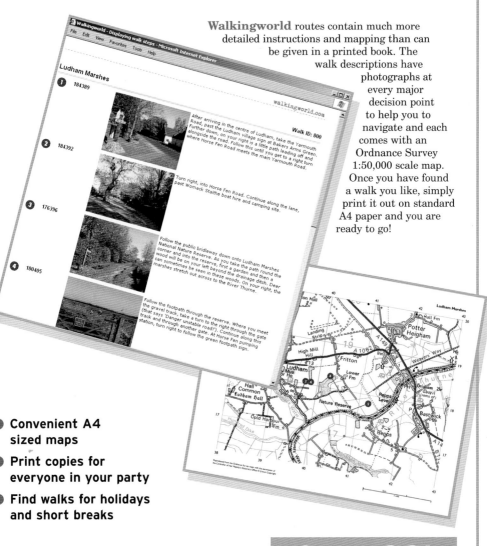

Walkingworld routes contain much more detailed instructions and mapping than can be given in a printed book. The walk descriptions have photographs at every major decision point to help you to navigate and each comes with an Ordnance Survey 1:50,000 scale map. Once you have found a walk you like, simply print it out on standard A4 paper and you are ready to go!

- Convenient A4 sized maps
- Print copies for everyone in your party
- Find walks for holidays and short breaks

A modest annual subscription gives you access to over 2000 walks, all in Walkingworld's easy to follow format. The database of walks is growing all the time and as a subscriber you gain access to new routes as soon as they are published.

Visit the Walkingworld website at *www.walkingworld.com*

ORDER FORM

To order any of our publications just fill in the payment details below and complete the order form. For orders of less than 4 copies please add £1 per book for postage and packing. Orders over 4 copies are P & P free.

Please Complete Either:

I enclose a cheque for £ [   ] made payable to Travel Publishing Ltd

Or:

CARD NO: [   ]   EXPIRY DATE: [   ]

SIGNATURE: [   ]

NAME: [   ]

ADDRESS: [   ]

TEL NO: [   ]

Please either send, telephone, fax or e-mail your order to:

Travel Publishing Ltd, Airport Business Centre, 10 Thornbury Road, Estover, Plymouth PL6 7PP
Tel: 01752 697280   Fax: 01752 697299   e-mail: info@travelpublishing.co.uk

	PRICE	QUANTITY		PRICE	QUANTITY
HIDDEN PLACES REGIONAL TITLES			**COUNTRY LIVING RURAL GUIDES**		
Cornwall	£8.99	....	East Anglia	£10.99	....
Devon	£8.99	....	Heart of England	£10.99	....
Dorset, Hants & Isle of Wight	£8.99	....	Ireland	£11.99	....
East Anglia	£8.99	....	North East of England	£10.99	....
Lake District & Cumbria	£8.99	....	North West of England	£10.99	....
Northumberland & Durham	£8.99	....	Scotland	£11.99	....
Peak District and Derbyshire	£8.99	....	South of England	£10.99	....
Yorkshire	£8.99	....	South East of England	£10.99	....
HIDDEN PLACES NATIONAL TITLES			Wales	£11.99	....
England	£11.99	....	West Country	£10.99	....
Ireland	£11.99	....			
Scotland	£11.99	....			
Wales	£11.99	....			
OTHER TITLES					
Off The Motorway	£11.99	....	**TOTAL QUANTITY**	[ ]	
Garden Centres and Nurseries of Britain	£11.99	....	**TOTAL VALUE**	[ ]	

READER REACTION FORM

The **Travel Publishing** *research team would like to receive readers' comments on any visitor attractions or places reviewed in the book and also recommendations for suitable entries to be included in the next edition. This will help ensure that the* **Country Living series of Rural Guides** *continues to provide its readers with useful information on the more interesting, unusual or unique features of each attraction or place ensuring that their visit to the local area is an enjoyable and stimulating experience. To provide your comments or recommendations would you please complete the forms below and overleaf as indicated and send to:*

The Research Department, Travel Publishing Ltd, Airport Business Centre, 10 Thornbury Road, Estover, Plymouth PL6 7PP

YOUR NAME:

YOUR ADDRESS:

YOUR TEL NO:

Please tick as appropriate: COMMENTS ☐   RECOMMENDATION ☐

ESTABLISHMENT:

ADDRESS:

TEL NO:

CONTACT NAME:

PLEASE COMPLETE FORM OVERLEAF

READER REACTION FORM

COMMENT OR REASON FOR RECOMMENDATION:

READER REACTION FORM

The **Travel Publishing** *research team would like to receive readers' comments on any visitor attractions or places reviewed in the book and also recommendations for suitable entries to be included in the next edition. This will help ensure that the* **Country Living series** *of* **Rural Guides** *continues to provide its readers with useful information on the more interesting, unusual or unique features of each attraction or place ensuring that their visit to the local area is an enjoyable and stimulating experience. To provide your comments or recommendations would you please complete the forms below and overleaf as indicated and send to:*

The Research Department, Travel Publishing Ltd, Airport Business Centre, 10 Thornbury Road, Estover, Plymouth PL6 7PP

YOUR NAME:

YOUR ADDRESS:

YOUR TEL NO:

Please tick as appropriate: COMMENTS ☐   RECOMMENDATION ☐

ESTABLISHMENT:

ADDRESS:

TEL NO:

CONTACT NAME:

PLEASE COMPLETE FORM OVERLEAF

READER REACTION FORM

COMMENT OR REASON FOR RECOMMENDATION:

....

....

....

....

....

....

....

....

....

....

....

READER REACTION FORM

The **Travel Publishing** *research team would like to receive readers' comments on any visitor attractions or places reviewed in the book and also recommendations for suitable entries to be included in the next edition. This will help ensure that the* **Country Living series of Rural Guides** *continues to provide its readers with useful information on the more interesting, unusual or unique features of each attraction or place ensuring that their visit to the local area is an enjoyable and stimulating experience. To provide your comments or recommendations would you please complete the forms below and overleaf as indicated and send to:*

The Research Department, Travel Publishing Ltd, Airport Business Centre, 10 Thornbury Road, Estover, Plymouth PL6 7PP

YOUR NAME:

YOUR ADDRESS:

YOUR TEL NO:

Please tick as appropriate: COMMENTS ☐   RECOMMENDATION ☐

ESTABLISHMENT:

ADDRESS:

TEL NO:

CONTACT NAME:

PLEASE COMPLETE FORM OVERLEAF

READER REACTION FORM

COMMENT OR REASON FOR RECOMMENDATION:

....

....

....

....

....

....

....

....

....

....

....

READER REACTION FORM

The **Travel Publishing** *research team would like to receive readers' comments on any visitor attractions or places reviewed in the book and also recommendations for suitable entries to be included in the next edition. This will help ensure that the* **Country Living** *series of* **Rural Guides** *continues to provide its readers with useful information on the more interesting, unusual or unique features of each attraction or place ensuring that their visit to the local area is an enjoyable and stimulating experience. To provide your comments or recommendations would you please complete the forms below and overleaf as indicated and send to:*

The Research Department, Travel Publishing Ltd, Airport Business Centre, 10 Thornbury Road, Estover, Plymouth PL6 7PP

YOUR NAME:

YOUR ADDRESS:

YOUR TEL NO:

Please tick as appropriate: COMMENTS ☐   RECOMMENDATION ☐

ESTABLISHMENT:

ADDRESS:

TEL NO:

CONTACT NAME:

PLEASE COMPLETE FORM OVERLEAF

READER REACTION FORM

COMMENT OR REASON FOR RECOMMENDATION:

....

....

....

....

....

....

....

....

....

....

....

....

READER REACTION FORM

The **Travel Publishing** *research team would like to receive readers' comments on any visitor attractions or places reviewed in the book and also recommendations for suitable entries to be included in the next edition. This will help ensure that the* **Country Living series of Rural Guides** *continues to provide its readers with useful information on the more interesting, unusual or unique features of each attraction or place ensuring that their visit to the local area is an enjoyable and stimulating experience. To provide your comments or recommendations would you please complete the forms below and overleaf as indicated and send to:*

The Research Department, Travel Publishing Ltd, Airport Business Centre, 10 Thornbury Road, Estover, Plymouth PL6 7PP

YOUR NAME:

YOUR ADDRESS:

YOUR TEL NO:

Please tick as appropriate: COMMENTS ☐   RECOMMENDATION ☐

ESTABLISHMENT:

ADDRESS:

TEL NO:

CONTACT NAME:

PLEASE COMPLETE FORM OVERLEAF

READER REACTION FORM

COMMENT OR REASON FOR RECOMMENDATION:

TOWNS, VILLAGES AND PLACES OF INTEREST

TOWNS, VILLAGES AND PLACES OF INTEREST

TOWNS, VILLAGES AND PLACES OF INTEREST

TOWNS, VILLAGES AND PLACES OF INTEREST

TOWNS, VILLAGES AND PLACES OF INTEREST

TOWNS, VILLAGES AND PLACES OF INTEREST

TOWNS, VILLAGES AND PLACES OF INTEREST

TOWNS, VILLAGES AND PLACES OF INTEREST